APPLICATIONS OF SELF-ORGANIZING MAPS

Edited by **Magnus Johnsson**

Applications of Self-Organizing Maps

http://dx.doi.org/10.5772/3464
Edited by Magnus Johnsson

Contributors

Wattanapong Kurdthongmee, Dimitris Kontogiorgos, Hector Benitez-Perez, Hiroshi Dozono, Flavius Gorgonio, Huliane Silva, Cícero Silva, Ji Zhang, Jennifer Francis, Natasa Skific, Ryotaro Kamimura, Lydwine Gross, Arnaud Quesney, Suzanne Angeli, Marina Resta, Yuan-Chao Liu, Masaki Ishii, Fernando Bacao, Victor Lobo, Roberto Henriques, João Carlos Soares de Mello, Eliane Gomes, Lidia Angulo Meza, Sérgio De Zen, Thiago Bernardino De Carvalho, Urbano Gomes Abreu, Luiz Biondi Neto

Published by InTech

Janeza Trdine 9, 51000 Rijeka, Croatia

Publishing Process Manager Iva Lipovic
Typesetting InTech DTP Team
Cover InTech Design Team

Additional hard copies can be obtained from orders@intechopen.com

Applications of Self-Organizing Maps, Edited by Magnus Johnsson
p. cm.
ISBN 978-953-51-0862-7

For EU product safety concerns:
IN TECH d.o.o., Prolaz Marije Krucifikse Kozulić 3, 51000 Rijeka, Croatia,
info@intechopen.com or visit our website at intechopen.com.

Meet the editor

Dr. Magnus Johnsson is a researcher from Sweden. He studied mathematics, computer science and cognitive science and received a bachelor of science in computer science in 2003, a master of science in computer science in 2004, a master of arts in cognitive science in 2004 and a PhD in cognitive science in 2009. He is currently a researcher at Lund University in Sweden. His research interests include artificial neural networks, artificial intelligence, computational cognitive neuroscience, cognitive robotics, and the philosophy of mind. Dr Johnsson has experience from working in the industry and he has a keen interest in the application of neural networks and artificial intelligence to fields like industry, finance and medicine.

Contents

Preface

The self-organizing map is an unsupervised neural network first described by the Finnish scientist Teuvo Kohonen. By a self-organizing adaptation process this neural network learns to map the input space onto a discretized representation which preserves the topology and reflects the probability distribution of the input. This book is about how the original self-organizing map as well as variants and extensions of it can be applied in different fields. In fourteen chapters, a wide range of applications of the Self-Organizing Map is discussed. To name a few, these applications include the analysis of financial stability, the fault diagnosis of plants, the creation of well-composed heterogeneous teams and the application of the self-organizing map to the atmospheric sciences.

Dr. Magnus Johnsson
Lund University,
Sweden

Chapter 1

Graph Mining Based SOM: A Tool to Analyze Economic Stability

Marina Resta

Additional information is available at the end of the chapter

http://dx.doi.org/10.5772/51240

1. Introduction

Living in times of Global Financial Crisis (GFC) has offered new challenges to researchers and financial policy makers, in search of tools assuring either to monitor or to prevent the incurrence of critical situations. This issue, as usual, can be managed under various perspectives.

Under the economic profile, two basic strands emerged: various contributions debated on the central role of systemic risk in conditioning countries financial fragility; a second vein concerned the role (either in positive or negative sense) of financial sector on economic growth. Provided the relevance for our work, we will discuss each of them in a deeper way.

For what it concerns the first aspect, there are several definitions of systemic risk (see for instance: [1]; [2], [3] and [4]), but there is not any widely accepted definition for it. Nevertheless, we agree with the position of [5] who claimed that systemic risk can be identified by the presence of two distinct elements: an initial random shock, as the source of systemic impact, and a contagion mechanism (such as the interbank market or the payment system), which spread the negative shock wave to other members of the system. Along this vein, a growing body of empirical research has already bloomed: [6] suggested a network approach to analyze the impact of liquidity shocks into financial systems; a similar approach was followed by [7] discussing the case of United Kingdom, Boss [8] for Austria, and [9] for Switzerland; more recently Soramaki et. al. (2012) developed a software platform[1] that employs graphs models for various purposes, including to monitor financial contagion spreading effects.

A second related point concerns the evaluation of how financial sector can condition countries' economic growth. There is a general agreement in financial economics literature about

1 Financial Network Analysis (fna): free web version available at: http://www.fna.fi/products/list.

the existence of a link between bankruptcies and the business cycle. However, the same does not apply when one is asked to identify the methods and the variables by which bankruptcies and the business cycle interact. Basic streams of research moved along four directions. A number of papers focused on the application of discriminant analysis over a bunch of accounting variables (see for instance: [10], [11], [12]; [13]). A second group of papers (see among the others: [14]) employs the methodology initiated by [15], who used logistic regression models (logit) on macroeconomic variables. A third strand focuses on duration models, i.e. models that measure how long the economic system remains in a certain state. This is the line joined, for example, by [16], and [17]. Finally, there is a plenty of (more or less) sophisticated econometric techniques aided to estimate bankruptcies by means of macroeconomic variables. Interested readers may take a look to [18], and [19].

From all the above research streams dealing with crisis and financial (in)stability we extract three discussion issues. As first remark, our review highlighted that in general, in all periods of crisis there is always a strong financial component. As second remark, we may observe that the economic literature addressed the analysis mainly by means of either macroeconomic or accounting data. Finally, we want to focus on a methodological issue: quantitative papers generally studied the problem by means of econometric techniques; only over the past decade soft computing methods (namely: graphs models) have become of some interest for economic researchers and policy makers. Starting from this point, we think that there is enough room to add something newer towards the following directions: (i) studying the emergence of instability by way of financial markets data; (ii) using a hybrid approach combining graphs models together with non-linear dimension reduction techniques, in detail: with Self Organizing Maps [20]. To such purpose, it aids to remember that Self Organizing Maps (SOM) are nowadays a landmark among soft computing techniques, with applications which virtually span over all fields of knowledge. However, while the use of SOM in robotics, medical imaging, characters recognition, to cite most important examples, is celebrated by a consistent literature corpus (interested readers may take a look to [21], [22], and [23]), economics and financial markets seem relatively less explored, with some notable exceptions (from the pioneering works of [24], [25] to, more recently, [26] and [27]). Such lack of financial applications is quite non-sense, provided the great potential that relies on this kind of technique.

The rationale of this contribution is to offer some insights about the use of SOM to explore how financial markets organize during critical periods i.e. deflation, recession and so on. Something similar has been already discussed in [28] and [29], who deal with the use of SOM as support tool for Early Warning Systems (EWS), alerting the decision maker in case of critical economic situations. However, the present contribution goes one step forward under various points of view. The first element of innovation relies on the examined data. We studied the situation of markets characterized by different levels of (in)stability, but instead of using either financial or macroeconomic indicators as it is generally done in literature, we employed historical time-series of price levels for every enterprise quoted in the related stock exchanges, and we then trained a SOM for each market. A second innovative item relied on the use of the so obtained SOM best matching units, to build the corresponding Minimum Spanning Tree (MST). In this way we were able to capture both the clusters structure of every market and to analyze the impact of emerging patterns over the economic situation of the country. This was done both in a static way, i.e. by observing the situation with data referring to a fixed one year long period (from December 2010 to December 2011), and in a dynamic way, by comparison of MST obtained for each countries with data extracted by means of a 300 days long moving window over a time interval of overall length of 3000 days (approximately ten years).

Our major findings may be then summarised as follows: (i) using SOM we got an original representation of financial markets; (ii) by building from SOM winning nodes the corresponding MST it was possible both to emphasize the relations among various quoted enterprises, and to check for the emergence of critical patterns; (iii) we provided a global representation of countries financial situation that generates information that can be of help to policy makers, in order to realize more efficient interventions in periods of higher instability.

2. Methodology

As stated in Section 1, we examined financial markets data by means of a hybrid technique which assumes the joint use of both SOM and graphs formalism. In order to assure a better understanding of this framework, we will recall some basic definitions and notational conventions for both the aforementioned tools.

2.1. Self Organizing Maps: Basic principles

A Self Organizing Map (SOM) is a single layer neural network, where neurons are set along an n-dimensional grid: typical applications assume a 2-dimensions rectangular grid, but hexagonal as well as toroidal grids are also possible. Each neuron has as many components as the input patterns: mathematically this implies that both neuron and inputs are vectors embedded in the same space. Training a SOM requires a number of steps to be performed in a sequential way. For a generic input pattern x we will have:

1. to evaluate the distance between x and each neuron of the SOM;
2. to select the neuron (node) with the smallest distance from x. We will call it winner neuron or Best Matching Unit (BMU);
3. to correct the position of each node according to the results of Step 2., in order to preserve the network topology.

Steps 1.- 3. can be repeated either once or more than once for each input pattern: a good stopping criterion generally consists in taking a view to the so called Quantization Error (QE), i.e. a weighted average over the Euclidean norms of the difference between the input vector and the corresponding BMU. When QE goes below a proper threshold level, say for instance 10^{-2} or lower, it might be suitable to stop the procedure.

In this way, once the learning procedure is concluded, we get an organization of SOM which takes into account how the input space is structured, and projects it into a lower dimensional space where closer nodes represent neighboring input patterns.

2.2. Graphs models: A brief review and some notational conventions

In order to understand how graphs theory can be used in clusters analysis, it is worth to review some basic terminology.

From the mathematical point of view, a graph (network) G = (V,E) is perfectly identified by a (finite) set V, and a collection $E \subseteq V \times V$, of unordered pairs $\{u, v\}$ of distinct elements from V. Each element of V is called a vertex (point, node), and each element of E is called an edge (line, link). Edges of the form (u,u), for some $u \in V$, are called self-loops, but in practical applications they typically are not contained in a graph.

A sequence of connected vertices forms a *path*; the number n of vertices, (i.e. the cardinality of V), defines the *order of graph* and it is denoted by $|V|:=n$. In a similar way, the number m of edges (the cardinality of E), is called the *size of the graph* and denoted by: $|E|:= m$. Finally, the number of neighbors of any vertex $v \in V$ in the graph identifies its *degree.*

Moreover, the graph G will be claimed to be:

- *directed,* if the edges set is composed of ordered vertex (node) pairs; *undirected* if the edge set is composed of unordered vertex pairs;
- *simple,* if it has no loops or multiple edges;
- *acyclic* if there is not any possibility to loop back again from every vertex; *cyclic* if the contrary holds.
- *connected,* if there is a path in G between any given pair of vertices, otherwise it is *disconnected;*
- *regular,* if all the vertices of G have the same degree;
- *complete,* if every two distinct vertices are joined by exactly one edge;
- a *path,* if consisting of a single path.
- *bipartite,* if the vertex–set can be split into two sets in such a way that each edge of the graph joins a vertex in first set to a vertex in second;
- a *tree,* if it is connected and it has no cycles. If G is a connected graph, the spanning tree in G will be a subgraph of G which includes every vertex of G and is also a tree. The minimum length spanning tree is called Minimum Spanning Tree (MST).

Our brief explanation highlights that Minimum Spanning tree is nothing but a particular graph with no cycles, where all nodes are connected and edges are selected in order to minimize the sum of distances.

Graphs representation passes through the building of the *adjacency matrix,* i.e. the matrix that marks neighbor vertexes with one, and with zero not adjacent nodes. Figure 1 provides an explanatory example.

In a number of real world applications there is the common habit to use graphs theory formalism, representing the problem data through an undirected graph. Each node is associated to a sample in the feature space, while to each edge is associated the distance between

http://dx.doi.org/10.5772/51240

nodes connected under a suitably defined neighborhood relationship. A cluster is thus defined to be a connected subgraph, obtained according to criteria peculiar of each specific algorithm. Algorithms based on this definition are capable of detecting clusters of various shapes and sizes, at least for the case in which they are well separated. Moreover, isolated samples should form singleton clusters and then can be easily discarded as noise in case of cluster detection problems.

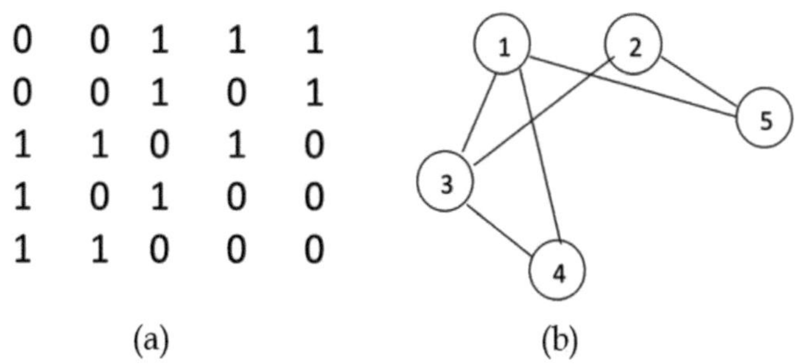

Figure 1. From left to right: the adjacency matrix (a) for an undirected graph, and the corresponding graph (b). The ones in the matrix indicate the existence of a connection among nodes, while zeroes mean no connection.

With this in mind, one can easily understand that coping SOM (that satisfy topology preservation features) to graphs (that do not require any a priori assumption about the input space distribution) should result in a very powerful tool to analyze data domains.

2.3. A hybrid model combining SOM to MST

SOM achieves a bi-dimensional representation of the input domain, maintaining unchanged the basic relations among neighbor patterns: closer points in their r-dimensions ($r>>2$) initial space are still nearer one to each other in the SOM grid; in addition, they are projected into a space where relations can be easily visualized and understood. However, sometimes this cannot be enough.

Consider the issue to represent basic relations among quoted societies in a market (for example: in the Italian market). Figure 2 shows SOM, once the relations among Italian quoted companies have been learned.

Here we have a SOM assuring an overall good performance, in terms of quantization error ($QE<10^{-3}$), but the winner nodes are even too much closer than desired, thus making difficult to understand the effective significance of their closeness.

Moving one step forward, we suggested a hybrid procedure that combines together SOM and MST (see also [31]). The idea by itself is not totally newer: [32], for instance, suggested a variant of SOM where neighborhood relationships during the training stage were defined along the MST; [33], and, more recently, [34] applied a MST to SOMs to connect similar nodes with each other, thus visualizing related nodes on the map. In all cited cases this was done by calculating the square difference between neighbor units on the trained map, and using this value to color the edge separating the units.

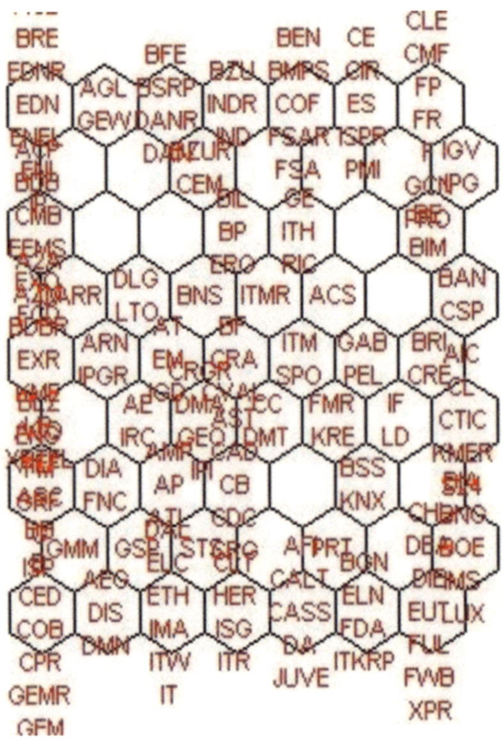

Figure 2. SOM representation of Italian quoted companies.

In a likewise manner, we applied a clustering procedure whose main steps can be summarized as follows:

1. Define a SOM M (made of a number n of neurons w) over the input space and run it.

2. For each input sample extract the corresponding BMU. We set:

   a. $$\mathrm{B} = \{w : w \in M \wedge w \text{ is a BMU}\} \tag{1}$$

3. Build the correlation matrix C among the nodes belonging to B.

4. Use C as starting point to compute the MST. In particular, since C is symmetric, one can consider only the lower (L) or Upper (U) triangular part of the matrix, and:

   i. sort the elements of L (U) in decreasing order, thus moving from L to the list *Lord* (from U to *Uord*).

   ii. ii.Set the coordinates in C of the first element of *Lord* (*Uord*) as those of the first two nodes of the MST.

iii. For each element in *Lord* (*Uord*) add the corresponding couple from *C* to MST; in particular, if the graph is still acyclic (i.e. no loops are added to MST), then hold the inserted link, otherwise discard it.

iv. Repeat step iii. until all the elements in *Lord* (*Uord*) have been examined, and then stop the procedure

The result is a filtering of available information, letting only more significant patterns to emerge.

3. Experimental settings and results discussion

Our work is aimed to demonstrate how a fully data-driven approach can be helpful to analyze complex financial situations in quite an intuitive way, thus making SOM-MST a very reliable tool also for policy makers.

We performed both static and dynamic analyses, as we are going to explain. As starting point for the static analysis we selected a market and for each quoted enterprise we took all available price levels (*pl*) from December 2010 to December 2011. In this way for the generic i-th stock (i=1,…,N, where N is the overall number of quoted enterprises) we got the time-series $S^{(i)}=\{pv_k^{(i)}\}$ with length T-1, being:

$$pv_k^{(i)}=log\frac{pl_{k+1}^{(i)}}{pl_k^{(i)}},\ k=1,\ \cdot,\ T-1 \tag{2}$$

The transformation described in (2) turns price levels into price log-returns: this is a common practice in empirical financial studies to avoid any trend effect in data. The final result was a matrix Σ of dimensions $N \times T$-1, containing T-1 log-returns for each quoted enterprise (for an overall number of *N*). As final step, we performed on Σ the procedure we explained in Sec.2.3, coping SOM to MST.

The dynamical procedure is similar to the static one, but instead of considering last year sample for each stock, we examined a number of fixed length samples, going back in time (when possible) up to ten years. In practice, assuming as starting point t=3000 the day Dec. 30 2011, we build for each stock the block B1 going from t=2701 to t=3000; the block B2 with data from t=2401 to t=2700; and so on towards the block B10 that goes from t=1 to t=300. In practice, instead of having a single block of data to analyze, in the dynamical procedure we can monitor the situation of the country with different sets of data. Moreover, taking advantage of the networks representation, one can have a look to graphs statistics for every year and to compare them over the ten years time horizon.

We applied our methodology to the German and Spanish markets. Our choice obeys to a precise motivation: we have examined countries characterized by different levels of (in)stability: at the end of 2011 Spanish financial equilibrium seemed heavily compromised, while Germany still maintained its leading role in Europe.

4. Results and discussion

Before going to separately discuss various cases, we will spend a few words about some common features shared by our simulation study.

Starting from the static case, we examined German, Italian and Spanish markets from 30 December 2010 to 30 December 2011. For each market we considered data of quoted enterprises, transforming them according to the formula given in (2). Table 1 highlights some basic details concerning the markets we have considered.

Country	Idx	NrS	MD
Germany	CDAX	207	207 × 245
Spain	IGBM	85	85 × 245

Table 1. Markets main features.

The column *Country* reports the name of the countries whose assets have been examined, while *Idx* indicates the name of the national market index that has been employed to pick up quoted stocks; *NrS* is the number of stocks we included for every market; finally *MD* highlights input matrix dimensions in our simulation study. In particular, we referred to the CDAX (*Composite Deutscher Aktienindex*) index for the German market, and the IGBM (*Index General de Bolsa Madrid*) index in the case of Spain. As a straightforward observation, one can argue that the overall number of quoted enterprises in those markets should be higher than the one we have reported in the third column of Table 1. However, for sake of comparison among graphs, we needed to eliminate from the markets those stocks for which it was not possible to go back in time enough (at least 600 days, approximately corresponding to two years and half of market tradings).

4.1. The case of Germany

Applying our procedure led us to obtain the skeleton framework of the German stock exchange that is shown in Figure 3.

Our procedure found out 14 clusters. At first glimpse the clusters seem to be *natural,* in the sense discussed in [35], i.e.:

- each node is member of exactly one group;
- each node has many edges to other members of its group;
- each node has few or even no edges to nodes of other groups.

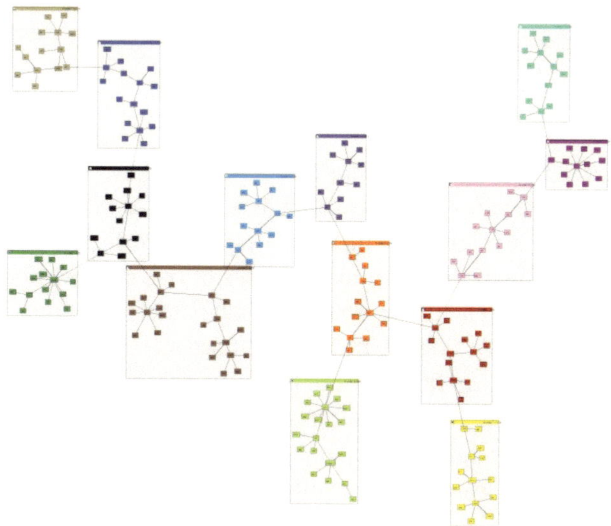

Figure 3. German Market topology, as resulting in the static case. Natural clusters are highlighted with different colors.

This cluster structure is partly due to the filtering procedure operated on SOM BMUs after the learning stage, but the resulting organization makes sense also if we look at the statistical features of the clusters (Table 2) as well as at their composition, by industrial reference sector (Table 3).

CL. ID.	mu	std	sk	ku	SR
CL01	0.0001270	0.045235	1.651532	411.3881	0.281%
CL02	0.0002923	0.055717	10.48408	2521.463	0.525%
CL03	0.0001208	0.143701	9.605624	906.0551	0.084%
CL04	0.0002904	0.056795	10.3774	2448.29	0.511%
CL05	0.0003361	0.056718	10.14951	2386.374	0.593%
CL06	0.0004759	0.057566	11.4447	2608.218	0.827%
CL07	0.0003254	0.056369	10.4055	2471.74	0.577%
CL08	0.0003683	0.05673	10.54512	2485.83	0.649%
CL09	0.0003223	0.056334	10.14833	2402.134	0.572%
CL10	0.0004811	0.057746	11.11191	2515.727	0.833%
CL11	0.0002920	0.05616	10.06927	2395.238	0.520%
CL12	0.0005635	0.058396	11.85686	2655.044	0.965%
CL13	0.0002770	0.058349	11.88501	2663.531	0.475%
CL14	0.0003343	0.056866	10.46831	2462.213	0.588%

Table 2. Statistical properties of the network of German stocks in the period December 2010-December 2011.

We examined basic clusters statistics: mean (*mu*), standard deviation (*std*), skewness (*sk*), and kurtosis (*ku*). We also evaluated the Sharpe Ratio of every cluster (SR):

$$SR = \frac{mu - rf}{std}$$

where *rf* is the risk free rate, and *mu*, *std* are as above described. According to financial literature, SR is a profitability index that measures how much attractive a risky investment is with respect to a riskless investment with return equal to *rf*: the ratio, in fact, opposes the excess of return (upper side of the ratio) to the excess of risk the investor assumes in charge when/if he decides to move his money from the riskless asset (whose standard deviation is zero) to the riskier one (lower side of the ratio), whose standard deviation is greater than zero. The beauty of SR stands in the fact it can be easily interpreted, giving an idea about the general attractiveness/profitability of the companies included in each group; at the same time, if we assume rf=0, the index turns to be the reciprocal of the coefficient of variation and it has also a (quite) trivial statistical interpretation.

The analysis of the results evidenced that all clusters have positive mean, relatively low variability, and good profitability (with the exception of CL01 and CL03 whose Sharpe Ratio is the lowest over all examined cases). Besides, companies returns are positively skewed.

Moving to Table 3, we checked whether companies tend to aggregate according to the sector they belong to or not, as well as if clusters composition may have affected the results that we have shown in Table 2.

Sector	**CL01**	**CL02**	**CL03**	**CL04**	**CL05**	**CL06**	**CL07**	**CL08**	**CL09**	**CL10**	**CL11**	**CL12**	**CL13**	**CL14**
Mkt	0.00	7.14	0.00	0.00	0.00	0.00	0.00	0.00	0.00	0.00	7.14	7.69	0.00	0.00
B&F	6.67	14.29	30.77	16.67	42.86	6.67	13.04	21.43	4.76	7.14	21.43	7.69	23.08	9.09
HI	0.00	7.14	7.69	0.00	0.00	0.00	4.35	0.00	9.52	14.29	0.00	15.38	0.00	4.35
Serv	20.00	0.00	0.00	0.00	0.00	6.67	4.35	15.00	9.52	0.00	14.29	0.00	15.38	9.09
Fash	13.33	0.00	0.00	16.67	0.00	13.33	5.88	0.00	0.00	7.14	0.00	7.69	15.38	0.00
HT	0.00	0.00	7.69	25.00	14.29	0.00	9.52	0.00	9.52	28.57	7.14	0.00	15.38	27.27
HC	13.33	14.29	0.00	8.33	14.29	6.67	17.39	27.28	9.52	14.29	0.00	0.00	0.00	0.00
Log	20.00	14.29	15.38	8.33	0.00	0.00	4.35	0.00	0.00	0.00	21.43	0.00	4.35	4.52
Lux	0.00	0.00	0.00	0.00	0.00	0.00	0.00	0.00	5.00	0.00	0.00	0.00	0.00	4.52
Hou	13.33	7.14	7.69	8.33	14.29	13.33	8.70	7.14	4.76	0.00	7.14	0.00	7.69	0.00
Comp	0.00	14.29	0.00	8.33	0.00	0.00	4.52	0.00	0.00	7.14	14.29	7.14	0.00	9.09
Re. Serv	0.00	0.00	0.00	0.00	0.00	6.67	0.00	0.00	0.00	0.00	0.00	0.00	0.00	0.00
F&D	0.00	7.14	7.69	0.00	0.00	0.00	9.52	0.00	0.00	0.00	0.00	0.00	7.69	0.00
En	0.00	7.14	7.69	0.00	0.00	20.00	0.00	7.14	14.29	7.14	0.00	0.00	0.00	9.09
Ent	0.00	0.00	0.00	0.00	7.14	6.67	0.00	0.00	2.50	7.14	0.00	30.77	0.00	0.00

http://dx.doi.org/10.5772/51240

Sector	CL01	CL02	CL03	CL04	CL05	CL06	CL07	CL08	CL09	CL10	CL11	CL12	CL13	CL14
Press	0.00	0.00	7.14	0.00	7.14	6.67	0.00	0.00	10.00	0.00	0.00	7.69	4.14	0.00
Imp/Exp	0.00	0.00	0.00	0.00	0.00	0.00	4.35	0.00	0.00	0.00	0.00	0.00	0.00	9.09
PU	0.00	0.00	0.00	0.00	0.00	0.00	0.00	0.00	0.00	0.00	0.00	4.52	0.00	4.79
TCom	0.00	7.14	8.24	0.00	0.00	0.00	0.00	0.00	13.33	0.00	7.14	0.00	6.89	0.00
Auto	6.67	0.00	0.00	0.00	0.00	0.00	9.52	0.00	2.50	0.00	0.00	7.14	0.00	9.09
Gard	0.00	0.00	0.00	0.00	0.00	0.00	0.00	0.00	0.00	0.00	0.00	0.00	0.00	0.00
Man	6.67	0.00	0.00	8.33	0.00	13.33	4.52	7.14	4.76	7.14	0.00	4.28	0.00	0.00

Table 3. Clusters percentage composition according to the reference industrial sector.

In general, clusters did not show an exclusive, but rather a dominant composition. Looking at Table 3, in fact, CL01 exhibits a dominant percentage of companies from both Services (Serv) and Logistics (Log) sector (20%), CL02 is equally divided into firms belonging to Banking and Finance (B&F), Health-Care (HC), Logistics and Components (Comp) sectors which share the same 14.29% percentage. B&F dominates (30%) cluster CL03 as well as CL05 (42.86%), CL11 (21.43%), and CL13 (23.08%). Hi-Tech companies (HT) are preferably grouped into clusters CL04 (25%) and CL10 (28.57%). Companies working in the Health Care sector (HC) are more numerous in clusters CL07 and CL08 (17.39% and 27.28% respectively). Finally, clusters CL06 and CL09 have their most representative elements in societies of energy sector (En) (20% and 14.29%), while CL14 is dominated by Heavy Industry (HI) companies.

This seems to suggest that despite of the variety of sectors represented in German Stock Exchange, only a reduced number of them (i.e. clusters dominant sectors) may be considered the very driving engine of the German economy. Such information together with the one retrieved by looking at the Sharpe Ratio scores has strengthened the belief that Hi-Tech and Energy are, at present, the most challenging areas for investors in German market.

As a counterpart, we observed that there is a plenty of sectors[2] whose incidence on clusters composition is lower, or better, they did not seem to cluster anyway. If this sounds reasonably for some niche-wise sectors (Luxury and Gardening, to make some examples), this is more surprising for other sectors (mainly Automotive and Telecommunications) that are worldwide known as strengths of German economy. This evidence, however, is somewhat aligned to the policy strategy that the German government has adopted in most recent times.

We can then conclude that Germany did not particularly suffer for the critical situation common to greater part of European countries. The role played by both Hi-Tech and Energy sectors has been probably a key issue. However, from now on Germany should carefully monitor the state of B&F companies that are those that actually are performing worse. Other

2 Fashion (Fash), Luxury Goods (Lux), Housing (Hou), Retail Services (Ret Serv.), Food and Drinking (F&D), Entertrainment (Ent), Press (Press), Import/Export (Imp/Exp), Public Utilities (PU), Telecommunications (TCom), Automotive (Auto), Gardening (Gard) and Manifacturing (Man).

sectors like F&D, Hou, Press, and Auto need to be constantly checked as well since they seem to be in a stage whose evolution (towards either better or worse phases) is uncertain.

At this point it makes sense to test whether or not the actual snapshot we have captured for Germany is the result of either a strategic issue, or a kind of natural evolution from previous situations. To do this we performed a dynamical analysis going back in time from December 2011 to December 2001. As explained in Section 3, we scanned data by means of a moving window, thus obtaining 10 matrices of dimensions 207×300, where 207 is the number of companies included into the simulation and 300 is the number of log-returns we took for each of them.

In order to make the discussion as clear as possible, we focused on the analysis of the periods: 2004-2005 and 2007-2008. The period 2004-2005, in fact, is a starting point of some symptoms anticipating the world financial crisis; while the period 2007-2008 is generally acknowledged as the one where deepest effects of the crisis were felt.

Figure 4 shows the market skeleton frame obtained for the German Stock Exchange in the periods 2007-2008 and 2004-2005 respectively. Tables 4-7 detail basic statistics and clusters composition.

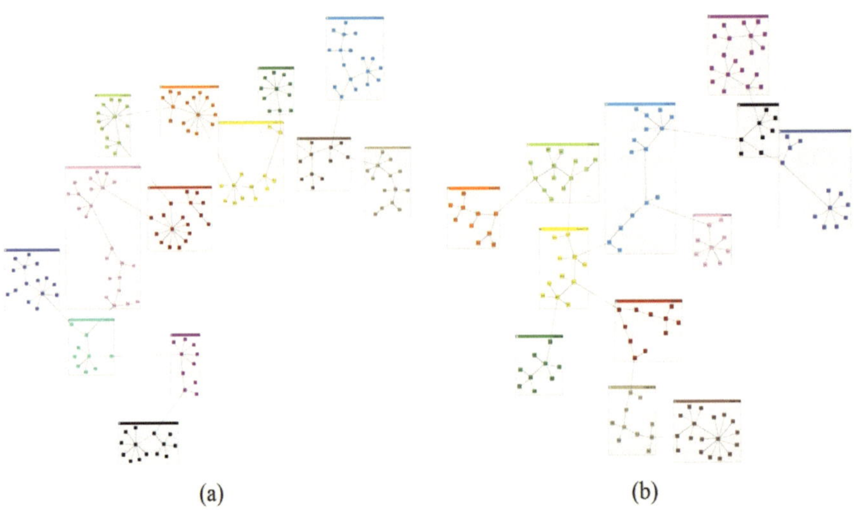

Figure 4. German market topology in 2008 (a) and 2004 (b).

CL.ID	mu	std	sk	ku	SR
CL01	0.0003094	0.057005	10.44936	2451.638	0.543%
CL02	0.0003942	0.057219	10.25497	2390.428	0.689%
CL03	0.0002678	0.05579	9.94812	638.8266	0.480%
CL04	0.0002824	0.056436	10.02534	2373.059	0.500%
CL05	0.0003270	0.056945	10.9984	2587.711	0.574%

CL.ID	mu	std	sk	ku	SR
CL06	0.0002756	0.055918	10.00477	2389.595	0.493%
CL07	0.0002644	0.055723	10.02986	2411.497	0.475%
CL08	0.0004753	0.058852	11.32831	2525.394	0.808%
CL09	0.0003157	0.056422	10.36997	2460.894	0.559%
CL10	0.0005666	0.059179	11.77725	2602.168	0.957%
CL11	0.0005439	0.058084	11.26676	2532.204	0.936%
CL12	0.0003427	0.056806	10.10251	2371.656	0.603%
CL13	0.0004168	0.057255	10.66783	2490.513	0.728%

Table 4. Clusters percentage composition for the German market in the period 2007-2008.

CL.ID	mu	std	sk	ku	SR
CL01	0.0003849	0.056505	10.48629	2485.513	0.681%
CL02	0.0004037	0.057215	1.653466	2378.495	0.706%
CL03	0.0008787	0.061519	12.6148	2713.425	1.428%
CL04	0.0002657	0.055689	9.951796	2394.033	0.477%
CL05	0.0003660	0.056965	10.57433	2485.67	0.642%
CL06	0.0003745	0.056659	10.46166	2471.775	0.661%
CL07	0.0003209	0.056475	10.12393	2390.405	0.568%
CL08	0.0001570	0.045558	1.733983	413.5084	0.345%
CL09	0.0003237	0.056749	10.47651	2469.166	0.570%
CL10	0.0003062	0.056178	10.10382	2404.7	0.545%
CL11	0.0005619	0.058529	11.85308	2648.211	0.960%

Table 5. Clusters percentage composition for the German market in the period 2004-2005.

Sec.	CL01	CL02	CL03	CL04	CL05	CL06	CL07	CL08	CL09	CL10	CL11	CL12	CL13
Mkt	0.00	0.00	0.00	8.33	0.00	0.00	4.35	0.00	11.76	0.00	0.00	8.33	0.00
B&F	23.81	8.33	15.38	0.00	22.22	0.00	17.39	37.50	11.76	7.69	14.29	8.33	36.36
HI	4.76	0.00	0.00	8.33	0.00	6.29	0.00	0.00	12.75	0.00	0.00	0.00	0.00
Serv	0.00	8.33	7.69	8.33	0.00	7.14	4.35	12.50	0.00	0.00	0.00	0.00	7.14
Fash	4.76	8.33	7.69	8.33	5.56	7.14	4.35	12.50	5.88	15.38	0.00	16.67	0.00
HT	4.76	12.00	7.69	0.00	0.00	21.43	4.35	0.00	11.76	23.08	21.43	25.00	9.09
HC	0.00	16.67	8.33	0.00	16.67	0.00	0.00	0.00	0.00	15.38	0.00	0.00	0.00

Sec.	CL01	CL02	CL03	CL04	CL05	CL06	CL07	CL08	CL09	CL10	CL11	CL12	CL13
Log	4.76	0.00	8.33	16.67	0.00	7.14	4.35	12.50	0.00	0.00	0.00	0.00	4.75
Lux	0.00	8.33	0.00	0.00	0.00	0.00	0.00	0.00	0.00	0.00	0.00	7.14	0.00
Hou	19.05	0.00	7.69	0.00	5.56	7.14	8.70	12.50	5.88	0.00	14.29	8.33	9.09
Comp	4.76	0.00	0.00	8.33	0.00	0.00	4.00	0.00	0.00	7.69	0.00	0.00	9.09
Ret Serv	0.00	0.00	0.00	0.00	0.00	5.00	0.00	0.00	11.76	0.00	4.21	0.00	0.00
F&D	4.76	0.00	7.69	8.33	5.56	0.00	16.67	0.00	0.00	0.00	0.00	8.33	4.75
En	4.76	0.00	4.76	0.00	16.67	0.00	9.20	0.00	0.00	0.00	0.00	0.00	4.76
Ent	0.00	0.00	0.00	8.33	0.00	7.14	0.00	7.14	5.88	23.08	14.29	0.00	0.00
Press	4.76	0.00	8.33	8.33	0.00	0.00	0.00	0.00	0.00	0.00	0.00	0.00	7.14
Imp/Exp	0.00	16.67	3.94	8.33	0.00	7.14	0.00	0.00	0.00	0.00	7.14	0.00	0.00
PU	4.76	1.00	0.00	0.00	0.00	0.00	0.00	0.00	0.00	0.00	0.00	0.00	0.00
TCom	0.00	0.00	7.69	0.00	0.00	7.14	12.41	0.00	16.67	7.69	7.69	0.00	0.00
Auto	9.52	12.00	0.00	8.33	11.11	7.14	5.90	5.36	5.88	0.00	16.67	16.67	9.09
Gard	0.00	0.00	0.00	0.00	0.00	3.00	0.00	0.00	0.00	0.00	0.00	1.19	0.00
Man	4.76	8.33	4.76	0.00	16.67	7.14	4.00	0.00	0.00	0.00	0.00	0.00	0.00

Table 6. Clusters percentage composition during the period 2007- 2008.

Sec.	CL01	CL02	CL03	CL04	CL05	CL06	CL07	CL08	CL09	CL10	CL11
Mkt	0.00	6.25	12.50	6.67	0.00	6.25	0.00	0.00	0.00	0.00	0.00
B&F	20.00	12.50	0.00	0.00	18.18	25.00	41.67	35.00	0.00	40.00	14.29
HI	0.00	0.00	7.50	16.80	5.00	0.00	0.00	0.00	16.43	0.00	0.00
Serv	0.00	6.25	0.00	0.00	9.09	0.00	0.00	10.00	0.00	10.00	0.00
Fash.	10.00	25.00	0.00	6.67	0.00	6.25	0.00	5.00	0.00	0.00	14.29
HT	10.00	0.00	12.50	26.67	18.18	0.00	8.33	0.00	14.29	0.00	41.43
HC	5.00	0.00	0.00	0.00	0.00	12.50	0.00	0.00	0.00	0.00	0.00
Log	0.00	18.50	0.00	0.00	10.00	0.00	8.33	20.00	0.00	0.00	12.00
Lux	0.00	0.00	12.50	0.00	0.00	0.00	0.00	0.00	0.00	0.00	0.00
Hou	10.00	6.25	0.00	6.67	0.00	5.50	8.33	0.00	41.43	0.00	0.00
Comp	0.00	11.50	0.00	6.67	0.00	6.25	0.00	5.00	0.00	0.00	0.00
Ret Serv	0.00	0.00	10.00	0.00	0.00	0.00	0.00	0.00	0.00	15.00	0.00
F&D	0.00	0.00	0.00	6.67	0.00	6.25	0.00	5.00	0.00	0.00	0.00
En	10.00	0.00	7.50	0.00	0.00	0.00	0.00	0.00	0.00	0.00	0.00

Sec.	CL01	CL02	CL03	CL04	CL05	CL06	CL07	CL08	CL09	CL10	CL11
Ent	0.00	6.25	25.00	6.67	0.00	12.50	0.00	0.00	0.00	10.00	7.14
Press	0.00	0.00	0.00	0.00	10.00	0.00	0.00	10.00	0.00	10.00	0.00
Imp/Exp	0.00	0.00	0.00	9.86	0.00	0.00	0.00	0.00	5.71	0.00	5.00
PU	0.00	0.00	0.00	0.00	0.00	0.00	0.00	0.00	0.00	5.00	0.00
TCom	0.00	7.50	0.00	0.00	0.00	0.00	16.67	0.00	0.00	0.00	0.00
Auto	30.00	0.00	12.50	6.67	9.09	12.50	16.67	10.00	15.00	0.00	0.00
Gard	5.00	0.00	0.00	0.00	10.00	0.00	0.00	0.00	0.00	0.00	0.00
Man	0.00	0.00	0.00	0.00	10.00	7.00	0.00	0.00	7.14	10.00	3.00

Table 7. Clusters percentage composition during the period 2004- 2005.

In both cases cluster statistics evidence (once again) positive mean and skewness, and lower variability. The Sharpe Ratio is generally higher than that evidenced in the static analysis. Looking at clusters composition, we primarily observe that, moving from one period to another, it did not maintain unchanged. However, it has been possible to isolate dominant sectors. In particular, in the period 2007- 2008, B&F companies prevail in five over thirteen clusters (CL01, CL03, CL07, CL08 and CL13); HC and Imp/Exp firms share dominance in CL02; Hi-Tech is the dominant sector in cluster CL06, CL10, CL11 and CL12. Finally, Logistics and TCom societies are concentrated in CL04 and CL09 respectively. Coping such results to the values of Sharpe Ratio, it seems possible to claim that good performances are mainly due to the leading activity of the High-Tech sector. Besides, by comparison with the performances discussed in the static analysis, Germany gave the impression to have suffered for the global crisis with some delay.

	2004-2005 (NETG1)	2007-2008 (NETG2)	2010-2011 (NETG3)
Average Degree	1.990	1.989	1.990
Density	0.010	0.011	0.010
Modularity	0.767	0.757	0.755

Table 8. Measures of network organization. A comparison among German market topologies during the periods under examination. NET.

Most interesting results, in our opinion, come by the analysis of the period: December 2004-December 2005. The first element to highlight is that in this case we have only 11 clusters (versus 13 in the period: 2007-2008, and 14 in the period: 2010-2011). For what is concerning clusters composition now we have: B&F companies dominating clusters CL01, CL05, CL06, CL07, CL08, and CL10; fashion sector prevails in CL02, entertainment companies in CL03, housing societies in CL09, while Hi-Tech is the king of remaining clusters (CL04, CL05 and CL11). If we compare the results to those we have previously discussed, it is quite clear that during the observed period we have been witnesses of various companies reactions to the crisis: while Hi-Tech as well as financial companies maintained similar behaviors (and this is confirmed by the tendency to be clustered together), companies in other sectors did not group in any way. A possible explanation might stay in some policy action made by the national government, in order to address the economy, and to protect sectors with higher exposure.

To conclude, the joint use of SOM and MST makes also possible to analyze the results from a network (graphs theory) perspective. To such aim, Table 8 shows some relevant measures of network organization for the German market in the periods under examination.

Before discussing the values, we briefly explain the meaning of the observed variables. The Average Degree (AD) expresses the average number of ties of the networks nodes and measures how much immediate is the risk of nodes for catching whatever is flowing through the network. In the examined cases higher scores should mean an exposure to abrupt changes in the market arrangement. However, the AD values we have obtained are low and very similar one to each other. The Graph Density (GD) measures how close the network is to be complete: since a complete graph has all possible edges, its GD will be 1: the lower this value, the farther the graph is to be complete. The values in our nets are at least the same and lower. Both NetG1, NetG2 and NetG3 are far to be complete. Note that the reason is in the filtering procedure acted by MST on SOM that cleaned the original map from lesser significant ties. The Modularity, on the other hand, is a concept close to that of clustering, since it examines the attitude to community formation in the net, and it is then strictly related to the possibility to disclose clusters in a net. In order to be significant, values need to be higher than 0.4. This threshold has been largely exceeded in all examined nets.

4.2. The case of Spain

As done for Germany, we begin by the static analysis during the period: December 2010-December 2011. Our procedure identified eight clusters, as shown in Figure 5.

Figure 5. Skeleton framework of the Spanish stock exchange in the period: 30 December 2010 - 30 December 2011.

CL.ID	mu	std	sk	ku	SR
CL01	0.0004	0.023	-1.803	189.280	1.9%
CL02	0.0005	0.022	-1.400	175.611	2.4%
CL03	0.0005	0.022	-1.235	162.575	2.4%
CL04	0.0005	0.022	-1.353	169.223	2.4%
CL05	0.0005	0.022	-1.209	161.611	2.3%
CL06	0.0005	0.023	-1.321	164.853	2.3%
CL07	0.0006	0.022	-1.345	180.364	2.8%
CL08	0.0004	0.023	-1.705	179.979	1.8%

Table 9. Basic statistics for clusters in the Spanish stock exchange. The reference period is: Dec. 2010 - Dec. 2011.

At the first glance cluster statistics are not as dramatic as to justify the present critical situation of the Spanish market: mean is positive and so the Sharpe Ratio is. Obviously it is quite low, and hence it can be explained as a signal of overall reduced market profitability. Nevertheless, a warning comes matching mean to skewness. Skewness, in fact, is negative: under this light the positivity of the mean can be justified only by the presence of bursts (and hence speculative movements), like viewing at the Spanish market behavior (Fig 6) over the past year confirms.

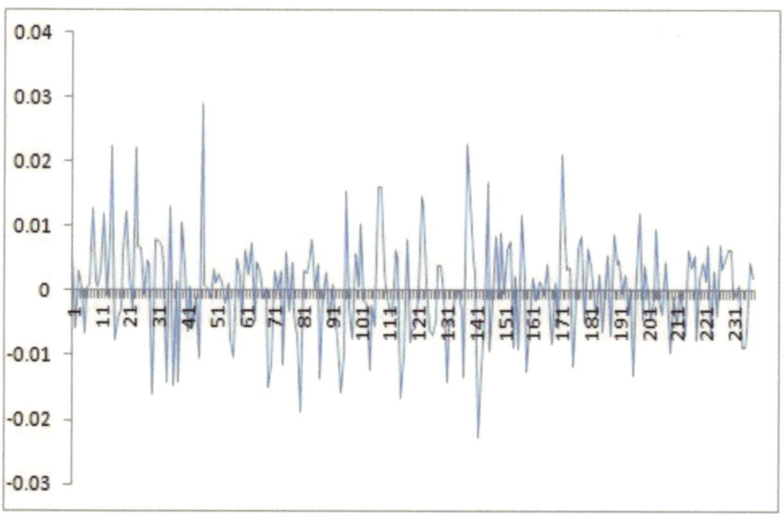

Figure 6. The behaviour of Spanish market (log returns) in the period December 2010-December 2011.

Fig 6, in fact, shows the log returns dynamics in the Spanish market in the period December 2010-December 2011. It sticks out immediately the *spiky* nature of the observed time series.

Moving to the analysis of clusters composition (Table 10), by comparison to the situation discussed for Germany a number of sectors is now missing[3]. In addition, companies in the

B&F sector are widely disseminated and dominate five over eight clusters. In the remaining three clusters Housing (Hou) and Paper Factories (Pap, a new entry with respect to what already seen for Germany) have a dominant position.

The aforementioned clusters structure suggests a key to understand present financial instability in Spain: the highest number of financial companies in the market makes it weak and prone to speculation (as the bursts one can see by looking at Fig 6 confirms in turn). One the other hand, since the Housing sector has been the driving engine of the global crisis, it is reasonable that its higher influence in the Spanish market composition has negatively conditioned its behaviour.

	CL01	CL02	CL03	CL04	CL05	CL06	CL07	CL08
Aero	0%	0%	14.29%	0.00%	0%	0%	0%	0%
Agr	0%	0%	7.14%	0.00%	0%	0%	0%	0%
Auto	0%	0%	0.00%	0.00%	11.11%	0%	0%	0%
B&F	40%	22.22%	21.43%	12.50%	11.11%	44.44%	0.00%	20%
Chem	0%	0%	7.14%	0.00%	0.00%	11.11%	10%	0%
En	10%	11.11%	14.29%	12.50%	0.00%	11.11%	10%	0%
F&D	10%	11.11%	0.00%	0.00%	22.22%	22.22%	10%	10%
Fas	10%	0%	0%	12.50%	0%	0%	0%	10%
Hi	10%	0%	0%	0%	0%	0%	0%	10%
Hou	10%	22.22%	7.14%	0.00%	22.22%	0%	20%	0%
It	0%	0%	0%	12.50%	0%	0%	0%	0%
Log	0%	0%	0%	12.50%	0%	0%	0%	0%
Lux	0%	11.11%	0%	0%	11.11%	0%	0%	0%
Pap	0%	0.00%	0.00%	25.00%	0%	11.11%	10%	10%
Pharm	0%	11.11%	7.14%	0%	0%	0%	10%	10%
Pu	0%	0%	7.14%	0%	0%	0%	0%	0%
Tcom	10%	0%	0%	12.50%	0%	0%	20%	0%
Ter	0%	0%	7.14%	0%	22.22%	0%	10%	30%
Transp	0%	11.11%	7.14%	0%	0%	0%	0%	0%

Table 10. Cluster percentage composition for Spain in the period December 2010-December 2011.

Replicating for Spain the analysis we have already performed for Germany, suggests a number of additional issues to be discussed. Figure 7 shows the market organization in the periods: 2007-2008 and 2004-2005, while Tables 11-14 report the corresponding basic statistics and clusters composition.

3 This is the case, for instance, of Imp/Exp, Ret. Serv., and High Tech.

(a) (b)

Figure 7. Skeleton framework of Spanish market in the periods: 2007-2008 (a), and 2004-2005.

CL.ID	mu	std	sk	ku	SR
CL01	0.00142	0.018	1.156	14.442	8%
CL02	-0.00023	0.016	0.702	13.033	-1.5%
CL03	-0.00028	0.026	-10.400	354.521	-1.1%
CL04	0.0014	0.020	0.948	7.377	7.1%
CL05	-0.0005	0.025	-0.267	13.392	-2.1%
CL06	0.0009	0.017	0.375	4.462	5.3%
CL07	0.0015	0.024	7.952	185.964	6.2%
CL08	0.0002	0.022	-0.122	14.941	0.7%

Table 11. Clusters statistics for Spain in the period: 2007-2008.

CL.ID	mu	std	sk	ku	SR
CL01	-0.00006	0.021	1.888	19.464	-0.3%
CL02	0.00150	0.018	1.327	18.261	8.4%
CL03	-0.00019	0.021	0.209	2.673	-0.09%
CL04	0.0012	0.015	0.782	6.485	7.7%
CL05	0.0013	0.017	0.939	7.531	7.6%
CL06	-0.0006	0.026	-11.489	396.951	-2.1%
CL07	0.0014	0.029	6.702	132.794	5%
CL08	-0.0001	0.024	-0.249	12.979	-0.5%

Table 12. Clusters statistics for Spain in the period: 2004-2005.

	CL01	CL02	CL03	CL04	CL05	CL06	CL07	CL08
Aero	14%	0%	0.00%	12.50%	0%	0%	0%	0%
Agr	0%	0%	0.00%	0.00%	0%	0%	9%	0%
Auto	0%	0%	8.33%	0.00%	0.00%	0%	0%	0%
B&F	0%	0.00%	33.33%	25.00%	22.22%	22.22%	18.18%	36%
Chem	0%	0%	0.00%	0.00%	0.00%	11.11%	9%	9%
En	29%	18.18%	0.00%	12.50%	0.00%	0.00%	18%	0%
F&D	14%	9.09%	16.67%	12.50%	0.00%	11.11%	18%	0%
Fas	0%	0%	8%	0.00%	11%	11%	0%	0%
Hi	0%	0%	0%	0%	0%	11%	9%	0%
Hou	14%	9.09%	8.33%	12.50%	33.33%	0%	0%	9%
It	0%	0%	0%	0.00%	11%	0%	0%	0%
Log	0%	0%	8%	0.00%	0%	0%	0%	0%
Lux	0%	9.09%	0%	0%	0.00%	0%	0%	9%
Pap	14%	9.09%	8.33%	0.00%	0%	0.00%	9%	9%
Pharm	0%	18.18%	0.00%	0%	0%	0%	0%	18%
Pu	0%	0%	0.00%	13%	0%	0%	0%	0%
Tcom	14%	9%	0%	12.50%	0%	11%	0%	0%
Ter	0%	9%	8.33%	0%	22.22%	22%	9%	0%
Transp	0%	9.09%	0.00%	0%	0%	0%	0%	9%

Table 13. Cluster percentage composition for Spain in the period 2007-2008.

Looking to Table 11, basic statistics for 2008 highlight a situation that cannot be interpreted in an precise way: clusters CL01, CL04, CL06, and CL07 have positive mean, skewness and Sharpe Ratio, CL08 has positive mean and SR, CL03 and CL05 has gone negative, while CL02 is a hybrid of all above states, with negative mean and SR, and positive skewness. Going back to 2004, Table 12 sees two clusters (CL06, CL08) negative both in mean, SR and skewness, two negative only in mean and SR (CL01, CL03), and all remaining clusters with positive statistics.

The turning point to understand the crisis of Spain is in clusters composition. While in 2004 (Table 14) the Spanish market exhibited a strongest component in the Energy sector, this disappeared when we look to Table 13 that shows market organization in 2008. The snapshot we took by looking at this period, shows a market dominated by banks (i.e. an exposure to speculation), as well as by sectors like luxury goods, and fashion that did not assure any protective shield in period of global crisis.

	CL01	CL02	CL03	CL04	CL05	CL06	CL07	CL08
Aero	0%	8%	0.00%	0.00%	10%	0%	0%	0%
Agr	0%	0%	0.00%	10.00%	0%	0%	0%	0%
Auto	0%	0%	0.00%	0.00%	0.00%	8%	0%	0%
Bkf	17%	33.33%	11.11%	20.00%	0.00%	41.67%	0.00%	26%
Chem	0%	25%	0.00%	10.00%	0.00%	0.00%	0%	0%
En	0%	16.67%	22.22%	10.00%	10.00%	0.00%	13%	5%
F&D	0%	0.00%	11.11%	20.00%	10.00%	16.67%	38%	0%
Fas	17%	0%	11%	0.00%	10%	0%	13%	0%
Hi	0%	8%	0%	10%	0%	8%	0%	0%
Hou	0%	0.00%	11.11%	0.00%	10.00%	8%	13%	26%
It	0%	0%	0%	0.00%	0%	0%	0%	5%
Log	0%	0%	0%	0.00%	0%	8%	0%	0%
Lux	17%	0.00%	0%	0%	0.00%	0%	0%	5%
Pap	17%	0.00%	11.11%	0.00%	30%	0.00%	0%	0%
Pharm	17%	0.00%	0.00%	0%	0%	0%	0%	16%
Pu	0%	0%	0.00%	10%	0%	0%	0%	0%
Tcom	0%	0%	0%	0.00%	20%	0%	13%	5%
Ter	0%	8%	22.22%	10%	0.00%	8%	13%	5%
Transp	17%	0.00%	0.00%	0%	0%	0%	0%	5%

Table 14. Cluster percentage composition for Spain in the period 2004-2005.

Moving the attention towards networks statistics (Table 15), we may observe that the values of NETS2 and NETS3 are quite similar; conversely, they differ from those referring to the first period under examination (NETS1). In the attempt to give the data an economic interpretation, we can say that NETS2 and NETS3 mirror a steady situation. Moreover, looking to Density values the Spanish market gives the impression of a place where each company is undertaking its own way. Such *de-clustering* orientation confirms the present exposure of the country to external speculation attacks.

	2004-2005 (NETS1)	2007-2008 (NETS2)	2010-2011 (NETS3)
Average Degree	1.75	1.974	1.974
Diameter	16	19	22
Density	0.25	0.026	0.026
Modularity	0.132	0.697	0.701

Table 15. Measures of network organization. A comparison among market topologies during the periods under examination.

5. Conclusion

In this chapter we provided an example of how to use Self Organizing Maps (SOMs) as a tool to analyze financial stability.

We moved from row data (price levels) of quoted enterprises to provide a snapshot of countries financial situation, and then we applied a hybrid procedure coping together SOMs and Minimum Spanning Tree (MST). We checked our approach on two markets featuring different levels of (in)stability: the German and the Spanish Stock Exchange.

Our study made us possible to highlight most important relations among quoted societies, as well as the natural clusters that tend to be created into those markets.

In particular, in the case of Germany we captured the country situation in three periods (2004-2005, 2007-2008 and 2010-2011). The study suggested that the German government was able to pay attention to warning signals emerging from the market. In this way Germany applied measures that allowed it to face last year critical situation. Protecting sectors with a strength tradition and promoting the challenge in emerging sectors Germany played a game that seems to maintain the country at the marginal side of current global crisis.

On the other hand, the case of Spain suggests the existence of a weak market dominated by banks that has been highly exposed to investors speculation. Local governors neither did take into account in the right way alerting signals or did apply correction/protection measures. In a positive sense our procedure highlighted some direction towards which policy makers could operate in order to reduce instability.

To conclude the joined SOM-MST approach seems able to suggest proper recipes that governments might consider in order to address their policy efforts.

Author details

Marina Resta*

Address all correspondence to: resta@economia.unige.it

Department of Economics, University of Genova, Italy

References

[1] Kaufman, G. Ed. (1995). Banking, Financial Markets, and Systemic Risk Research in Financial Services Greenwich/London , 7

[2] de Bandt, O., & Hartmann, P. (2000, December). Systemic Risk: a Survey. *Discussion Paper 2634*, Centre for Economic Policy Research.

[3] European Central Bank. (2004). *Annual Report.*

[4] Schwarcz, S. L. (2008). Systemic risk. *Duke Law School Legal Studies Paper 163*, Duke University.

[5] Martinez-Jaramillo, S., Perez, O., Embriz, F., & Dey, F. (2010). Systemic risk, financial contagion and financial fragility. *Journal of Economic Dynamics & Control*, 34(11), 2358-2374.

[6] Allen, F., & Gale, D. (2000). Financial contagion. *Journal of Political Economy*, 108, 1-33.

[7] Nier, E., Yang, J., Yorulmazer, T., & Alentorn, A. (2006). Network models and financial stability. *Journal of Economic Dynamics & Control*, 31, 2033-2060.

[8] Boss, M., Elsinger, H., Summer, M., & Thurner, S. (2004). The network topology of the interbank market. *Quantitative Finance*, 4, 677-684.

[9] Muller, J. (2006). Interbank credit lines as a channel of contagion. *Journal of Financial Services Research*, 29, 37-60.

[10] Altman, E. I., & Saunders, A. (1998). Credit risk measurement: developments over the last 20 years. *Journal of Banking and Finance*, 21, 1721-1742.

[11] Benito, A., Delgado, F., & Pagés, J. (2004). A synthetic indicator of financial pressure for Spanish firms. *Banco de Espana, Working paper* [411].

[12] Bernhardsen, E. (2001). A Model of Bankruptcy Prediction. *Norges Bank Working Paper 2001/10.*

[13] Bunn, P., & Redwood, V. (2003). Company Accounts-Based Modelling of Business Failures and the Implications for Financial Stability. *Bank of England Working Paper* [210].

[14] Chava, S., & Jarrow, R. A. (2004). Bankruptcy prediction with industry effects. *Review of Finance*, 8(4), 537-569.

[15] Allison, P. (1982). Discrete-time methods for the analysis of event history. *Sociological Methodology*, 61-99.

[16] Bonfim, D. (2009). Credit risk drivers: evaluating the contribution of firm level information and of macroeconomic dynamics. *Journal of Banking and Finance*, 33(2), 281-299.

[17] Bhattacharjee, A., Higson, C., Holly, S., & Kattuman, P. (2009). Macroeconomic instability and business exit: determinants of failures and acquisitions of UK Firms. *Economica*, 76, 108-131.

[18] Qu, Y. (2008). Macro Economic Factors and Probability of Default. *European Journal of Economics, Finance and Administrative Sciences* [13], 1450-2275.

[19] Pederzoli, C., & Torricelli, C. (2005). Capital requirements and business cycle regimes: forward-looking modelling of default probabilities. *Journal of Banking and Finance*, 29(12), 3121-3140.

[20] Kohonen, T. (2001). Self-Organizing Maps. Third, extended edition, Springer.

[21] Kaski, S., Kangas, J., & Kohonen, T. (1998). Bibliography of Self-Organizing Map (SOM) Papers: 1981-1997. *Neural Computing Surveys*, 1, 102-350.

[22] Oja, M., Kaski, S., & Kohonen, T. (2003). Bibliography of Self-Organizing Map (SOM) Papers: 1998-2001 Addendum. *Neural Computing Surveys*, 3, 1-156.

[23] Polla, M., Honkela, T., & Kohonen, T. (2009). Bibliography of Self-Organizing Map (SOM) Papers: 2002-2005 Addendum. *TKK Reports in Information and Computer Science, Report TKK-ICS-R23*, Helsinki University of Technology.

[24] Martin, B., & Serrano, Cinca. C. (1993). Self Organizing Neural Networks for the Analysis and Representation of Data: some Financial Cases. *Neural Computing & Applications*, 1(2), 193-206.

[25] Deboeck, G., Kohonen, T., & Edrs, . (1998). Visual Explorations in Finance: with Self-Organizing Maps. Springer Finance, New York.

[26] Montefiori, M., & Resta, M. (2009). A computational approach for the health care market. *Health Care Management Science*, 12(4), 344-350.

[27] Resta, M. (2011). Assessing the efficiency of Health Care Providers: A SOM perspective. *In: Laaksonen J., Honkela T. Advances in Self Organizing Maps. LNCS 6731*, Springer, Heidelberg, 30-39.

[28] Resta, M. (2009). Early Warning Systems: an approach via Self Organizing Maps with applications to emergent markets. *Proceedings of the 2009 conference on New Directions in Neural Networks: 18th Italian Workshop on Neural Networks: WIRN 2008*, IOS Press, Amsterdam, The Netherlands.

[29] Sarlin, P., & Eklund, T. (2011). Fuzzy clustering of the self-organizing map: some applications on financial time series. *In: Laaksonen J., Honkela T. Advances in Self Organizing Maps. LNCS 6731*, Springer, Heidelberg, 40-50.

[30] Resta, M. (2012). The Shape of Crisis: lessons from Self Organizing Maps. *Forthcoming in C. Kahraman Ed.: Computational intelligence applications in industrial engineering*, Springer, Atlantis.

[31] Kangas, J. A., Kohonen, T., & Laaksonen, J. (1990). Variants of self-organizing maps. *IEEE Trans Neural Netw*, 1(1), 93-99.

[32] Kleiweg, P. (1996). *Neurale netwerken: Een inleidende cursus met practica voor de studie Alfa-Informatica, Master thesis*, Rijksuniversiteit Groningen.

[33] Mayer, R., & Rauber, A. (2010). Visualising Clusters in Self-Organising Maps with Minimum Spanning Trees. *Proceedings of the International Conference on Artificial Neural Networks (ICANN'10)*, Springer-Verlag, Berlin, Heidelberg, 364-2-15821-842-6, 426-431.

[34] Girvan, M., & Newman, M. E. J. (2002). Community structure in social and biological networks. *Proc. Natl. Acad. Sci.*, USA, 99, 7821-7826.

Chapter 2

Social Interaction and Self-Organizing Maps

Ryotaro Kamimura

Additional information is available at the end of the chapter

http://dx.doi.org/10.5772/51705

1. Introduction

In this chapter, we consider neuron societies where there are many different types of interactions. In one society, a neuron is connected with others only by the distance between two neurons. In another one, a neuron is connected with others by similarity between neurons, and so on. We here choose a special case where the interaction between neurons is weighted by the distance between them. This simplification aims to apply the new method to the creation of self-organizing maps. With this research, we expect new types of self-organizing maps to appear, ones which take into account the interactions between neurons.

The self-organizing map (SOM) [1] is one of the most well-known techniques in neural networks. In particular, the SOM is commonly used for the visualization of complex data. Contradictorily, one of the main problems of the SOM is that it is difficult to represent final SOM knowledge. This is because self-organizing maps are generally only concerned with competition and cooperation between neurons, without due attention being paid to visualization in the course of learning. Thus, there have been many attempts to visually represent SOM knowledge [1], [2], [3], [4], [5], [6], [7], [8], [9]. However, it is still presently difficult to visualize SOM knowledge clearly; thus, the present study is an additional attempt at clearly visualizing SOM knowledge. The hypothetical improved visualization is possible by enhancing the characteristics common to neurons based upon their interactions. In addition, our method can be used to control the degree of interaction or cooperation, which contributes to the better visualization of SOM knowledge.

We applied our method to the analysis of Japanese automobile production for a period of twenty years. The automobile industry underwent drastic changes during these years due to severe competition in the development of environmentally friendly and fuel-efficient cars, and in reducing production costs. However, because of the lack of the methods to clarify the overall characteristics of the automobile industry, it has been difficult to clarify the main characteristics of automobile production. Our method is expected to focus upon the important characteristics of the automobile industry through social interaction, because two neurons with similar outputs interact with each other. Even if the conventional

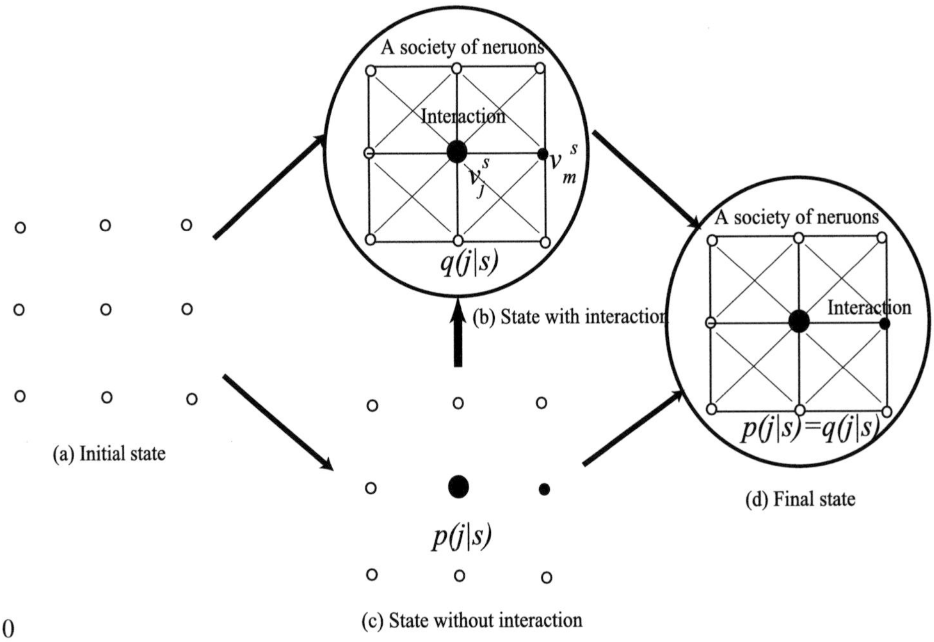

Figure 1. Social interaction from an initial state (a) to a final state (d).

SOM does not create interpretable representations, our method can be used to create interpretable representations by controlling the degree of interaction.

In Section 2, we explain a concept of social interaction and how to compute social interaction. Then, we apply the method to the self-organizing maps. We define the KL-divergence between neurons in interaction and usual neurons. By minimizing the KL-divergence, we derive the optimal outputs and connection weights. In Section 3, we present the experimental results applied to the extraction of characteristics of automobile production from the period of 1993 to 2011 in Japan. We first determine the optimal representation to maximize mutual information between neurons and input patterns. Then, we try to interpret connection weights. In the discussion section, we try to interpret the final representations based on the events and incidents of this period.

2. Theory and computational methods

2.1. Social interaction

In this chapter, we consider societies formed by the interaction of neurons. Suppose that two neurons' outputs are represented by v_j and v_m, respectively as shown in Figure 1. Then, the interaction is defined by the product of two neurons' outputs:

$$\text{interact}_{jm} = v_j v_m. \tag{1}$$

In addition, the distance between two neurons should be considered. Now, suppose that the distance is represented by h_{jm}. Then, the interaction is modified as

$$\text{interact}_{jm} = v_j h_{jm} v_m. \tag{2}$$

The output from the jth neuron is defined by the sum of all interaction of the jth neuron and computed by

$$\text{interact}_j = \sum_{m=1}^{M} v_j h_{jm} v_m. \tag{3}$$

The relative output after the interaction becomes

$$q(j) = \frac{\text{interact}_j}{\sum_{m=1}^{M} \text{interact}_m} \tag{4}$$

Then, we suppose that neurons gradually transform from an initial state of society without interaction in Figure 1(a) to a final state with interaction in Figure 1(d). Thus, we should develop a method to model this transformation. Now, let $p(j)$ denote the relative output without the interaction of the jth neuron. Then, this neuron must imitate the corresponding neuron with interaction. The difference between two types of neurons can be defined by the KL-divergence:

$$D = \sum_{j=1}^{M} p(j) \log \frac{p(j)}{q(j)}. \tag{5}$$

A society of neurons is formed by minimizing this KL-divergence. By minimizing this divergence, the relative output $p(j)$ becomes closer to the output after the interaction.

2.2. Application to SOM

Let us apply the concept of a society of neurons to the self-organizing maps. The sth input pattern of total S patterns can be represented by $\mathbf{x}^s = [x_1^s, x_2^s, \cdots, x_L^s]^T$, $s = 1, 2, \cdots, S$. Connection weights into the jth neuron of total M neurons are computed by $\mathbf{w}_j = [w_{j1}, w_{j2}, \cdots, w_{jL}]^T$, $j = 1, 2, \ldots, M$. Then, the jth neuron's output can be computed by

$$v_j^s \propto \exp\left\{ -\frac{1}{2} (\mathbf{x}^s - \mathbf{w}_j)^T \mathbf{\Lambda} (\mathbf{x}^s - \mathbf{w}_j) \right\}, \tag{6}$$

where $\mathbf{x}^s$ and $\mathbf{w}_j$ are supposed to represent L-dimensional input and weight column vectors, where L denotes the number of input units. The $L \times L$ matrix $\mathbf{\Lambda}$ is called a "scaling matrix," and the klth element of the matrix denoted by $(\mathbf{\Lambda})_{kl}$ is defined by

$$(\mathbf{\Lambda})_{kl} = \delta_{kl} \frac{1}{\sigma_\alpha^2}, \quad k, l = 1, 2, \cdots, L. \tag{7}$$

where σ_α is a spread parameter and defined by

$$\sigma_\alpha = \frac{1}{\alpha}. \tag{8}$$

Let us consider the following neighborhood function usually used in self-organizing maps:

$$h_{jc} \propto \exp\left(-\frac{\|\mathbf{r}_j - \mathbf{r}_c\|^2}{2\sigma_\gamma^2}\right), \tag{9}$$

where $\mathbf{r}_j$ and $\mathbf{r}_c$ denote the position of the jth and the cth unit on the output space and σ_γ is a spread parameter. Using this neighborhood function, we have

$$\text{interact}_j^s = \sum_{m=1}^{M} h_{jm} \exp\left\{-\frac{1}{2}(\mathbf{x}^s - \mathbf{w}_j)^T \mathbf{\Lambda}(\mathbf{x}^s - \mathbf{w}_j)\right\}. \tag{10}$$

The relative output of the jth neuron with interaction can be obtained by

$$q(j \mid s) = \frac{\text{interact}_j^s}{\sum_{m=1}^{M} \text{interact}_m^s}. \tag{11}$$

Let $p(j \mid s)$ denote the relative output from the jth neuron without interaction; then KL divergence is defined by

$$D = \sum_{s=1}^{S} p(s) \sum_{j=1}^{M} p(s) p(j \mid s) \log \frac{p(j \mid s)}{q(j \mid s)}. \tag{12}$$

By minimizing this divergence, we have

$$p^*(j \mid s) = \frac{q(j \mid s) \exp\left\{-\frac{1}{2}(\mathbf{x}^s - \mathbf{w}_j)^T \mathbf{\Lambda}(\mathbf{x}^s - \mathbf{w}_j)\right\}}{\sum_{m=1}^{M} q(m \mid s) \exp\left\{-\frac{1}{2}(\mathbf{x}^s - \mathbf{w}_m)^T \mathbf{\Lambda}(\mathbf{x}^s - \mathbf{w}_m)\right\}}. \tag{13}$$

Then, by substituting $p(j \mid s)$ for $p^*(j \mid s)$, we have the well-known free energy function [10], [11]

$$F = -2\sigma_\alpha^2 \sum_{s=1}^{S} p(s) \log \sum_{j=1}^{M} q(j|s) \exp\left\{-\frac{1}{2}(\mathbf{x}^s - \mathbf{w}_j)^T \mathbf{\Lambda}(\mathbf{x}^s - \mathbf{w}_j)\right\}. \tag{14}$$

By differentiating the free energy, we can have connection weights

$$\mathbf{w}_j = \frac{\sum_{s=1}^{S} p^*(j \mid s)\mathbf{x}^s}{\sum_{s=1}^{S} p^*(j \mid s)}. \tag{15}$$

http://dx.doi.org/10.5772/51705

3. Experiments

3.1. Data description and network architecture

The automobile industry has undergone drastic changes these days because of the increasing interest in environmental problems and severe competition between different automobile manufacturers around the world. In particular, the Japanese automobile industry has undergone major changes in developing advanced technologies and lowering the costs of manufacturing. In advanced technologies, much focus has been upon more fuel-efficiency automobiles, like electric, hybrid, and fuel cell vehicles. In addition, the high appreciation of the Japanese yen has made it impossible to produce automobiles with lower costs in Japan. Thus, it is certain that these drastic changes have been observed in the production and sales of automobiles in Japan. However, it has been difficult to extract the overall characteristics from complex automobile production and sales data. We here focus upon the analysis of automobile production and try to show the main characteristics of the production over these twenty years.

The total data for automobile production ranged between the years 1993 and 2011. The numbers of variables were eight, namely, standard, small, and mini passenger cars; standard, small, and mini trucks; and large and small buses. The data was normalized to range between zero and one. We examined what kinds of characteristics could be obtained by visualizing the data by our method and compared the results with those by the conventional SOM. Figure 2 shows the network architecture for the automobile data. In the network, we had eight input units, corresponding to the eight variables used. The number of neurons in the output layer was 288 (24×12). We used the large size of the network to clearly visualize the final results.

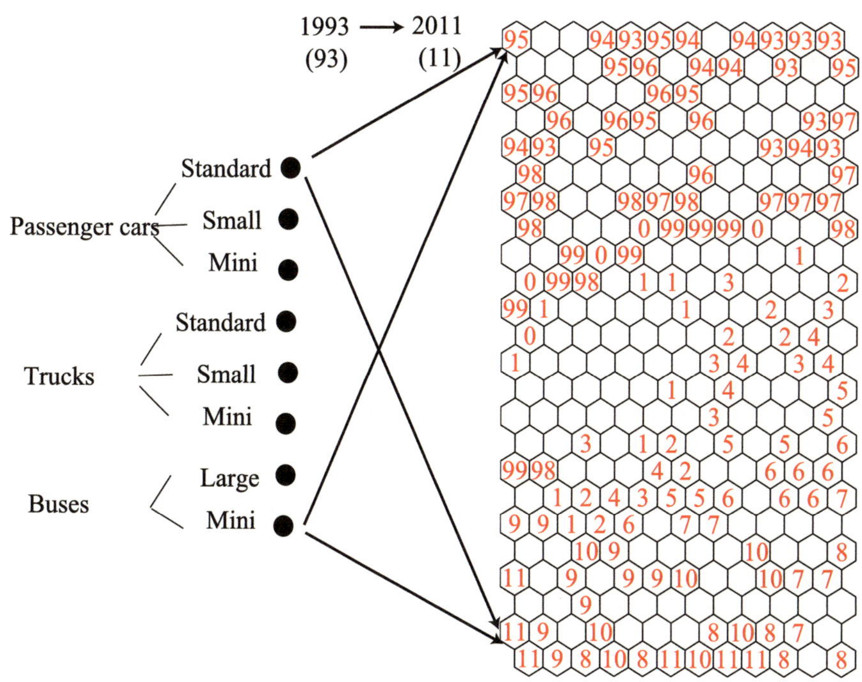

Figure 2. Network architecture for the automobile data.

3.2. Optimal representation and mutual information

The social interaction method can produce many different types of networks by taking into account the degree of interaction and competition. The degree of interaction can be changed through the parameter α. Thus, we must choose an appropriate representation among them. One of the possibilities is to use mutual information between neurons and input patterns. When this mutual information is increased, neurons tend to contain more information on input patterns. Mutual information can be defined by

$$I(\alpha) = \sum_{s=1}^{S} p(s) \sum_{j=1}^{M} p(s)p(j \mid s;\alpha) \log \frac{p(j \mid s;\alpha)}{p(j;\alpha)}. \tag{16}$$

One of the problems with this mutual information is that it increases constantly when the Gaussian width decreases or the parameter α increases, as shown in Figure 3(a). Thus, we must assign a constant value to the parameter α. Note that in actual learning, the parameter α was changed from one to ten, and the parameter was fixed only for computing mutual information. Figure 3(b) shows this mutual information when the parameter α was set to 1/10. As can be seen in the figure, mutual information increased initially and reached its highest point when the parameter α was 4. Then, mutual information gradually decreased. Though mutual information increased when the parameter α was increased in Figure 3(a), the actual mutual information did not increase when the parameter α was increased from 4 in Figure 3(b). Thus, we can say that when the parameter α was 4, we could obtain an optimal representation which had the maximum amount of information on input patterns.

Figure 4 shows the U-matrices when the parameter α was changed from 1 (a) to 10 (i). When the parameter α was 1 in Figure 4(a), the centralized class boundary was too huge. When the parameter α was 2, the huge class boundary became smaller, see Figure 4(b). When the parameter α was further increased to 3 in Figure 4(c), a class boundary in warmer colors on the upper side of the matrix became clearer, and other class boundaries began to appear on the lower side of the matrix. When the parameter α was 4 in Figure 4(d), the class boundary on the upper side of the matrix became the clearest and the other boundaries on the lower side became much clearer. Then, when the parameter α was further increased from 5 in Figure 4(e) to 10 (i), the class boundaries began to gradually deteriorate. These results corresponded to those of mutual information in Figure 3(b). When mutual information was 4, we could obtain maximum information, and then mutual information gradually decreased. When mutual information reached its maximum, the clearest representation in Figure 4(d) could be obtained.

3.3. Interpretation of optimal representation

We interpret the optimal representation with maximum mutual information when the parameter α was 4. Figure 5 shows the U-matrix and labels with class boundaries when the parameter α was 4. As shown in Figure 5(1), a clear class boundary in warmer color could be detected on the upper side of the matrix. Additionally, several minor class boundaries were located on the lower side of the matrix. From these boundaries and labels in Figure 5(2), the data was classified into three classes (periods). The first period (a) represented the production from 1993-1998. The second period ranged between 1999 and 2006, and the third period between 2007 and 2011. In the third period, the period between 2007 and 2008 and the year 2011 were separated from the period in the middle. In addition, we can see that in the first and the third periods, the data were arranged from right to left. On the other hand, in the second period, the data were arranged from left to right.

http://dx.doi.org/10.5772/51705

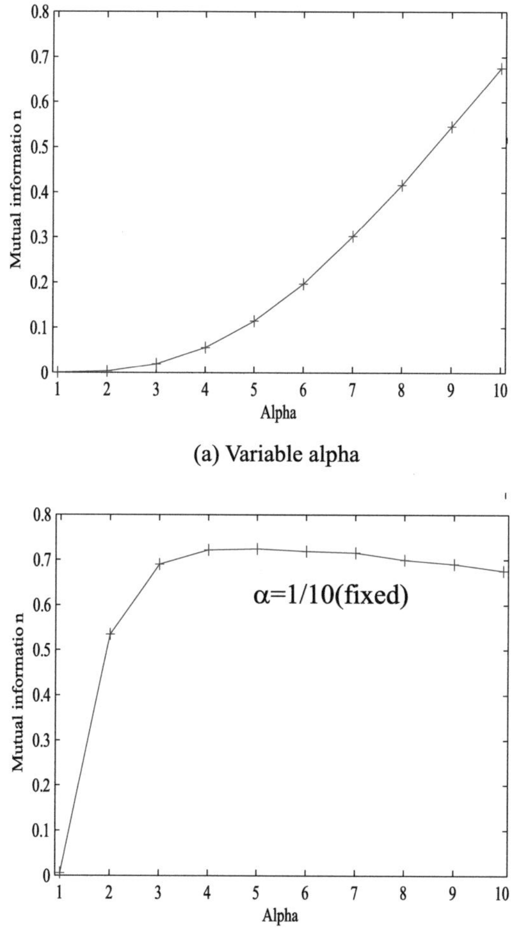

(a) Variable alpha

(b) Fixed alpha

Figure 3. Mutual information as a function of the parameter α (a) and with a fixed value (1/10) of the parameter α (b).

Figure 6 shows connection weights from the eight variables. As shown in Figure 6(a3), in the second and third periods, the production of mini-cars was very large, shown in warmer colors. On the other hand, standard, small and mini trucks were more heavily produced in the first period, in Figure 6 (b1), (b2) and (b3). In the third period, standard passenger cars and small buses were produced largely, represented by warmer colors in Figure 6(a1) and (c2). In addition, for all variables, the parts on the left hand at the bottom were very low in dark blue. This means that the production of automobiles was the lowest around 2011.

Figure 7 shows connection weights in nine typical neurons located and shown on the map in Figure 5(2). In the first period, the production of small passenger cars and trucks was large and the levels of production decreased gradually from (a3) to (a1). In the second period, the production gradually increased. In particular, the production of mini-cars increased from left (b1) to right (b3). In the beginning of the third period, in Figure 7(c3), the production of standard passenger cars and small buses were much higher than that of any other type of cars. However, the production decreased gradually in Figure 7(c2). Finally, in 2011, shown in Figure 7(c1), though overall production was very low, the production of mini-cars remained relatively higher.

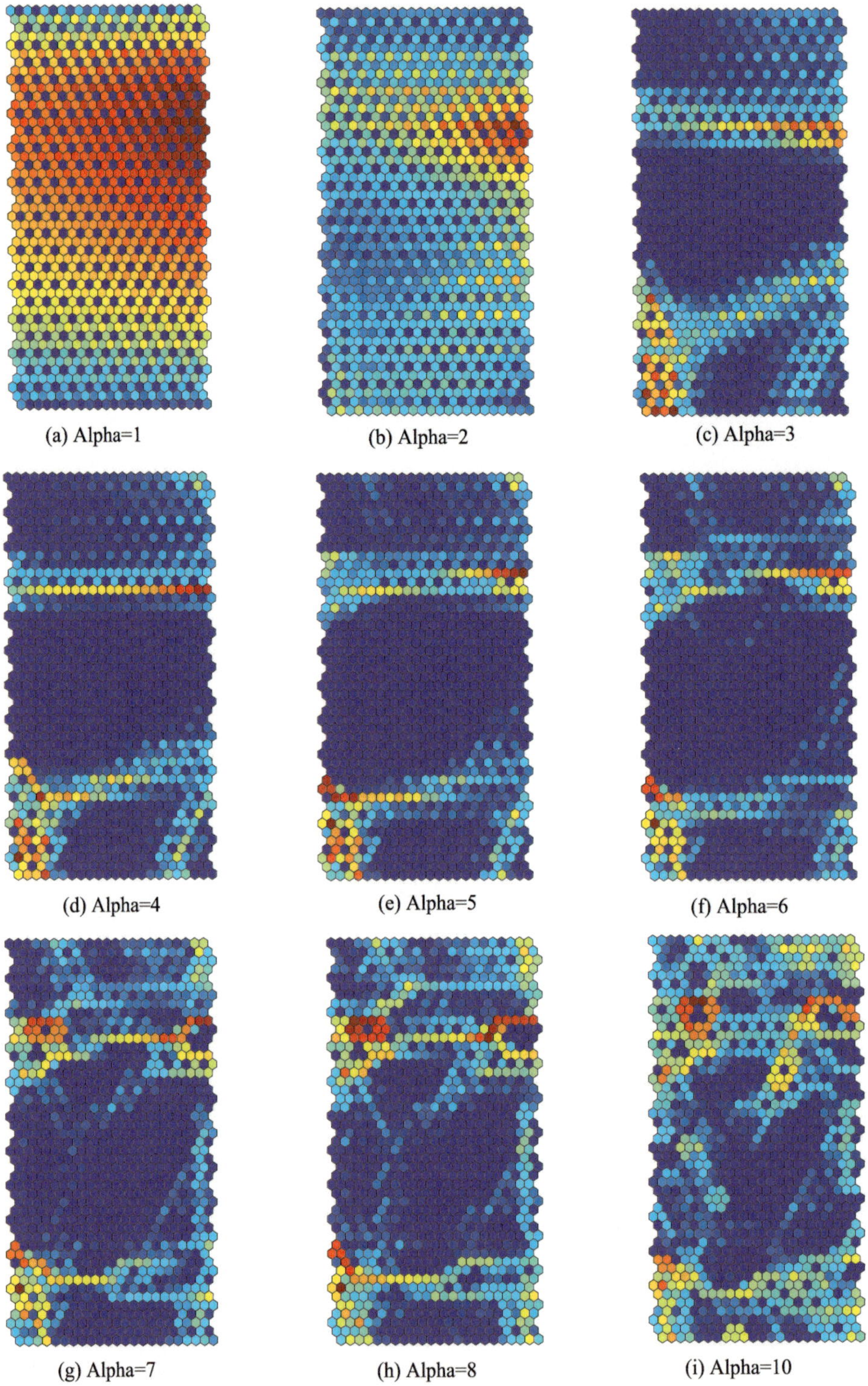

Figure 4. U-matrices when the parameter α was changed from 1 (a) to 10 (i).

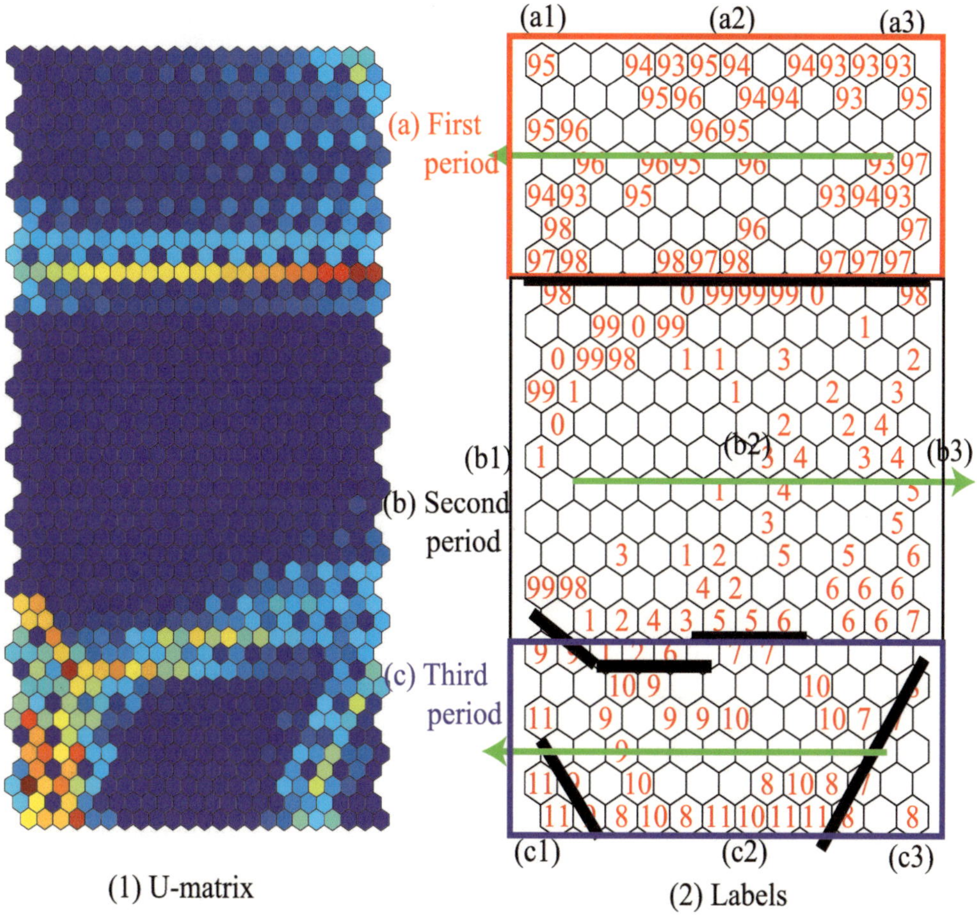

Figure 5. U-matrices (1) and labels (2) when the parameter α was 4.

3.4. Comparison with SOM and PCA

We here compare the results of our method with those obtained by the standard SOM and PCA. Figure 8 shows the U-matrix and labels by the conventional SOM. We used the SOM toolbox for the experiments [4]. As can be seen in Figure 8(a), two class boundaries in warmer colors appeared on the upper side and the lower left hand side of the matrix, but they were rather ambiguous. Labels in Figure 8(b) show that the class boundaries in Figure 8(b) corresponded to those in Figure 5(2).

Figure 9 shows information contained in the jth neuron on the input neurons. Let $p(k \mid j)$ denote the relative output of the kth input neuron for the jth neuron; then, information for the jth neuron on the input neurons is defined by

$$I_j = \log L + \sum_{k=1}^{L} p(k \mid j) \log p(k \mid j), \tag{17}$$

where

$$p(k \mid j) = \frac{w_{jk}}{\sum_{l=1}^{L} w_{jl}}. \tag{18}$$

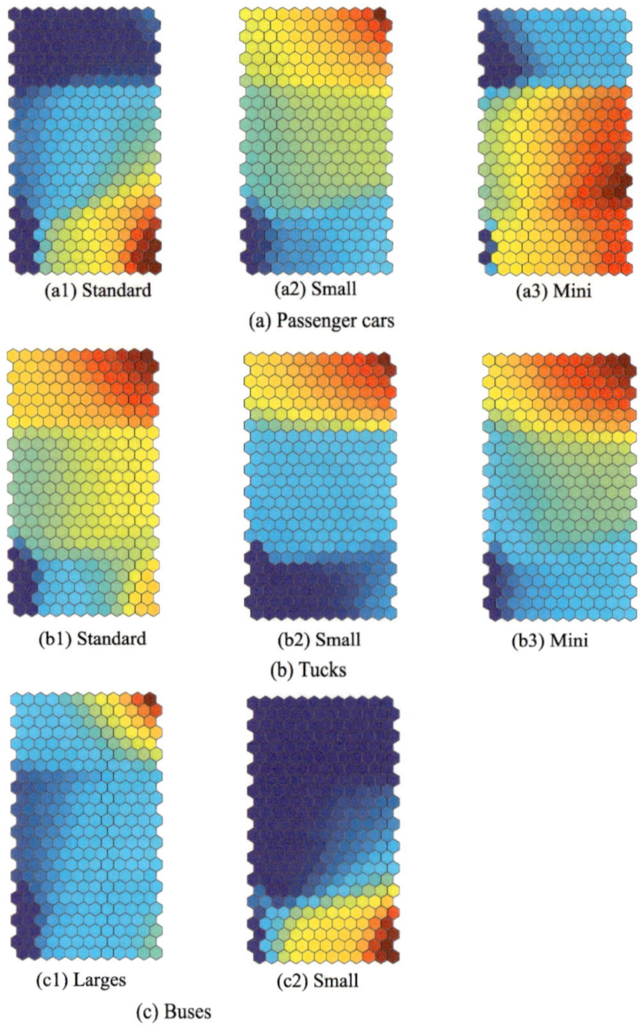

Figure 6. Connection weights from all variables when the parameter α was 4.

Figure 9 shows this information computed by the social interaction (a) and SOM (b). As shown in Figure 9(a), we could see three classes on the map by the social interaction. On the other hand, by the SOM, as in Figure 9(b), boundaries between three classes were not always clear. On the lower left hand side of the maps by the social interaction and SOM, neurons with the highest information on input neurons appeared. This part corresponded to year 2011, where only mini-car was produced largely. This proves that the year 2011 showed the most explicit characteristic of all periods. Namely, the number of mini cars was much larger than any other cars in terms of production.

Figure 10 shows the results of PCA applied to data itself (a), connection weights by the conventional SOM (b) and social interaction (c). With the PCA applied to the data itself, seen in Figure 10(a), three classes were observed but they were extensively overlapping. Figure 10(b) shows the results of PCA applied to the connection weights by the conventional SOM. Though three classes could be observed, many weights were scattered between boundaries. Finally, when the social interaction was used in Figure 10(c), the classes were clearly separated.

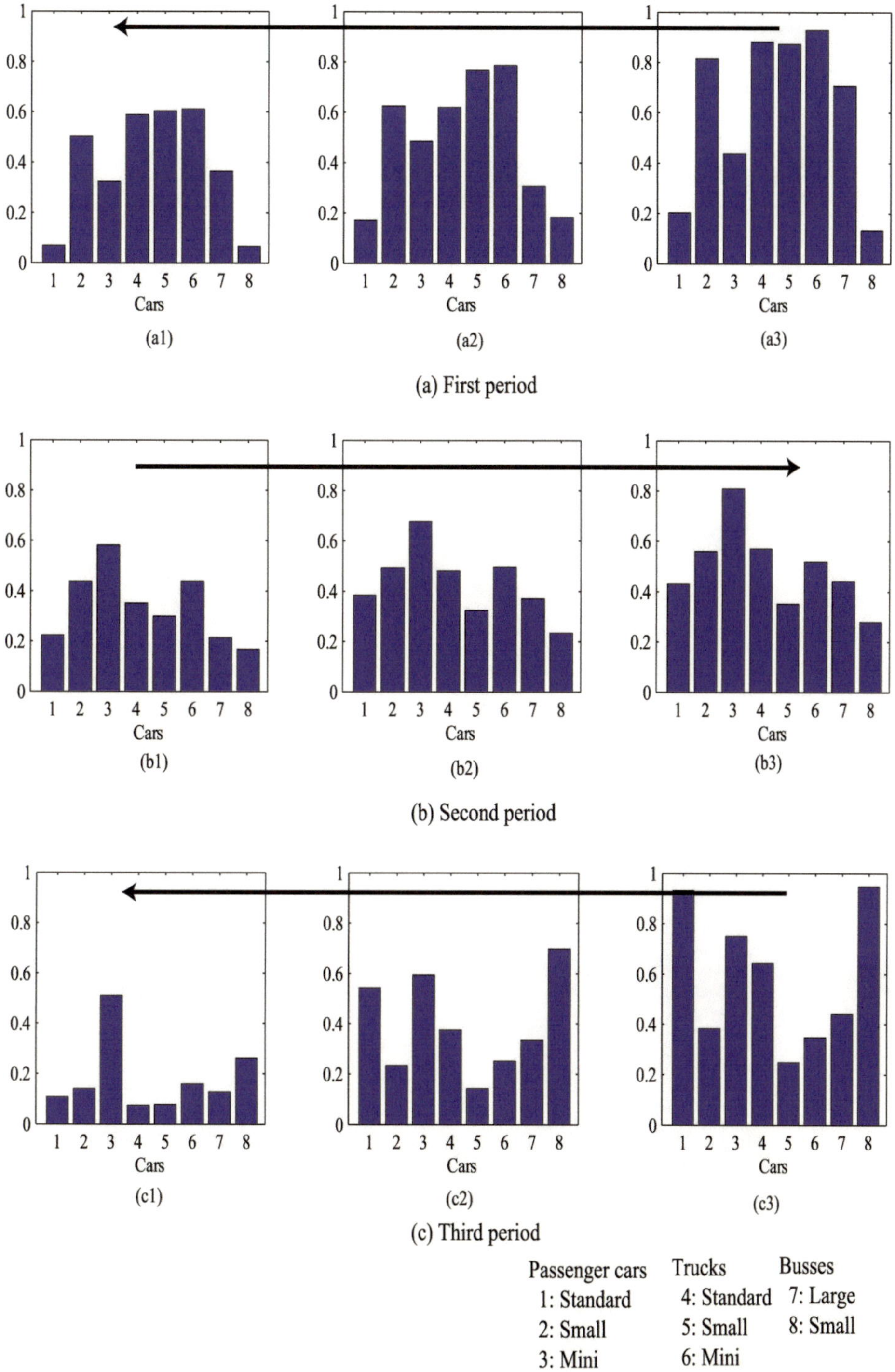

Figure 7. Connection weights into six typical neurons in Figure 5(2).

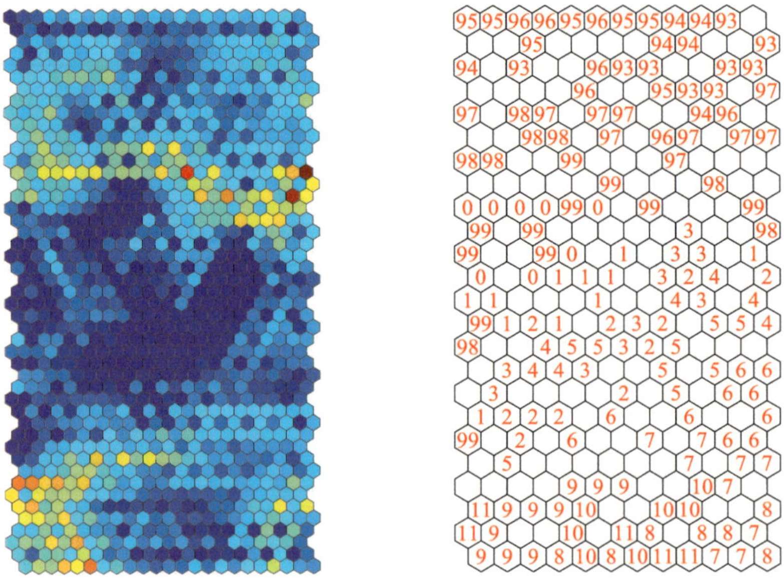

(a) Umatrix (b) Label

Figure 8. U-matrix (a) and labels (b) by the conventional SOM.

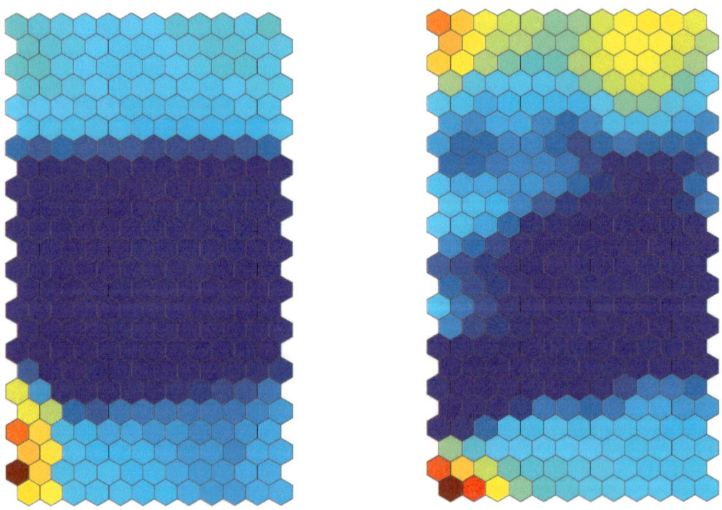

(a) Social interaction (b) SOM

Figure 9. Information content of neurons on input neurons by social interaction (a) and SOM (b).

3.5. Discussion

3.5.1. Summary of Results

Let us summarize the main results of the automobile production. In 2000s, the automobile production gradually decreased as shown in Figure 7(a3) to (a1). In the second period (the beginning of 1990s), the production inversely increased, and in particular, the production of mini-cars increased as shown

http://dx.doi.org/10.5772/51705

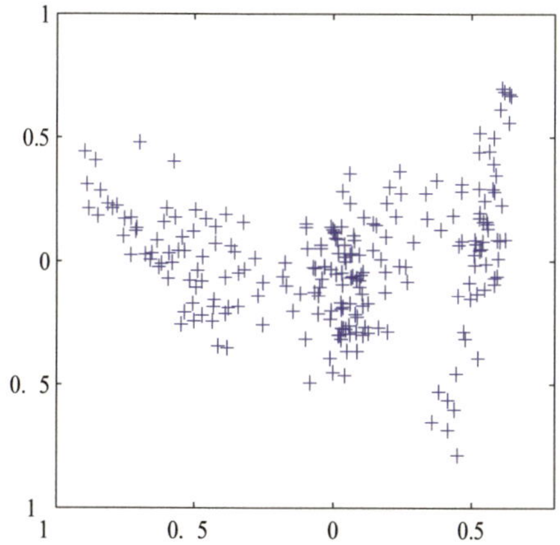

(a) Data

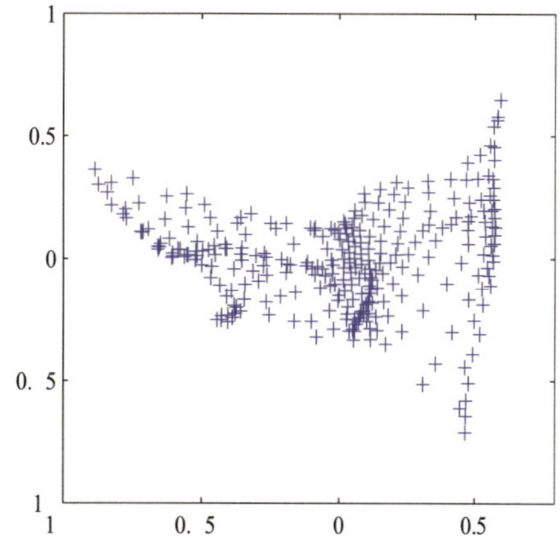

(b) Weights by SOM

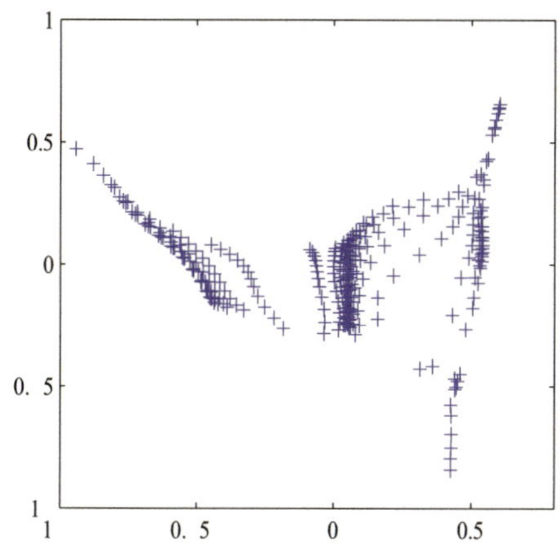

(b) Weights by social interaction

Figure 10. Results of PCA analysis applied to the data (a), connection weights by SOM (b) and those by social interaction (c).

in Figure 7(b3) to (b1). Then, in the beginning of the third period (2007 and 2008), the production of standard passenger cars and small buses increased significantly, shown in Figure 7(c3). The production then decreased again in Figure 7(c2). Finally, in 2011, only the production of mini-cars maintained relatively high production rates, while all the other types of car showed rather low production rates, as shown in Figure 7(c1).

3.5.2. Explaining by Actual Events

These characteristics can be explained by the two important factors occuring in these periods: the revised regulation law for mini cars and the economic crisis called the "Lehman shock."

First, the class boundary between the first and second period could be explained by the revised regulation law for mini cars in 1998. In the first period, all types of cars were being produced equally, except standard and mini-cars and small buses. In the 2000s, only the production of mini-cars increased, albeit gradually. We examined the events and incidents around this boundary period, and found that the automobile regulation by the Japanese government was revised in 1998. In the revision of the safety regulation for the mini-cars in 1998, the size of mini-cars became larger and the safety levels became higher, obtaining performance comparable to that of larger cars. Because of this revision of the regulation, the Japanese automobile market was drastically changed around 1998.

Second, the third period was explained by the economic crisis of 2008. We could observe the high production in standard passenger cars and small buses in the beginning of the third period in Figure 7(c3) around 2007 and 2008. In this period, we recognized the well-known "Lehman Shock" phenomenon following the economic crisis, which damaged the Japanese automobile industry. In particular, the increase in the production of standard passenger cars in this period was one of the main causes of troubles in the automobile industry.

3.5.3. Implication for Automobile Industry

Considering these results and facts, we can point out two factors concerning the automobile industry, namely, policy and planning.

First, one important factor in the development of automobile industry is the policy for the industry. It is necessary to guide the industry through the effective and industrial policy, conceptualized and implemented by the government. In our experimental results, the revised regulation law for the mini-cars drastically changed the market, leading to a sharp increase in the production of mini cars.

Second, production should be more carefully planned. The increase in production in the beginning of 2000s had long lasting negative effects on the automobile industry. We observed that the production in the beginning of 2000s was focused on mini cars, meaning that smaller cars were generally preferred. Despite this, standard passenger cars were largely produced in the beginning of the period. Even if the majority were for export purposes, more restrained production should have been expected, which would have led to lessened damages from the economic crisis.

3.5.4. Problems of the method

Though our method has shown better performance in visualization, we should point out two problems, namely, optimality and topological preservation.

First, we used mutual information to obtain optimal representations. In other words, mutual information was used to choose the optimal values of the parameter α. When mutual information increases, neurons tend to respond very specifically to input patterns. By increasing mutual information, representations become simpler. However, one of the problems is that we did not increase this mutual information, but rather decreased KL-divergence. Thus, we need to examine the relation between KL-divergence and mutual information more carefully.

Second, we should examine the relations between visualization and topological preservation. We have shown that the method worked better to clarify class boundaries. When visualization can be improved, it may happen that topological relations cannot be maintained. This is because better visualization enhances some parts of input patterns, reducing topological preservation. However, we have not yet finished examining the relations between the improved performance and topological preservation. Even if the performance in visualization is improved, if topological relations are not preserved, then the reliability of the final maps decreases. Thus, we should more precisely examine the relationship between visual performance and topological preservation.

3.5.5. Possibilities of the Method

The main possibilities of the method are summarized by two points, namely, flexibility and new self-organizing maps.

First, one of the main beneficial characteristics of our method is its flexibility. Fundamentally, we aim to create a general theory of social interaction. For that, we must take into account many types of interactions. For simplification, social interaction is supposed to be the product of two neurons; thus, in this study, only the distance between two neurons was taken into account. However, it is easy to include any kind of interaction only by substituting the present probabilities $q(j \mid s)$ by new ones. For example, we can imagine a case where even if the distance between neurons is very large, they still may strongly be connected with each other. We can take into account this kind of interaction.

Second, we can create new types of self-organizing maps based upon the social interaction. As mentioned above, our method can create a variety of interactions between neurons. Based upon these different types of interaction, it is possible for networks to self-organize, leading to characteristics different from those by the conventional SOM. If we take into account the different types of cooperation between neurons, new types of self-organizing maps can be created.

4. Conclusion

In this chapter, we proposed a new type of information-theoretic method in which neurons are supposed to form a society. In this society, the interaction of neurons is the product of all neighboring neurons' outputs weighted by their distance. The individual neuron tries to imitate this interaction as much as possible. The difference between neurons with and without interaction is computed by the KL-divergence. By minimizing the KL-divergence, we can obtain the optimal outputs of the neuron and the free energy. By differentiating the free energy, we can obtain the re-estimation rules for connection weights.

We applied our method to the data of the production of Japanese automobiles during the period of 1993 and 2011. We can summarize the final results from two points of view. Technically, the new method showed better performance in clarifying class boundaries, compared with the conventional SOM. Explicit class boundaries were due to the interaction of neurons, similar neurons interacting strongly with each other in terms of distance and firing rates. Second, the strong class boundaries were traced back to the important events or incidents which occurred in the period. For example, the class boundary between the first and the second period was due to the revision of regulation law for mini-cars. Thanks to this revision, the number of mini-cars in production increased gradually. In the third period, a significant production increase at the beginning of the period was accompanied by a decrease in production of other models, with only mini-cars being largely produced in the end. This period was well explained by the economic crisis in 2008.

Though there are some problems such as optimality and topological preservation, as explained in the discussion section, we have shown that it is possible to create different types of neuron societies, where different kinds of interaction can be implemented.

Author details

Ryotaro Kamimura

Ryotaro Kamimura IT Education Center Tokai University, Japan

References

[1] J. W. Sammon. A nonlinear mapping for data structure analysis. *IEEE Transactions on Computers*, C-18(5):401–409, 1969.

[2] A. Ultsch and H. P. Siemon. Kohonen self-organization feature maps for exploratory data analysis. In *Proceedings of International Neural Network Conference*, pages 305–308, Dordrecht, 1990. Kulwer Academic Publisher.

[3] A. Ultsch. U*-matrix: a tool to visualize clusters in high dimensional data. Technical Report 36, Department of Computer Science, University of Marburg, 2003.

[4] J. Vesanto. SOM-based data visualization methods. *Intelligent Data Analysis*, 3:111–126, 1999.

[5] S. Kaski, J. Nikkila, and T. Kohonen. Methods for interpreting a self-organized map in data analysis. In *Proceedings of European Symposium on Artificial Neural Networks*, Bruges, Belgium, 1998.

[6] I. Mao and A. K. Jain. Artificial neural networks for feature extraction and multivariate data projection. *IEEE Transactions on Neural Networks*, 6(2):296–317, 1995.

[7] Hujun Yin. ViSOM-a novel method for multivariate data projection and structure visualization. *IEEE Transactions on Neural Networks*, 13(1):237–243, 2002.

[8] Mu-Chun Su and Hsiao-Te Chang. A new model of self-organizing neural networks and its application in data projection. *IEEE Transactions on Neural Networks*, 123(1):153–158, 2001.

[9] Lu Xu, Yang Xu, and Tommy W.S. Chow. PolSOM-a new method for multidimentional data visualization. *Pattern Recognition*, 43:1668–1675, 2010.

[10] R. Kamimura. Self-enhancement learning: target-creating learning and its application to self-organizing maps. *Biological cybernetics*, pages 1–34, 2011.

[11] R. Kamimura. Constrained information maximization by free energy minimization. *International Journal of General Systems*, 40(7):701–725, 2011.

Chapter 3

Using Wavelets for Feature Extraction and Self Organizing Maps for Fault Diagnosis of Nonlinear Dynamic Systems

Héctor Benítez-Pérez, Jorge L. Ortega-Arjona and
Alma Benítez-Pérez

Additional information is available at the end of the chapter

http://dx.doi.org/10.5772/50235

1. Introduction

Fault diagnosis has been established in two main approaches: model-based fault diagnosis and model-free fault diagnosis. Present paper focuses on the later, mainly as an extension of the approach proposed in [17]. The challenge here is to classify faults at early stages, with an accurate response. However, as the term model-free implies, a model for the plant is not available neither for fault-free nor for fault-present scenarios. The objective, thus, is to classify faults based on system's response and the related signal analysis, in terms of dilation and shift decomposition, as obtained by a wavelets approach. So, self-organizing maps (SOM) are proposed as a powerful nonlinear neural network to achieve such a fault classification.

Several strategies have been proposed for feature extraction using wavelets. For instance, [1] presents a wavelet packet feature extraction, based on the analysis and measure of a "distance" between the energy distribution of some signal classes and the proper classification by the use of fuzzy sets. Alternatively, [2] proposes the use of wavelets as a strategy of parametric system identification, giving prime emphasis to wavelet properties and parameter relations. The idea of using wavelets for fault classification is a powerful procedure for feature extraction of several scenarios, even in the case of frequency and power shifts. [3] and [4] have explored this approach for process system, in which practical results are satisfactory, regardless of the classification. Moreover, several other strategies using wavelets have been proposed for abnormal signal detection, like that presented in [5], in which a parasitic wavelet transform is proposed. Further research in the same direction is followed in [6], in which a cubic spline methodology is proposed for the boundary problem, although the results of this approach tend to be just local, linear models. An alternative strategy for auto-correlation and signal discovery is proposed in [7], following some multi-class wavelet support vector machines. In all these methodologies, wavelets are used as a technique for feature extraction; however, none of the above have presented any enhancement for pattern classification. Here, an enhancement for pattern classification is proposed, in order to isolate different scenarios.

On the other hand, the use of neural networks for feature extraction only presents the disadvantage of inherent data uncertainties and large quantity of necessary data. Different proposals have previously explored similar strategies. For example, [8] proposes feature extraction using local parametric models, giving valuable results; however, there is a drawback of a bounded system response. This strategy for fault diagnosis integrates an ART2A network and a Kohonen neural network. The objective is to combine both strategies in order to generate two subsystems capable of overcoming glitches and redundant data representations [8]. Both subsystems, based on the ART2A topology and the Kohonen neural network, are used to perform a learning strategy. This strategy allows on-line fault diagnosis, with the inherent uncertainty of SOM variation due to the plasticity-stability dilemma. A fundamental work has been introduced in [9], in which an extended review is provided regarding topics related to sensors patterns and stability-plasticity trade-offs, inherent to an ART2A network. Interesting comments have been included about how a time window data can be monitored, in order to identify abnormal situations, as well as how data should be treated in terms of normalization, time scaling, and filtering, and their comparison prior to declare a winner selection. Further developments are addressed in [10], focusing on the use of a parallel ART2A network approach, based on a wavelet decomposition in which clustering is defined in the wavelet domain, although it is not proposed for a dynamical system.

Feature extraction for dynamical systems based on wavelets presents the advantage of scale decomposition, allowing several possibilities of fault detection depending on the scale of the fault. Similarly, fault detection can be easily engaged if a source of information is decomposed into several fruitful components. These components are taken as parameter vectors, where several signal conditions are highlighted depending on the resolution. Further, these components need to be combined in a fair strategy, in order to classify similar behaviors. To do so, the use of SOM is proposed, in which each vector is processed as a consecutive input. The result of this classification gives a number of selected patterns, depending on the learning rate, and regarding a time window. Nevertheless, using this technique, the plasticity-stability dilemma is still not solved.

As stated before, feature extraction presents an inherently extrapolated method to determine several characteristics (like geometry differences) related to the monitored signal, based on a scale factor. The most typical characteristics are those related to frequency and phase modification, which are multiplicative faults in terms of fault detection. Amplitude change is detected on the general modification from wavelets scales, and the consequent change on the selected patterns. The importance of the methodology is the capacity for fault isolation at unknown scenarios, with enough time to pursue modification in terms of system safety. In this sense, time response is determined in terms of the sampled window and the classification of current analyzed data. It is necessary to establish a feasible relationship among the sampling window, the time taken to process information, and the accuracy to classify a particular scenario. This can be achieved by following a frequency analysis of some selected scenarios, in order to find such a relationship. However, this is a non-homogeneous strategy for any scenario. Further work needs to be done in terms of data analysis and sampling capabilities to recognize scenarios, either known or unknown.

Based on this extensive review, the current approach divides the process of fault isolation using SOM techniques into a two stages process. The first stage is a basic construction of the map, as pattern clusters, using SOM. The second stage is a labeling process that identifies scenarios of the system. Following this, the current approach proposes the classification of time-varying faults within a bounded time window, using the wavelet decomposition inherent response. The objective, hence, is to establish an approach for fault localization, based on feature extraction and clustering, by considering diverse fault-present and fault-free scenarios. The novelty of this approach is on signal classification for time varying scenarios, under unknown consideration. The proposed system is limited to certain signals conditions, such as coupled noise and frequency response. In this case, frequency dispersion should be bounded, regardless of time variance. The main advantage of this approach is related to fault isolation through signal decomposition, and classification in a bounded time response.

2. Background

2.1. The Wavelet Transform

Wavelet transform (WT) is an alternative method for processing transient, non-stationary signals simultaneously in time-scale domains [11]. Wavelets are used to decompose a signal into different *scale factors*. Wavelet approach provides a more natural description of the signal, in terms of a composition of a set of "typical signals", or wavelets. In fact, the WT is the correlation between a signal and a set of basic wavelets, proposed from a basic "mother wavelet" $h(t)$, chosen in order to analyze a specific transient signal of finite energy. Thus, a complete orthogonal set of "daughter wavelets" $h_{a,b}(t)$ is generated from $h(t)$ by two operations: a dilation a and shift b.

Formally, the dilation and shift, as wavelet coefficients of the signal, are defined by:

$$W_S(a, b)=\int_{-\infty}^{\infty} s(t)h^{*}_{a,b}(t)dt \tag{1}$$

where $s(t)$ is the current signal, and the function $h_{a,b}(t)$ defined as:

$$h_{a,b}(t)=a^{-1/2}h\left(\frac{t-b}{a}\right) \tag{2}$$

The information used in this approach is based on both a and b, as expansion coefficients. Commonly, the mother wavelet is considered as a Daubechies signal. The wavelets automatically adapt to the different components of a signal, using a small window (large scale) to search for brief high-frequency components, and large window (low scale) to look for long lived, low-frequency components. The shape of low- and high-frequency components is determined by the mother wavelet. A further and deeper revision of the wavelet technique may be found in [12].

Wavelets can be represented using a function ψ, and the family $\Im$ of expanded and translated wavelets are expressed as :

$$\Im=\left\{\psi_{j,n}(t)=\frac{1}{\sqrt{2^j}}\psi\left(\frac{t-2^j n}{2^j}\right): j,\, n\in\mathbb{Z}\right\} \tag{3}$$

which performs an orthogonal base $L^2 ¢$. Orthonormal wavelets are obtained by expanding this by a factor 2^j, allowing variations of the signal in a 2^{-j} resolution. The construction of these bases permits the study of multi-resolution of a signal. Formally, the approximation of a function with a resolution 2^{-j} is defined as an orthogonal projection over a space $V_j \subset L^2 ¢$ The space V_j groups every possible approximation with resolution 2^{-j}. Remember that an orthogonal projection from function f is a function $f_j \in V_j$ which is minimized $\| f - f_j \|$.

Definition. (Multi-Resolution) A family of closed subspaces $\{V_j : j \in \mathbb{Z}\}$ *of* $L^2 ¢$ *is a multi-resolution approximation, if it satisfies the following properties:*

i. *For* $j,\, k \in \mathbb{Z}, f(t) \in V_j \cdot f(t-2^j k) \in V_j$

ii. *For* $j \in \mathbb{Z}, V_{j+1} \subset V_j$

iii. *For* $j \in \mathbb{Z}, f(t) \in V_j \cdot f\left(\frac{t}{2}\right) \in V_{j+1}$

iv. $\lim_{j\to+\infty} V_j = \bigcap_{j=-\infty}^{+\infty} V_j = \{0\}$

v. $\lim_{j\to-\infty} V_j = \bigcup_{j=-\infty}^{+\infty} V_j = L^2 ¢$

vi. *there is* θ *such that* $\{\theta(t-n) : n \in \mathbb{Z}\}$ *is a Riesz base of* V_0 .

Property (i) states that the subspace V_j is invariant in any translation proportional to scale 2^j Property (ii) is causal, since the resolution 2^{-j} owns the necessary information to calculate a

http://dx.doi.org/10.5772/50235

raw resolution 2^{-j-1}. If the functions are dilated in V_j by 2, then the details are amplified by a factor of 2. So (iii) defines an approximation of a raw resolution when the resolution 2^{-j} tends to be cero. (iv) implies that all the details have been lost, meaning that the projection of signal f over the space V_j when $j \to +\infty$ is zero:

$$\lim_{j\to+\infty} \| P_{V_j} f \| = 0. \tag{4}$$

On the other hand, if the resolution 2^{-j} tends to $+\infty$ property (v) forces that the approximation of the signal converges to the original signal:

$$\lim_{j\to-\infty} \| f - P_{V_j} f \| = 0. \tag{5}$$

Finally, the existence of a Riesz base $\{\theta(t-n) : n \in \mathbb{Z}\}$ of V_0 provides a discretization theorem. Function θ can be interpreted as a cell with unitary resolution. To compute several resolutions of signal, it is necessary then to compute the orthogonal components over different spaces $\{V_j : j \in \mathbb{Z}\}$ of $L^2 ¢$ According to the definition of a Riesz base, there are $A, B > 0$ that if $f \in V_0$, it may be decomposed as:

$$f(t) = \sum_{n=-\infty}^{+\infty} a[n]\theta(t-n) \tag{6}$$

with

$$A \| f \|^2 \leq \sum_{n=-\infty}^{+\infty} | a[n] |^2 \leq B \| f \|^2 \tag{7}$$

This last expression guarantees that the expansion of the signal over $\{\theta(t-n) : n \in \mathbb{Z}\}$ is numerically stable.

The approximation of f in the resolution 2^{-j} is defined as the orthogonal projection $P_{V_j} f$ over V_j. To compute this projection, an orthogonal base should be find over the space V_j. Hence, the following theorem allows for an orthogonal Riesz base $\{\theta(t-n) : n \in \mathbb{Z}\}$, and it builds an orthogonal basis for each space V_j where dilation and transferring over a function ϕ, named *scale*.

Theorem (Goswami Jaideva, 1999). Being $\{V_j : j \in \mathbb{Z}\}$ an approximation of multi-resolution and ϕ a scale function, where the Fourier Transformation is:

$$\hat{\varphi}(\omega) = \frac{\hat{\theta}(\omega)}{\left(\sum_{k=-\infty}^{+\infty} | \hat{\theta}(\omega + 2k\pi) |^2 \right)^{1/2}} \tag{8}$$

Defining

$$\varphi_{j,n}(t)=\frac{2}{\sqrt{2^j}}\varphi\left(\frac{t-n}{2^j}\right) \tag{9}$$

Then the family $\{\theta_{j,n}:n\in\mathbb{Z}\}$ *is an orthonormal base of* $V_j \forall j\in\mathbb{Z}$

Demonstration

The objective is to build an orthonormal base, and therefore, a function $\varphi\in V_0$. Now, this function is expanded in terms of the Reisz base $\{\theta(t-n):n\in\mathbb{Z}\}$:

$$\varphi(t)=\sum_{k=-\infty}^{+\infty} a[n]\theta(t-n) \tag{10}$$

Computing the Fourier transform for this last function, it is obtained that:

$$\hat{\varphi}(\omega)=\hat{a}(\omega)\hat{\theta}(\omega) \tag{11}$$

where $\hat{a}$ is a Fourier series with period 2π and finite energy; $\hat{a}$ is expressed in terms of the orthogonal condition of $\{\varphi(t-n):n\in\mathbb{Z}\}$ into the Fourier dominion, being $\bar{\varphi}(t)=\varphi^*(-t)$ It is necessary that for any $n,\ p\in\mathbb{Z}$:

$$\langle\varphi(t-n),\ \varphi(t-p)\rangle=\int_{-\infty}^{+\infty}\varphi(t-n)\varphi^*(t-p)dt=\varphi*\bar{\varphi}(p-n)=\delta[n] \tag{12}$$

If the Fourier transform is obtained from this, it determines the following equation:

$$\sum_{k=-\infty}^{+\infty} |\hat{\varphi}(\omega+2k\pi)|^2=1 \tag{13}$$

On the other hand, the Fourier transform of $\varphi(t)*\bar{\varphi}(t)$ is $|\hat{\varphi}(\omega)|^2$, and therefore:

$$\hat{a}(\omega)=\frac{1}{\left(\sum_{k=-\infty}^{+\infty} |\hat{\theta}(\omega+2k\pi)|^2\right)^{\frac{1}{2}}} \tag{14}$$

To find an approximation of f over the space V_j, it is necessary to expand the function in terms of the orthogonal base from the scale function:

$$P_{V_j}f=\sum_{n=-\infty}^{+\infty}\langle f,\varphi_{j,n}\rangle\varphi_{j,n} \tag{15}$$

where the inner products are:

$$a_j[n] = \langle f, \varphi_{j,n} \rangle \tag{16}$$

giving a discrete approximation of scale 2^j. This last equation can be expressed as the convolution product:

$$a[n] = \int_{-\infty}^{+\infty} f(t) \frac{1}{\sqrt{2^j}} \varphi\left(\frac{t - 2^j n}{2^j}\right) dt = f * \bar{\varphi}_j(2^j n) \tag{17}$$

with $\bar{\varphi}_j(t) = \sqrt{2^{-j}}\varphi(2^{-j}t)$.The energy of the Fourier Transform $\hat{\varphi}$ is typically concentrated in $[-\pi, \pi]$, and as a consequence, the Fourier Transform $\sqrt{2^j}\hat{\varphi}^*(2^j\omega)$ of $\bar{\varphi}_j(t)$ concentrates its energy in the interval $\lfloor -2^{-j}\pi, 2^{-j}\pi \rfloor$. Then, the discrete approximation is $a_j[n]$, as a low pass filter of function *f*, from sampling 2^j.

2.2. Self Organizing Maps (SOM)

The purpose of Kohonen's SOM is to capture the topology and probability distribution of some input data (Figure 1) [13][14]. First, a topology of SOM is defined as a rectangular grid [15].

Different types of grid may be used to represent data, although the one shown in Figure 2 presents a homogenous response suitable for noise cancellation.

The neighborhood function regarding a rectangular grid, such as this one, is based on a set of bi-dimensional Gaussian functions, as described by Equation 18.

$$h(i_1, i_2) = \exp\left(-0.5 * \frac{(i_1^{win} - i_1)^2 + (i_2^{win} - i_2)^2}{\sigma^2}\right) \tag{18}$$

where i_1 and i_2 represent the indices of each neuron, and $\sigma$is the standard deviation of each Gaussian distribution, which determines how the neighbor neurons of a winner neuron are modified. Each neuron also has a weight vector (w_i^j), which represents how the actual neuron is modified by an input updating. Thus, $h(i_1, i_2)$ is the Gaussian representation that allows for modifications of neighbor neurons of a SOM.

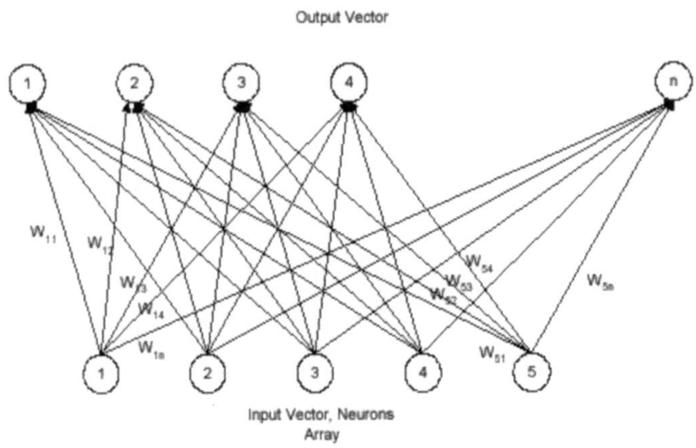

Figure 1. Topology Network of a SOM.

Equation 20 is the basis of the SOM. In this equation, the weight matrix is updated based on the bi-dimensional indexing, namely $h(i_1, i_2)$. This equation is used during training (offline) stage of the SOM. Moreover, this bi-dimensional function allows the weight matrix to be updated in a global way, rather than just to update the weight vector associated to a winner neuron.

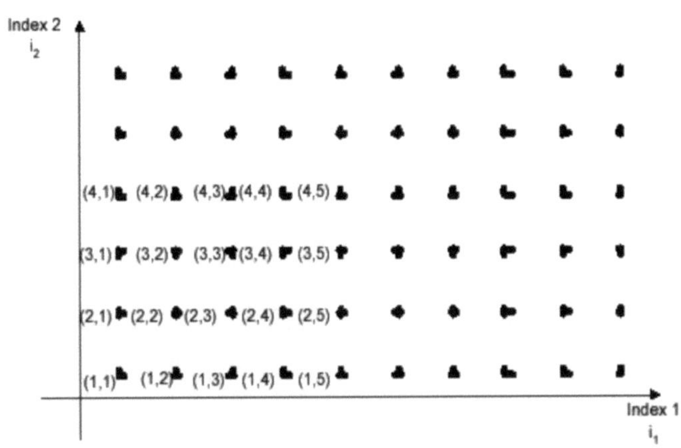

Figure 2. Index Grid for noise cancellation.

For updating the SOM, an inner product is performed between the weight matrix W and the input vector (I), in order to define a winner neuron. Having calculated this product, the maximum value is determined by the comparison between each scalar from resultant vector. This value is declared as the winner, just as in the technique known as "the winner take all". The related bi-dimensional index (Figure 2) is calculated in order to determine how the weight matrix is modified.

http://dx.doi.org/10.5772/50235

The updating process of the weight matrix is performed as shown by Equation 19.

$$w_j^{new} = w_j^{old} + \eta * h(i_1, i_2) * \left(I - w_j^{old}\right) \tag{19}$$

whereη represents a constant value equals to 0.7. This parameter can be tuned as a learning parameter. Here, I represents the current input vector.

3. Main approach

The proposed organization for the actual model is shown in Figure 3. The model is divided into two stages: first, it is performed offline, where the SOM is trained; second, the fault diagnosis procedure is performed online.

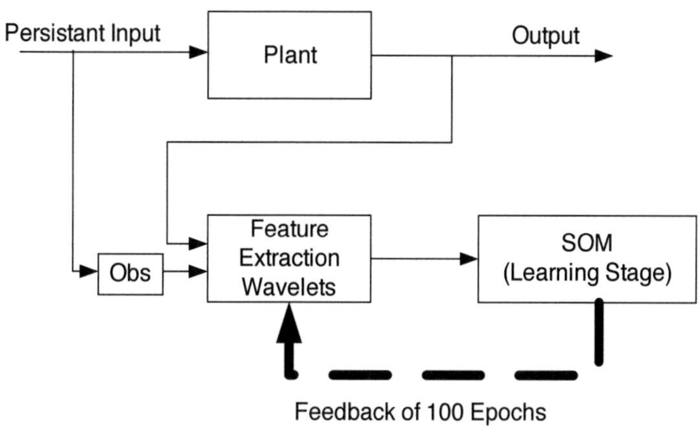

Figure 3. Organization for the model.

The SOM is trained offline, following the output signal, which is decomposed into several levels, as proposed by wavelets feature extraction scales. The observed dynamical system decomposition should perform this regarding its input, by considering a diversity of frequencies. The decomposition is proposed for several wavelets scales as feature extraction, where just one is chosen based on repeatability in similar scenarios, either fault-present or fault-free.

Several parameters need to be tuned for the SOM and wavelet feature extraction, such as:

- Length of the sampling window k.
- Number of wavelet decomposition levels.
- Learning value η.
- Vigilance threshold β.

During the offline stage, the SOM is trained based on known fault-present and fault-free scenarios with a local decomposition wavelet strategy, using a mother wavelet known as Daubechies 4. This means that four decomposition levels (scales) are produced. The Daubechies 4 is a wavelet particularly chosen here due to the case study response, as it is discussed later.

For fault-free scenarios, four decomposed levels have a particular powerful response, being different of the fault-present scenarios, as shown in the next section. In this case, similar patterns are stated to occur when a bounded fault scenario is presented. In both, fault-free and fault-present cases, and for four levels, Daubechies 4 presents a trustable response.

Current data has a pre-treatment as input/output responses from the plant. Input and output are locally normalized before they are processed by wavelets, to extract certain features. To take the advantage of this situation, it is necessary that the learning law of the SOM is suitable to perform an accurate response with respect to the case study.

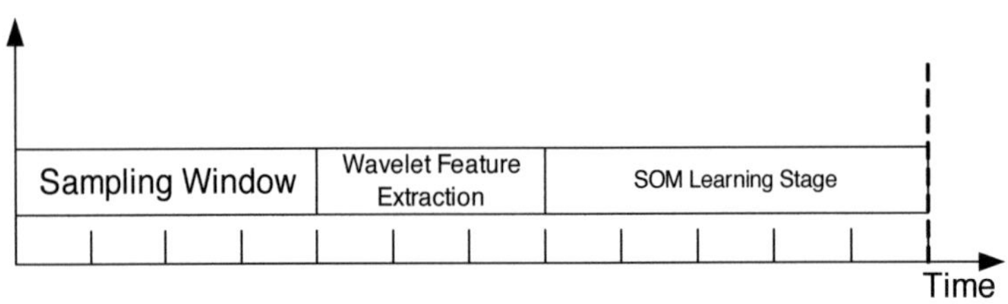

Figure 4. Three steps of the offline stage.

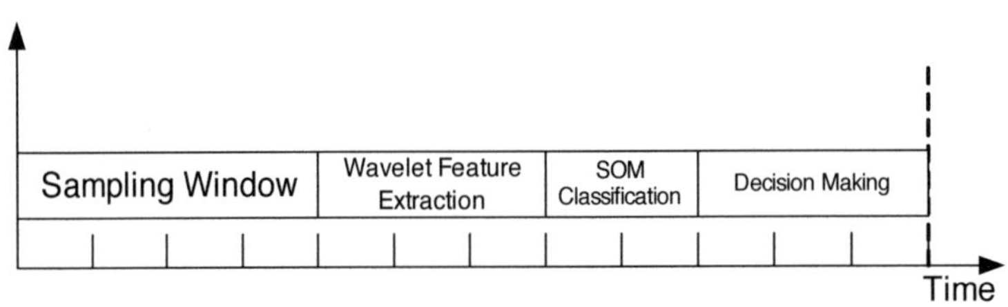

Figure 5. Three steps of the online stage.

Three steps are defined during the offline stage, as shown in Figure 4, in terms of data processing: first, a sampling window of input and output data is taken and normalized; next, this information is processed by the wavelet module, to perform feature extraction; finally, the local matrix is classified by the SOM in learning mode. In this case, it is necessary to provide with enough information and a diversity of scenarios (fault-present and fault-free) to the SOM, in order to ensure a suitable fault identification.

http://dx.doi.org/10.5772/50235

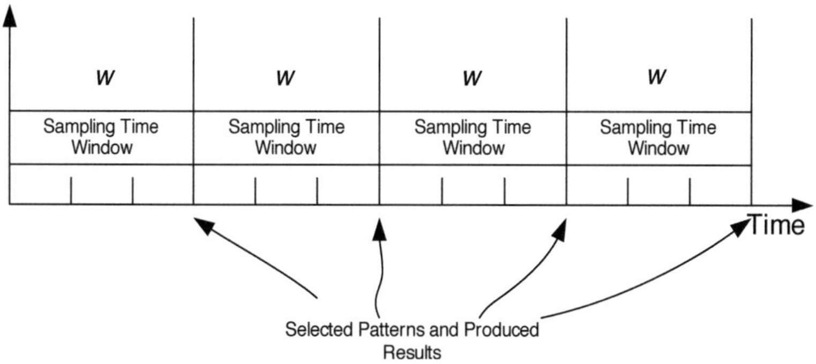

Figure 6. Results produced during the online stage.

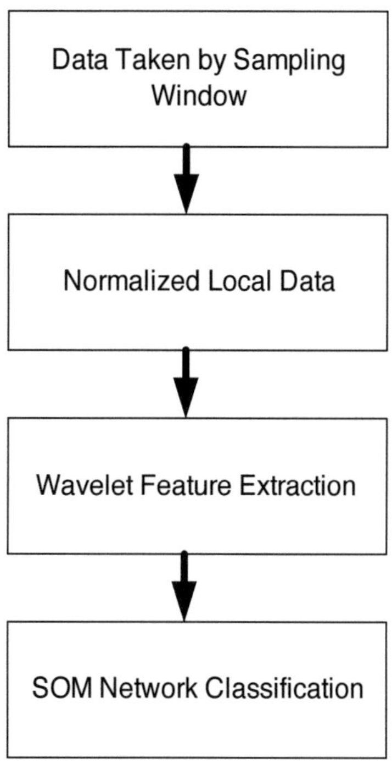

Figure 7. Proposed main procedure for the model-free fault diagnosis.

During the online stage, the SOM does not perform any learning procedure. The comparison between already classified patterns against current scales vectors, produced by wavelets, is performed by an inner product, where the minimal value obtained amongst all patterns is defined as the winner, and compared with β. If the winner value is smaller than β, this is a correct winner; otherwise, the SOM is not capable of performing this comparison. The value β is called *error*, for the purposes of model evaluation. Similarly to the offline stage, the online stage takes four major steps, as shown in Figure 5, in order to produce a result. The main difference, thus, is that here SOM does evaluate the resultant local model, generated by wavelet feature extraction. The decision making module inherent in SOM determines if this classification is valid or not. Notice that for the current purposes, time consumption is neglected.

The results of the online stage are produced every w sampling time windows, which is the time taken by the application in order to produce a result (Figure 6). Such a time window w becomes crucial in terms of the frequency of the plant. Further, the sampling window is a multiple of inherent period of the system. In fact, the plant response during fault-present and fault-free scenarios need to be bounded to this parameter, in order to guarantee a reliable response.

The main procedure followed here is shown in Figure 7, in which the normalized, local preprocessing stage is executed per local sample data; after that, the wavelet feature extraction is performed as data decomposition. The results related to different levels are processed by the SOM per level, where just one would be the winner, and learned by the SOM.

4. The case study

The case study is integrated by a system, as it is shown in Figure 8. It consists of a multiple-input, single-output (MISO) system, with a PID controller, and a switching fault injection procedure. As it may be noticed, the dynamics of this plant tends to be quite slow in comparison with the occurrence of faults, according to the dynamics of the plant and the fault scenarios. This characteristic is crucial for the construction of the local model and the feature extraction, in order to produce a fruitful fault diagnosis procedure. Case study is linear and modeled through model-based techniques; however, when a fault is present, its dynamics becomes nonlinear. This nonlinear behavior tends to be extremely difficult to be diagnosed by classical strategies, like for example, unknown input observers [8]. This scenario has been presented for local system identification techniques and for a global classification strategy, in order to have an accurate fault diagnosis strategy [16]. However, the strategy is dependent on the persistent excitation of certain frequency responses. Alternatively, the proposed strategy here overcomes such a frequency dependency, since the only obvious dependency is the sampling period. This strategy is based on the sensibility of the feature extraction strategy, which uses Daubechies 4 wavelets (db4).

The dynamics of the case study are expressed as vectors of the state space representation:

k1= [0.1; -20.000];

e=[0; 0.001];

b=[1.8000 -2.1000; 0.9000 0.8600];

A=[1.1000 0; 0 2.1000];

c=[0 1];

where A, b, c, and e belong to the case study model, and k1 to the PID controller. The types of faults are:

http://dx.doi.org/10.5772/50235

Fault 1: Backlash of 0.01, followed by a dead zone between {-0.1 0.1}

Fault 2: Backlash of 0.91, followed by a dead zone between {-0.3 0.4}

For this case study, the parameters to be tuned (such as β, η, a, b and k) are bounded to specific ranges:

$0.01\beta 0.99$

$0.01\eta 0.99$

$2a,\ b6$ where η =0.1952 for this case study

$k=10$

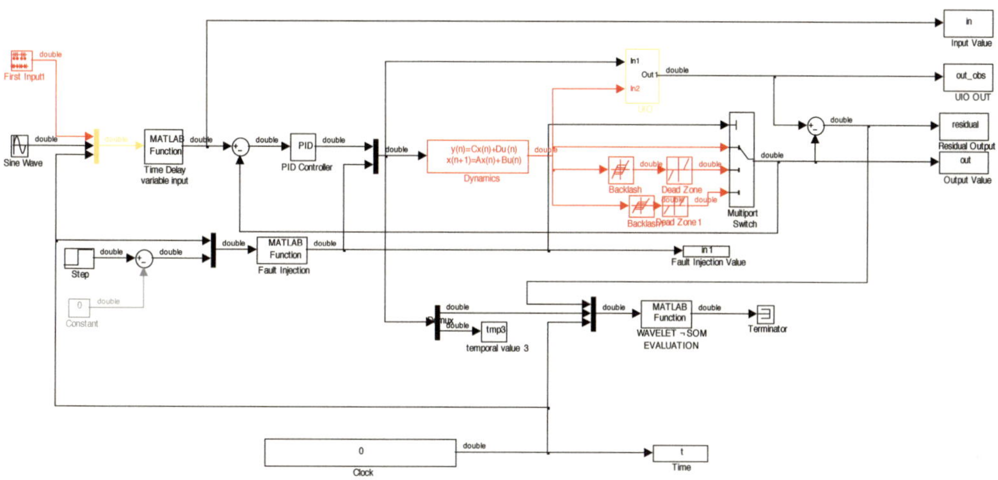

Figure 8. Schematic diagram of the system for the case study.

These ranges are arbitrarily fixed, since there is no further information regarding these values. In order to obtain certain selection according to fault presence and dynamic system response, a testing (response) from the tuples integrated by the combination of these values is performed, as shown in the next section. Notice that the pattern selected by the SOM is a representation of the most suitable approximation of current feature extraction, that is, a model of the current response.

5. Case study results

The present results are referred in terms of pattern construction and feature extraction, considering several known fault-present and fault-free scenarios. Regarding this, Figure 9 shows the output response of the benchmark during a fault-free scenario. The response of the system is inherently stable, due to the inner local control. In this case, the sampling time window has a duration of 10 seconds, representing a period of system response. This response produces the level decomposition presented in Figure 10, in which four wavelet levels are used to decompose the data. Since response is fairly stable, the main differences amongst levels are not significant neither regarding to power, nor regarding to frequency selection. Based on this approximation, the selected patterns should be similar, equidistant, and close related; otherwise, an unknown response has appeared.

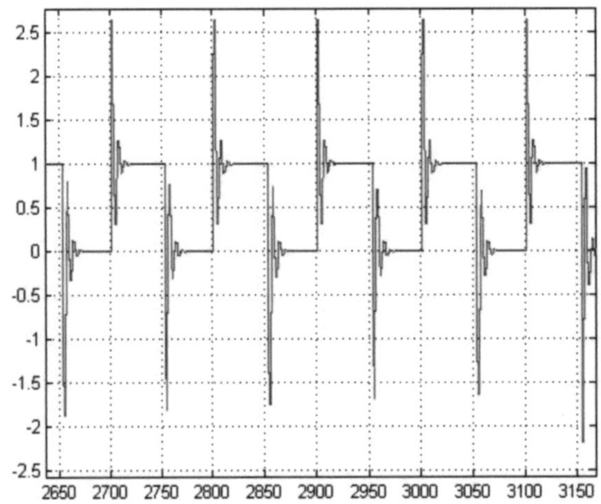

Figure 9. Fault-free response for the current example.

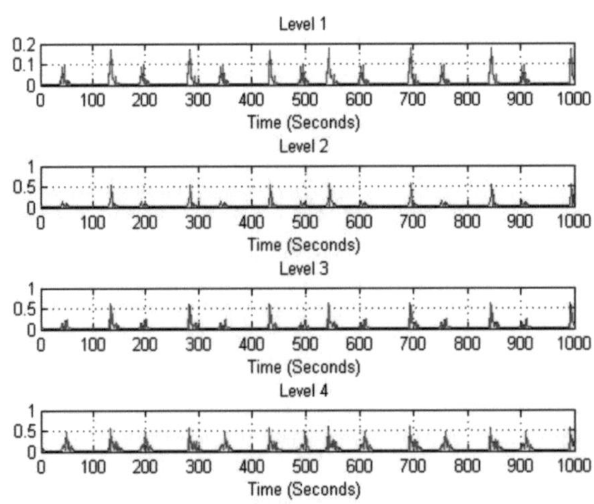

Figure 10. Wavelets feature extraction for fault-free scenario.

http://dx.doi.org/10.5772/50235

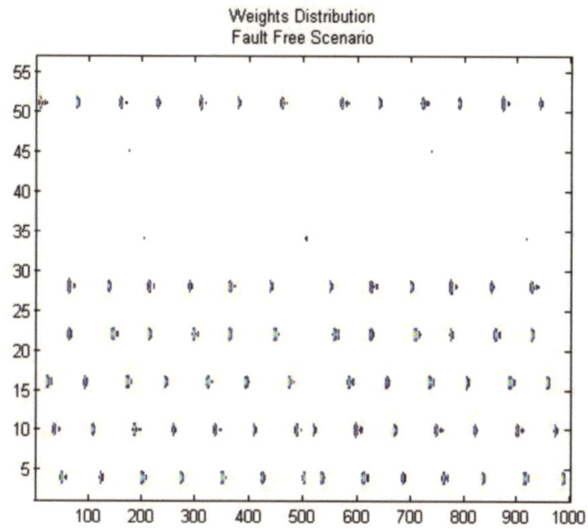

Figure 11. SOM for the fault-free scenario.

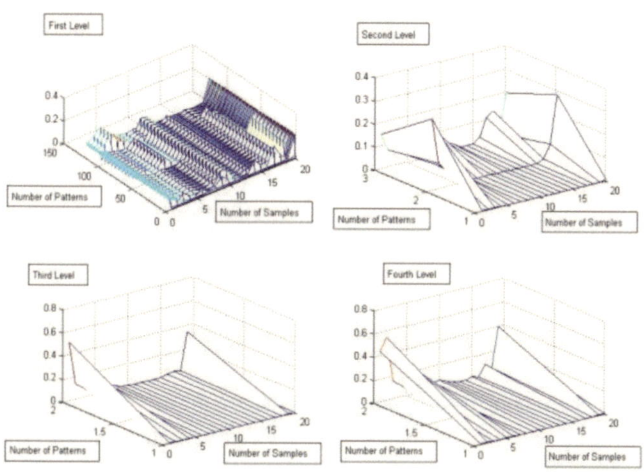

Figure 12. Selected patterns per level for the fault-free scenario. The winner patterns are at the first level.

The fault-free scenario shows the response of a damped system, in which four decomposed levels tends to be similar in terms of power values. For this scenario, the patterns are classified by the SOM as shown in Figure 11. The total number of patterns is 125, from which 55 patterns are "zoom" (enlarged) patterns with a similar power response, given the wavelets feature extraction. Remember that Daubechies 4 has been selected for feature extraction, since this wavelet is stable enough in terms of feature extraction repetition for same scenarios. In Figure 11, the amplitude of 55 patterns reflects a similar response amongst them. Moreover, there is a region around patterns 30 to 45, whose amplitude is close to zero. Notice that the pattern response tends to be similar through time. In Figure 12, the related patterns per level are classified by the SOM for this fault-free scenario. In this case, level 1 presents most of the variations with respect to the observer scenario. This is reflected by the number of created patterns regarding the rest of the levels: level 1 proposes 125 patterns, while the rest of the levels propose mostly 2.

Figure 13 presents the response of the system and the selected patterns that vary from 0.1 to 0.8, in magnitude terms, presenting a close relation between the winner patterns. It is interesting to observe that the most selected pattern has a magnitude of 0.6.

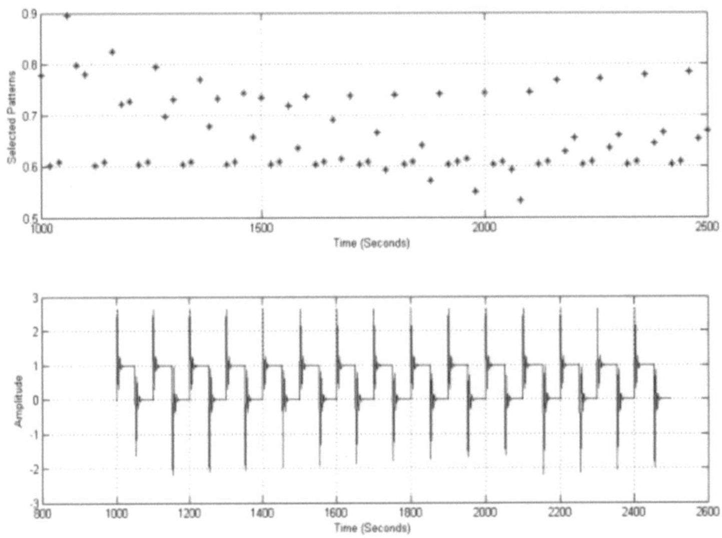

Figure 13. Fault-free scenario and selected patterns for the case study.

For the fault-present scenario, two types of faults are injected to the system (see Section 4). First, let us consider Fault 1, which is an increment of sudden amplitude, as shown in Figure 14. In this case, the fault scenario is presented from 400 to 800 seconds, and it is related to a 10% increment of the amplitude. A detail of the response for this scenario is shown in Figure 15. Observe that the system response presents just an oscillation, and not a clear stage of fault condition. However, the expected response is not desirable according to system dynamics.

Figure 16 shows the features extraction results for this scenario. In this case, power values are modified around 500 seconds, in comparison with the fault-free response (Figure 10). This difference is a clear modification of phase around the 500 seconds. This slight phase modification is the result of the increment of amplitude for this fault scenario. Regarding the patterns that are classified by the SOM for this fault scenario, the number of patterns simply does not augment, but the feature extraction results are different. This is shown in the amplitude of the patterns and the selected patterns, especially in pattern number 15,

http://dx.doi.org/10.5772/50235

which clearly exposes the presence of the fault. In Figure 16, the first level presents a very noticeable difference between the two responses of the whole scale presentation. Moreover, the response in terms of patterns classified by the SOM tends to increase, but it is still stable (Figure 17).

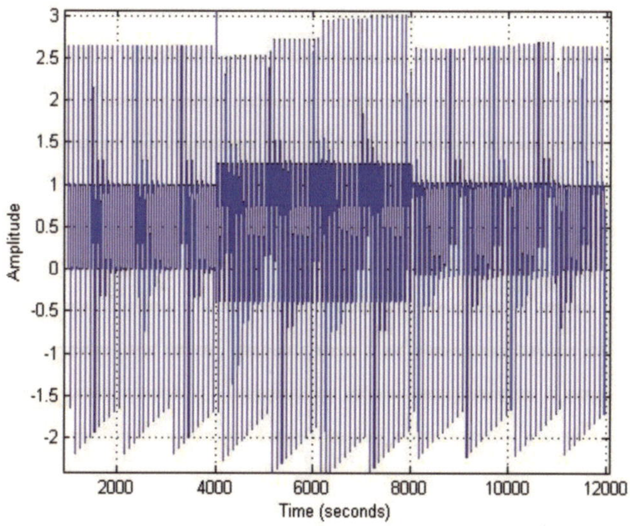

Figure 14. System response during fault present scenario.

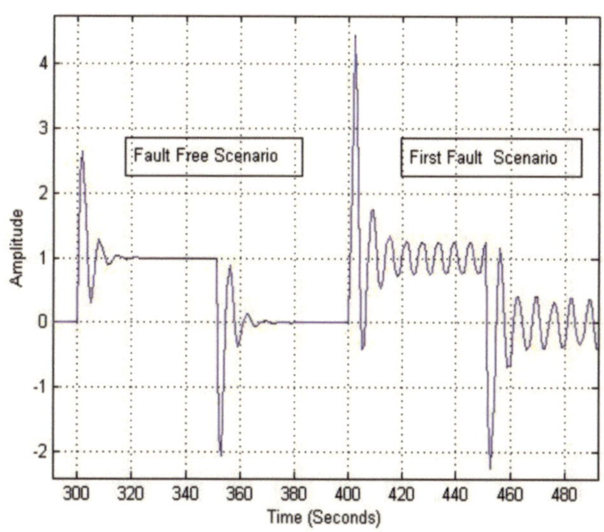

Figure 15. Detail of the response for the first fault present scenario.

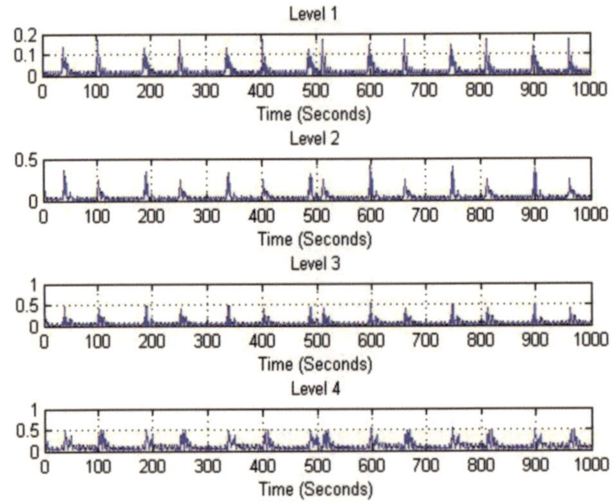

Figure 16. Wavelets feature extraction for the fault present scenario.

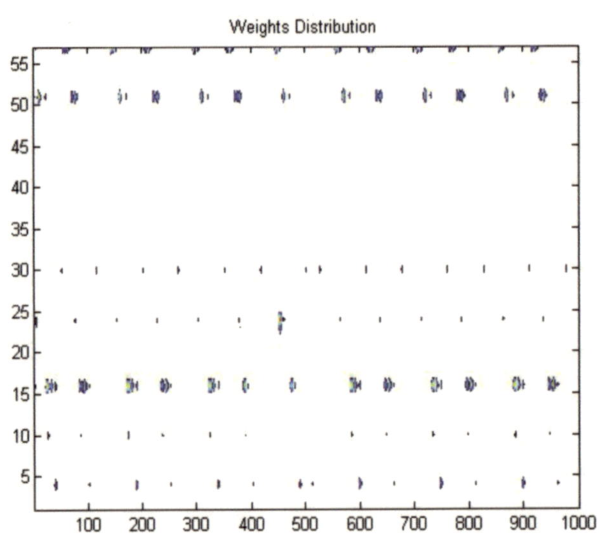

Figure 17. SOM for the fault present scenario.

For the case second fault scenario, Fault 2, Figure 18 shows a detail of the output response of the system, in which an oscillation tends to be larger than that present in the first fault scenario. Although, this behavior is quite erratic, the case study is still measurable, as shown in Figure 19. In this figure, the patterns are selected and quite defined in terms of the presence

http://dx.doi.org/10.5772/50235

of the fault in fast response. There is a small magnitude variation around patterns 2 to 3, at the beginning of the fault scenario, which is resolved at the fifth sampling window. The values of the selected patterns in terms of magnitude are quite defined around 3, which is clearly different in comparison with the other two previous scenarios.

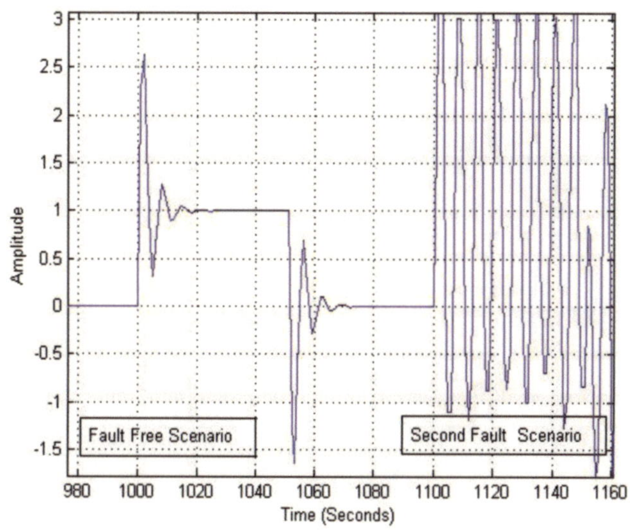

Figure 18. Detail of the response for the second fault present scenario.

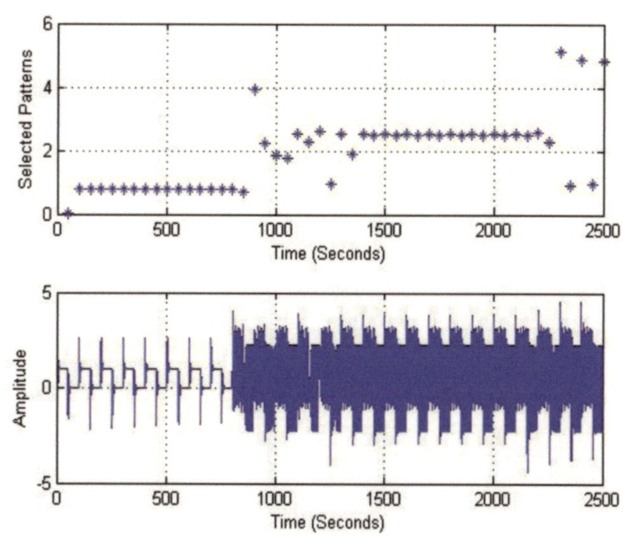

Figure 19. General response for the second fault present scenario and the selected pattern.

Figure 20 shows the selected patterns per level, which present an increment in the number of patterns. Now, the first level has 200 patterns, while the rest of three levels have around 80 patterns. Moreover, the amplitude of learned and winner patterns are around 0.15 for the first level, and close to zero for the second, third, and fourth levels, in the majority of learned patterns (red patterns).

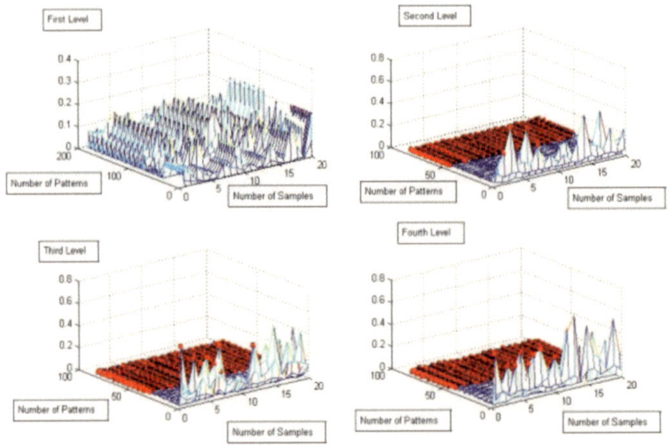

Figure 20. Selected patterns per level for the second fault present scenario.

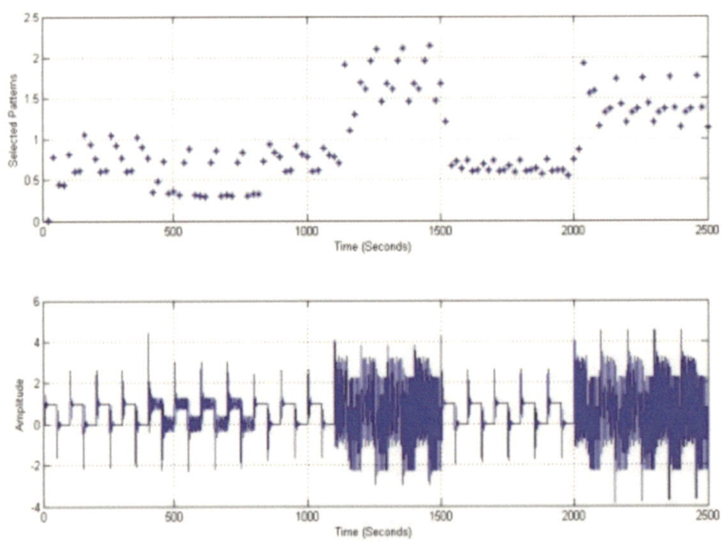

Figure 21. Current output response for the fault-present and fault-free scenarios.

Figure 21 shows a combination of the three scenarios: the fault-free scenario from time 0 to 400 seconds, the first fault scenario from 400 to 700 seconds, and the second fault scenario from 1100 to 1500 seconds, and again from 2000 to 2500 seconds. From this combination, several patterns have been selected, as shown by the upper diagram of Figure 21. These selected patterns, depicted with their amplitude, show a clear definition of the three fault scenarios: the fault-free scenario is related to the patterns measured at 0.7, the first fault-present scenario is related with the two patterns measured at 0.4 and 0.9, respectively, and the second fault-present scenario is related with the three patterns whose values are 1.4, 1.6 and 2.0. The richness is quite obvious in this scenario, due to the oscillation present in it.

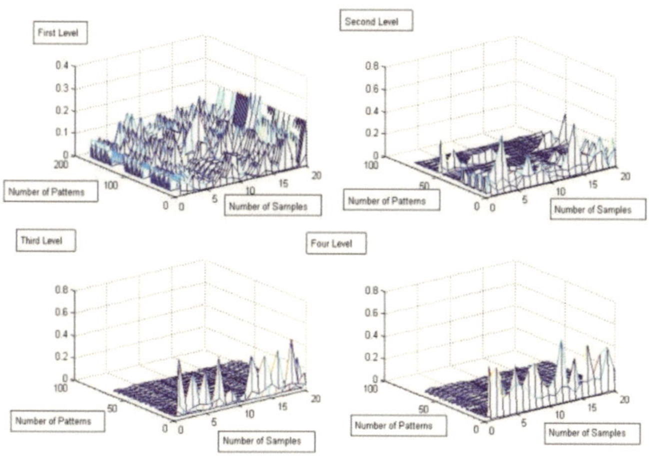

Figure 22. Selected patterns per wavelet levels for the three scenarios.

Finally, Figure 22 shows the levels of the four wavelets, depicted as learned patterns, in which the first level has 190 winner patterns, while the other three levels have 60 winner patterns. Observe that the richness of the combined winner patterns determines a clear classification of the patterns, as shown in Figure 21. Moreover, the current amplitude is quite similar and rich for the first level, as presented in the three scenarios.

6. Concluding remarks

The present work shows a strategy for fault diagnosis based on local feature extraction and global system classification, in which different parameters play an important role in this condition monitoring proposal. The number of samples with respect to sampling window, the learning and vigilance parameters, and the number of extracted features has been tuned by an extensive review of every possible scenario. This approach enhances the capabilities of the simple use of a neural network for pattern classification. This strategy has shown an alternative for classification of abnormal situations, with no information from current case study as state space response. Furthermore, pattern databases have been constructed, based on several selected scenarios, which have been obtained offline per scenario. This initial information is basic in order to obtain an accurate model of the system under study. This strategy shows how model-free techniques can be implemented for fault diagnosis, and the need of a large amount of data, as well as the extensive review of multiple parameters. The main contribution here is the use of several pre-processing data stages, in order to conform suitable and accurate information to be processed by the neural network. In addition, a database of several scenarios needs to be used for a trustable fault diagnosis strategy. In fact, it is necessary to define a heuristic index that allows the differentiation between scenarios. Here, the use of one specific time frequency distribution approach over the rest of the current algorithms is pursued. Moreover, this strategy could address a proper dynamic non-linear system for online classification of unknown scenarios.

Acknowledgements

The authors would like to thank the financial support of DISCA-IIMAS-UNAM, ICYTDF PICCO10-53, and UNAM-PAPIIT (IN103310) Mexico, in connection with this work. Furthermore, authors would like to thank the valuable help of Mr. Adrian Duran during the construction of this chapter.

Author details

Héctor Benítez-Pérez[1*], Jorge L. Ortega-Arjona[2] and Alma Benítez-Pérez[3]

*Address all correspondence to: hector@uxdea4.iimas.unam.mx

1 Departamento de Ingeniería de Sistemas Computacionales y Automatización, Instituto de Investigaciones en Matemáticas Aplicadas y en Sistemas, Universidad Nacional Autónoma de México, México

2 Departamento de Matemáticas, Facultad de Ciencias, Universidad Nacional Autónoma de México, México

3 CECYT 11 "WILFRIDO MASSIEU", Instituto Politécnico Nacional, México

References

[1] Li, D., Pedrycz, W., & Pizzu, N. (2005). Fuzzy Wavelet Packet based Feature Extraction Method and Its Application to Biomedical Signal Classification. *IEEE Transaction on Biomedical Engineering*, 52(6), 1132-1139.

[2] Billings, S., & Wei, H. (2005). A New Class of Wavelet Networks for Nonlinear System Identification. *IEEE Transaction on Neural Networks*, 14(4), 862-874.

[3] Wang, X., Chen, B., Yang, S., & Mc Greavy, C. (1999a). Application of Wavelets and Neural Networks to Diagnostic Systems Development, 2, an Integrated Framework and its Application. *Computers and Chemical Engineering*, 23, 945-954.

[4] Chen, B. H., Wang, X. Z., Yang, S. H., & Mc Greavy, C. (1999). Application of wavelets and neural networks to diagnostic system development, 1, feature extraction. Computers & Chemical Engineering , July 1999, 23(7), 899-906.

[5] Zhan, Z., Ikeuchi, H., Saiki, N., Imamura, T., Miyake, T., Toda, H., & Horihata, S. (2008). Fast Wavelet Instantaneous Correction and its Application to Abnormal Signal Detection. *International Journal of Innovative Computing Information and Control*, 4(10), 2697-2710.

[6] Cheng, Y., Junxian, L., Feng, B., & Guan, W. (2009). Hermite Cubic Spline Multi-Wavelet Natural Boundary Element Method. *ICIC Express Letters*, 3(2), 213-217.

[7] Xing, Y., Wu, X., & Zhiliang, X. (2008). Multiclass Least Squares Auto-Correlation Wavelet Support Vector Machines. *ICIC Express Letters*, 2(4), 345-350.

[8] Benítez-Pérez, H., & Benitez-Perez, Alma. (2009). The use of ARMAX strategy and Self Organizing Maps for Feature Extraction and Classification for Fault Diagnosis. *International Journal of Innovative Computing, Information and Control, IJICIC*, 5(2), 1-ISIII08-025.

[9] Whiteley, J., Davis, A., & Mehrotra, Ahalt S. (1996). Observations and Problems Applying ART2 for Dynamic Sensor Pattern Interpretation. IEEE Transactions on Systems, Man, and Cybernetics- Part A: Systems and Humans, 26, 4, July.

[10] Moisen, C., Benítez-Pérez, H., & Medina, L. (2008). Non-contact Ultrasound for Flaw Characterisation using ARTMAP and Wavelet Analysis. DOI: 10.1504/IJMPT.2008.022517, *International Journal of Materials and Product Technology*, 33(4), 387-403.

[11] Abbate, A., Koay, H., Frankel, J., Schroeder, S., & Das, P. (1997). Signal Detection and Noise Suppression Using a Wavelet Transform Signal Processor: Application to Ultrasonic Flaw Detection. IEEE Transactions on Ultrasonics, Ferroelectrics, and Frequency Control , January 1997, 44(1), 14-26.

[12] Frazier, M. (1999). *An Introduction to Wavelets Through Linear Algebra*, Springer-Verlag.

[13] Kohonen, T. (1989). *Self-Organization and Associative Memory*, Springer-Verlag, Berlin, Germany.

[14] Hassoum, H. (1995). *Fundamentals of Artificial Neural Networks*, Massachusetts Institute of Technology, USA.

[15] Nelles, O. (2001). *Non-Linear Systems Identification*, Springer-Verlag, Berlin, Germany.

[16] Blanke, M., Kinnaert, M., Lunze, J., & Staroswicki, . (2003). *Diagnosis and Fault Tolerant Control*, Springer-Verlag.

[17] Benítez-Pérez, Héctor, & Benitez-Perez, Alma. (2010). The use of WAVELET strategy and Self Organizing Maps for Feature Extraction and Classification for Fault Diagnosis. *International Journal of Innovative Computing, Information and Control, IJICIC*, 6(11), 4923-4936.

Chapter 4

Ex-Post Clustering of Brazilian Beef Cattle Farms Using Soms and Cross-Evaluation Dea Models

João Carlos Correia Baptista Soares de Mello,
Eliane Gonçalves Gomes, Lidia Angulo Meza,
Luiz Biondi Neto, Urbano Gomes Pinto de Abreu,
Thiago Bernardino de Carvalho and Sergio de Zen

Additional information is available at the end of the chapter

http://dx.doi.org/10.5772/51324

1. Introduction

The beef cattle production system is the set of technologies and management practices, animal type, purpose of breeding, breed group and the eco-region where the activity is developed. The central structure in the beef cattle production chain is the biological system of beef production, including the stages of creation (cow-calf production, stocker production, feedlot beef production) and their combinations. The cow-calf phase is the less profitable activity and the one that has the higher risk. However, it supports the entire structure of the production system.

Although it is undeniable that a systemic view in agriculture is important, it is not yet established in the Brazilian agricultural research. In this study, by using a non parametric technique known as Data Envelopment Analysis (DEA) and Self-Organizing Maps (SOMS), we intend to cluster cattle breeders of some Brazilian municipalities. The objective is to group the farmers according to their efficiency profiles regarding the decisions related to the composition of their production systems, which are focused on the cow-calf phase. The farmers' decisions have direct impacts on the expenditures and on the income reached.

Efficiency is a relative concept: we compare the amount produced by a productive unit or firm given the available resources, to the maximum quantities that would have been produced with the same amount of resources. There are different approaches to measure efficiency. The so-called parametric methods assume a pre-defined functional relationship between resources (inputs) and products (outputs). These methods usually use averages to determine the amount that would have been produced. The non-parametric approaches, among which DEA, do not make any assumption about the functional form of the relationship between inputs and outputs. DEA assumes that the maximum that could have been produced is obtained in the sample under evaluation, by observing the firms that better perform. DEA was initially presented in [1] and computes the efficiency of productive units, the so-called decision making units (DMUs). The DMUs, here the farms, use the same types of inputs to produce the same sort of outputs, and this set must be homogenous.

Mathematically and in the presence of multiple inputs and multiple outputs, efficiency is the ratio between the weighted sum of outputs and the weighted sum of inputs. In the DEA approach, each firm chooses the most appropriate set of weights with the view to maximize that ratio. This choice is neither arbitrary nor subjective, as it is based on some restrictions. The result of the ratio must mean efficiency, i.e., it must be a number between 0 and 1. Thus, it is necessary that the weights that a firm chooses when applied to itself and to the others (in total of k firms) cannot give a number bigger than one. These considerations are set in a mathematical programming problem that formalizes the DEA model. In this context, we may say that DEA scores are a benevolent measure of efficiency.

SOMS are a special case of neural networks. In the literature we can find some papers that discuss the joint use of neural networks and data envelopment analysis. SOMS are often used with DEA to perform an ex-ante clustering, in order to allow DEA to evaluate only homogeneous units. For instance, in [2] Neural Networks and DEA were used to determine if the differences among efficiency scores were due to environmental variables or to the management process. The use of Neural Network for clustering and benchmarking container terminals was done in [3]. In [4], authors used Kohonen self-organizing maps to cluster participating countries in the Olympics and then applied DEA for producing a new ranking of participating teams. In references [5, 6] they used the back propagation neural network algorithm to accelerate computations in DEA. In [7] authors applied Neural Networks to estimate missing information for suppliers evaluation using DEA. In [8], SOMS were used to cluster the CEDERJ distance learning centers before applying DEA models to assess the efficiency of these centers. The differences between the clusters were taken into account by a homogenization of the centers for the purpose of comparing them in one single cluster.

In this chapter we propose a different approach. SOMS are used for ex-post evaluation, as discussed in [9]. In our approach we first perform a DEA evaluation and then we cluster the DMUs into groups based on DEA efficiencies. In our case we compute the farmers' efficiency profiles and the SOMS are used to group the DMUs according to their common characteristics. The efficiency profiles are derived from the DEA cross-efficiency matrix. In the cross-evaluation approach [10] each DMU is assessed by its own set of multipliers as well as by the other DMUs' multipliers. Thus, the column vector of efficiencies calculated for each DMU in the cross-evaluation matrix is assumed as the efficiency profile. It is important to note that the DEA cross-efficiency technique is usually used for ranking purposes. Here, however, it is not used as a ranking tool but as the input to a SOM that will be used to cluster the units according to the way their efficiencies were obtained.

Our discussion proceeds as follows. In Section 2 we discuss the theoretical aspects of DEA and of cross-evaluation analysis. Section 3 is about the fundamental aspects of SOMS: Kohonen Neural Networks. In Section 4 we present the proposed approach: DEA and SOMS in an ex-post evaluation. The case study is detailed in section 4. In Section 5 we discuss the results. Finally, we summarize our conclusions and list the references.

2. Dea and cross-efficiency evaluation

DEA is a mathematical programming approach developed to compute the comparative efficiency of productive units (firms or DMUs). The DMUs perform similar tasks and use different amounts of inputs to produce different quantities of outputs. In order to maximize the efficiency of each DMU, DEA models allow each one to choose the weight assigned to each variable in complete freedom, subject to some restrictions. In the case the firms under evaluation operate under different scales, it is possible to consider these differences in a DEA formulation. This model is known in the DEA literature as VRS (variable returns to scale) or BCC model (from Banker, Charnes and Cooper), as firstly discussed in [11]. On the other hand, if it is possible to assume that the DMUs operate under constant return to scale, i.e., there is a proportional relationship in increments or decrements between inputs and outputs, the suitable model is the CRS (constant returns to scale) or CCR (from Charnes, Cooper and Rhodes), as presented in the seminal paper [1].

The mathematical linear formulation for DEA CCR model is shown in model (1), where h_1 is the efficiency of the DMU '1' under evaluation; $x_{ik}$and y_{jk} are the *i-th* input and *j-th* output of the *k-th* DMU, *k*=1…*n*; μ_j and $v_i$are the output and the input weights or multipliers, respectively.

$$\begin{aligned}
&\max h_1=\sum_{j=1}^{s}\mu_j y_{j1}\\
&\text{subject to}\\
&\sum_{i=1}^{r} v_i x_{i1}=1\\
&\sum_{j=1}^{s}\mu_j y_{jk}-\sum_{i=1}^{r} v_i x_{ik}\le 0\\
&\mu_j,\ v_i\ge 0,\quad k=1\ldots n,\ \ j=1\ldots s,\ \ i=1\ldots r
\end{aligned} \tag{1}$$

As previously mentioned, DEA allows each DMU to perform its self-evaluation, in other words, to choose its own set of multipliers in such a way that its efficiency score is maximized. In [10], it was proposed that the optimal weights for each DMU can be used to evaluate its peers, i.e., to compute alternative efficiency scores for every other DMU. This evaluation performed by the complete set of DMUs is called cross-evaluation [12, 13] and the resulting measures of performance are the cross-efficiencies. In (2), $h_{k1}$is the cross-efficiency of DMU '1' using the weights of the DMU 'k'; μ_{jk} is the weight of output j obtained for DMU 'k'; v_{ik} is the weight of input i obtained for DMU 'k'. The final cross-efficiency index is the average of all peer and self-evaluations.

$$h_{k1} = \frac{\sum_{j=1}^{s} \mu_{jk} y_{j1}}{\sum_{i=1}^{r} v_{ik} x_{i1}} \tag{2}$$

As discussed in [14], the use of cross-evaluation has spread to a number of different areas, as in multiple criteria decision making to improve discrimination among alternatives, in a preferential election, in the ranking and selection of projects and technologies, among others. As discussed in [15-17] cross-evaluation commonly uses the CCR model due to the existence of negative efficiencies when choosing the BCC model. The usage of the BCC model for cross-evaluation imposes the inclusion of an additional set of restrictions to ensure positive efficiencies [16, 17].

As was noticed in [10], in the DEA context the optimal set of weights for a DMU is not unique. Therefore it is necessary to choose one set of weights among all the possibilities. In the original cross-evaluation formulation these approaches led to nonlinear problems. In [12] two linear models were introduced, that are approximations to the original formulation. There are some other alternative models for the cross-efficiency evaluation. We mention the DEA-Game [18], among others [19]. These models may use two approaches. The first one, called "aggressive model", minimizes the cross-evaluation indexes of all DMUs. The second approach, known as "benevolent model", maximizes the cross-evaluation scores of all DMUs. The so-called aggressive C_k formulation is shown in model (3), as presented in [12].

$$\begin{aligned}
&\min C_k = \sum_{j=1}^{s} \mu_{jk} \sum_{m \neq k} y_{jm} \\
&\text{subject to} \\
&\sum_{i=1}^{r} v_{ik} \sum_{m \neq k} x_{im} = 1 \\
&\sum_{j=1}^{s} \mu_{jk} y_{jm} - \sum_{i=1}^{r} v_{ik} x_{im} \leq 0, \quad \forall m \neq k \\
&\sum_{j=1}^{s} \mu_{jk} y_{jk} - h_{kk} \sum_{i=1}^{r} v_{ik} x_{ik} = 0 \\
&\mu_{jk},\ v_{ik} \geq 0
\end{aligned} \tag{3}$$

After determining the set of weights to be used in the cross-evaluation, a cross-efficiency matrix is calculated, as shown in Table 1. This matrix contains the self-evaluation (h_{kk}) and the peer-evaluation (h_{kl}, $k \neq l$) of each DMU. The efficiency scores of a given DMU will be in the column of this matrix.

http://dx.doi.org/10.5772/51324

DMU	1	2	3	...	*n*
1	h_{11}	h_{12}	h_{13}	...	h_{1n}
2	h_{21}	h_{22}	h_{23}	...	h_{2n}
3	h_{31}	h_{32}	h_{33}	...	h_{35}
...	...	...	...	...	...
n	h_{n1}	h_{n2}	h_{n3}	...	h_{n5}

Table 1. Cross-efficiencies matrix for *n* DMUs.

We may point out that DMUs sharing similar weights distribution (with similar characteristics) will evaluate each other with high efficiency scores. On the contrary, those who have dissimilar characteristics will evaluate each other with low efficiency scores. The efficiency scores of a DMU (the column of the matrix) are limited by the efficiency score obtained in the self-evaluation (the diagonal of the matrix, h_{kk}). In the self-evaluation, provided by the classic DEA models, a DMU is shown in the best possible way as to maximize its efficiency. Therefore, all peer-evaluations will be lower or equal to that efficiency score.

3. Fundamental aspects of som: kohonen neural network

The human brain organizes information in a logic way. A paramount aspect of the self-organized networks is motivated by the organization of the human brain in such a way that the sensory inputs are represented by topologically organized maps. The Kohonen self-organizing map emulates the unsupervised learning in a simple and elegant way taking into account the neuron neighborhood [20].

From topographic map development principle came up two feature mapping models: the model presented in [21, 22], having strong neurobiological motivations, and the Kohonen model [23], not as close to neurobiology as the previous one but enabling a simple computing treatment stressing the essential characteristics of the brain maps. Moreover, the Kohonen model or Kohonen Self-Organizing Map yields a low input dimension.

The SOMS are artificial neural networks special structures in a grid form that work in a similar way of the human brain, as far as the information organization is concerned, and are based on competitive learning. The most used SOM is the topologically interconnected two-dimensional, where the neurons are represented by rectangular, hexagonal and random grid knots of neighbor neurons. Higher dimensional maps can also be modeled.

In order to analyze the competitive process, let us suppose that the input space is m-dimensional and that X represents a random input pattern [24] such that one can write $X=[X_1, X_2, X_3, ..., X_m]$. Assuming that the weight vector W of each neuron has the same dimension of the input space, for a given neuron j of a total of l neurons the weight vector can be written as$W=[W_{j1}, W_{j2}, W_{j3}, ..., W_{jm}]$, j=1...l.

For each input vector, the scalar product is evaluated in order to find the X vector which is closest to the weight vector W. By comparison, the maximum scalar product $\max\left(W_j^t \cdot X\right)$ is chosen, representing the location in which the topological neighborhood of excited neurons should be centered. Maximizing this scalar product is equivalent to minimizing the Euclidian distance between X and W. Other metrics could also be used.

The neuron with the weight vector closest to the input vector X is called the winner neuron, whose index $V(X)$ is given by$V(X)=\min\| X - W_j\|$. In the cooperative process the winner neuron locates the centre of a topological neighborhood of cooperating neurons. The active winner tends to strongly stimulate its closest neighbor neurons and weakly the farthest ones. It is essential to find a topological neighborhood function $N_{j,V(X)}$ that is independent from the winner neuron location. That neighborhood function should represent the topological neighborhood centered in the winner neuron, denoted by V, having as closest lateral neighbors a group of excited and cooperative neurons, from which a representative j neuron can be chosen. The lateral distance $D_{j,V}$ between the winner neuron, indexed by V, and the excited neuron, indexed by j, can be written as in (4), where is the neighborhood width [24].

$$N_{j,V(X)}=\exp\left(-\frac{D_{j,V}^2}{2\sigma^2}\right) \tag{4}$$

The more dependent is the lateral distance$D_{j,V}$, the greater will be the cooperation among the neighborhood neurons. So, for a two-dimensional output grid, the lateral distance can be defined as in (5), for which the discrete vector $\wp_j$ represents the position of the excited neuron, and $\wp_V$ the position of the neuron that won the competition.

$$D_{j,V}=\sqrt{\| \wp_j - \wp_V \|^2} \tag{5}$$

The topological neighborhood should decrease with discrete time t. In order to accomplish that, the width σ of the topological neighborhood $N_{j,V(X)}$ should decrease in time. The width could be written as in (6), where σ_0 represents the initial value of the neighborhood width and τ_1 a time constant. Usually σ_0 is adjusted to have the same value as the grid ratio, i.e.,$\tau_1=1,\ 000/\log\sigma_0$.

$$\sigma(t)=\sigma_0\exp\left(-\frac{t}{\tau_1}\right), \quad t=0,\ 1,\ 2,\ 3,\ \ldots \tag{6}$$

The expression of the topological neighborhood in time can be written as in (7).

$$N_{j,V(X)}(t)=\exp\left(-\frac{D_{j,V}^2}{2\sigma^2(t)}\right), \quad t=0,\ 1,\ 2,\ 3,\ \ldots \tag{7}$$

The adaptive process is the last phase of the SOM procedure. During this phase is carried out the adjustment of the connection weights of the neurons. In order the network succeed in the self-organization task, it is necessary to update the weights W_j of the excited j neuron relatively to the input vector X.

The change to the weight vector of the excited neuron j in the grid can be written as $\Delta W_j = \eta \ y_j X - g(y_j) W_j$, where is the learning rate parameter, $\eta \ y_j X$ is the Hebbian term, and $g(y_j)W_j$ is called forgetting term [23-25].

In order to satisfy the requirement, a linear function for $g(y_j)$ is chosen as$g(y_j) = \eta \ y_j$. If $y_j = N_{j,V(X)}$, then the expression can be written as (8).

$$\Delta W_j = \eta \ N_{j,V(X)}(X - W_j) \tag{8}$$

Using discrete-time notation, a weight updating equation can be written, which applies to all neurons that are within the topographic neighborhood equation of the winner neuron [23, 24], as in (9).

$$W_j(n+1) = W_j(n) + \eta(n) \ N_{j,V(X)}(n)(X - W_j(t)) \tag{9}$$

In (9) the learning rate parameter changes in each iteration, with an initial value around 0.1 and decreases with increasing discrete-time t up to values above 0.01 [20]. To that end, equation (10) is written in which decays exponentially and τ_2 is another time-constant of the SOM algorithm. For the fulfillment of the requirements one could choose for instance, $\eta_0 = 0.1$and$\tau_2 = 1,\ 000$.

$$\eta(t) = \eta_0 \exp\left(-\frac{t}{\tau_2}\right), \quad t = 0,\ 1,\ 2,\ 3,\ \ldots \tag{10}$$

4. Dea and soms in an ex-post evaluation

As discussed in Section 2, in the cross-evaluation approach each DMU is assessed by its own set of multipliers (self-evaluation) as well as by the other DMUs' multipliers (peer-evaluation). The cross-efficiency matrix provides the cross-efficiencies of every DMU, each column providing the efficiencies of each DMU, i.e., is the evaluation performed by the other DMUs. As previously discussed, DMUs with the same characteristics will evaluate each other with high efficiencies, or with low efficiencies otherwise. Therefore, we can assume that each column of the cross-evaluation matrix is the efficiency profile of each DMU.

When high value of weights are assigned to the variables of DMU A this implies that DMU A will have a good efficiency score (ratio between the weighted sum of the outputs and the weighted sum of the inputs). In the context of cross-evaluation, when these weights are assigned to DMU B and it also has high efficiency score we may say that DMU B has similar characteristics to DMU A. We can observe the case in which a DMU have a good performance in all variables (or in the majority of them), but it is not unusual the case where the efficiency score is computed based only on two variables (one input and one output). This occurs when the DMU have a low performance on some variables and null weights (or near zero) are assigned to them. Therefore, considering DMUs A and B, DMU A may evaluate DMU B positively, but when DMU B evaluates DMU A, its efficiency may be low. In other words, cross-evaluation may not bring the same results for both.

In this chapter we will use SOMS to cluster the farmers with similar characteristics using the cross-efficiency matrix information. However, the cross-efficiencies are dependent on the DMU self-evaluation. The cross-efficiency scores may be smaller compared to those obtained by other DMUs (lines in the matrix), but they may be consistent or very similar to the efficiency score obtained by the DMU (column in the matrix). Therefore, as our clusters will be defined by the efficiency profile, we need to remove the self-evaluation effect of each DMU. In this approach this is accomplished by normalizing each column of the matrix by the self-evaluation, i.e., all values are divided by the CCR DEA efficiency of the DMU. This is shown in Table 2. The self-evaluation is the highest efficiency score of the DMU, located in the diagonal of the cross-evaluation matrix. As a consequence, we will have unitary values in the matrix diagonal. The objective of this operation is to group the DMUs by the way they are evaluated by the others rather than by their efficiency level. This minimizes the benevolent characteristic of the classic DEA models.

DMU	1	2	3	...	*n*
1	$\frac{h_{11}}{h_{11}}$	$\frac{h_{12}}{h_{22}}$	$\frac{h_{13}}{h_{33}}$	...	$\frac{h_{1n}}{h_{nn}}$
2	$\frac{h_{21}}{h_{11}}$	$\frac{h_{22}}{h_{22}}$	$\frac{h_{23}}{h_{33}}$	...	$\frac{h_{2n}}{h_{nn}}$
3	$\frac{h_{31}}{h_{11}}$	$\frac{h_{32}}{h_{22}}$	$\frac{h_{33}}{h_{33}}$	...	$\frac{h_{3n}}{h_{nn}}$
...	...	...	...	...	...
n	$\frac{h_{n1}}{h_{11}}$	$\frac{h_{n2}}{h_{22}}$	$\frac{h_{n13}}{h_{33}}$	...	$\frac{h_{nn}}{h_{nn}}$

Table 2. Normalized cross-efficiency matrix.

In the traditional cross-evaluation applications, the resulting average cross-efficiency index is commonly used for ranking purposes. Here, in contrast, the square matrix of normalized efficiencies will be submitted to the SOMS procedure (as its input) to generate the homogeneous clusters. In other words, the normalized cross-evaluation matrix will be used to cluster the DMUs according to their efficiency profile.

An approach based on cross-evaluation and cluster technique was used in [26] to group participating countries in Summer Olympics Games. The authors used the average cross-efficiencies and cluster analysis to group the nations and to select more appropriate targets for poorly performing countries to use as benchmarks.

5. Case study

The beef complex in Brazil is consolidated as an important link in the production and in the international trade: Brazil is the largest exporter and the second largest producer of beef. Considering this scenario, the study and the evaluation of beef cattle production systems are important tools for enhancing the performance of this sector.

In Brazil, the cow-calf beef cattle phase occurs predominantly in extensive continuous grazing, with native or cultivated pastures, encompassing: calves (until weaning or even one year old), cows, heifers and bulls. The cow-calf phase supports the entire structure of the beef production chain.

This case study seeks to assess the comparative performance of extensive livestock modal production systems in its cow-calf phase, in some Brazilian municipalities. The objective is to measure their performance and to group them according to the decisions regarding the composition of the production system. This has a direct impact on the expenditures and on the income generated.

5.1 Data Source

Primary data were collected through the panel system, which allows the definition of representative farms, as proposed in [27].

In this approach, based on the experience of the participating farmers, it is characterized the property that is the most commonly found in the region, i.e., a property or a production system that is representative of the locality under study. In some cases it is not possible to determine this typology and more than one representative property or production system are specified.

The panel is a less costly procedure of obtaining information than the census or the sampling of farms. The technique is applied during a meeting with a group of one or more researchers, one technician and eight regional farmers. Meetings are scheduled in advance, with the support of rural unions and regional contacts. At the end of that debate one can say that any characterization of the typical farm in the region has the consent of the farmers. Thus, productivity rates, establishment costs, fixed and variable costs, i.e., all the numbers resulting from the panel, tend to be fairly close to the regional reality.

It is noteworthy that the rates and the costs reported by each participant are not related to their properties, but with a single farm, declared at the beginning of the panel as the one that best represents the scale of operation and the production system of most of the local properties.

This study evaluated 21 beef cattle modal production systems that performed only the cow-calf phase, in seven states of Brazil. The data, derived from the indicators of the project developed by the Centro de Estudos Avançados em Economia Aplicada and the Confederação da Agricultura e Pecuária do Brasil, were collected in municipalities of these seven states: Mato Grosso do Sul - MS (eight), Goiás - GO (four), Rio Grande do Sul - RS (one), Minas Gerais - MG (four), Tocantins - TO (two), São Paulo - SP (one) and Bahia - BA (one). Panels with the farmers, with the support of the local rural technical assistance, were performed to collect the data, according to the methodology described in [28].

5.2 Modeling

5.2.1 DMUs

The objective of the DEA model is to measure the performance of the farmers' decision regarding the composition of the rearing production system. Thereby, the DMUs are the 21 modal systems, identified from the panel discussions in 21 cities in seven Brazilian states. Table 3 presents the dataset.

DMUs			Breeders	Calves	Cull cows
Municipality	State	Code	(input)	(output)	(output)
Alvorada	TO	#1	12	147	30
Amambai	MS	#2	15	143	40
Aquidauana	MS	#3	92	713	214
Bonito	MS	#4	14	166	75
Brasilândia	MS	#5	31	290	178
Camapuã	MS	#6	9	65	33
Carlos Chagas	MG	#7	19	297	160
Catalão	GO	#8	8	81	42
Corumbá	MS	#9	69	455	200
Itamarajú	BA	#10	4	44	18
Lavras do Sul	RS	#11	5	58	30
Montes Claros	MG	#12	5	47	28
Niquelândia	GO	#13	4	35	18
Paraíso do Tocantins	TO	#14	12	123	35
Porangatu	GO	#15	5	46	23
Ribas Rio Pardo	MS	#16	15	143	70
Rio Verde	GO	#17	23	196	82
São Gabriel d'Oeste	MS	#18	11	95	40
Tupã	SP	#19	5	46	30
Uberaba	MG	#20	5	66	36
Uberlândia	MG	#21	2	20	10

Table 3. DMUs, inputs and outputs.

5.2.2 Variables

The technicians and the researchers mentioned in 5.1, analyzed the variables set and immediately identified those relevant to our study. They selected "number of bulls" as the input variable, since this variable represents a significant portion of all total expenditures of the ranchers that produce calves. It is directly linked to the quality of animals that will be sold in these systems. This is also the only category that is purchased from other herd, especially in ranches with herds of genetic selection.

The products of the system that are responsible for the main revenue from the cow-calf systems were chosen as the output variables. These are the "number of calves on the herd" and the "number of cull cows". All calves produced are sold on the property and generate income. Cull cows are those that are sold, as they are not part of the production system either by higher age or by reproductive performance lower than desired. The decision to fit between these variables is important because it will provide the dynamics structure of the breeding herd. This is the fundamental factor for keeping the economic viability of the beef cattle production system.

The variables indicated by experts need to be examined by analysts to determine whether they conform to the properties required by the DEA models. In particular, there must be a causal relationship between each input-output pair [29]. There is a clear causal relationship between the output "number of calves on the herd" and the input "number of bulls". The same cannot be said of the relationship between the input and the output "number of cull cows". Actually, there is no direct causal relationship between these variables; however there is a cost-benefit relationship. In the case the rancher has a big number of bulls (that represent an expense) he must earn more, either through the sale of calves or cows. Therefore, the "bulls – cull cows" ratio makes sense when using DEA to analyze cost-benefit ratios, and not just pure productive relations. This interpretation of DEA was introduced in [30] and was used in [31, 32]. Generalizations of this usage can be seen in [33].

6. Results and discussion

Figure 1 shows the cross-evaluation matrix. It was computed using the SIAD software [34]. As previously mentioned, we used the DEA CCR as the BCC model can generate negative efficiency scores [17].

The values of the Figure 1, cross-evaluation matrix, were normalized before using SOMS, as explained in Section 4. Four different grid dimensions were tested: the 5x5 grid, the 3x3 grid, the 2x2 grid and the 2x1 grid. We began our analysis with the 5x5 grid since it yields 25 neurons against the 21 DMUs of the data set.

	#1	#2	#3	#4	#5	#6	#7	#8	#9	#10	#11	#12	#13	#14	#15	#16	#17	#18	#19	#20	#21
#1	0.7837	0.6099	0.4958	0.7585	0.5985	0.4620	1.0000	0.6477	0.4219	0.7037	0.7421	0.6013	0.5598	0.6557	0.5886	0.6099	0.5452	0.5525	0.5886	0.8444	0.6397
#2	0.7837	0.6099	0.4958	0.7585	0.5985	0.4620	1.0000	0.6477	0.4219	0.7037	0.7421	0.6013	0.5598	0.6557	0.5886	0.6099	0.5452	0.5525	0.5886	0.8444	0.6397
#3	0.7837	0.6099	0.4958	0.7585	0.5985	0.4620	1.0000	0.6477	0.4219	0.7037	0.7421	0.6013	0.5598	0.6557	0.5886	0.6099	0.5452	0.5525	0.5886	0.8444	0.6397
#4	0.7837	0.6099	0.4958	0.7585	0.5985	0.4620	1.0000	0.6477	0.4219	0.7037	0.7421	0.6013	0.5598	0.6557	0.5886	0.6099	0.5452	0.5525	0.5886	0.8444	0.6397
#5	0.2969	0.3167	0.2762	0.6362	0.6819	0.4354	1.0000	0.6234	0.3442	0.5344	0.7125	0.6650	0.5344	0.3464	0.5463	0.5542	0.4234	0.4318	0.7125	0.8550	0.5938
#6	0.7837	0.6099	0.4958	0.7585	0.5985	0.4620	1.0000	0.6477	0.4219	0.7037	0.7421	0.6013	0.5598	0.6557	0.5886	0.6099	0.5452	0.5525	0.5886	0.8444	0.6397
#7	0.2969	0.3167	0.2762	0.6362	0.6819	0.4354	1.0000	0.6234	0.3442	0.5344	0.7125	0.6650	0.5344	0.3464	0.5463	0.5542	0.4234	0.4318	0.7125	0.8550	0.5938
#8	0.7837	0.6099	0.4958	0.7585	0.5985	0.4620	1.0000	0.6477	0.4219	0.7037	0.7421	0.6013	0.5598	0.6557	0.5886	0.6099	0.5452	0.5525	0.5886	0.8444	0.6397
#9	0.7837	0.6099	0.4958	0.7585	0.5985	0.4620	1.0000	0.6477	0.4219	0.7037	0.7421	0.6013	0.5598	0.6557	0.5886	0.6099	0.5452	0.5525	0.5886	0.8444	0.6397
#10	0.7837	0.6099	0.4958	0.7585	0.5985	0.4620	1.0000	0.6477	0.4219	0.7037	0.7421	0.6013	0.5598	0.6557	0.5886	0.6099	0.5452	0.5525	0.5886	0.8444	0.6397
#11	0.7837	0.6099	0.4958	0.7585	0.5985	0.4620	1.0000	0.6477	0.4219	0.7037	0.7421	0.6013	0.5598	0.6557	0.5886	0.6099	0.5452	0.5525	0.5886	0.8444	0.6397
#12	0.2969	0.3167	0.2762	0.6362	0.6819	0.4354	1.0000	0.6234	0.3442	0.5344	0.7125	0.6650	0.5344	0.3464	0.5463	0.5542	0.4234	0.4318	0.7125	0.8550	0.5938
#13	0.7837	0.6099	0.4958	0.7585	0.5985	0.4620	1.0000	0.6477	0.4219	0.7037	0.7421	0.6013	0.5598	0.6557	0.5886	0.6099	0.5452	0.5525	0.5886	0.8444	0.6397
#14	0.7837	0.6099	0.4958	0.7585	0.5985	0.4620	1.0000	0.6477	0.4219	0.7037	0.7421	0.6013	0.5598	0.6557	0.5886	0.6099	0.5452	0.5525	0.5886	0.8444	0.6397
#15	0.7837	0.6099	0.4958	0.7585	0.5985	0.4620	1.0000	0.6477	0.4219	0.7037	0.7421	0.6013	0.5598	0.6557	0.5886	0.6099	0.5452	0.5525	0.5886	0.8444	0.6397
#16	0.7837	0.6099	0.4958	0.7585	0.5985	0.4620	1.0000	0.6477	0.4219	0.7037	0.7421	0.6013	0.5598	0.6557	0.5886	0.6099	0.5452	0.5525	0.5886	0.8444	0.6397
#17	0.7837	0.6099	0.4958	0.7585	0.5985	0.4620	1.0000	0.6477	0.4219	0.7037	0.7421	0.6013	0.5598	0.6557	0.5886	0.6099	0.5452	0.5525	0.5886	0.8444	0.6397
#18	0.7837	0.6099	0.4958	0.7585	0.5985	0.4620	1.0000	0.6477	0.4219	0.7037	0.7421	0.6013	0.5598	0.6557	0.5886	0.6099	0.5452	0.5525	0.5886	0.8444	0.6397
#19	0.2969	0.3167	0.2762	0.6362	0.6819	0.4354	1.0000	0.6234	0.3442	0.5344	0.7125	0.6650	0.5344	0.3464	0.5463	0.5542	0.4234	0.4318	0.7125	0.8550	0.5938
#20	0.2969	0.3167	0.2762	0.6362	0.6819	0.4354	1.0000	0.6234	0.3442	0.5344	0.7125	0.6650	0.5344	0.3464	0.5463	0.5542	0.4234	0.4318	0.7125	0.8550	0.5938
#21	0.7837	0.6099	0.4958	0.7585	0.5985	0.4620	1.0000	0.6477	0.4219	0.7037	0.7421	0.6013	0.5598	0.6557	0.5886	0.6099	0.5452	0.5525	0.5886	0.8444	0.6397

Figure 1. Cross-evaluation matrix. In the diagonal are the scores computed by the self-evaluations. Other cells show the peer-evaluations.

Cluster	DMUs		
	Municipality	**State**	**Code**
1	Alvorada	TO	#1
2	Amambai	MS	#2
3	Aquidauana	MS	#3
4	Bonito	MS	#4
5	Brasilândia	MS	#5
5	Montes Claros	MG	#12
6	Camapuã	MS	#6
7	Carlos Chagas	MG	#7
8	Catalão	GO	#8
9	Corumbá	MS	#9
10	Itamarajú	BA	#10
11	Lavras do Sul	RS	#11
12	Niquelândia	GO	#13
13	Paraíso do Tocantins	TO	#14
14	Porangatu	GO	#15
14	Ribas Rio Pardo	MS	#16
15	Rio Verde	GO	#17
15	São Gabriel d'Oeste	MS	#18
16	Tupã	SP	#19
17	Uberaba	MG	#20
18	Uberlândia	MG	#21

Table 4. Clusters obtained with the 5x5 grid.

The 5x5 grid provided the results shown in Table 4. There were obtained 18 clusters and almost all contained one municipality (DMU). The exceptions were cluster 5 (which contains Brasilândia and Montes Claros), cluster 14 (compounded of Porangatu and Ribas Rio Pardo), and cluster 15 (with Rio Verde and São Gabriel d'Oeste).

Figure 2 shows the resulting allocation for the 5x5 grid. The clusters with two DMUs were the ones in which the municipalities had the most similar efficiency profiles, i.e., strongest similarities. If these six DMUs hadn't met their similar pairs they would had been allocated in the empty clusters, each DMU in one cluster, instead of being grouped in pairs in three clusters.

These three clusters were formed mainly due to the similarity of the decision profile in regards to the cows' culling age in the production systems of Brasilândia and Montes Claros (8.2 and 8.5 years), Ribas Rio Pardo and Porangatu (9.2 and 9.0 years), Rio Verde and São Gabriel d'Oeste (10.3 and 10.7 years). In practice, however, the 5x5 grid didn't perform well, as it hadn't grouped other production systems with similar profiles. Thus, this grid didn't provide the basis for an accurate synthesis of convergence points among the other systems under assessment.

The 5x5 grid allocated many single municipalities in the clusters, i.e., one DMU in one cluster. Therefore, this topology was not suitable for this study. We also analyzed the 4x4 grid. We inferred that the 4x4 typology was also not adequate for this study as we obtained similar results to the 5x5 grid.

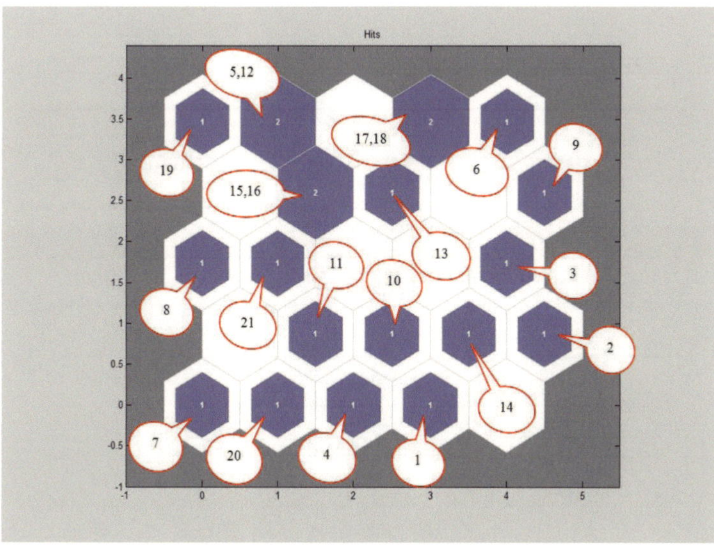

Figure 2. DMUs' distribution for the 5x5 grid.

The set shown in Table 5 is from the 3x3 grid. We observe that some DMUs were in the same clusters they were allocated in the 5x5 grid. This was the case of the cluster composed of Brasilândia and Montes Claros. In this cluster were added the DMUs Catalão, Ribas Rio Pardo, Tupã and Uberlândia. The same occurred with the group Rio Verde – São Gabriel d'Oeste that in the 3x3 grid was also consisted of Niquelândia and Porangatu municipalities. We may point out that Porangatu and Ribas Rio Pardo were no longer in the same cluster, which was a consequence of this new grid.

Cluster	DMUs		
	Municipality	**State**	**Code**
1	Alvorada	TO	#1
2	Amambai	MS	#2
2	Paraíso do Tocantins	TO	#14
3	Aquidauana	MS	#3
3	Camapuã	MS	#6
3	Corumbá	MS	#9
4	Bonito	MS	#4
4	Lavras do Sul	RS	#11
5	Brasilândia	MS	#5
5	Catalão	GO	#8
5	Montes Claros	MG	#12
5	Ribas Rio Pardo	MS	#16
5	Tupã	SP	#19
5	Uberlândia	MG	#21
6	Carlos Chagas	MG	#7
7	Itamarajú	BA	#10
8	Niquelândia	GO	#13
8	Porangatu	GO	#15
8	Rio Verde	GO	#17
8	São Gabriel d'Oeste	MS	#18
9	Uberaba	MG	#20

Table 5. Clusters obtained with the 3x3 grid.

This situation was probably a result of the same decision-making profile of the municipalities that were grouped, in regards the dispose of cows and bulls in their production systems. The 3x3 grid provided balanced groups concerning the variables, especially in relation to the profile of discarding cows and bulls. Bulls' disposal is directly related to purchase: the higher is the annual discard, it increases the need for annual replacements.

By limiting the number of clusters to nine (3x3 grid) we obtained three clusters with only one municipality: cluster 1 (Alvorada), cluster 6 (Carlos Chagas) and cluster 7 (Itamarajú). These three municipalities had unique profiles of decision- making with respect to the culling of cows and bulls. In Alvorada, cows and bulls culling rates were the lowest among the municipalities analyzed (8 and 13%, respectively). In Carlos Chagas, the rates were higher (18 and 21%). In Itamarajú, the cows disposal rate was small (12%), but the bulls disposal rate was the highest among the production systems evaluated (24%).

Figure 3 shows the DMUs' distribution for the 3x3 dimension grid.

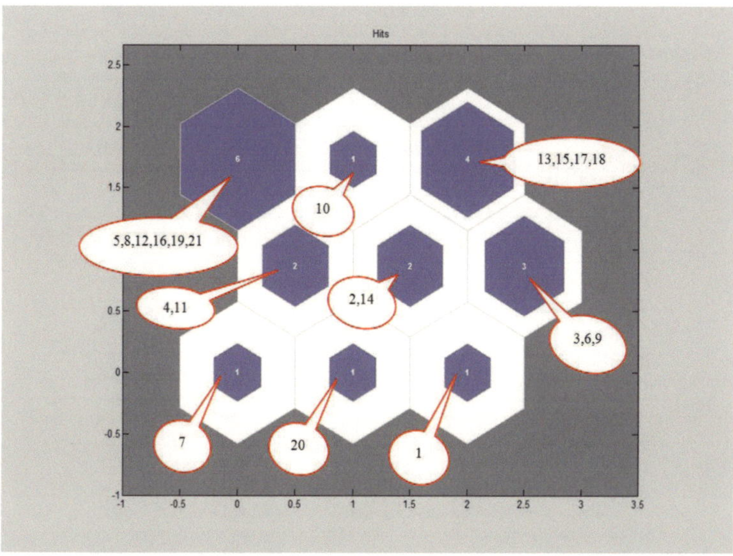

Figure 3. DMUs' distribution for the 3x3 grid.

The third grid used was the 2x2. The results are displayed in Table 6. Comparing these results with the ones from the 3x3 grid we observe that most of the previous allocation remained unchanged and there were mergers according to the clusters similarities. The exception is cluster 8 in the 3x3 grid (Niquelândia, Porangatu, Rio Verde and São Gabriel d'Oeste): in the current configuration its DMUs were inserted into other clusters (Niquelândia and Porangatu are in cluster 3 along with Bonito, Brasilândia, Catalão, Itamarajú, Lavras do Sul, Montes Claros, Ribas Rio Pardo, Tupã and Uberlândia; Rio Verde and São Gabriel d'Oeste were in cluster 2 along with Aquidauana, Camapuã and Corumbá).

Although these clusters were different from the ones obtained with the 3x3 grid, they were compatible with the results from 5x5 configuration, where the pairs Rio Verde – Gabriel d'Oeste and Porangatu – Ribas Rio Pardo were allocated in different groups.

Cluster	DMUs		
	Municipality	State	Code
1	Alvorada	TO	#1
1	Amambai	MS	#2
1	Paraíso do Tocantins	TO	#14
2	Aquidauana	MS	#3
2	Camapuã	MS	#6
2	Corumbá	MS	#9
2	Rio Verde	GO	#17
2	São Gabriel d'Oeste	MS	#18
3	Bonito	MS	#4
3	Brasilândia	MS	#5
3	Catalão	GO	#8
3	Itamarajú	BA	#10
3	Lavras do Sul	RS	#11
3	Montes Claros	MG	#12
3	Niquelândia	GO	#13
3	Porangatu	GO	#15
3	Ribas Rio Pardo	MS	#16
3	Tupã	SP	#19
3	Uberlândia	MG	#21
4	Carlos Chagas	MG	#7
4	Uberaba	MG	#20

Table 6. Clusters obtained with the 2x2 grid.

The DMUs' allocation in regards to the 2x2 grid is shown in Figure 4. The biggest cluster had 11 municipalities: Bonito, Brasilândia, Catalão, Itamarajú, Lavras do Sul, Montes Claros, Niquelândia, Porangatu, Ribas Rio Pardo, Tupã and Uberlândia. In this group, cows and bulls discard rates had medium values (19 and 14%, respectively).

The smallest group was composed of two municipalities: Carlos Chagas and Uberaba. These municipalities exhibited higher rates for the discarding of cows and bulls (18% and 21%), which is a characteristic of production systems with a more dynamics profile, when compared to other clusters.

The clusters composed of three (Alvorada, Amambai and Paraíso do Tocantins) and five municipalities (Rio Verde, Aquidauana, Camapuã, São Gabriel d'Oeste and Corumbá) had

http://dx.doi.org/10.5772/51324

discard rates of cows and bulls of 10% and 13%, and 18% and 15%, respectively. This implies that the former group (with lower rates) probably had herds with a lower replacement dynamics. In the latter cluster, which had a lower rate of bulls' replacement, there was less investment in improving the genetic quality of the herd.

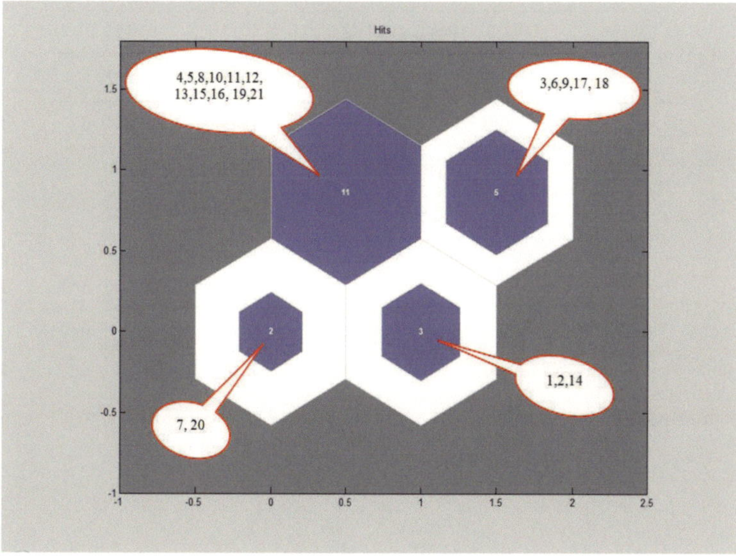

Figure 4. DMUs' distribution for the 2x2 grid.

Finally, the 2x1 dimension grid was used and the results are depicted in Table 7 and Figure 5 shows its DMUs' distribution.

Cluster	DMUs		
	Municipality	**State**	**Code**
1	Alvorada	TO	#1
1	Amambai	MS	#2
1	Aquidauana	MS	#3
1	Brasilândia	MS	#5
1	Camapuã	MS	#6
1	Catalão	GO	#8
1	Corumbá	MS	#9
1	Itamarajú	BA	#10
1	Montes Claros	MG	#12
1	Niquelândia	GO	#13

Cluster	DMUs		
	Municipality	State	Code
1	Paraíso do Tocantins	TO	#14
1	Porangatu	GO	#15
1	Ribas Rio Pardo	MS	#16
1	Rio Verde	GO	#17
1	São Gabriel d'Oeste	MS	#18
1	Tupã	SP	#19
1	Uberlândia	MG	#21
2	Bonito	MS	#4
2	Carlos Chagas	MG	#7
2	Lavras do Sul	RS	#11
2	Uberaba	MG	#20

Table 7. Clusters obtained with the 2x1 grid.

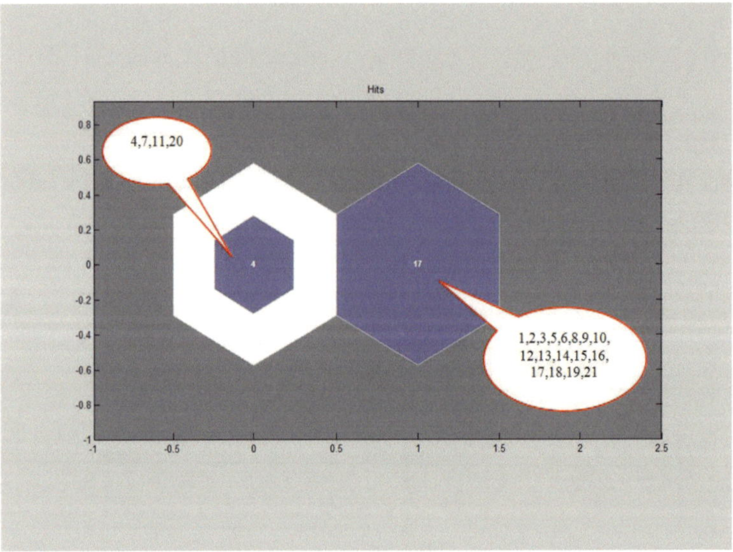

Figure 5. DMUs' distribution for the 2x1 grid.

We notice that a small cluster was formed with Bonito, Carlos Chagas, Lavras do Sul and Uberaba. Bonito and Lavras do Sul were part of one cluster in the 3x3 grid and in the 2x2 grid they were included in cluster 3 along with Brasilândia, Catalão, Itamarajú, Montes Claros, Niquelândia, Porangatu, Ribas Rio Pardo, Tupã and Uberlândia, which were in clus-

http://dx.doi.org/10.5772/51324

ter 1. This was a result of the new grid used. Both groups had no outstanding difference between the culling rates of cows and bulls (14 and 17% in cluster 1, 14 and 18% in cluster 2).

This grid was not satisfactory to support the analysis of similarities and dissimilarities of the beef cattle production systems profiles evaluated.

7. Conclusions

In this paper we used Data Envelopment Analysis with SOMS to cluster the 21 beef cattle modal production systems into homogeneous groups according to their efficiency profiles. The efficiency profiles are derived from the cross-evaluation DEA approach. This approach allows a peer-evaluation instead of only considering the self-evaluation performed by the classic DEA models.

The approach used here is different from the previous ones in the literature, in which SOMS are used to group the DMUs into homogeneous sets and then use DEA models to evaluate the DMUs belonging to each cluster. In our approach rather than performing ex-ante clustering we carried out ex-post grouping. We used the DEA cross-efficiencies as inputs to the SOMS procedure. It is important to stress that we didn't use the classic DEA efficiency scores, but the efficiency profiles of each DMU derived from the cross-evaluation matrix.

The proposed approach yielded interesting results for 3x3 and 2x2 grids. In using these grids, the production systems developed in the 21 assessed municipalities were grouped, particularly, in relation to the inlet-outlet dynamics of important animals' categories of the breeding herd. The different decision-making profiles of culling of cows and bulls, and consequently of the purchase of bulls, were satisfactorily grouped relative to the efficiency profile observed in each production system.

Acknowledgements

To National Council for Scientific and Technological Development (CNPq) for the financial support.

Author details

João Carlos Correia Baptista Soares de Mello[1*], Eliane Gonçalves Gomes[2], Lidia Angulo Meza[1], Luiz Biondi Neto[3], Urbano Gomes Pinto de Abreu[4], Thiago Bernardino de Carvalho[5] and Sergio de Zen[5]

*Address all correspondence to: jcsmello@producao.uff.br

1 UFF. Passo da Pátria 156, Brazil

2 Brazilian Agricultural Research Corporation (Embrapa), Brazil

3 UERJ. Rua São Francisco Xavier 524, Brazil

4 Embrapa Pantanal. Caixa Postal 109, Brazil

5 Center for Advanced Studies on Applied Economics (CEPEA/ESALQ/USP), Brazil

References

[1] Charnes, A., Cooper, W. W., & Rhodes, E. (1978). Measuring the efficiency of decision-making units. *European Journal of Operational Research*, 2, 429-44.

[2] Samoilenko, S., & Osei-Bryson, K. M. (2010). Determining sources of relative inefficiency in heterogeneous samples: Methodology using Cluster Analysis, DEA and Neural Networks. *European Journal of Operational Research*, 206(2), 479-87.

[3] Sharma, M. J., & Yu, S. J. (2009). Performance based stratification and clustering for benchmarking of container terminals. Expert Systems with Applications PART 1) , 5016-5022.

[4] Churilov, L., & Flitman, A. (2006). Towards fair ranking of olympics achievements: The case of Sydney 2000. *Computers and Operations Research*, 33(7), 2057-2082.

[5] Biondi, Neto. L., Lins, M. P. E., Gomes, E. G., Soares de Mello., J. C. C. B., & Oliveira, F. S. (2004). Neural data envelopment analysis: a simulation. *International Journal of Industrial Engineering*, 11, 14-24.

[6] Emrouznejad, A., & Shale, E. (2009). A combined neural network and DEA for measuring efficiency of large scale datasets. *Computers and Industrial Engineering*, 56(1), 249-54.

[7] Çelebi, D., & Bayraktar, D. (2008). An integrated neural network and data envelopment analysis for supplier evaluation under incomplete information. *Expert Systems with Applications*, 35(4), 1698-710.

[8] Angulo-Meza, L., Biondi Neto., L., Brandão, L. C., Andrade, F. V. S., Soares de Mello, J. C. C. B., & Coelho, P. H. G. (2011). Modelling with self-organising maps and data envelopment analysis: A case study in educational evaluation. *Self organizing maps, new achievements*, Vienna, Intech, 71-88.

[9] Paschoalino, F. F., & Soares de, Mello. J. C. C. B., Angulo-Meza L., Biondi Neto L. (2011). DMU clustering based on Cross Efficiency Evaluation. International Conference on Data Envelopment Analysis and Its Applications to Management. Lima (Peru).

[10] Sexton, T. R., Silkman, R. H., & Logan, A. J. (1986). Data Envelopment Analysis: Critique and extensions. In: Silkman H, ed. Measuring efficiency: An assessment of data envelopment analysis. San Francisco Jossey-BassEditor: , 73-105.

[11] Banker, R. D., Charnes, A., & Cooper, W. W. (1984). Some models for estimating technical scale inefficiencies in data envelopment analysis. *Mngmt Sc.*, 30(9), 1078-92.

[12] Doyle, J. R., & Green, R. H. (1994). Efficiency and cross-efficiency in DEA derivations, meanings and uses. *Journal of the Operational Research Society*, 45, 567-78.

[13] Doyle, J. R., & Green, R. H. (1995). Cross-Evaluation in DEA: Improving Discrimination Among DMUs. *Information Systems and Operational Research*, 33(3), 205-22.

[14] Appa, G., Argyris, N., & Williams, H. P. (2006). A methodology for cross-evaluation in DEA. Working Paper: London School of Economics and Political Science November 7.

[15] Soares de, Mello. J. C. C. B., Lins, M. P. E., & Gomes, E. G. (2002). Construction of a smoothed DEA frontier. *Pesquisa Operacional.*, 28(2), 183-201.

[16] Wu, J., Liang, L., & Chen, Y. (2009). DEA game cross-efficiency approach to Olympic rankings. *Omega*, 37(4), 909-18.

[17] Gomes, E. G., Soares de Mello, J. C. C. B., Angulo-Meza, L., Silveira , J. Q., Biondi Neto, L., & Abreu, U. G. P. d. (2012). Some Remarks About Negative Efficiencies in DEA Models. In: Holtzman Y, ed. Advanced Topics in Applied Operations Management. Rijeka InTech , 113-32.

[18] Liang, L., Wu, J., Cook, W. D., & Zhu, J. (2008). The DEA game cross-efficiency model and its nash equilibrium. *Operations Research*, 56(5), 1278-88.

[19] Liang, L., Wu, J., Cook, W. D., & Zhu, J. (2008). Alternative secondary goals in DEA cross-efficiency evaluation. *International Journal of Production Economics*, 113(2), 1025-30.

[20] Mitra, P., Murthy, C. A., & Pal, S. K. (2002). Unsupervised feature selection using feature similarity. *IEEE Transactions on Pattern Analysis and Machine Intelligence*, 24(3), 301-12.

[21] Willshaw, D. J., Buneman, O. P., & Longuet-Higgins, H. C. (1969). Non-holographic associative memory. *Nature*, 222, 960-2.

[22] Willshaw, D. J., & Von der, Malsburg. C. (1976). How patterned neural connections can be set up by self-organization. *Proceedings of the Royal Society of London Series B*, 194, 431-45.

[23] Kohonen, T. (2001). Self-organizing maps. rd ed. ed. Berlin: Springer-Verlag.

[24] Haykin, S. (1999). Neural networks: a comprehensive foundation. nd ed. ed. New Jersey Prentice Hall

[25] Bishop, C. M. (1995). Neural networks for pattern recognition. New York, Oxford University Press.

[26] Wu, J., Liang, L., Wu, D., & Yang, F. (2008). Olympics ranking and benchmarking based on cross efficiency evaluation method and cluster analysis: the case of Sydney 2000. *International Journal of Enterprise Network Management*, 2(4), 377-92.

[27] Plaxico, J. S., & Tweeten, L. G. (1963). Representative farms for policy and projection research. *Journal of Farm Economics*, 45, 1458-65.

[28] Centro de Estudos Avançados em Economia Aplicada. (2010). Metodologia do índice de preços dos insumos utilizados na produção pecuária brasileira. [cited 2010 March, 24]; Available from: http://www.cepea.esalq.usp.br/boi/metodologiacna.pdf

[29] Gomes, E. G., Soares de Mello, J. C. C. B., Souza, L., Angulo-Meza, G. D. S., & Mangabeira, J. A.d. C. (2009). Efficiency and sustainability assessment for a group of farmers in the Brazilian Amazon. *Annals of Operations Research.*

[30] Womer, N. K., Bougnol, M. L., Dulá, J. H., & Retzlaff-Roberts, D. (2006). Benefit-cost analysis using data envelopment analysis. *Annals of Operations Research*, 145(1), 229-50.

[31] Kuosmanen, T., & Kortelainen, M. (2007). Valuing environmental factors in cost-benefit analysis using data envelopment analysis. *Ecological Economics*, 62(1), 56-65.

[32] Kuosmanen, T., Bijsterbosch, N., & Dellink, R. (2009). Environmental cost-benefit analysis of alternative timing strategies in greenhouse gas abatement: A data envelopment analysis approach. *Ecological Economics*, 68(6), 1633-42.

[33] Bougnol, M. L., Dulá, J. H., Estellita, Lins. M. P., & Moreira da Silva, A. C. (2010). Enhancing standard performance practices with DEA. *Omega*, 38(1-2), 33-45.

[34] Angulo-Meza, L., Biondi, Neto. L., Soares de Mello, J. C. C. B., & Gomes, E. G. (2005). ISYDS- Integrated System for Decision Support (SIAD Sistema Integrado de Apoio a Decisão): A Software Package for Data Envelopment Analysis Model. *Pesquisa Operacional.*, 25(3), 493-503.

Chapter 5

A Self – Organizing Map Based Strategy for Heterogeneous Teaming

Huliane M. Silva, Cícero A. Silva and
Flavius L. Gorgônio

Additional information is available at the end of the chapter

http://dx.doi.org/10.5772/52776

1. Introduction

Even though education and knowledge are processes inherent to human development and are present in all cultures since the earliest and most remote age, the educational model adopted today had its origins in Ancient Greece, where the first signs of appreciation of cultural knowledge took place [1]. At the time, the most traditional way to prepare young individuals of any social class to social integration was through individual processes of teaching, whether in daily life, with their parents, or in contact with masters and artisans. Although, the more privileged classes enjoyed other types of learning, such as access to reading, writing and other areas of knowledge, this process was always conducted on an individual basis.

The need to generalize the teaching of reading, writing and the so-called general culture among the less privileged social strata caused an increase in the number of students in relation to the number of teachers available. This fact prompted educators that time to seek a teaching model that could bring knowledge from the educators to a maximum number of individuals at the same time. Given this need, the Greeks developed the earliest forms of grouping students in order to maximize their teaching activities [2].

The school and the way students are organized in the classroom have also undergone various transformations throughout history [2]. Initially, they were organized in large groups in a single classroom, and guided by a teacher or tutor who had different concepts that he judged to be of common interest, combined with specific content, targeted to smaller groups or individual students. Later, new forms of organization of schools and classrooms emerged, such as the structuring of the content presented according to age, the division of students into fixed and/or mobile groups along with learning from interaction with other individuals through the formation of study groups.

Throughout the evolution of the teaching-learning process, interaction between members of a group in order to encourage mutual learning, has become increasingly valued. Currently, learning from the development of team activities is very encouraging, since it facilitates the sharing of experiences and ideas among group members and allows the realization of some activities that are not possible to be carried out individually. From the socio-educational viewpoint, it is considered a means to promote socialization and cooperation among different levels, in order to solve problems of group dynamics and facilitate learning among peers.

From the pedagogical point of view, the distribution of students in heterogeneous teams allows the exchange of knowledge among peers and, consequently, enhances mutual learning, given that individuals can share different kinds of knowledge. However, the procedures commonly adopted by teachers and educators in the process of forming academic teams usually do not favor such heterogeneity, since in most cases, students choose their own teams considering their affinities and common interests. In other instances, it is the teacher who leads the process of teaming through some selection criterion, which can range from random choice (through a "draft") to appointing some students to be team leaders, trying to better distribute students within teams, and thus make them more heterogeneous.

In this context, a problem arises: how to partition a set of n students into k teams, maximizing the heterogeneity among the members of each team, to allow students share their individual knowledge with each other? This chapter presents a strategy to partition a class into several teams that enables the formation of heterogeneous teams, with the goal of enabling knowledge sharing and mutual learning on the part of the team members. The proposed strategy is based on using of well-known clustering algorithms, such as self-organizing maps and K-means algorithm, and using the Davies-Bouldin cluster validity index to measure the results.

The remainder of the chapter is presented in the following way. Section 2 presents a literature review on the process of forming heterogeneous teams and its difficulties in educational settings. This second section was divided into three parts: the first argues about the importance of team work, the second discusses about the complexity of teaming process, while the third presents several works related to the area of educational data mining. Section 3 introduces the clustering process and its stages, according to three different approaches and presents the clustering algorithms to be used in the proposed strategy: self-organizing maps and k-means, and a brief discussion of similarity measures and clustering validation indices, with the presentation of the Davies-Bouldin index. Section 4 presents and discusses the strategy proposed in this paper. Section 5 presents the methodology used in the experiments, a brief discussion of the databases used and discusses the results obtained. Finally, section 6 presents the conclusions and proposals for future works.

2. Theoretical basis

2.1. The importance of team work

Society is changing faster and faster; along with these changes new ways of social living, interacting with people, teaching and learning are emerging. The way the teaching-learning process is currently conducted in the classroom is not what it used to be some years ago, since teaching and learning have been undergoing several modifications. The use of new information and communication technologies have contributed significantly to these changes, offering new ways of learning and abandoning the old ways of studying, which is becoming, – if not less important – at least as one more among many other alternatives available.

Traditional pedagogy was based on transmission of general culture, i.e., the great discoveries of mankind, as well as aiming on the formation of reasoning and training the mind and will [3]. The methods and practices adopted in this approach overburden the student with merely memorized knowledge, without seeking to establish relations with the everyday life and without encouraging the formation of critical thinking and intellectual capacities.

According to traditional pedagogy, the teaching activity is focused on the teacher who explains and interprets the matter for the students to understand. Besides, this approach assumes that students, by listening and doing repetitive exercises, end up memorizing the subject in order to later reproduce it, whether it is through by questions from the teacher or via tests [3]. This old paradigm, currently seen as outdated, was based on the knowledge transmission performed by teachers, on memorization and competitive and individualistic learning by the students, more and more out of favor [4].

Nowadays, it is defended that the practice of teaching centered on the teacher is not the best approach; and that the methodologies and practices widely adopted by teachers – which are based on repetition and rote memorization – undermined the objectives of traditional pedagogy. That is why, over time, difficulties found in the teaching process became more evident and this methodology, gradually, was modified.

In opposition to this approach, this new pedagogy changes the focus towards students instead of teachers. Therefore, students now become the center of school activity and are placed under favorable conditions in order to learn by themselves from their own needs. In this conception what becomes crucial is the issue of learning. The challenge posed to teachers is changing teaching axis towards paths that lead to learning, and also make it essential for teachers and students to be in a constant process of continual learning [4].

Methodologies such as collaborative learning and cooperative learning have often been advocated in the academic field, since, it recognizes these methodologies to have potential to promote a more active learning, by encouraging critical thinking, development of capabilities in interaction, information exchange and problem solving, as well as development of the self-regulation of the teaching-learning process [5].

Using these methods of learning is not something new. For years, educators have been using these practices of collaborative and cooperative learning, along with group work, because they believed in the potential that these methods have to prepare students to face work demands [5]. Despite being longstanding methodologies, the terms collaborative learning and cooperative learning are often confused in literature. Both have similar definitions but they are different in theoretical and practical perspectives.

The terms collaboration and cooperation can be differentiated as it follows: Collaboration as a certain philosophy of interaction and personal lifestyle, where individuals are responsible for their actions, including learning and respect regarding skills and contributions of each member of the group, while cooperation is a structure of interaction designed to facilitate the achievement of a specific product or goal by means of people working together in teams [6]. The same author also discusses the differences of both terms when used in the classroom. In the cooperative model, it is the teacher who retains full control of the class. Although students work in groups, the teacher is responsible for guiding the tasks performed in the room, i.e., it is a teacher focused process. However, the collaborative model is more open; the responsibility of guiding the tasks is on the group itself and not on the teacher – who can be consulted – but the group needs to interact in order to achieve the shared goal.

It is, then, possible to say that both the concepts of cooperation and collaboration are applied to group activities. Although they possess fundamental differences concerning the dynamics of working together, their goals are common and both practices are complementary, representing, therefore, opposition to the teacher-centered education system, on which Traditional Pedagogy is based [5]. The school has considerably developed lately and, therefore, the need for teamwork becomes more and more a matter of métier than a personal choice. This need occurs due to multiple reasons, such as the increasing intervention in school, by educators, psychologists and educational psychologists, division of pedagogic work in primary school, the evolution towards learning cycles among other reasons justifying the need for teamwork [7].

Through group or team work, therefore, it is possible for people to get into contact with different visions of worlds, learn to socialize knowledge, listen to and give opinions on a particular subject, accept suggestions, develop a group mentality and be proactive, among others. The same author also stresses that teamwork, in general, makes the activity more enjoyable and enables the realization of a common activity, with common goals, allowing the enrichment experiments and experiences [8].

It is common to find in literature different terms for the concepts of group and team. A team can be defined as a group gathered around a common project, whose implementation involves various ways of agreement and cooperation [7]. In [9], team is defined as a group of people, who besides working together, cooperate one with another, sharing common goals. Thus, we can say that team is a group of people working together towards a common goal. In this work, in order to keep terminology simple and following the standard adopted by [8], there will be no differentiation made about them, even though the term team is used more often than group.

2.2. The teaming process

Teamwork is a practice commonly adopted in carrying out various tasks, whether simple or complex. In [7], it is argued that teamwork is a matter of skill, and also requires conviction that cooperation is a professional value. Teamwork can be justified based on three main reasons: i) the collaborative work allows assigning tasks to be performed simultaneously by team members, enabling the completion of the activity in a shorter period of time; ii) the existence of activities that have no possibility of being individually performed, because they demand multiple skills; iii) teamwork allows the exchange of experiences among team members, encouraging mutual learning.

The first two reasons justify the use of teamwork in the commercial sector, while the latter justifies its use in academia. In fact, the main reason for the usage of teamwork in academia is to allow the exchange of knowledge among its members, enabling knowledge pre-existing or acquired during the learning process by each individual to be shared by others.

Although in the commercial sector teaming is driven by productivity, where the most efficient teams are those that produce faster results, in academic fields, the goal is mutual learning and knowledge sharing, even though the final result is achieved in a longer period of time. Thus, many researchers argue that the more heterogeneous teams in a learning process are, the more exchange of knowledge among its members is going to happen, fostering mutual learning [2,10,11].

In academia teachers may adopt different ways to teach a class, as well as they may use different techniques to evaluate students in the performance of activities. A common way of evaluation is promoting teamwork, which is used as a means for students to carry out academic activities. In this process the students are grouped into different teams and each team is responsible for executing the task assigned by the teacher.

However, an important question, to which not always due attention is paid by teachers is the method used to determine which students are going to be part of each team. In academia, such process can be influenced by several factors, especially by preference and personal motivation from the students themselves. The most commonly used methods are:

a. Mutual choice: each team is chosen by its own members, usually subject to a minimum and maximum amount of participants that is defined by the educator. The main advantage of this method is usually the affinity between team members. The main disadvantage is that the method tends to form too homogeneous teams, where members have a profile very similar to each other's;

b. Random choice: the teams are chosen at random, usually through some kind of random draw or lottery. Despite allowing a less homogenous distribution than in the previous method, we cannot guarantee that all teams remain equally heterogeneous, given the large amount of possibilities of dividing a class into teams. Another disadvantage of this method is that students often have little or no affinity with each other, which makes the connectedness of the group difficult;

c. Choice guided by the educator: in this case, it is the teacher who defines the teams, seeking to balance these teams and make the more heterogeneous possible, considering the prior knowledge he or she has on the students, while they can meet individual preferences of students to participate in either of the teams. This method has the same problem as the previous one, given an explosion of combinatorial possibilities to choose the teams. Therefore, not all the teams are equally balanced.

One of the problems associated with the development of activities in teams is little engagement and commitment of some members with the performance of activities. This may partly be caused by deficiencies in the teaming process. Teams whose individuals have very similar profiles, i.e. very homogeneous teams, tend to gather students with the same abilities and limitations, so that there will always be activities that none of the individuals in the team have the skills necessary to perform it. Another common problem in this process is that it tends to lead to the formation of a few teams composed of individuals who possess academic performance quite above average and other teams with individuals who have performance below the average, contributing to a certain segregation of students based on their academic performance.

Analyzing the three teaming methods presented above, it is possible to see that none of them directly addresses these problems, i.e. none of them guarantees the heterogeneity of the teams. Taking the method of random choice as an example, where teams are formed from a random selection, and considering a classroom composed of n students, the number of different possibilities of dividing the class into$k$ teams, each consisting of n/k members, is given by the equation(1),derived from the combinatorial analysis:

$$C_{n,k} = \frac{n!}{k!(n-k)!} \tag{1}$$

If it is noticed that teams can have any number of students, flexibility normally allowed by some teachers, the number of possibilities is greater, since it corresponds to the number of possible partitions of a set, being given by the Stirlingnumber of the second kind [12], given by the equation (2),

$$S_n^{(k)} = \sum_{k=1}^{n} \frac{1}{k!} \sum_{i=0}^{k} \left[(-1)^{k-i} C_{k,i} i^n \right] \tag{2}$$

where,n represents the number of students and k represents the number of teams.

For purposes of illustration of how these values can be extremely large, even considering relatively small-sized classes, Table 1 shows the number of different possible ways to divide a class with n students into k teams.

Number ofstudents	Numberof teams	Number of fix-sized teams	Number ofvariable-sized teams
10	2	45	511
12	3	220	86926
12	4	495	611501
25	5	53130	2.4 x 1015
50	5	2118760	7.4 x 1032

Table 1. Quantity of different configuration of students in teams

The values shown in Table 1 demonstrate that, even though teachers use mechanisms to measure the heterogeneity of each team formed, the complexity of finding the ideal combination of students and teams for maximizing the criteria of heterogeneity by performing an exhaustive search in the set of possible solutions makes this task impossible to be performed in a feasible time frame. Thus, a possible alternative to circumvent these difficulties is the use of computational methods in finding approximate (quasi-optimal) solutions which, although not the ways of doing it, represent a viable possibility for solving the problem.

2.3. Educational data mining

The term data mining may be defined as a set of automated techniques for exploration of large data sets in order to discover new patterns and relationships that, due to the volume of data, would not be easily discovered by human beings with bare eye, due to great amount of data. Data mining isdefinedas a process of automatic discovery of useful information in large data warehouses[13,14]. In [15],authors describe it as a process of extracting information that emerged from the intersection of three areas: classical statistics, artificial intelligence and machine learning, which can be used both to identify and describe past events and analyze and predict future trends.

The methods and data mining techniques have been applied to a wide variety of subject areas, such as commercial and industrial sectors, the analysis and understanding of data from research institutions, in medicine and bioinformatics, in text analysis as well as in identification of feelings and opinions on social networks, among others. More recently, researchers in the field of educational computing have been using these techniques in order to investigate problems in computer-mediated learning environments, including the identification of factors that affect learning and developing more effective educational systems. [16-18].

This new area of research, called educational data mining, is primarily focused on developing methods for exploring data sets collected in educational settings [19]. Thus, the area of educational data mining uses computational techniques derived from traditional data mining – classification, regression, density estimation and clustering being some of them – in order to provide mechanisms to optimize the learning process [20].

Literature review shows a growing number of recently published works on this subject, where researchers have sought, in computing, solutions to problems encountered in education. In this context, data mining has been widely used to solve problems with difficult resolution and great importance, not only related to teaming, rather including, also, several other areas of education [14]. One can cite, for example, the development of a methodology for student monitoring based on objective tests on the web [21] and the use of data mining techniques to find association rules and extract patterns about information of students [22], among other works.

In [23], it isshownan agent architecture, integrated to a distance education environment, as a way to solve the problem of formation of collaborative groups, allowing the establishment of the roles that individuals in a group will play in the development of a collaborative activity. To perform the work referred above, the author uses an agent modeled with genetic algorithms, which enables the formation of collaborative study groups in distance learning courses via the web. Finally, the author demonstrates, through the results, that the teams formed from the proposed approach in the work had a superior performance in their activities, compared to the ones that formed teams at random.

Another work in the context of distance education is presented in [24], in which data mining techniques are used in order to identify the profile of students at risk of dropout or failure, and then generate alerts that aware and assist teachers/tutors with monitoring and interacting with these students. Thus, the author proposed an architecture for virtual learning environments – based on information extracted through processes of data mining – in order to identify students with characteristics and behaviors that can be considered as belonging to risk group (dropout and/or failure). The results obtained from the use of the architecture described in the work proved satisfactory, since the warnings contributed positively in the communication and involvement of teachers with students, providing an educational action that improved quality of education in this scenario.

Two works stand out in the literature due to the use of clustering to identify individuals with similar profiles and seek the formation of homogeneous teams, contrary to the purpose described in this chapter. The first aims to identify groups of students with similar profiles in a classroom, in order that the teacher can make use of a differentiated pedagogy adequate to meet groups of students having the same learning difficulty [25]. This method was applied to students in regular classroom teaching and the data were collected from forms filled out by students, in which they identify their degree of certainty in the understanding of every topic addressed by the teacher. The authors cite the use of algorithms K-means and Self-Organizing Maps for these experiments, stating that such algorithms are very useful in the formation of homogeneous teams of students and the identification of groups of similar students in a particular class is an important tool when the teacher wants to apply a differentiated pedagogy on these groups.

Another study which uses educational data mining and also statistical techniques of clustering is presented in [26], which aims to identify and generate homogeneous groups to perform tasks in educational settings. The main objective of the study is to research and implement a clustering tool for distance education platforms, in order to allow the increase of interactions among students with similar profiles in virtual learning environments, allowing better conditions for the learning desired in these environments. According to the author, the methodology adopted for undertaking the work has proved satisfactory, meeting the expected results, since interaction in distance education environments occurred more easily.

In [27], the authors conducted a study focused on improving education, trying to identify a new and smaller set of variables that may influence the quality of teaching and learning the discipline of mathematics, so that mathematics teachers improve activities undertaken in the classroom. In this context, the technique of clustering was useful because, according to the authors, a large amount of information was obtained through the data collected via questionnaires, and this information would be meaningless unless they were classified into groups which one can handle, therefore the advantages of applying a Ward clustering algorithm, in order to group the variables.

This brief literature review revealed some papers belonging to the growing and diverse field of research in educational data mining. The following section describes the task of clustering in the context of data mining, as well as two of the most widely used clustering algorithms that process.

3. Clustering

The task of analyzing and clustering similar objects in a given group, taking into consideration one or more common characteristic(s) existent among them, is an important activity inherent to human behavior, since it, in a general way, permits the organization of objects or everyday activities. People are, daily, faced with the need to group a set of data: either at a supermarket, organizing products complying with the criteria of category or brand; in organizing books in a bookcase, following an order according to subjects, or even the choice of friends in social network, taking into account, for example, the affinity between them – such as belonging to the same classroom at school or even musical taste. Thus, the clustering is often performed intuitively and ends up unnoticed by the user.

3.1. Definitions

Cluster may be defined as a set of cohesive entities, so that internal entities (belonging to the group) are more similar to each other, and more different from external entities (not belonging to the group) [28]. Thus, clustering may be understood as a technique able to divide a data set into one or more sub-sets, taking into account the similarity existing among its elements. However, far from a consensus, this is not the only definition adopted for the term, it is common to find in literature a variety of definitions for this technique, result of studies performed by different researchers in different areas where clustering can be applied [29,31].

Clustering is a statistical technique with general use, applied in different fields of knowledge and widely used in activities involving data analysis. Some of the numerous applications of clustering in different contexts include their use: in psychology, to identify different types of depression; in biology, to identify groups of genes with similar functions; in medicine, to detect patterns in spatial or temporal distribution of a particular disease; in sales, to identify customer profiles and determine sales strategies, among others [14,29].

Most of its applications is the analysis of large databases on which there is limitedor non-existent information about its structure and the main goal of its use is precisely to allow in understanding and description of data unknown up to then [12,32]. Thus, clustering can be regarded as a data mining task associated with data description activities, having a wide range of applications. However, it is necessary to be careful in its use, for instance, in analyzing attributes that make up the database and determine in advance the goals desired with the application, to thereby obtain satisfactory results.

3.2. Stages in clustering

The clustering process is usually comprised of several steps, and some authors present these stages more succinctly [28,29], while others have to do it in a more detailed way, divided into more stages [30]. Figure 1 presents the five steps included in the clustering process, as described in [29], which includes the following stages: data preparation, proximity, clustering, validation and interpretation of results, described below:

i. First stage: data preparation involves aspects related to the pre-processing of data, as well as adequate representation for being used by a clustering algorithm;

ii. Second stage: called proximity, it is consisted of the proximity measures proper to the application, as well as the information you want to obtain from data extraction. These measures can be classified as a measure of similarity and dissimilarity;

iii. Third stage: formation of clusters is the central stage of the clustering process. It is at this stage that one or more clustering algorithms are applied on the data in order to identify structures existing in the same cluster;

iv. Fourth stage: the validation consists of assessing the results. In general, it determines if the clusters obtained are significant, i.e., if the solution obtained is representative to the set of analyzed data and the expected solution;

v. Fifth stage: the interpretation refers to the process of examining and labeling each cluster according to its goals, describing its nature. The interpretation goes beyond a simple description, since it still corresponds to a validation process of the clusters found based on the initial hypotheses, as well as other subjective assessments that are of interest to the specialist.

In [28], five steps to the clustering process are also presented, namely: development of the dataset, data preprocessing and standardization, cluster identification, cluster interpretation and, finally, conclusions. These steps, as described below and illustrated in Figure 2, have several similarities with the process described in [29], although some activities described in a particular stage of a process happen in a different stage in another process.

http://dx.doi.org/10.5772/52776

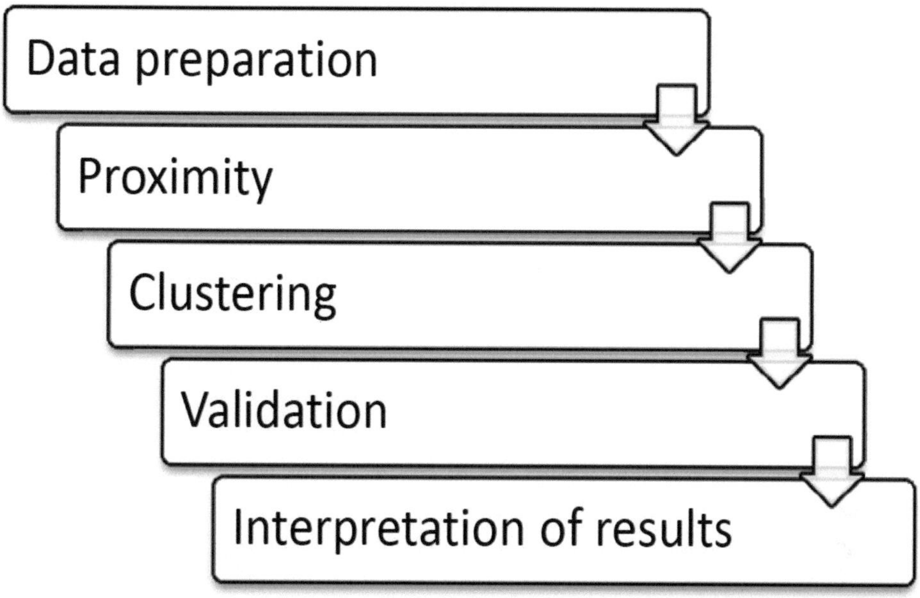

Figure 1. Stages in the clustering process, according to [29]

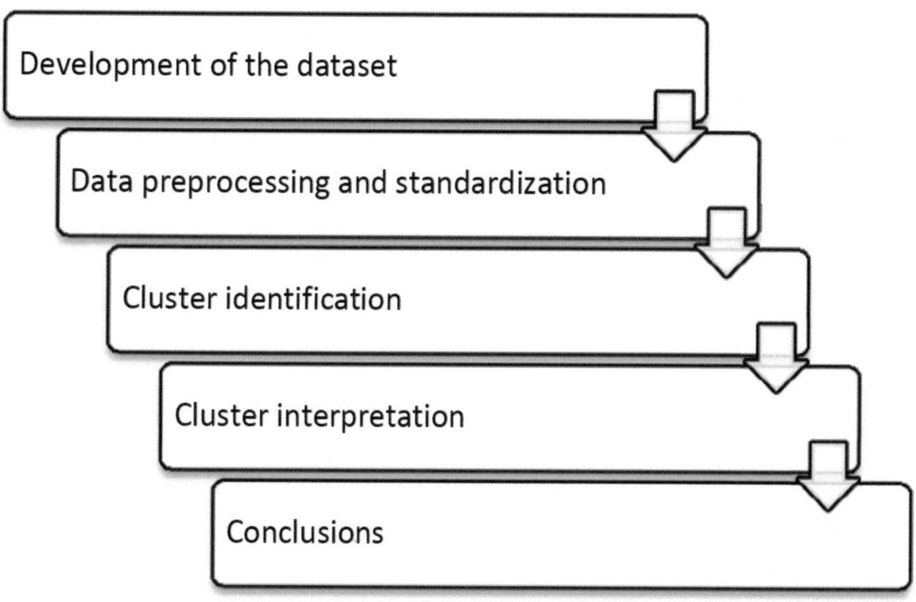

Figure 2. Stages in the clustering process, according to [28]

i. First stage: the development of the data set includes the problem definition, and the choice of the data to be analyzed;

ii. Second stage: the pre-processing is the stage of data preparation, which includes the standardization of variables used in the process;

iii. Third stage: the stage cluster identification consists of applying an algorithm to the data set, resulting in a cluster structure;

iv. Fourth stage: the stage of interpretation must be performed by specialists, who analyze the characteristics used in the cluster to verify the relevance of the obtained results and, if necessary, suggest modifications in the data, followed by reapplication of the previous stages;

v. Fifth stage: the final stage corresponds to the interpretation of results and formulation of conclusions, focusing on the regularities implicit in the results.

In [30], it is described a third clustering process, based on a model slightly different, with six stages,is shown in Figure 3 and described below:

i. First stage: in this stage the objectives to be achieved with the task of clustering and the selection of variables used to characterize the clusters are defined. Objectives cannot be separated from the variable selection, because the researcher restricts the possible results through selected variables;

ii. Second stage: in this stage some matters regarding the procedures to be adopted in case of outliers detection are evaluated, and decisions are taken about how to measure the similarity of objects and if there is any need for data standardization of;

iii. Third stage: in this stage, it is performed an evaluation of the assumptions that were made during the previous steps, which concerns the representativeness of the sample and the impact of variable multicollinearity in the clustering process;

iv. Fourth stage: in this stage cluster definition is performed, where it is necessary to determine which algorithm is used, the number of clusters to be formed, and identify, from the results obtained, if it will be necessary to set the clustering process again;

v. Fifth stage: This stage involves the interpretation of the obtained clusters, where the specialist will examine each cluster formed for the purpose of appointing or designating a label that accurately describes its fundamental characteristics;

vi. Sixth stage: This stage is responsible for validating the solution obtained and by clusters of clusters found. Validation aims to ensure that the solution of clusters is representative for the general population, and thus is generalizable to other objects and stable over time. The profile of clusters involves the description of the characteristics of each cluster to explain how they may differ in important dimensions.

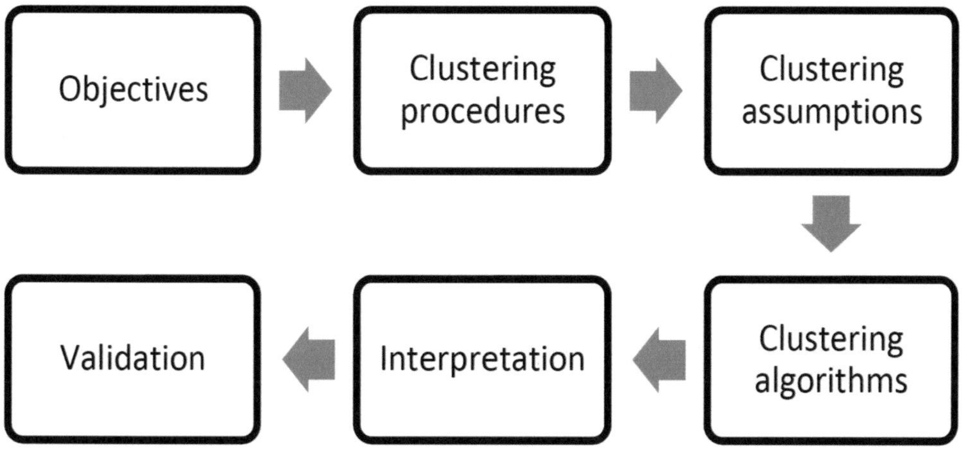

Figure 3. Stages in the clustering process, according to [30]

3.3. Similarity and dissimilarity measures

The task of identifying similar items from the existing ones in an input set requires the adoption of a metric distance between the items that can determine the proximity between them. There are two types of distance metrics: similarity shows the similitude between items, i.e., the greater the similarity, more alike (or near) the items are. Dissimilarity measures the difference between items, the greater the dissimilarity, the more different (or far) they are [31].

Considering each item of the input set as a vector in the *p*-dimensional space, a distance function between two items x_i and x_j of the set X may be defined as in equation (3):

$$d : X \times X \rightarrow \mathrm{R} \tag{3}$$

$d_{ij} = d(x_i, x_j)$

where d_{ij} is a real value associated with each pair of items in the input set and is calculated from a measure of similarity (or dissimilarity) that meets the following assumptions:

i. $d(x_i, x_j) = d(x_j, x_i), \quad \forall x_i, x_j \in X$

ii. $d(x_i, x_j) \geq 0, \quad \forall x_i, x_j \in X$

iii. $d(x_i, x_j) = 0 \leftrightarrow x_i = x_j, \quad \forall x_i, x_j \in X$

iv. $d(x_i, x_j) \leq d(x_i, x_k) + d(x_k, x_j), \quad \forall x_i, x_j, x_k \in X$

In the literature, various metrics of similarity and dissimilarity are presented which meet these conditions. The choice of a metric is associated with characteristics of the input set, such as the nature of the variables (discrete, continuous, binary, etc.), the scale of measurements (nominal, ordinal, intervallic, etc.)., The format of the clusters in *p*-dimensional space (spherical, square, elliptical, etc..) and even the preference of the researcher [33, 34].

In this work, the similarity metric used was Euclidean distance, because it is the most widely used in classification and clustering tasks, which is a generalization of the distance between two points on a Cartesian plane and is given by the square root of the sum of squares of differences of values of each attribute. Mathematically, it is defined by:

$$d_{ij} = \left(\sum_{f=1}^{p} \left| x_{if} - x_{jf} \right|^2 \right)^{1/2} \tag{4}$$

wherex_i and x_j are two input vectors in *p*-dimensional space and x_{if} corresponds to the fth attribute of the vectorx_i.

3.4. Metrics for the evaluation of results

One of the difficulties in clustering tasks is to measure whether the results are satisfactory, since in most cases, not much is known about the data being analyzed. Several metrics have been proposed for evaluation of results in clustering tasks [31,35-42], most of them are based on the application of cluster validation indices, which measure the average intra-cluster distances (between objects belonging to the same cluster) and inter-cluster (between objects belonging to different clusters). According to [52], the index most used for this purpose are: Silhouette index, Dunn index and the Davies-Bouldin index, and among these, the Davies-Bouldin index is more robust for use in tasks whose data sets have hyperspherical clusters, with no outliers, features common in applications that use the K-means and SOM algorithms.

Being $C = \{C_1, C_2, \cdots, C_k\}$a partition of the input set$X$. The Davies-Bouldin index for the partition C_i is calculated as defined in equation (5):

$$db(i) = \frac{1}{K} \sum_{i=1}^{K} R_i \tag{5}$$

where$K$ is the number of existing partitions and R_i is the relative similarity between the cluster C_i and the other clusters. The similarity R_{ij} between clusters C_i and C_j is computed as described in equation (6):

$$R_{ij} = \max_{i \neq j} \frac{\left(\frac{e_i}{\sqrt{n_i}}\right) + \left(\frac{e_j}{\sqrt{n_j}}\right)}{d_{ij}} \tag{6}$$

where d_{ij} is the distance between the mean element (centroid) of the clusters i and j, n_k is the number of elements of the cluster k and e_k is the average square distance between elements in cluster k and its centroid, given byequation (7):

$$e_k = \frac{1}{n_k} \sum_{i=1}^{n_k} \left(x_i - w_\xi\right)^2 \tag{7}$$

where n_k is the number of elements in cluster k, x_i is an element in cluster k and w_ξ represents the centroid in cluster k.

3.5. Self-organizing mapsalgorithm

Self-organizing maps (SOM) are a class of neural networks for unsupervised, collaborative and competitive learning, which have been widely used in automatic data classification tasks, visualization of high dimension data and dimensionality reduction [43]. Self-organizing maps, like other clustering algorithms, are used to identify clusters of objects based on similarities found in their attributes, i.e., features. Thus, in the end of a clustering process, it is possible to identify which objects have greater similarity to each other and which are more different.

The architecture of a SOM neural network is extremely simple, consisting of only two layers of neurons (Figure 4). The first input layer, comprising a vector with p neurons, is the dimensionality of the input set (i.e., the number of features of the data table). Each input neuron is connected to all neurons of the next layer. The second layer, also known as the output layer, the map which represents the set of input will be projected, and comprises a set of neurons, usually arranged in the form of a vector (unidimensional) or a matrix (two-dimensional), where each neuron is connected only to its neighbors.

During the training phase of a SOM neural network, each representative of the input set is randomly selected and presented to the input layer of the network. An activation function computes the similarity between the input vector and all neurons of the map. The neuron of the output layer which is most similar to the input neuron is declared the winner and their synaptic weights, as well as the synaptic weightsof their neighbors, are updated. The process is repeated with the other vectors of the input set, several times, until the network is trained.

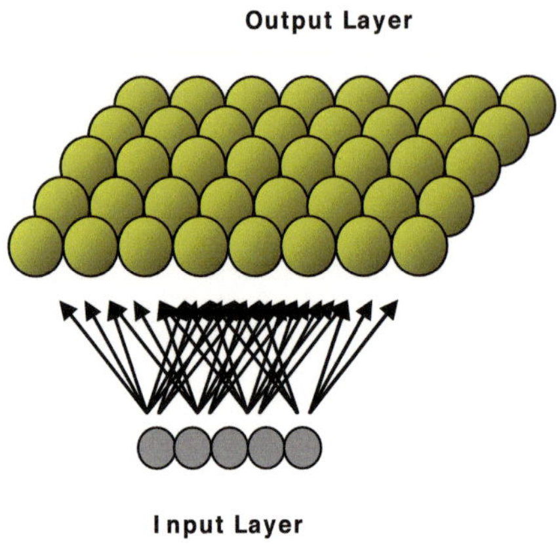

Figure 4. Architecture of a SOM neural network

The similarity function commonly used to calculate the distance between the input vector and the neuron network is the Euclidean distance as shown in equation (8) given by:

$$d_{ij} = \left(\sum_{f=1}^{p} \left| x_{if} - w_{jf} \right|^2 \right)^{1/2} \tag{8}$$

wherex_i is an input vector in the *p*-dimensional space,w_j is a neuron of the output layer and x_{if} represents the fth attribute of the vectorx_i.

To identify the winning neuron (*bmu*, i.e., best match unit), it is necessary to check all the neurons of the output layer, in order to identify which of them has the shortest distance to the input vector, by using the equation (9):

$$w_{\xi} = \min\left(d_{ij}\right) \tag{9}$$

wherew_{ξ} represents the winner neuron and d_{ij} is the Euclidean distance between an element of the input set and an output layer neuron.The synaptic weights of the neuron and its neighborhood are updated using the equation (10):

$$m_i(t+1) = m_i(t) + h_{ci}(t) \cdot \left[x(t) - m_i(t) \right] \tag{10}$$

where$t$ represents time, $x(t)$represents any element in the input set and h_{ci} determines the neighborhood radius to be modified, usually being reduced while the training algorithm progresses.

In pattern recognition tasks, which are a major application for this type of network, being the winner neuron means to be the most similar neuron, from the existing in the output map, to the value presented to the input of the network. The winner neuron has, along with its neighborhood, its values enhanced, so that if the same input is subsequently presented to the network, that region of the map will be further enhanced.

3.6. K-means algorithm

Initially proposed in [44], the K-means is a partition clustering algorithm, one of the most known and used in clustering tasks, especially due to its simplicity and easy implementation.

As with other clustering algorithms, the goal of K-means algorithm is to cluster a set of n items into k groups, based on a given similarity measure, which is usually the Euclidean distance. The basic idea of the K-means clustering is based on the centroids, which are the average of a group of points. Its training process takes place considering all the vectors in each iteration, and the process is repeated until convergence [45]. Convergence occurs when there is no change in value of the centroids or when the processing reaches the limit of iterations, normally very high. At the end of processing, each element is said to belong to the cluster represented by its centroid.

Then the K-means algorithm is described, presenting its stages, as follows:

1. Set the value of k, corresponding to the number of groups of the sample;
2. Randomly select a set of centroid to represent the k groups;
3. Calculate a matrix of distances between each set of data elements and each centroid;
4. Assign each element to its nearest centroid;
5. Recalculate the value of each centroid from the average values of the elements belonging to this centroid, generating a new matrix of distances;
6. Return to step 4 and repeat until convergence.

The K-means algorithm has linear complexity $O(npk)$, where n and p are, respectively, the number of elements and the dimensionality of the data set, and k is the number of desired clusters. The K-means has good scalability, since the values of p and k are, in most cases much smaller than n [46]. In addition, being based on the principle of vector quantization, the algorithm works well on compact, hyperspherical and well defined clusters.

Among the disadvantages of K-means there is a need to provide a pre-set value to k, the number of clusters, which often is done randomly. The main strategy to overcome this difficulty is to run the algorithm several times, for different values of k and measure up the cohesion of clusters detected by cluster validation indices. In [47], several other techniques are presented to approach this problem.

In [48], it is indicated as the main disadvantage of the K-means the fact that it is a nondeterministic algorithm, strongly influenced by both the initialization values as well as small changes in the training set, which can influence major alterations in solution which the algorithm converges, which makes this algorithm a rather unstable one. As the choice of initial values of the centroids is usually done at random or from elements that compose the set of input data, this strategy is widely criticized and some changes have been proposed to improve the performance of this algorithm [28].

In [49], it is emphasized that the K-means is not an appropriate method to deal with non-convex shaped clusters or of different sized clusters as well as being very sensitive to noise and distortion (outliers), so that a small number of data having such characteristics can significantly influence the values of the centroids.

Despite all the criticism, K-means is one of the most studied clustering algorithms, having a large number of variants that differ in small details, such as in the way of selecting the initial centroids, in calculating the similarity between the centroids and elements of the input set and the strategies used to compute the centroid of each cluster [49].

Examples of variations of the K-means are K-modes, which uses the concept of fashion, rather than average, to cluster categorical data; and K-medoids, which uses real components of the input set to represent the cluster centroids, reducing the influence of noise and distortion. In addition, other algorithms that were later developed, such as LBG, Expectation-Maximization and SOM, share common ideas with the K-means.

4. The proposed strategy

The problem addressed earlier in this chapter concerns the formation of heterogeneous teams, aiming to encourage integration of students with different profiles and thus promote knowledge sharing and mutual learning. However, clustering algorithms, as described in the previous section, act in a contrary way, identifying clusters of objects based on common features and similarities found in their attributes, i.e., these algorithms identify homogeneous groups. What at first glance may seem contradictory is resolved through the use of a strategy of teaming that promotes diversity in each team.

The strategy of this approach can be divided into two stages: in the first stage, clustering algorithms are used to identify individuals having a similar academic profile, according to a selection criterion, such as performance at school activities; in the second stage, an algorithm for the distribution of students into teams is applied, which allocates students with similar profile in different teams, favoring heterogeneity of teams.

Clustering tasks using K-means algorithm tend to establish a direct relationship between the number of centroids and the expected number of clusters, so that each centroid represents a group of individuals. Unlike this, self-organizing maps generally utilize a two-dimensional grid, with a much higher number of neurons than the expected number of groups, which allows obtaining more detailed results than those obtained with K-means centroids. Taking this point in consideration, self-organizing maps have a superior performance than K-means in clustering tasks, since they provide information about the proximity between objects in the results presented.

However, while the K-means algorithm, at its output, provides labels corresponding to each object in the input set, allowing the direct relationship of each object to the group it belongs to, self-organizing maps provide more subjective information, suggesting that objects that are mapped to a single neuron or adjacent neurons in the output map, have a close relationship in the input set and belong to the same group. Thus, the association of objects from the input set to the clustering they belong to is not performed directly.

One of the approaches traditionally used to label the elements of the input set in clustering tasks which use the SOM algorithm is to perform a new clustering process on the neurons of the map in order to identify groups of neurons and assign similar elements that are associated with those neurons as belonging to a same cluster. This approach is presented in [54], using K-means algorithm to segment the output map of the SOM algorithm in distinct k regions, where k represents the number of desired groups.

A similar approach is proposed in this paper, which uses a combination of SOM and K-means to segment the input set, corresponding to the students in the class, in k groups, where k represents the desired number of students on each team. Then the strategy is applied to separate the teams, which selects one element from each group for the formation of a heterogeneous team. Figure 5 summarizes the process, which is detailed below:

1. Initially, the data of the students are gathered in a single set, from which a subset of attributes to represent each individual is selected;

2. In stage 1, the SOM algorithm is applied on the selected attributes, organizing individuals in accordance with the similarity which they have to each other. Also in this stage, K-means algorithm is applied on the SOM obtained results in order to segment the groups obtained;

3. In stage 2, a distribution algorithm is applied, which allocates similar individuals into distinct groups, favoring the formation of heterogeneous groups;

4. In step 3, final adjustments are made and each team is allocated.

5. Used methodology and obtained results

In order to validate the strategy proposed in this chapter, this section presents the results of using this approach on two databases selected for the experiments: the Iris database and a real database with academic performance of undergraduates from the course of Bachelorship in Information Systems at Federal University of Rio Grande do Norte, superior education institution located in the northeastern region of Brazil.

Iris is one of the most popular data sets publicly available and has been widely used in testing algorithms for pattern recognition, machine learning and data mining. Although this database is not related to the context of applications proposed in this chapter, it waschosendue to its being a dataset widely known and used, whosereference values are known a priori and can be used for validity comparison of the proposed strategy.

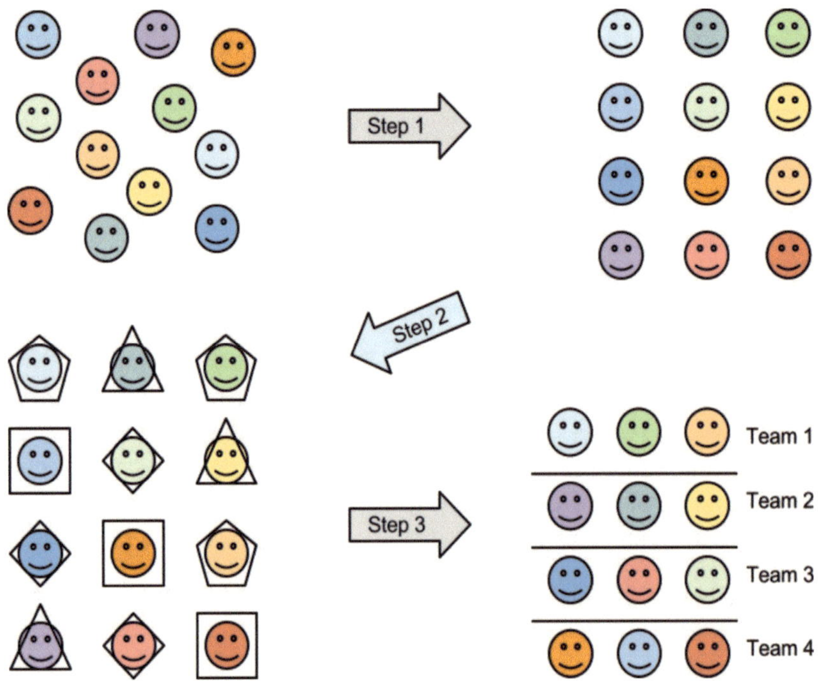

Figure 5. The proposed strategy

This database has 150 instances containing data from measurements of the width and length of three species of the flower Iris, namely, *Setosa, Versicolor* and *Virginica* [53]. Each instance of the base has four attributes, corresponding to length and width of sepal, length and width of petal, as well as additional information about class and order number that are not considered in the experiments. The 150 instances are equally divided, so that each species has 50 records. A sample of Iris database is shown in Table 2.

Instance	Sepal length	Sepal width	Petal length	Petal width	Class
1	5.1	3.5	1.4	0.2	Setosa
2	4.9	3.0	1.4	0.2	Setosa
3	4.7	3.2	1.3	0.2	Setosa
...	...	...	...	...	...
150	5.9	3.0	5.1	1.8	Virginica

Table 2. Sample of the Iris dataset structure

In the experiments with the Iris database, the main objective was to determine whether the strategy worked correctly, actually forming heterogeneous groups, consisting of instances belonging to different species. For the experiments described here, we considered only the four attributes related to the length and width of sepals and petals, and ignored the attributes related to the number and class to which the instance belongs.

Initially, the experiment simulated the process of teaming in the classroom, which is usually conducted by draw, with groups being formed randomly. For this, the Iris dataset was divided into 50 groups, each containing three instances of the database. Then, the process of teaming was repeated with the same numbers as the previous experiment, but applying the strategy proposed in this paper.

For the proposed approach, the data were originally submitted to the SOM algorithm, and then the map obtained at the output of SOM was segmented using the K-means algorithm. All experiments in this paper were implemented from the use of the package SOM Toolbox 2.0 [54]. In all cases, the size of the maps was established automatically from estimates made by the algorithm available on the implementation of the SOM Toolbox, which also used the method of linear initialization of maps [43] and batch training. For training the SOM, we used sheet shaped maps, with 11 x 6 neurons dispersed in hexagonal shape. Figure 6 shows the maps obtained during the experiment. The left map represents the U-matrix obtained directly from the SOM algorithm, while the map on the right shows the segmentation of neurons derived from the application of K-means algorithm.

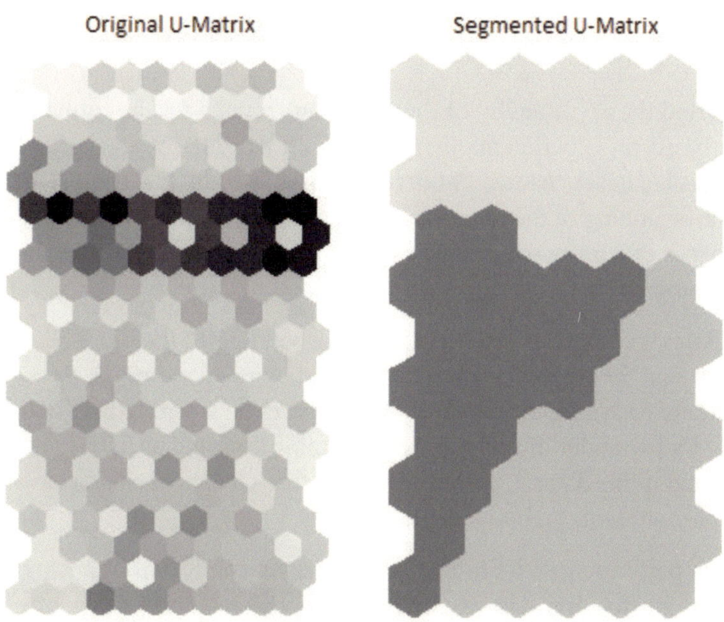

Figure 6. Original and segmented U-Matrix relating to Iris dataset

The comparison between the two approaches was performed both qualitatively and quantitatively. Through visual observation, we found that many of the groups formed by random strategy, had two or three elements belonging to the same class, suggesting the presence of homogeneous groups in the formation of teams. By repeating the experiment with the proposed approach, this condition of existence of more than one instance of a group belonging to the same class is minimized, being reduced to a few instances, from classification errors of the algorithm. The Iris dataset has an interesting characteristic, the class *Setosa* can be linearly separated from the others, but the classes *Versicolor* and *Virginica* are not linearly separable and, in general, clustering algorithms for classification and clustering make mistakes in erroneously assigning some instances belonging to these classes.

From the quantitative point of view, intra-cluster and inter-cluster dispersion measures were used to measure the heterogeneity of the groups formed using the Davies-Bouldin index (db). Table 3 presents the results of minimum, maximum and average db index, and the standard deviation of these measures, obtained in 20 executions of the algorithms, using both approaches.

Methodology	Minimum db index	Maximum db index	Average db index	Standard deviation
Homogeneous clustering	0.61	0.68	0.64	0.02
Random approach	10.06	14.16	12.12	1.13
Proposed strategy	18.63	21.28	19.82	1.35

Table 3. Heterogeneity of groups for the Iris dataset measured by the Davies-Bouldin index

Once demonstrated the applicability of the proposed strategy for the formation of heterogeneous groups, based on experiments performed with Iris dataset, the second set of experiments used a real dataset, named Students dataset, within the context of the problem discussed in the beginning of the chapter. The dataset used contains information on the academic performance of a group of students in a particular class, in various disciplines of the undergraduate program in Information Systems UFRN.

The Students dataset comprises 43 samples, corresponding to the students comprising the examined group and 39 attributes were considered, corresponding to the course subjects. The performance of each student is expressed as a score between 0.0 and 10.0. If the student has not attended a particular discipline, that discipline is scored as 0.0. Since there is no prior information about this dataset, we do not know the number of clusters available. A sample of the database students is shown in Table 4.

The experiments performed with Students dataset were conducted in analogous manner to that performed with the Iris dataset. In this case, the main objective was to determine whether the proposed strategy could form heterogeneous teams composed of students with different profiles and different academic performance. As in the previous experiment, two approaches were taken, the first using a random teaming process, and the second, application of SOM and K-means clustering algorithms and then a strategy for distributing students with similar performances in different teams. The results were also compared through the same criteria used previously, qualitative analysis of the teams formed, based on comparison of profiles of the selected students on the same team, and quantitative assessment, measured through the use of the Davies-Bouldin index. Table 5 presents the results of minimum, maximum and average intra-cluster and inter-cluster dispersion measures,and standard deviation of these measures, obtained in 20 executions of the algorithms, using both approaches and the db index to measure the heterogeneity of the groups formed.

Instance	Discipline 1	Discipline 2	Discipline 3	...	Discipline 39
Student 1	8.4	9.8	9.5	...	0.0
Student 2	6.4	8.0	7.2	...	0.0
Student 3	9.8	9.2	9.3	...	10.0
...	...	...	...	...	...
Student 39	8.5	7.2	7.1	...	0.0

Table 4. Structure of Students dataset

For training the SOM, sheet shapedmaps, with 11 x 6 neurons dispersed in hexagonal shape were used. In all cases, the size of the maps was set automatically from estimates made by the algorithm, available on the implementation of the SOM Toolbox, which also used the method of linear maps startup and batch training.

Methodology	Minimum db index	Maximum db index	Average db index	Standard deviation
Random approach	2.87	4.09	3.49	0.32
Proposed strategy	4.01	5.04	4.52	0.45

Table 5. Heterogeneity of groups for the Students dataset measured by the Davies-Bouldin index

6. Conclusions and final thoughts

Throughout human history, there are several approaches that contributed to the improvement of teaching and learning. However, virtually all of these approaches have one thing in common: the ability of humans to learn from their peers. Within this context, the development of team activities is often a common practice in society, adopted in performing various daily tasks. In school, this practice has been widely used due to its fostering mutual learning. In fact, the formation of heterogeneous teams facilitates the sharing of ideas and experiences among members of a team, allowing the exchange of knowledge between them and carrying out of activities that are not likely to be done individually.

However, the procedures commonly adopted by teachers in the classroom for teaming do not always contribute to knowledge exchange and mutual learning. Teams formed at random or from affinities between its members do not favor the heterogeneity. Furthermore, individuals with the same academic profile and who have knowledge in the same areas have less information and content to provide and share with each other. Thus the process of teaming must be guided so as to prioritize heterogeneity among members of the teams.

The use of computational tools to solve problems in the area of education has been an increasingly common practice. In this context, a research field that has received recent attention is the educational data mining, which seeks to use data mining techniques in order to investigate problems that affect learning, as well as the development of educational systems. Such surveys are presented as an alternative to solving these problems that are focused primarily on exploring the dataset collected in educational settings. However, analyzing the literature available in the area, one can identify a lack of algorithms and tools to improve the process of academic teaming, since most of the available algorithms search homogeneous groups.

Thus, this paper presents a strategy capable of forming heterogeneous teams by using traditional clustering algorithms, such as K-means and self-organizing maps, contributing to the process of forming study groups and conducting works in academia. By using cluster validation indices, such as Bouldin-Davies index, the results obtained from the experiments carried out show that the teams formed by the use of the proposed strategy are more heterogeneous than those obtained with the methods conventionally used in classroom, such as random or affinity-based approaches, demonstrating its efficiency in the formation of heterogeneous groups of objects, both in educational and other datasets.

Future work may include optimizations in the proposed strategy, in order to even more heterogeneous teaming to be achieved. Using genetic algorithms to organize teams during the second stage of the strategy appears to be a viable alternative to evaluate different possible combinations of individuals, thus promoting heterogeneity. On the other side, the use of other clustering algorithms, more stable and with improved performance, can also contribute to better results in the team allocation process. Finally, assessments in relation to learning and performance of students through the process of developing team activities can prove the greater efficiency of utilization of diverse teams, compared to homogeneous teams.

Author details

Huliane M. Silva, Cícero A. Silva and Flavius L. Gorgônio

*Address all correspondence to: flavius@ufrnet.br

Laboratory of Computational Intelligence Applied to Business Federal Universityof Rio Grande do Norte, Caicó, RN, Brazil

References

[1] Fonseca MJ. A Paideia Grega Revisitada. RevistaMillenium 1998;3(9) 56-72.

[2] Zabala A. A Prática Educativa: Como Ensinar. Porto Alegre: Artmed; 1998.

[3] Libâneo JC. Didática. São Paulo: São Paulo; 1994.

[4] Behrens MA. Projetos de Aprendizagem Colaborativa num Paradigma Emergente. In: Moran JM, Masetto MT, Beherens MA. (eds.) Novas Tecnologias e Mediação Pedagógica. Campinas: Papirus; 2000. p67-132.

[5] Torres PL, Irala EAF. Aprendizagem Colaborativa. In: Torres PL. (ed.) Algumas Vias para Entretecer o Pensar e o Agir. Curitiba: SENAR-PR; 2007. p65-97.

[6] Panitz T. Collaborative versus cooperative learning: A comparison of the two concepts which will help us understand the underlying nature of interactive learning, Cooperative Learning and College Teaching 1997;8(2) 1-13.

[7] Perrenoud P. Dix NouvellesCompétences pour Enseigner. Paris: ESF Éditeur; 1999.

[8] Colenci AT. O ensino de engenharia como uma atividade de serviços: a exigência de atuação em novos patamares de qualidade acadêmica. MSc thesis. Universidade de São Paulo; 2000.

[9] Maybi S. Team Building: comoconstruirequipeseficazes. Specialist thesis. Universidade de Passo Fundo; 2000.

[10] Gillies RM. Cooperative Learning: Integrating Theory and Practice. Thousand Oaks: Sage Publications; 2007.

[11] Millis B, Rhem J. Cooperative Learning in Higher Education: Across the Disciplines, Across the Academy. Sterling: Stylus Publishing; 2010.

[12] Costa JAF. Classificação automática e análise de dados por redes neurais auto-organizáveis. DSc thesis. UniversidadeEstadual de Campinas; 1999.

[13] Amorim T. Conceitos, técnicas, ferramentas e aplicações de Mineração de Dados para gerar conhecimento a partir de bases de dados. Undergraduatethesis. Universidade Federal de Pernambuco; 2006.

[14] Tan PN, Steinbach M, Kumar V. Introduction to Data Mining. Boston: Addison Wesley; 2005.

[15] Sferra HH, Corrêa AMCJ. Conceitos e Aplicações de Data Mining: Data Mining ConceptsandApplications. Revista de Ciência&Tecnologia 2003;11(22): 19-34.

[16] Ha SH, Bae SM, Park SC. Web mining for distance education. In: IEEE Engineering Management Society (eds.) ICMIT 2000: Management in the 21st Century: proceedings of the IEEE International Conference on Management of Innovation and Technology, v2, p715-719, ICMIT2000, 12-15 Nov 2000, Orchard Hotel, Singapore. IEEE Engineering Management Society; 2000.

[17] Machado AP, Ferreira R, Bittencourt II, Elias, E, Brito P, Costa E. Mineração de Texto em Redes Sociais Aplicada à Educação a Distância. Colabor@ - Revista Digital da CVA 2010; 6(23). http://pead.ucpel.tche.br/revistas/index.php/colabora/article/download/132/115 (accessed 20 May 2012).

[18] Paiva R, Bittencourt II, Pacheco H, Silav AP, Jaques P, Isotani S. Mineração de Dados e a Gestão Inteligente da Aprendizagem: Desafios e Direcionamento. In: SBC proceedingsofthe I Workshop de Desafios da Computação Aplicada à Educação, DesafIE'2012, 17-18 July 2012, Curitiba, Brazil. Curitiba: UFPR; 2012.

[19] Baker RSJ, Isotani S, Carvalho AMJB. Mineração de Dados Educacionais: Oportunidades para o Brasil. RevistaBrasileira de InformáticanaEducação2011;19(2) 3-13.

[20] Baker RSJ. Date Mining for Education. In: McGaw B, Peterson P, Baker E. (eds.) International Encyclopedia of Education. Oxford: Elsevier; 2010. p112-118.

[21] Zaina LAM, Ruggiero WV, Bressan, G. Metodologia para Acompanhamento da Aprendizagem através da Web, Revista Brasileira de Informática na Educação 2004;12(1): 20-28. http://www.lbd.dcc.ufmg.br/colecoes/rbie/12/1/002.pdf (accessed 22 May 2012).

[22] Milani F, Camargo SS. Aplicação de Técnicas de Mineração de Dados na Previsão de Propensão à Evasão Escolar. In: Congresso Sul Brasileiro de Computação: proceedingsofthe V Congresso Sul Brasileiro de Computação, V SULCOMP, 29 Sept - 1 Oct 2010, Criciúma, Brazil. Criciúma: Ed. UNESC; 2010.

[23] Silveira SR. Formação de grupos colaborativos em um ambiente multiagente interativo de apredizagem na internet: um estudo de caso utilizando sistemas multiagentes e algoritmos genéticos. DScthesis. Universidade Federal do Rio Grande do Sul; 2006.

[24] Kampff AJC. Mineração de dados educacionais para geração de alertas em ambientes virtuais de aprendizagem como apoio à prática docente. DSc thesis. Universidade Federal do Rio Grande do Sul; 2009.

[25] Pimentel EP, França V, Omar N. A identificação de grupos de aprendizes no ensino presencial utilizando técnicas de clusterização. In: Sampaio FF, Motta CLR, Santoro FM (eds.) Proceedingsofthe XIV Simpósio Brasileiro de Informática na Educação, SBIE'2003, 12-14 November 2003, Rio de Janeiro, Brazil. Rio de Janeiro: NCE/IM/UFRJ; 2003.

[26] Azambuja S. Estudo e implementação da análise de agrupamento em ambientes virtuais de aprendizagem. MScthesis. Universidade Federal do Rio de Janeiro; 2005.

[27] Zanella A, Lopes LFD. Melhoria da qualidade do ensino através da análise de agrupamento. In: ABEPRO (eds.) Proceedingsofthe XXVI Encontro Nacional de Engenharia de Produção, ENEGEP'2006, 9-11 October 2006, Fortaleza, Brazil. Fortaleza: ABEPRO; 2006.

[28] Mirkin B. Clustering for Data Mining: A Data Recovery Approach. Boca Raton: Chapman and Hall/CRC; 2005.

[29] Faceli K, Lorena AC, Gama J, Carvalho ACPLF. Inteligência Artificial: Uma Abordagem de Aprendizado de Máquina. Rio de Janeiro: LTC; 2011.

[30] Hair Jr. JF, Anderson RE, Tatham RL, Black WC. Multivariate Data Analysis. Upper Saddle River: Prentice Hall; 2005.

[31] Frei F. Introdução à Análise de Agrupamento: Teoria e Prática. São Paulo: Unesp; 2006.

[32] Gorgônio FL. Uma arquitetura para análise de agrupamentos sobre bases de dados distribuídas aplicadas a segmentação de mercado. DScthesis. Universidade Federal do Rio Grande do Norte; 2009.

[33] Kasznar IK, Gonçalves BML. Técnicas de Agrupamento: Clustering. EletroRevista: Revista Científica e Tecnológica 2007;6(20): 1-5. http://www.ibci.com.br/20Clustering_Agrupamento.pdf (accessed 22 May 2012).

[34] Bussab WO, Miazaki ES, Andrade DF. Introdução à análise de agrupamento. São Paulo: ABE/IME/USP; 1990.

[35] Kuncheva LI. Combining Pattern Classifiers: Methods and Algorithms. New Jersey: John Wiley & Sons; 2004.

[36] Pölzlbauer G. Survey and comparison of quality measures for self-organizing maps. In: Paralič J, Pölzlbauer G, Rauber A. (eds.) Proceedings of the Fifth Workshop on Data Analysis, WDA'04, 24-27 June 2004, VysokéTatry. Slovakia: Elfa Academic Press; 2004.

[37] Salazar Giron EJ, Arroyave G, Ortega Lobo O. Evaluating several unsupervised class-selection methods. In: Perez Ortega G, BranchBedoya, JW (eds.) Memorias Encuentro de Investigación sobre Tecnologías de Información Aplicadas a laSolución de Problemas: EITI-2001, Medellín: Universidad Nacional de Colombia, 2001. p1-6.

[38] Salazar Giron EJ, Vélez AC, Mario Parra C, Ortega Lobo O. A cluster validity index for comparing non-hierarchical clustering methods. In: Ortega Lobo O, BranchBedoya JW. (eds.) Memorias Encuentro de Investigación sobre Tecnologías de Información Aplicadas a laSolución de Problemas: EITI-2002, Medellín: Universidad de Antioquia, 2002. p115-120.

[39] Shim Y, Chung J, Choi, I. A comparison study of cluster validity indices using a nonhierarchical clustering algorithm. In: IEEE Computer Society Press (eds.) Proceedings

of the International Conference on Computational Intelligence for Modeling, Control and Automation CIMCA2005, 28-30 November 2005, Vienna, Austria; 2005.

[40] Kim M, Ramakrishna RS. New Indices for Cluster Validity Assessment. Pattern Recognition Letters 2005;26(5) 2353-2363.

[41] Gonçalves ML, Netto MLA, Costa JAF, ZulloJr J. Data clustering using self-organizing maps segmented by mathematic morphology and simplified cluster validity indexes. In: International Neural Network Society (eds.) proceedings of IEEE International Joint Conference on Neural Networks, IJCNN'06, 16-21 July 2006, Vancouver, Canada. Piscataway: IEEE Xplore; 2006.

[42] Saitta S, Raphael B, Smith IF. A bounded index for cluster validity. In: Perner P (ed.) LNCS: Lecture Notes in Artificial Intelligence 4571: proceedings of the 5th International Conference on Machine Learning and Data Mining in Pattern Recognition, MLDM'2007, 18-20 July 2007, Leipzig, Germany. Berlin: Springer-Verlag; 2007

[43] Kohonen T. Self-Organizing Maps. Berlin: Springer; 2001.

[44] MacQueen JB. Some methods for classification and analysis of multivariate observations. In: Le Cam LM, Neyman J. (eds.) Proceedings of the 5th Berkeley Symposium on Mathematical Statistics and Probability, Jun 21-Jul 18 1965 and Dec 27 1965-Jan 7 1966, Berkeley, USA. Berkeley: University of California Press; 1967.

[45] Linde Y, Buzo A, Gray RM. An Algorithm for Vector Quantizer Design. IEEE Transactions on Communications 1980;28(1) 84-95.

[46] Xu R, Wunsch II D. Survey of Clustering Algorithms. IEEE Transaction on Neural Networks 2005;16(3) 645-678.

[47] Chiang MMT, Mirkin B. Experiments for the number of clusters in K-means. In: Neves J, Santos MF, Machado JM (eds.) LNCS: Progress in Artificial Intelligence 4874: proceedings of the 13th Portuguese Conference on Artificial Intelligence, EPIA'2007, 3-7 December 2007, Guimaraes, Portugal. Berlin: Springer-Verlag; 2007.

[48] Leisch F. Ensemble methods for neural clustering and classification. PhD Thesis. TeschnischeUniversität Wien; 1998.

[49] Han J, Kamber M. Data Mining: Concepts and Techniques. San Francisco: Morgan Kaufmann; 2006.

[50] Ultsch A. Knowledge Extraction from Self-Organizing Neural Networks. In: Opitz O, Lausen B, Klar R. (ed.) Information and classification. Berlin: Springer-Verlag; 1993. p301-306.

[51] Davies DL, Bouldin DW. A Cluster Separation Measure. IEEE Transactions on Pattern Analysis and Machine Intelligence 1979;1(2) 224-227.

[52] Villanueva WJP, Vonzuben FJ. Índices de validação de agrupamentos. In: Wu ST (ed.) Proceedingsofthe I Encontro dos Alunos e Docentes do Departamento de En-

genharia de Computação e Automação Industrial, EADCA'2008, 12-13 March 2008, Campinas, Brazil. Campinas: UNICAMP; 2008.

[53] UCI repository of machine learning databases. Department of Information and Computer Science, University of California, Irvine, CA, USA. http://www.ics.uci.edu/~mlearn/MLRepository.html (accessed 28 July 2012).

[54] Vesanto J, Alhoniemi E. Clustering of the self-organizing map. IEEE Transactions Neural Networks 2000;11(3) 586–600.

Chapter 6

Application of Self Organizing Maps to Multi Modal Adaptive Authentication System Using Behavior Biometrics

Hiroshi Dozono

Additional information is available at the end of the chapter

http://dx.doi.org/10.5772/52100

1. Introduction

Password mechanisms are widely used for the authentication method. However, Password mechanism has many issues. For examples, Password can be stolen easily, Password may be guessed from personal information, such as birthday, families name or telephone number. Some users set unique password to different systems. If one system is hacked, all of the systems can be accessed. Some users feel troublesome to memorize the password. For these problems, biometric authentication is one of the solutions.

Biometric authentication [1] is classified into two types. The first one is the biometric authentication with biological characteristics, such as fingerprint, Vein patterns and Iris patterns. To measure these characteristics, the additional hardware is necessary, and it costs up the computer system. And, some users may feel mentally uncomfortable to register their fingerprint to the computer system. Furthermore, static information about biological characteristics may be imitated by dummy. For example, the fingerprint authentication is easily hacked in the TV show.

The second type is biometric authentications with behavior characteristics, such as keystroke timings [2], Signature [3], hand written pattern and mouse moving pattern. For these methods, the standard input equipments of computer are available. The dynamic information about behavior characteristics is hard to imitate even if it is looked by illegal one. However, the accuracy of authentication is worse compared with that of biological characteristics. For use behavior characteristics, it is necessary to select the pattern of behavior and the features used for authentication. For this selection, Self Organizingmap(SOM)s are used for the analysis in our research.

SOM [4] is the architecture of neural networks, which is feedforward type and single layer network. SOM organizes the map which reflects the similarities of input vectors; thus SOM can visualize the relations among the input vector on the lower dimensional, usually 2-dimensional map. SOM is often used for the visualization of the multidimensional data. SOM is also applied to the authentication with biological characteristics, such as facial recognition system.

At first, SOM is applied to the authentication systems of behavior biometrics of pen calligraphies [5] [6] and keystroke timing [7] in this research. SOM is used for the analysis of input data to select the appropriatepattern of behavior and featureswith visualizing the input data on the map, and also for constructing an authentication system.

However, the accuracy of single behavior biometrics is not enough. For this problem, Pareto learning SOM(P-SOM) and Supervised Pareto learning SOM(SP-SOM), which can integrate multi-modal behavior biometrics [8], is proposed, and applied to the authentication system using keystroke timing and pen calligraphy [9] [10].

Furthermore, the multi-modal authentication system using keystroke timing and key typing sound, which can be obtained at the same time, is proposed [11]. Additionally, the incremental learning of the biometric data during the authentication is applied to implement the adaptive authentication system which can follow the changes of the biometrics of time [12] [13].

SP-SOM shows satisfactory performance as authentication system. However, SP-SOM needs to learn data of some users. For mobile devices, the number of users is usually one; thus the system may need dummy data. For this problem, Concurrent Full Pareto learning SOM(CFP-SOM), which uses a small map for each user, is applied. CFP-SOM can detect the unregistered user using the size of the Pareto set as index, and shows better performance than the SP-SOM [14].

In this chapter, SOM and its application to biometric authentication system are mentioned in section 2 and 3,4 respectively. In section 5 and 6, application of the SP-SOM to multi-modal authentication system and its extension to adaptive authentication system are mentioned respectively. In section 7, application of CFP-SOM to the multi-modal authentication system is mentioned.

2. Self Organizing Map (SOM)

SOM [4] is a kind of neural network, which was proposed by Kohonen, and SOM can extract the feature on the multidimensional input vectors and can visualize the relations among them by unsupervised learning. SOM can integrate multi-modal input vectors and can extract relations among them in 2-dimensional plane. SOM can be used for clustering of unlabeled data or classification of labeled data with labeling the output units after learning.

Figure 1 shows the basic learning algorithm of SOM. For each input vector, the neuron, which is closest to the input vector, is searched from the neurons which are arranged on the 2 dimen-

http://dx.doi.org/10.5772/52100

sional map. The closest neuron is called as winner neuron. The winner neuron and the neurons in the region of the neighborhood are updated as to decrease the difference to the input vector depending on the learning rate and neighboring functions. These steps are iterated for each input vector with decreasing the region of the neighborhood and learning rate.

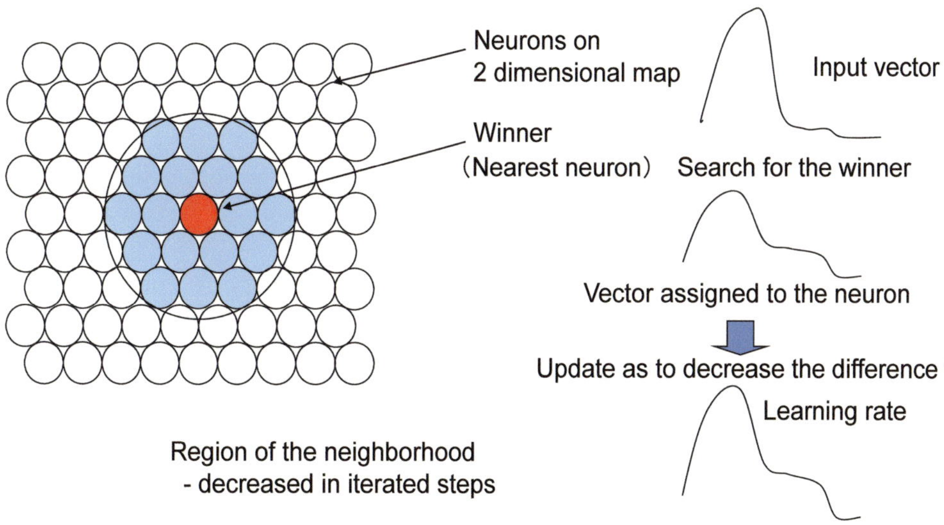

Figure 1. Schematic description of SOM algorithm

3. Application of SOM to the authentication system using handwritten patterns

Recently, many mobile devices, such as Smartphones, tablet devices and small computers, are equipped with touch screen. As the authentication method for touch screen devices, the password authentication is often used. But, on touch screen devices, password can be looked while typing on the screen. It is troublesome to enter the password using handwritten character recognition or screen keyboard. For the touch screen devices, handwritten signature authentication is often applied, because the touch screen is considered to be useful for signature input. However, the shape of the signature may be copied, and it is difficult to write the exact signature on slippery screen, especially for people who do not usually write signatures.

For this problem, we propose a user authentication method using the identical symbol for all users. Using this method, the symbol which is used for authentication is displayed on the touch screen and users simply trace it. However, the pen stroke data may not be enough for user authentications. We used the pen pressure data which may have enough information for user authentication. For this purpose, We analyzed the pen stroke data and pen pressure data using Self Organizing Map [5] [6].

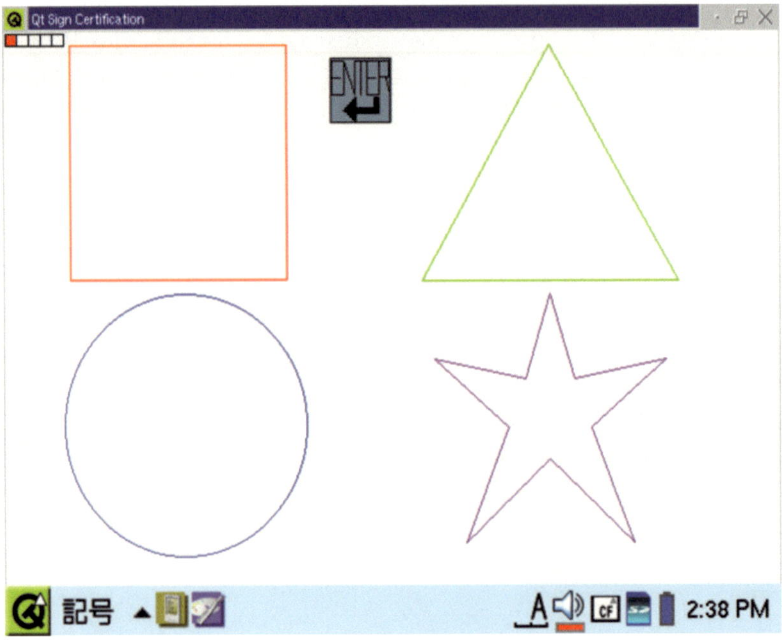

Figure 2. Test input screen

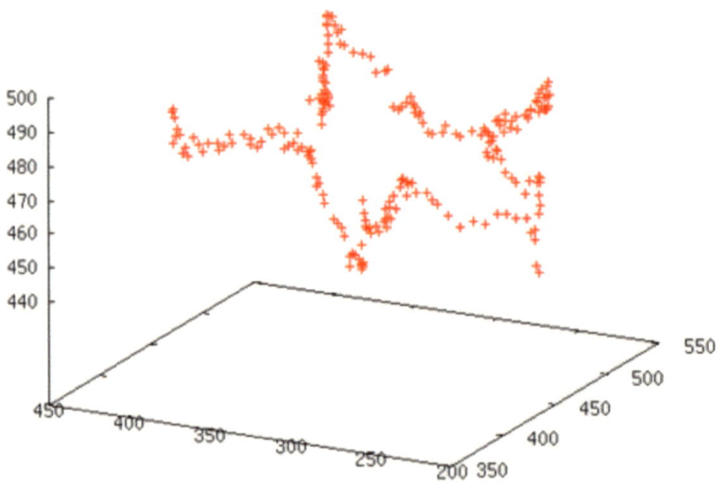

Figure 3. Pen input of symbol star

Figure 2 shows the screen of the application which measures the pen stroke data and pen pressure data of symbols square, circle triangle and star. Each symbol is written in a single stroke, and starting point is specified for all users. 5 samples are taken from each of 12 users. Figure 3 shows an example of symbol star taken from a user. This sample contains 232 points of x-axis, y-axis and pen pressure data in z-axis.

http://dx.doi.org/10.5772/52100

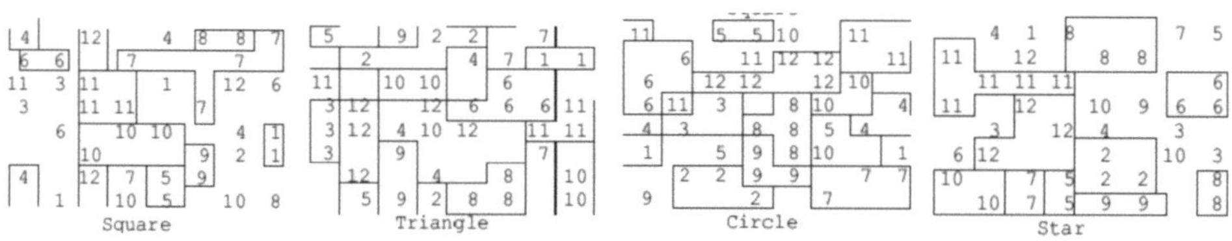

Figure 4. Organizied map for simple symbols

Figure 4 shows the maps of each symbol. The numbers in these figures denote the used-id. With these figures, the symbols of circle and star show better separations compared with others. We consider that the symbols comprised of oval lines or acute angle have more specific features of each user. The symbols of spiral and complex star are selected for next experiments.

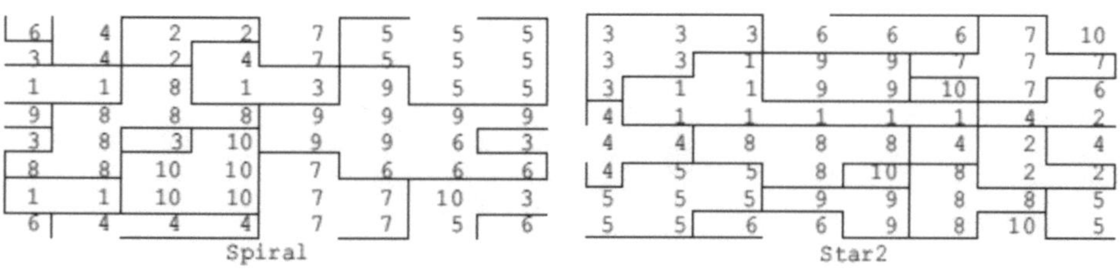

Figure 5. Organized map for symbols spiral and complex star

Figure 5 shows the maps of the symbols spiral and complex star. We use the torus map for this analysis, so the upper side of the map is connected to the lower side, and the right side is connected to the left side. Both of the symbols star and spiral show better separations compared with the simple symbols. It will be possible to authenticate the user using pen pressure data and pen speed data.

The authentication experiments using these symbols are conducted. As the authentication system, we used SOM. The settings of the experiments are as follows. 10 samples of spiral and complex star were taken from each of 10 users.

7 samples of each person were used for training SOM map, and 3 samples were used as test data. The maps were retrained by LVQ3 algorithm.

Spiral learned data	authenticated	false rejection	false acceptance
user-1	1.000	0.000	0.000
user-2	0.714	0.286	0.000
user-3	0.857	0.143	0.000
user-4	1.000	0.000	0.016
user-5	1.000	0.000	0.016
user-6	0.714	0.286	0.032
user-7	0.857	0.143	0.032
user-8	1.000	0.000	0.000
user-9	0.857	0.143	0.016
user-10	0.857	0.143	0.016
total	0.886	0.114	0.012

Spiral test data	authenticated	false rejection	false acceptance
user-1	0.667	0.333	0.000
user-2	1.000	0.000	0.000
user-3	1.000	0.000	0.037
user-4	1.000	0.000	0.037
user-5	0.667	0.333	0.037
user-6	0.000	1.000	0.037
user-7	1.000	0.000	0.074
user-8	1.000	0.000	0.074
user-9	0.333	0.667	0.000
user-10	0.333	0.667	0.037
total	0.700	0.300	0.033

Star-2 learned data	authenticated	false rejection	false acceptance
user-1	1.000	0.000	0.048
user-2	1.000	0.000	0.000
user-3	1.000	0.000	0.000
user-4	1.000	0.000	0.032
user-5	1.000	0.000	0.000
user-6	0.571	0.429	0.000
user-7	1.000	0.000	0.000
user-8	0.857	0.143	0.000
user-9	0.857	0.143	0.016
user-10	0.714	0.286	0.016
total	0.900	0.100	0.011

Star-2 test data	authenticated	false rejection	false acceptance
user-1	1.000	0.000	0.074
user-2	1.000	0.000	0.037
user-3	1.000	0.000	0.037
user-4	1.000	0.000	0.074
user-5	1.000	0.000	0.000
user-6	0.000	1.000	0.000
user-7	1.000	0.000	0.000
user-8	0.667	0.333	0.037
user-9	0.000	1.000	0.037
user-10	0.000	1.000	0.074
total	0.667	0.333	0.037

Table 1. Results of authentication experiments

Table 1 shows the result. For the learned data both of the spiral and complex star show high rate of authentication and low rate of false acceptance, but for the test data, rate of successful authentication was about 70%. From the table of spiral test data, users 6,9,10 show low rate of successful authentication, and from the table of star, same users are not authenticated at all. Both of the symbols can authenticate 7 users from 10 users. It depends of the characters of the users. The careful users tend to be authenticated better and careless users tend to be rejected falsely.

http://dx.doi.org/10.5772/52100

4. Application of SOMto the authentication method using keystroke timings

It is well known that keystroke timing is usable for user authentication. We propose an authentication method which uses the keystroke timings of identical phrase for all users. Users do not need to memorize phrases. For this purpose, the phrase, which is suitable for authentication, is selected by the analysis using SOM [7].

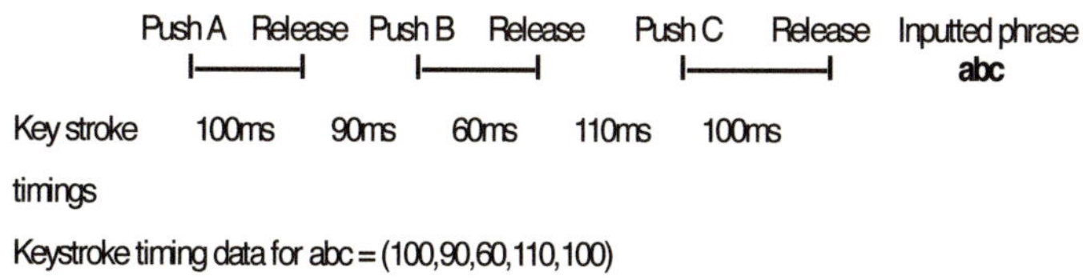

Figure 6. Keystroke timings

The method for taking keystroke timing is dependent on the Operating System(OS)s. The keystroke timing is the vector of intervals between pushing and releasing keys. We use this sequence as the vector of keystroke timing. The length of the vector is 2L-1, where the length of the phrase is L

The experiments are conducted using Romaji Phrases because the examinees are always typing Japanese using Romaji. As samples of phrases, „arigato"(Thank you in English), „kira-kira"(Twinkle Twinkle), „denatsu"(Voltage), „sagadai"(name of our university) and „kousatsu"(prospect) are used. The number of examinees is 10, and each examinee types each phrase in 8 times.

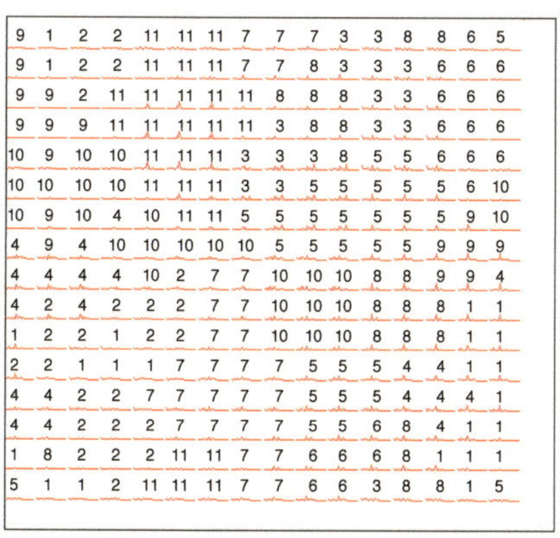

denatsup

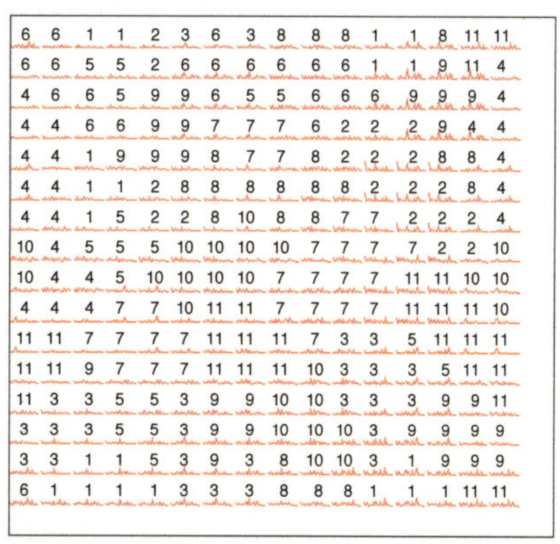

kirakita

Figure 7. Organized maps for keystroke timings „denatsu" and „kirakita"

Figure 7 shows the maps of the phrases "denatsu" and "kirakira". Comparing these 2 maps, the map of "kirakira" shows better clustering results of user-id. The simple phrase "kirakira" is considered to be suitable for authentication because users can type unconsciously.

Next, we conducted authentication experiments using the map organized by SOM. The half of the keystroke timing data is used for learning, and the remained half is used for authentication experiments.As the indexes for evaluation, FRR which is the rate of rejection of the regular user falsely and FAR which is the rate of acceptance of the irregular user falsely, are used.

denatsu

	Success	FRR	FAR
User 1	1.00	0.000	0.000
User 2	0.500	0.500	0.048
User 3	0.000	1.000	0.190
User 4	0.500	0.500	0.095
User 5	0.750	0.250	0.048
User 6	0.000	1.000	0.286
User 7	0.500	0.500	0.048
User 8	0.500	0.500	0.095
User 9	0.500	0.500	0.143
User 10	0.000	1.000	0.143
Average	0.425	0.575	0.081

kirakira

	Success	FRR	FAR
User 1	0.500	0.500	0.000
User 2	1.000	0.000	0.048
User 3	0.250	0.750	0.238
User 4	1.000	0.000	0.000
User 5	0.000	1.000	0.000
User 6	0.750	0.250	0.095
User 7	0.750	0.250	0.095
User 8	0.750	0.250	0.048
User 9	1.000	0.000	0.000
User 10	0.750	0.250	0.000
Average	0.675	0.325	0.052

Table 2. Results of authentication experiments using keystroke timings

Table 2 shows the results of authentication experiments using the phrases of "denatsu" and "kirakira". As expected from the map, the phase "kirakira" shows the better result. On average, rate of false rejections about 32%. Some users show a remarkably high rate of false rejection. It depends on the skill of typing.

5. Integration of muti-modal biometrics using pareto learning SOM

As shown before, accuracy of authentication using behavior characteristics is worse compared with biological characteristics. It is due to the variation of the behavior characteristics and noise. We consider that Integration of some behavior characteristics will improve the accuracy.

We proposed the authentication methods using the integrated information of multi-modal behavior characteristics to improve the accuracy. For example, keystroke timing and handwritten symbol at login time, keystroke timing and key typing sound at login and keystroke timings and mouse moving patterns during the operating time. For the integration of multi-modal biometrics, we propose the Pareto learning SOM(P-SOM). Furthermore, we propose the Supervised P-SOM(SP-SOM) which can improve the accuracy of the authentication.

5.1. Pareto leatning SOM [15]

Generally speaking, the multi modal vector is the vector composed of multi-kind of vectors or attributes. For examples, in the authentication problem using key typing features, the keystroke timing vector and key typing intensity vector are composed. For face image classification, the image vector, age, gender, jobs and other features are composed. In multi-modal vector, each element of the vector and the attribute is described in a different unit and scale. Accuracy of each element may differ.

Conventional SOM can be applied for integrating multi-modal vectors. For example, the simple concatenated vector $(\boldsymbol{x}_1, \boldsymbol{x}_2, \ldots, \boldsymbol{x}_{\mathrm{m}})$ can be used as the input vector.

Then, the quantization error is calculated in (1).

$$\sum_n \left| x_n - m_n^{ij} \right|^2 \tag{1}$$

The map is organized based on the value of the error. So, the resulting map is dominated by the largely scaled vectors and easily affected by inaccurate vector. For this problem, the concatenated vector $(w_1\boldsymbol{x}_1, w_2\boldsymbol{x}_2, \ldots, w_m\boldsymbol{x}_{\mathrm{m}})$ with weight values is often used. Then the quantization error is calculated in (2).

$$\sum_n \left| w_n x_n - m_n^{ij} \right|^2 \tag{2}$$

So, the resulting map heavily depends on the weight values. It is difficult to select the optimal value of the weights.

Same situations occur in multi-objective optimization problem. Consider the problem, Subject to $x \in S$, minimize multiple objective functions Fi($\boldsymbol{x}$). To solve this problem as a single objective optimization problem, the weighted sum of multi objective functions.

$$F(x) = \sum_n w_n F_n(x) \tag{3}$$

is minimized. However, the quality of the solution depends on the setting of weight values.

For this problem, the concept of Pareto optimal is proposed in multi-objective optimization problem.

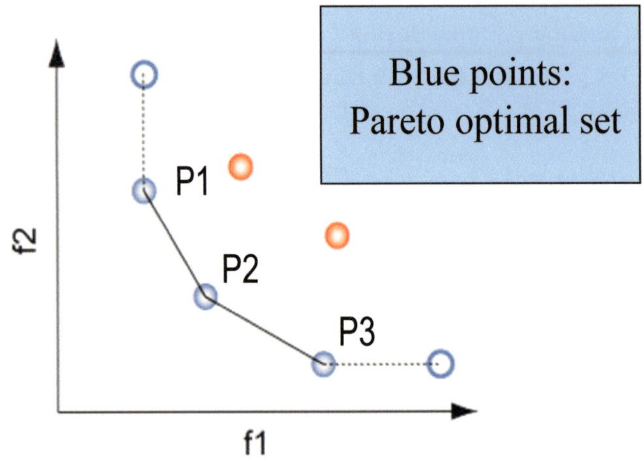

Figure 8. Pareto Optimality

Suppose that the objective function f1 and f2 should be minimized under the condition f1 and f2 should be the upper right side of this line. For this problem, P1 is better than P2 concerning f1, but P2 is better than P1 concerning f2. If no priority is given to f1 and f2, these 3 points P1, P2, P3 are not inferior to others among them. These points are named as Pareto optimal set, and they are the candidates of optimal solutions.

Pareto Learning Self Organizing Map(P-SOM) uses the concept of Pareo optimality for finding winner units. The error of each element of multi-modal vector is considered as the objective functions $f_n(\boldsymbol{x},U^{ij})=|\boldsymbol{x}_n-\boldsymbol{m}^{ij}_n|$, where $\boldsymbol{x}=(\{x_1\},\{x_2\},\ldots,\{x_m\})$ is the input vector and $\boldsymbol{m}^{ij}=(\{\boldsymbol{m}^{ij}_1\},\{\boldsymbol{m}^{ij}_2\},\ldots,\{\boldsymbol{m}^{ij}_m\})$ is the reference vector associated to the unit U^{ij}. Pareto optimal set P(x) is the set of units U^{ij} which are pareto optimal for the objective functions $f_n(\boldsymbol{x},U^{ij})$. So, the Pareto SOM is multi-winner SOM and all winner units and their neighbors are updated simultaneously.

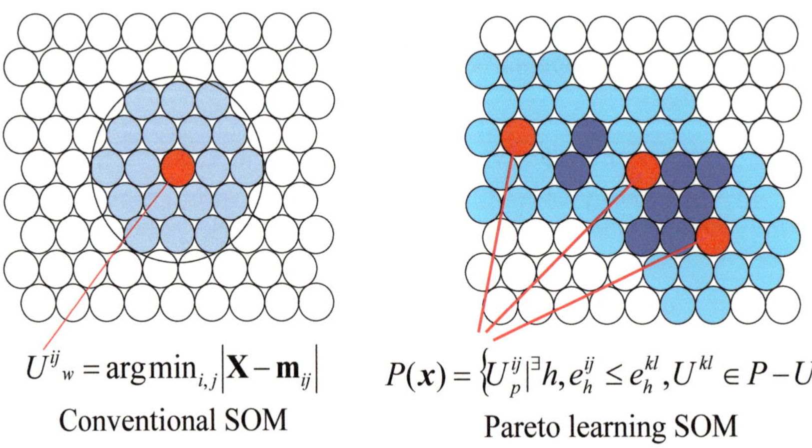

Figure 9. Difference between conventional SOM and Pareto learning SOM

http://dx.doi.org/10.5772/52100

Figure 9 shows the learning process of SOM and Pareto learning SOM. As for SOM, only one winner is selected and the winner and its neighbors are updated. As for pareto learning SOM, pareto winner set are selected, and they are updated simultaneously. For Pareto learning SOM, overlapped neighbors are updated more strongly, and it play an important role for integration of muti-modal vectors. In other word, conventional SOM integrates the multi-modal vector in a unit and P-SOM integrates the multi-modal vector in the region of Pareto optimal set. Algorithm of P-SOM is as follows.

P-SOM Algorithm

1. Initialization of the map: Initialize the vector $\mathbf{m}^{ij}$ which are assigned to unit U^{ij} on the map using the 1st and 2nd principal components as base vectors of 2-dimensional map.
2. Batch learning phase:
   - Clear all learning buffer of units U^{ij}.
   - For each vector xi, search for the pareto optimal set of the units $P = \{U^{ab}_p\}$. $U^{ab}p$ is an element of pareto optimal set P, if for all units $U^{kl} \in P - U^{ab}_p$ existing h such that $e^{ab}_h \leq e^{kl}_h$ where $e^{kl}_h = | \mathbf{x}^i_h - \mathbf{m}^{kl}_h |$.
   - Add $\mathbf{x}^i$ to the learning buffer of all units $U^{ab}_p \in P$.
3. Batch update phase: For each unit U^{ij} update the associated vector $\mathbf{m}^{ij}$ using the weighted average of the vectors recorded in the buffer of U^{ij} and its neighboring units as follows.

- For all vectors $\mathbf{x}$ recorded in the buffer of U^{ij} and its neighboring units in distance $d \leq Sn$, calculate weighted sum $\mathbf{S}$ of the updates and the sum of weight values W.

$$S = S + \eta fn(d)(x - m^{i'j'})$$

$$W = W + fn(d)$$

where $U^{i'j'}$'s are neighbors of U^{ij} including U^{ij} itself, η is learning rate, fn(d) is the neighborhood function which becomes 1 for d=0 and decrease with increment of d.

- Set the vector $\mathbf{m}^{ij} = \mathbf{m}^{ij} + \mathbf{S}/W$.

Repeat 2. and 3. with decreasing the size of neighbors Sn for pre-defined iterations.

As shown in step 2 of this algorithm, Pareto winner set for the integrated input vector $\mathbf{x}$ are searched for based on the concept of Pareto Optimality using the distance as the objective function $f_h(\mathbf{x})$ for each element x_h in $\mathbf{x}$. Thus, the multiple units become winners. The winners and their neighboring units are modified in the update process in step 3. Overlapped neighbors are updated multiply, and the overlapped region will contribute to generalization ability and integration ability of P-SOM.

5.2. Supervised paretolearning SOM (SP-SOM)

Because Pareto learning SOM can integrate any type of vectors, the category element can be introduced as an independent vector to each input vector x_i as follows.

$$x_i^S = (x_i, c_i)$$

where

$$c_i = \begin{cases} 1 & x_{i'} \in C_i \\ 0 & x_i \notin C_i \end{cases}$$

With introducing category element, it attracts the input vectors in the same category closely on the map corporately with other input vectors in the learning phase. In this meaning, P-SOM learning algorithm becomes supervised. In the recalling process, category of test vector $\mathbf{x}_t$ is determined by the following equation.

$$\arg\max_k \left\{ \sum_{U^{ij} \in P(x_t)} c_k{}^{ij} \right\}$$

where $P(\boldsymbol{x}_t)$ is the Pareto optimal set of units for $\mathbf{x}_t$

Considering the Further extension of Pareto learning SOM, anything which has its own metrics can be element of multi-modal input vector for P-SOM. Structured data and vectors can be integrated as input data. For example, in bioinformatics amino acid sequence data comprised of Hidden Markov Model(HMM) of the data, HMM of the structures and other features can be integrated. Furthermore, the map can be organized using the partial vectors which lack some attributes in the vectors.

5.3. Experiment of authentication system using multi-modal behavior biometrics

The experimental results of the authentication system using handwritten patterns and keystroke timings were shown in the previous section. Another experiments using both of handwritten patterns and keystroke timings were conducted [9] [10]. The experimental settings are as follows. 6 samples are taken from each of 11 examinees. Each sample is comprised of the keystroke timings and pen calligraphy data which is inputted alternately. For these experiments, tablet PC, which is equipped with keyboard and touch panel, is used.

The phrase "kirakira" which marked the best results in the previous experiments is used. The symbol Spiral is used as the handwritten symbol. SP-SOM is used for the analysis and authentication.

Figure 10 shows the map of SP-SOM using behavior biometrics data, key stroke timing, pen speed and pen pressure. Using keystroke timing, the users are clustered well except small fragmentations. Using pen speed and pen pressure, thefragmentations are increased compared with those of keystroke timings. Using the integrated biometrics of key stroke timing, pen speed and pen pressure, the fragmentations decreased compared with that of keystroke timings without affected by pen data.

The Authentication experiments are conducted using the map organized by SOM, P-SOM and SP-SOM for the comparisons. 4 of the 6 samples of each user are used to organize the map and 2 remainders are used for the test data. All of the combinations of training data and test data are examined. 6C2 x 10x2 =300 input vectors are tested.

Key stroke timing   Pen speed and pen pressure   Integration of key stroke timing, pen speed and pen

Figure 10. Organized map of SP-SOM with behavior biometrics data

	key		pen speed		pen pressure	
	FRR	FAR	FRR	FAR	FRR	FAR
User 1	0.167	0.0000	0.400	0.0000	0.467	0.0000
User 2	0.000	0.0000	0.133	0.0767	0.467	0.0083
User 3	0.000	0.0000	0.700	0.0000	0.100	0.0017
User 4	0.033	0.0000	0.000	0.0317	0.333	0.0200
User 5	0.033	0.0083	0.667	0.0100	0.700	0.0217
User 6	0.233	0.0083	0.567	0.0000	0.667	0.0333
User 7	0.167	0.0017	0.367	0.0100	0.200	0.0383
User 8	0.000	0.0000	0.167	0.0433	0.200	0.0167
User 9	0.167	0.0033	1.000	0.0217	0.000	0.0150
User 10	0.033	0.0033	0.200	0.0000	0.400	0.0067
User 11	0.000	0.0000	0.600	0.0283	0.600	0.0283
Average	0.076	0.0022	0.436	0.0202	0.376	0.0173

Table 3. Result of Authentication experiment using each of behavior biometrics

Table 3 shows the result of authentication using each data independently. In this experiment, FRR of keystroke timings is much better than that of the previous experiment because the typing skill of each user becomes much better. FRR of pen speed data and pen pressure data are much worse than that of keystroke timing.

Table 4 shows the results of authentication experiments using integrated vectors of keystroke timing, pen speed and pen pressure. The weight values for pen speed data and pen pressure data are studiously selected from many iterations of try and error for SOM. SP-SOM can achieve almost same authentication performance without tunings of parameters.

	SOM		P-SOM		SP-SOM	
	FRR	FAR	FRR	FAR	FRR	FAR
User 1	0.333	0.0000	0.467	0.0000	0.200	0.0000
User 2	0.000	0.0000	0.100	0.0083	0.000	0.0000
User 3	0.000	0.0000	0.333	0.0000	0.000	0.0000
User 4	0.000	0.0000	0.067	0.0033	0.000	0.0000
User 5	0.000	0.0000	0.033	0.0067	0.000	0.0167
User 6	0.000	0.0083	0.167	0.0033	0.133	0.0000
User 7	0.167	0.0000	0.033	0.0150	0.000	0.0083
User 8	0.000	0.0000	0.100	0.0267	0.000	0.0117
User 9	0.000	0.0000	0.333	0.0083	0.100	0.0000
User 10	0.000	0.0000	0.033	0.0050	0.033	0.0000
User 11	0.000	0.0000	0.200	0.0117	0.033	0.0000
Average	0.045	0.0008	0.170	0.0080	0.045	0.0020

Table 4. Result of authentication experiment using integrated biometrics

6. Adaptive authentication system using integrated biometrics of keystroke timing and key typing sound

In this section, the experiments on the Integration of Keystroke timings and Key Typing Sound, and adaptive authentication system is mentioned [11]. Key typing sound is used as the intensities of key typing. 10 samples are taken from each of 10 examinee. The phrase "kirakira" is used for sampling keystroke timings and typing sounds. Sampling rate of the sound is 44Khz, and the maximum amplitude for each key is used as a feature vector.

The setting of the authentication experiments is as follows. 5 of the 10 samples of each user are used to organize the map and 5 remainders are used for the test data. All of the combinations of training data and test data are examined. The results of the authentication using keystroke timing, using key typing sounds and using the integrated vector are examined.

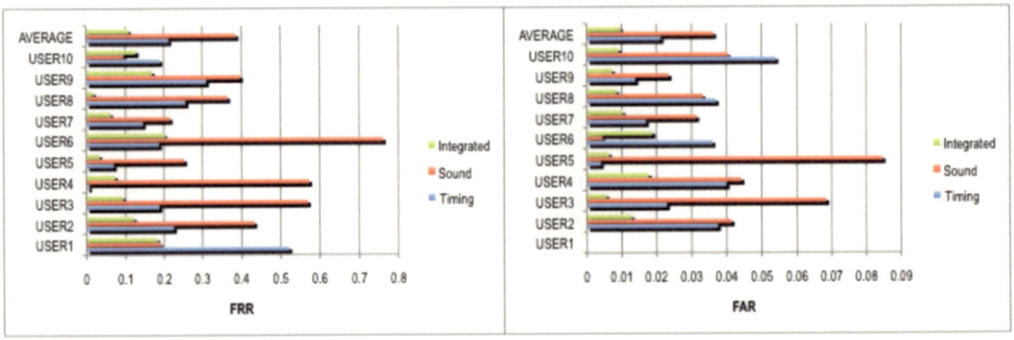

Figure 11. Result of authentication experiments using keystroke timing and key typing sound

Figure 11 shows the FRR and FAR of all user and their averages. In this experiments, average of FRR of keystroke timing is about 0.2. With integrating the typing sound, average of FRR is improved as about 0.1. For almost users, FRR and FAR is improved by integration.

As to adapt the changes of biometrics, incremental learning is introduced [15] [13]. At first, incremental learning of SP-SOM is examined using the test data. Incremental leaning is performed by updating the map after recalling process using the updating method of conventional SOM by the following equation.

$$m'_{ij} = \boldsymbol{m}'_{ij} + \eta' (\boldsymbol{x}' - \boldsymbol{m}'_{ij})$$

where $\boldsymbol{m}'_{ij}$ is the vector assigned to and P isPareto winner set for input vector $\boldsymbol{x}$. Two types of incremental learning, which are supervised learning using the input vector with category element and unsupervised learning without category element, are examined.

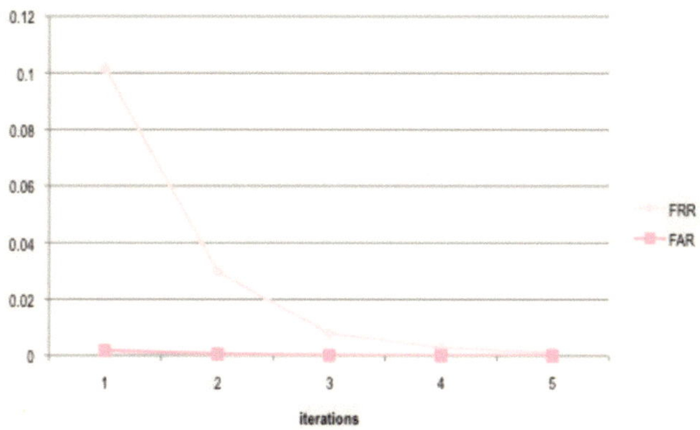

Figure 12. Result of iterated authentication with incremental learning

At first, test data is incrementally learned during the iterations of authentication. Figure 12 shows the result. Both of the FRR and FAR are improved by repeating incremental learning.

Changes of behavior biometrics by time, variation of the behavior biometrics and noise affect the accuracy of authentication. The authentication system will be able to adapt changes of behavior characteristics by the time with incremental learning of the input data for authentication. However, Incremental learning of the input data with variations or noises may affect the authentication system.

Next, we conducted experiments for changes of biometrics by the time of authentication input. It will take very long time to obtain the data which changes by the time from examinees. So, simulated data is made with changing the observed data at each authentication gradually. The experimental settings are as follows. Before authentication experiments, all data are learned by SP-SOM. For each authentication, 4 elements of the keystroke timing vector are selected randomly and multiplied by 0.8 and replaced with the new values. This case is very extreme case of changing the biometric input by the time. The results of supervised learning with used-id and unsupervised learning without user-id are examined.

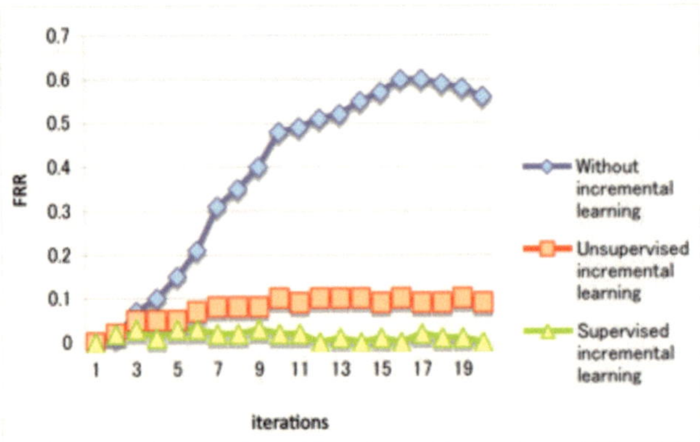

Figure 13. Result of authentication experiment of adaptive authentication system with changing the keystroke timing by time

Figure 13 shows the result. Average of the FRR becomes worse with iterations without incremental learning because the input for biometrics changing. Average of FRR is kept almost 0 with supervised incremental learning. Average of FRR becomes about 0.1 with unsupervised incremental learning. From this result, supervised incremental learning can adapt the changes by time almost perfectly.

Next, we conducted experiments for examining robustness to the noises and variations. Incremental learning may affect worse using the data with noise and variations because the noisy data is added to the map. The authentication data with noises is made artificially by adding the noise to the input vector. The experimental settings are as follows. For each authentication, 5 elements of the typing sound vector are selected, and 50% random noise is added at each authentication.

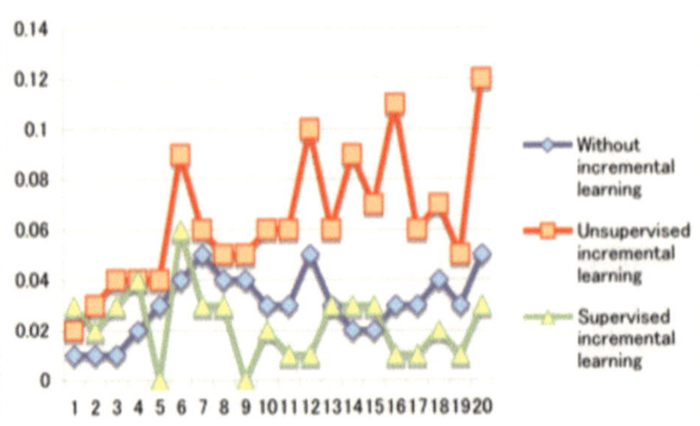

Figure 14. Result of authentication experiment with adding the noises to key typing sounds

The result for unsupervised incremental learning becomes worse by iterations. In contrast, supervised incremental learning is not affected by noises rather it becomes better than without incremental learning.

Next we conducted the experiment with changes of keystroke timings by time and adding the noises to key typing sounds simultaneously.

FRR for without incremental learning and unsupervised incremental learning becomes worse with iterations. FRR for supervised incremental learning is kept less than 0.1. In spite of the noises, supervised incremental learning can adapt to changes by time.

As the authentication system, unregistered user must be detected. Simple SP-SOM algorithm can classify the input vector to one of learned category, and cannot detect unlearned vector. For this problem, threshold values are introduced. As the features of SP-SOM, the size of Pareto set becomes large for unregistered user(unlearned data), and the magnitude of the category value becomes small for unregistered data. Thus, unregistered users can be identified with setting the threshold values to these values.

Figure 16 shows the result of authentication experiment with setting the threshold for size of Pareto set and category value as 10 and 0.5 respectively. Both of the FRR and FAR of registered users are remarkably small, and FAR of unregistered user is also small.

Figure 17 shows the result with adding changes by the time and noises. In this experiment, the authentication system can also adapt to the changes by time with incremental learning.

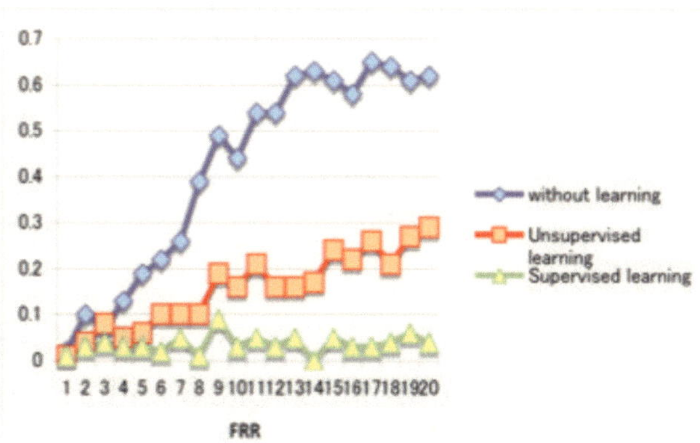

Figure 15. Result of authentication experiment with changing keystroke timing by time and adding noises to key typing sounds (x-axis: iterations, y-axis: FRR)

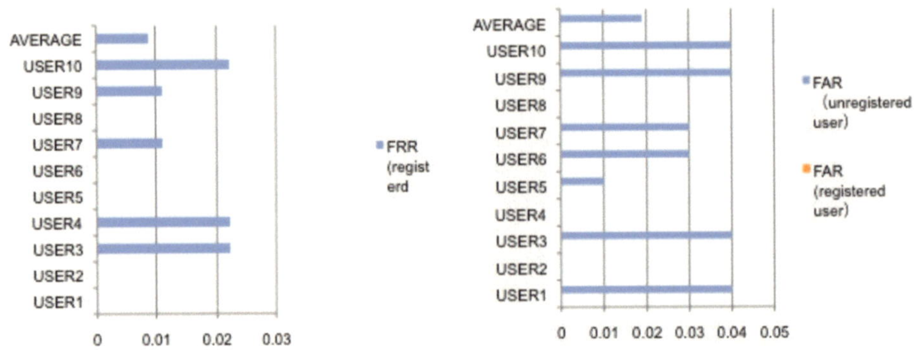

Figure 16. Result of authentication experiment with rejecting unregistered user

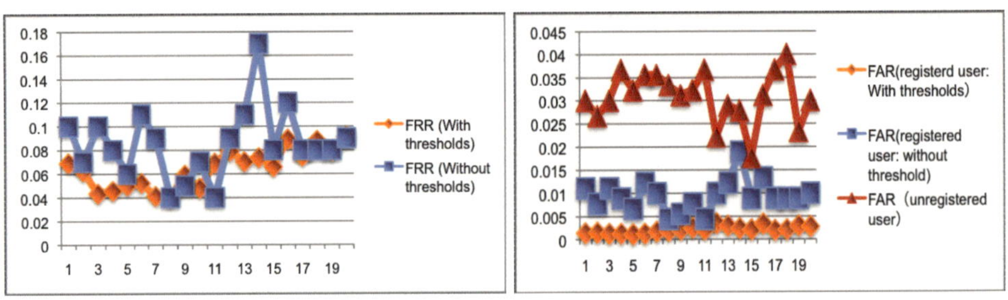

Figure 17. Result of authentication experiment with adding changes by time and noises using the threshold for rejecting unregistered user (x-axis: iterations, y-axis: FRR and FAR)

7. Concurrent paretolearning SOM and its application to the authentication system using multi-modal behavior biometrics

As mentioned in the previous section, we have proposed the authentication system using Supervised Pareto learning SOM(SP-SOM). However, SP-SOM needs the training data of multiple users for learning. For the device of single user, the authentication system, which requires the data of single user, is recommended. For this problem, Concurrent Pareto learning SOM (CP-SOM) is introduced [14]. CP-SOM is P-SOM which uses the small map for each user.

http://dx.doi.org/10.5772/52100

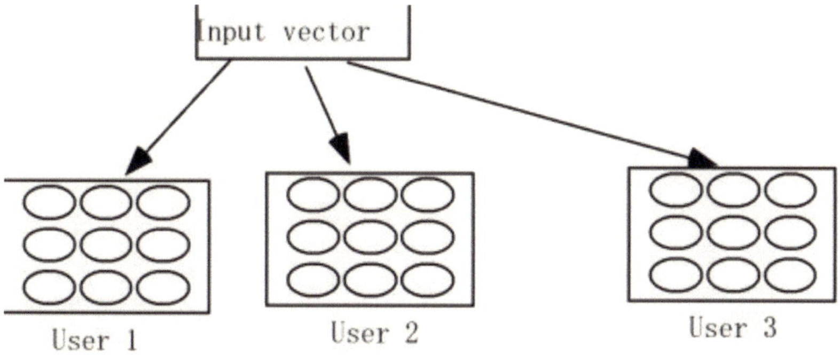

Figure 18. Concurrent P-SOM

Conventional concurrent SOM [16] uses threshold value of quantization error for classifying the learned data and unlearned data. Concurrent P-SOM uses the size of Pareto Optimal Set for detecting unregistered user.The threshold value of the size is set to TH_T*P_LAST, where P_LAST is the average size of Pareto optimal set in the last phase of learning.

The authentication experiment is conducted using the keystroke timing and key typing sound data used in the previous section. Each user data is learned as the registered user on the distinct map, and the data of other users is used as the test data of unregistered users. The experiments are conducted with changing map sizes and threshold values, TH_P. The size of Pareto sets are adaptively tuned as 1/4 and 1/2 of all units in initial learning step and last learning step respectively. The difference between registered user and unregistered users becomes larger using larger size of Pareto set in the last step.

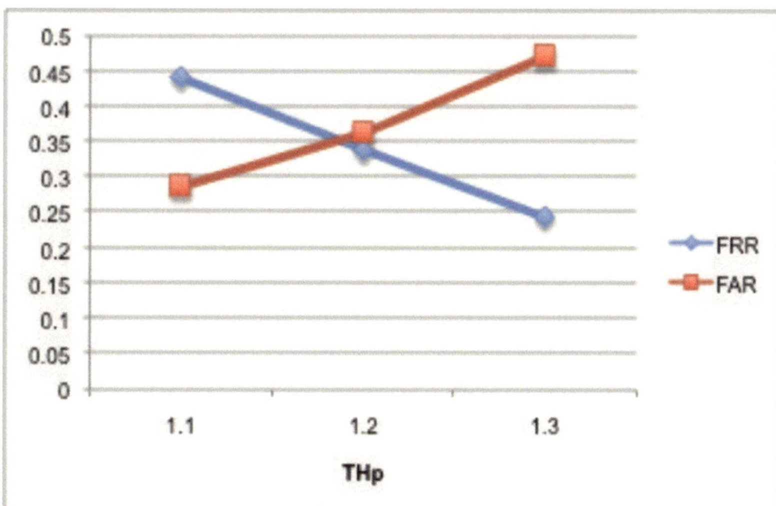

Figure 19. Experimental result of CP-SOM

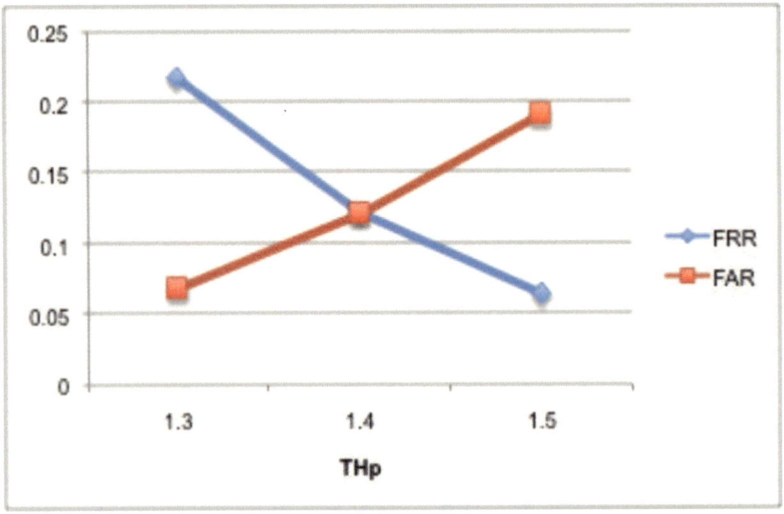

Figure 20. Experimental result of CFP-SOM

Figure 19 shows the experimental result of CP-SOM using the multi-modal vector composed of the 2 vectors, which are key stroke timing vector and key typing sound vector, with changing the threshold THp. The size of the map is 6x6. For typical tuning of authentication system, the threshold value is set to cross point of FRR and FAR. In this experiment, THp=1.2 and FRR=FAR=0.35 at the cross point, and this result is not adequate for authentication system. It is because of the small difference of the size of Pareto set between registered user and unregistered user, which are 6.22 and 7.77 respectively.

To enlarge the difference of the size of Pareto set, the number of integrated vectors should be increased. For this purpose, Full Pareto learning SOM(FP-SOM) is applied. FP-SOM is P-SOM which uses each element in the vector as independent 1-dimensional vector. Concurrent Full Pareto learning SOM(CFP-SOM) using multi-modal vector composed of 23 elements(15 keystroke timing and 8 typing sound) is applied to authentication system. Figure 20 shows the result. At the cross point, FRR=FAR=0.121, and the average size of the Pareto set for registered user and unregistered user are 17.95 and 27.95 respectively. FRR and FAR are much improved compared with the previous experiment because the difference of the size of Pareto set becomes larger.

Figure 20 shows the FRR and FAR of each user for experimental result of CFP-SOM. With checking each user, FARs of user 9 and user 6 are too large. Such users are called as "SHEEP" and are not adequate for this authentication method. Excluding user 6 and 9, average of FRR=0.112, FAR=0.070, and they are better than that of SP-SOM(FRR=0.187, FAR=0.065) which are conducted in the same setting of the experiment using CFP-SOM.

Figure 21 shows the experimental result with changing map size. TH_p is fixed to 1.4. With changing map size, FAR is not improved, however FRR is improved by enlarging map size. For map size 9x9, average of FAR=0.095, FAR=0.123, and FRR =0.090m FAR=0.061 excluding user 6 and 9.

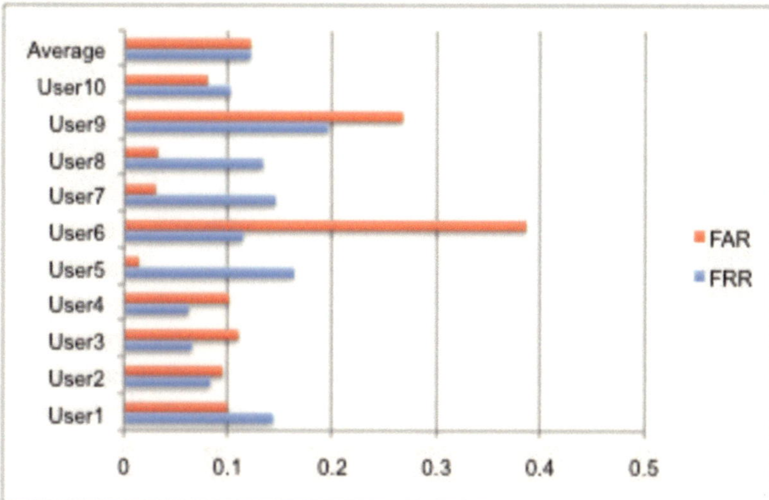

Figure 21. FRR and FAR of each user for experimental result of CFP-SOM

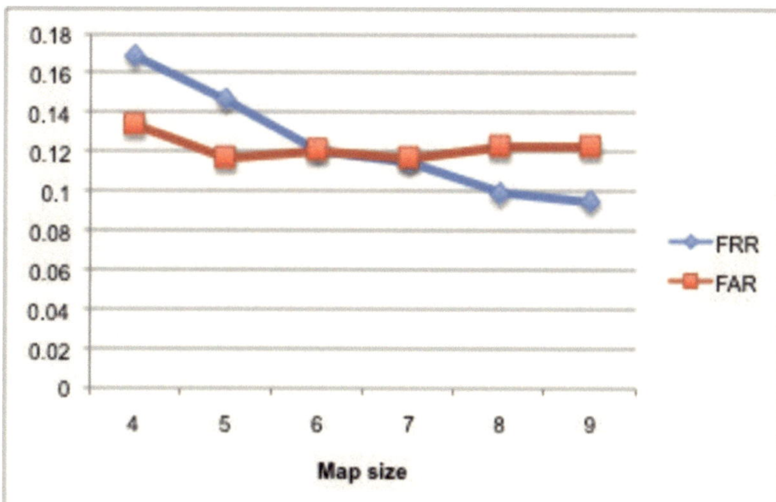

Figure 22. Experimental result with changing map size

8. Conclusions

In this chapter, application of Self Organizing Map(SOM)s to the authentication system using behavior biometrics is mentioned.

In section 3 and section 4, the application of SOM to the authentication systems using pen calligraphy and keystroke timing are mentioned respectively. SOM is used to visualize the relations among the biometrics data of users, and is used to select the appropriate feature, and to select the appropriate patterns of behavior for authentication. For the authentication system using pen calligraphy, the pen speed data and pen pressure data is selected as the features, and drawing spiral or star on the screen are selected as the patterns of behavior. For the authentication system using keystroke timing, keystroke timing data typing "kira-kira" is selected as the behavior. These systems show superior performance considering the simplicity of these methods. However, using single behavior biometrics, enough accuracy is hard to be accomplished.

In section 5, the application of SOM to the authentication system using multi-modal behavior biometrics is mentioned. As the multi-modal behavior biometrics, pen calligraphy drawing the symbols and keystroke timing which are measured on tablet PC are used. Supervised Pareto learning SOM(SP-SOM), which can integrate multi-modal vector naively with supervised learning, is proposed, and applied to the analysis of multi-modal biometric features and to the authentication system. The accuracy of authentication is improved compared with that of single behavior biometrics without disturbance from unreliable features.

In section 6, the application of SP-SOM to the authentication system using multi-modal behavior biometrics of keystroke timing and key typing sound is mentioned. These features can be measured simultaneously during typing a phrase. Additionally, the adaptive authentication system, which can follow the changes of biometrics by the time, is examined. The authentication system shows superior accuracy with following changes of keystroke timing by the time without disturbed by noises. As the practical authentication system, the unregistered users are detected using the size of the Pareto set and category magnitude of the user inputs.

In section 7, Concurrent Full P-SOM(CFP-SOM), which uses small map for each user, is applied to the authentication system using multi-modal behavior biometrics. CFP-SOM is suitable for mobile system because it only needs the learning data of single user, in contrast, SP-SOM needs the learning data of some users. CFP-SOM classifies the registered user from unregistered users using the size of Pareto set. With adjusting the threshold of size of Pareto set, the accuracy becomes almost same or better compared with that of SP-SOM.

As the future work, the adaptive algorithm for CFP-SOM should be developed. CFP-SOM needs the adjustment of threshold to apply to authentication system, thus adaptive scheme for the threshold is required. Furthermore, P-SOM and SP-SOM is a generic extension of SOM, and it can be applied to many applications, which need both of visualization and classification by supervised learning. P-SOM and SP-SOM can be used to integrate the multiple objects for which distance metric is defined. The novel application from this point of view should be explored.

Author details

Hiroshi Dozono

Faculty of Science and Engineering Saga University, Honjyo Saga, Japan

References

[1] Bolle R., Connell J., Pankanti S., Ratha N., Senior A.Guide to Biometrics, Springer; 2004

[2] Monrose F., Rubin A.D., Keystroke Dynamics as a Biometric for Authentication. Future Generation Computer Systems: March;2000

[3] Brault J.J., Plamondon R. A Complexity Measure of Handwritten Curves: Modelling of Dynamic Signature Forgery. IEEE Trans. Systems, Man and Cybernetics. 1993; 23 400-3

[4] Kohonen T. Self Organizing Maps, Springer;ISBN 3-540-67921-9

[5] Dozono H., Nakakuni M., et al. The Analysis of Pen Pressures of Handwritten Symbols on PDA Touch Panel using Self Organizing Maps. Proceedings of the International Conference on Security and Management; 2005: 440-5.

[6] Dozono H., Nakakuni M., et al. The Analysis of pen Inputs of Handwritten Symbols using Self Organizing Maps and its Application to User Authentication. Proceedings of 2006 International Joint Conference on Neural Networks: 2006; 4884-9.

[7] Dozono H., Nakakuni M., et al. The Analysis of Key Stroke Timings using Self Organizing Maps and its Application to Authentication. Proceedings of the International Conference on Security and Management; 2006: 100-5

[8] Dokic S., Kulesh A., et al. An Overview of Multi-modal Biometrics for Authentication. Proceedings of the International Conference on Security and Management; 2007: 39-44

[9] Nakakuni M., Dozono H., et al. Application of Self Organizing Maps for the Integrated Authentication using Keystroke Timings and Handwritten Symbols. WSEAS TRANSACTIONS on INFORMATION SCIENCE & APPLICATIONS. 2006; 2-4 413-420

[10] Dozono H., Nakakuni M., et al. Application of Self Organizing Maps to User Authentication Using Combination of Key Stroke Timings and Pen Calligraphy. Proceedings of the 5th WSEAS Int. Conf. on COMPUTATIONAL INTELLIGENCE; 2006: 105-10

[11] Dozono H., Nakakuni M., et al. Application of the Supervised Pareto Learning Self Organizing Maps to Multi-modal Biometric Authentication. Journal of Information Processing Society of Japan. 2008 49(9) 3028-37

[12] Dozono H., Nakakuni M., et al. Comparison of the Adaptive Authentication Systems for Behavior Biometrics using the Variations of Self Organizing Maps

[13] Dozono H., Nakakuni M., et al. The Adaptive Authentication System for Behavior Biometrics Using Pareto Learning Self Organizing Maps. Neural Information Processing Models and Applications ICONIP 2010. Springer; 2010 LNCS6444 383-90

[14] Dozono H., Nakakuni M., et al. The Authentication System for Multi-modal Behavior Biometrics Using Concurrent Pareto Learning SOM, Artificial Neural Networks and Machine Learning- ICANN 2011. Springer; 2011 LNCS6792 197-204

[15] Dozono H., Nakakuni M., et al. Application of Supervised Pareto Learning Self Organizing Maps and Its Incremental Learning. Advances in Self Organizing Maps WSOM 2009. Springer; 2009 LNCS 5629 54-62

[16] Neagoe, V., E., Ropot, A., D. Concurrent Self-Organizing Maps for Pattern Classification, Proceeding ICCI '02 Proceedings of the 1st IEEE International Conference on Cognitive Informatics; 2002: 304-12

Chapter 7

Quantification of Emotions for Facial Expression: Generation of Emotional Feature Space Using Self-Mapping

Masaki Ishii, Toshio Shimodate, Yoichi Kageyama,
Tsuyoshi Takahashi and Makoto Nishida

Additional information is available at the end of the chapter

http://dx.doi.org/10.5772/51136

1. Introduction

Facial expression recognition for the purpose of emotional communication between humans and machines has been investigated in recent studies [1-7].

The shape (static diversity) and motion (dynamic diversity) of facial components, such as the eyebrows, eyes, nose, and mouth, manifest expression. From the viewpoint of static diversity, owing to the individual variation in facial configurations, it is presumed that a facial expression pattern due to the manifestation of a facial expression includes subject-specific features. In addition, from the viewpoint of dynamic diversity, because the dynamic changes in facial expressions originate from subject-specific facial expression patterns, it is presumed that the displacement vector of facial components has subject-specific features.

On the other hand, although an emotionally generated facial expression pattern of an individual is unique, internal emotions expressed and recognized by humans via facial expressions are considered person-independent and universal. For example, one person may express the common emotion of happiness using various facial expressions, while another person may recognize happiness from these facial expressions. Pantic et al. argued that a natural facial expression always includes various emotions, and that a pure facial expression rarely appears [1]. Furthermore, they suggested that it is not realistic to classify all facial expressions into the six basic emotion categories: anger, sadness, disgust, happiness, surprise and fear. Instead, they proposed quantitative classification into many more emotion categories.

Pioneering studies on the quantification of emotions recognized from facial expressions have been conducted in the field of psychology. In particular, the mental space model of Russell et al. is well known: each facial expression is arranged in a space centering on "pleasantness" and "arousal," particularly addressing the semantic antithetical nature of emotion [8]. Russell et al. discovered that facial expression stimuli can be conceptualized as a circular arrangement in the mental space described above (the circumplex model). Yamada found a significant correlation between the "slantedness" and "curvedness/openness" of facial components and the "pleasantness" and "arousal" in the mental space [9]. This observation highlights the importance of clarifying a correspondence between changes in facial components accompanying emotional expressions (physical parameters) and recognized emotions (psychological parameters).

We address the following issues related to the recognition of emotions from facial expressions.

First, facial expression patterns are considered as physical parameters. Expressions convey personality, and as physical parameters, facial expression patterns vary among individuals. Hence, the classification of facial expressions is fundamentally a problem with an unknown number of categories. Accordingly, the extraction of subject-specific facial expression categories using a common person-independent technique is an important issue.

Second, emotions are considered as psychological parameters. The facial expression pattern of an individual is unique, but as a psychological parameter, emotion is person-independent and universal. Moreover, the grade of a recognized emotion changes according to the grade of physical change in a facial expression pattern. Therefore, it is important to match the amount of physical change in a subject-specific facial expression pattern with the corresponding amount of mental change in order to estimate the grade of emotion.

Previously, we proposed a method for generating a subject-specific feature space to estimate the grade of emotion, i.e., an emotional feature space that expresses the correspondence between physical and psychological parameters [10, 11]. In this chapter, we improve the abovementioned method. In addition, we develop a method for generating a feature space that can express a level of detailed emotion.

2. Previous studies

A method for generating a subject-specific emotional feature space using self-organizing maps (SOMs) [12] and counter propagation networks (CPNs) [13] has been proposed in previous studies [10, 11]. The feature space expresses the correspondence between the changes in facial expression patterns and the degree of emotions in a two-dimensional space centered on "pleasantness" and "arousal." For practical purposes, we created two types of feature spaces, a facial expression map (FEMap) and an emotion map (EMap), by learning facial images using CPNs. When a facial image is fed into the CPN after the learning process, the FEMap can assign the image to a unique emotional category. Furthermore, the

EMap can quantize the level of emotion in the image according to the level of change in the facial patterns.

Figures 1 and 2 respectively show the FEMap and EMap generated using the proposed method. Figure 3 shows the recognition result for the expressions of "fear" and "surprise". These results indicate that the pleasantness and arousal values gradually change with changes in facial expression patterns. Moreover, the changes in the pleasantness and arousal values of two individuals are similar, even though their facial expression patterns are different.

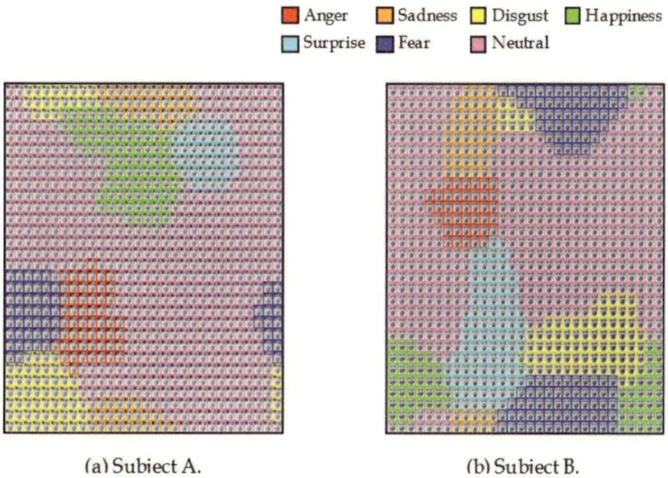

Figure 1. Generation results of FEMap.

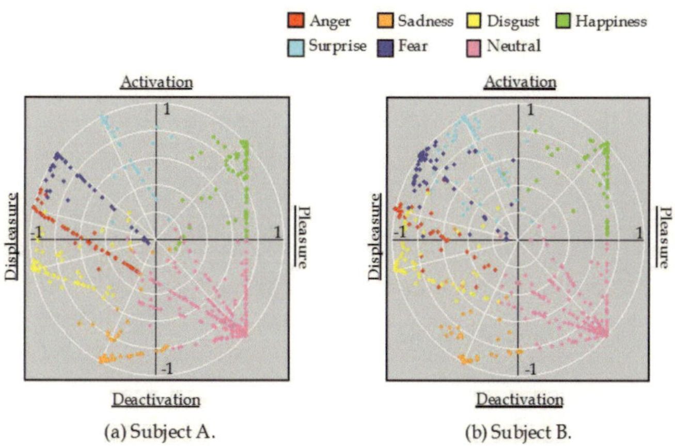

Figure 2. Generation results of EMap.

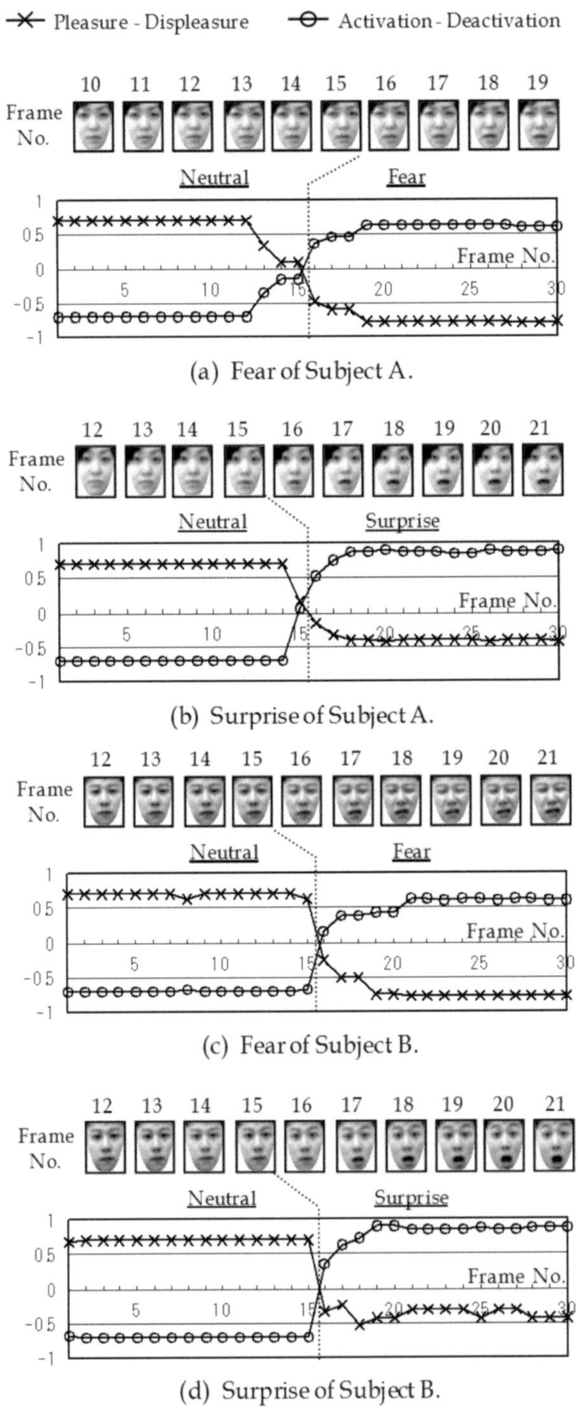

Figure 3. Recognition results for "fear" and "surprise".

3. Algorithms of SOM and CPN

3.1. Self-Organizing Maps (SOM)

An SOM is a learning algorithm that models the self-organizing and adaptive learning capabilities of the human brain [12]. It comprises two layers: an input layer, to which training data are supplied, and a Kohonen layer, in which self-mapping is performed via competitive learning. The learning procedure of an SOM is described below.

1. Let $w_{i,j}(t)$ be the weight from an input layer unit i to a Kohonen layer unit j at time t. Actually, $w_{i,j}$ is initialized using random numbers.

2. Let $x_i(t)$ be the data input to the input layer unit i at time t; calculate the Euclidean distance d_j between $x_i(t)$ and $w_{i,j}(t)$ using (1).

$$d_j=\sqrt{\sum_{i=1}^{I}(x_i(t)-w_{i,j}(t))^2} \tag{1}$$

3. Search for a Kohonen layer unit to minimize d_j, which is designated as the winner unit.

4. Update the weight $w_{i,j}(t)$ of a Kohonen layer unit contained in the neighborhood region of the winner unit $N_c(t)$ using (2), where $\alpha(t)$ is a learning coefficient.

$$w_{i,j}(t+1)=w_{i,j}(t)+\alpha(t)(x_i(t)-w_{i,j}(t)) \tag{2}$$

5. Repeat processes 2)–4) up to the maximum iteration of learning.

3.2. Counter Propagation Network (CPN)

A CPN is a learning algorithm that combines the Grossberg learning rule with a SOM [13]. It comprises three layers: an input layer to which training data are supplied, a Kohonen layer in which self-mapping is performed via competitive learning, and a Grossberg layer, which labels the Kohonen layer by the counter propagation of teaching signals. A CPN is useful for automatically determining the label of a Kohonen layer when the category to which training data belongs is predetermined. This labeled Kohonen layer is designated as a category map. The learning procedure of a CPN is described below.

1. Let $w^i_{n,m}(t)$ and $w^j_{n,m}(t)$ be the weights to a Kohonen layer unit (n, m) at time t from an input layer unit i and from a Grossberg layer unit j, respectively. In fact, $w^i_{n,m}$ and $w^j_{n,m}$ are initialized using random numbers.

2. Let $x_i(t)$ be the data input to the input layer unit i at time t, and calculate the Euclidean distance $d_{n,m}$ between $x_i(t)$ and $w^i_{n,m}(t)$ using (3).

$$d_{n,m}=\sqrt{\sum_{i=1}^{I}\left(x_i(t)-w^i_{n,m}(t)\right)^2} \tag{3}$$

3. Search for a Kohonen layer unit to minimize $d_{n,m}$, which is designated as the winner unit.

4. Update weights $w^i_{n,m}(t)$ and $w^j_{n,m}(t)$ of a Kohonen layer unit contained in the neighborhood region of the winner unit $N_c(t)$ using (4) and (5), where $\alpha(t)$, $\beta(t)$ are learning coefficients, and $t_j(t)$ is a teaching signal to the Grossberg layer unit j.

$$w^i_{n,m}(t+1)=w^i_{n,m}(t)+\alpha(t)\left(x_i(t)-w^i_{n,m}(t)\right) \tag{4}$$

$$w^j_{n,m}(t+1)=w^j_{n,m}(t)+\beta(t)\left(t_j(t)-w^j_{n,m}(t)\right) \tag{5}$$

5. Repeat processes 2)–4) up to the maximum iteration of learning.

6. After learning is completed, compare weights $w^j_{n,m}$ observed from each unit of the Kohonen layer, and let the teaching signal of the Grossberg layer with the maximum value be the label of the unit.

4. Proposed method

Figure 4 shows the procedure for generating the FEMap and EMap.

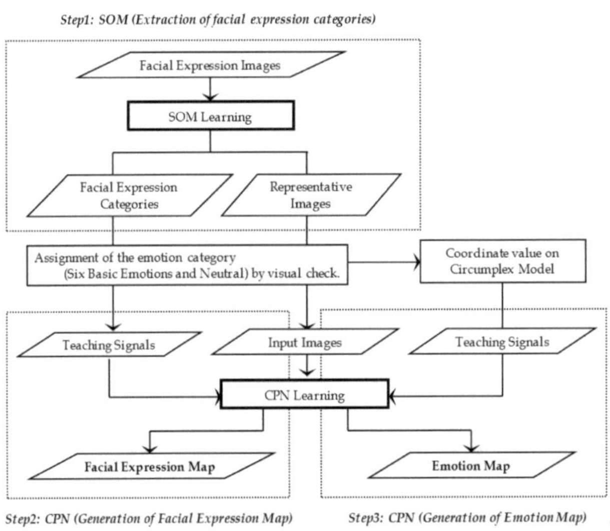

Figure 4. Flow chart of proposed method.

The proposed method consists of the following three steps. First, facial expression images are hierarchically classified using SOMs, and subject-specific facial expression categories are extracted. Next, the CPN is used for data expansion of the facial expression patterns on the basis of the similarity and continuity of each facial expression category. The CPN is a supervised learning algorithm that combines Grossberg's learning rule with the SOM. A category map generated by the method described above is defined as a subject-specific FEMap. Then, a subject-specific emotion feature space is generated. The space matches physical and psychological parameters by inputting the coordinate values to the circumplex model proposed by Russell [8] as teaching signals for the CPN. Then, this complex plane is defined as a subject-specific EMap.

4.1. Extraction of facial expression category

The proposed method was adopted to extract a subject-specific facial expression category hierarchically by using an SOM with a narrow mapping space. An SOM is an unsupervised learning algorithm, and it classifies the given facial expression images in a self-organizing manner, according to their topological characteristics. Hence, it is suitable for classification with an unknown number of categories. Moreover, an SOM compresses the topological information of facial expression images using a narrow mapping space, and it performs classification based on features that roughly divide the training data. We speculate that repeating these steps hierarchically renders the classified amount of change in facial expression patterns comparable; hence, a subject-specific facial expression category can be extracted. Figure 5 shows the extraction of a facial expression category, the details of which are provided below.

1. The expression images described in Section 5.1 were used as training data. The following processing was performed for each facial expression. The training data is assumed to constitute N frames.

2. Learning was conducted using an SOM with a Kohonen layer of five units and an input layer of 40 × 48 units (Fig. 5(a)), where the number of learning sessions was set to 10,000.

3. The weight of the Kohonen layer $W_{i,j}$ ($0 \leq W_{i,j} \leq 1$) was converted to a value of 0—255 at the end of learning, and visualized images were generated (Fig. 5(b)), where n_1—n_5 denote the training data classified into each unit.

4. Five visualized images can be considered as representative vectors of the training data classified into each unit (n_1—n_5). Therefore, a thresholding process was adopted to judge whether a visualized image was suitable as a representative vector. Specifically, for the upper and lower parts of the face shown in Fig. 5(c), a correlation coefficient between a visualized image and classified training data was determined for each unit. The standard deviation of these values was computed. When the standard deviation of both regions was 0.005 or less in all five units, the visualized image was considered to represent the training data, and the subsequent hierarchization processing was cancelled.

5. The correlation coefficient of weight $W_{i,j}$ between each adjacent unit in the Kohonen layer was computed. The Kohonen layer was divided into two parts between the units of the minimum correlation coefficient (Fig. 5(b)).

6. The training data (N_1 and N_2) classified into both sides of the partition were used as new training data; the processing described above was repeated recursively. Consequently, the hierarchical structure of the SOM was generated (Fig. 5(b) and Fig. 5(d)).

7. The lowest category of the hierarchical structure was defined as a facial expression category (Fig. 5(e)). Five visualized images were defined as representative images of each category at the end of learning. Then, the photographer of the facial expression images visually confirmed each facial expression category and conducted implication in emotion categories, such as a neutral facial expression and six basic facial expressions.

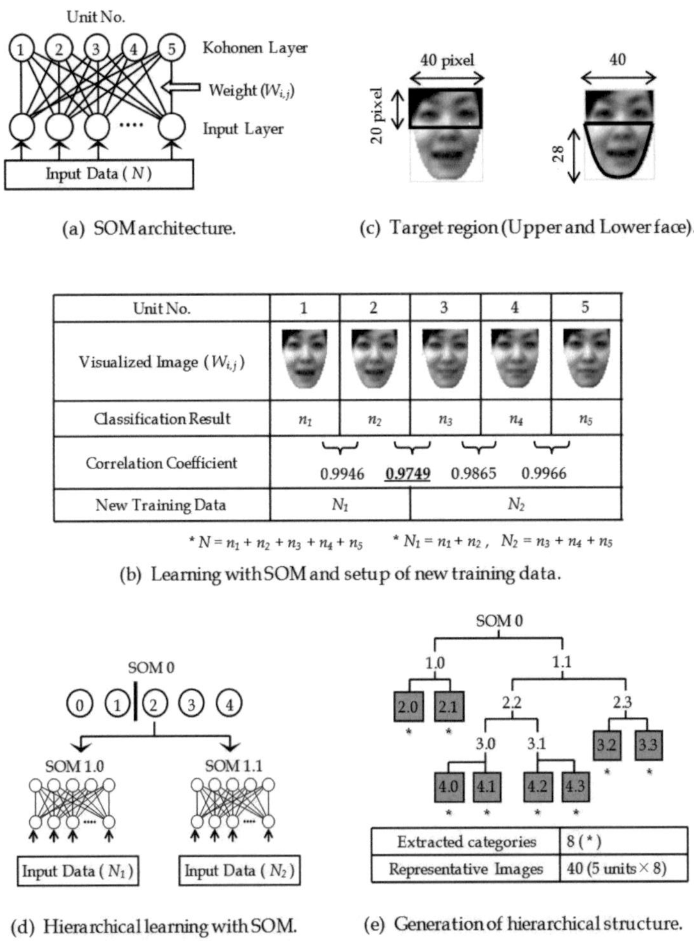

Figure 5. Extraction procedure of facial expression categories.

http://dx.doi.org/10.5772/51136

4.2. Generation of facial expression map

The recognition of a natural facial expression requires the generation of a facial expression pattern (mixed facial expression) that interpolates each emotion category. In the proposed method, the representative image obtained in Section 4.1 was used as training data, and data expansion of facial expression patterns between each emotion category was performed using a CPN with a large mapping space. A CPN is adopted because the teaching signal of the training data is known by the processing described in Section 4.1. The mapping space of the CPN comprises more units than the training data, and it has a torus structure because a large mapping space is assumed to enable the CPN to perform data expansion based on the similarity and continuity of the training data. Figure 6 shows the CPN architecture for generating an FEMap. The details of the processing are provided below.

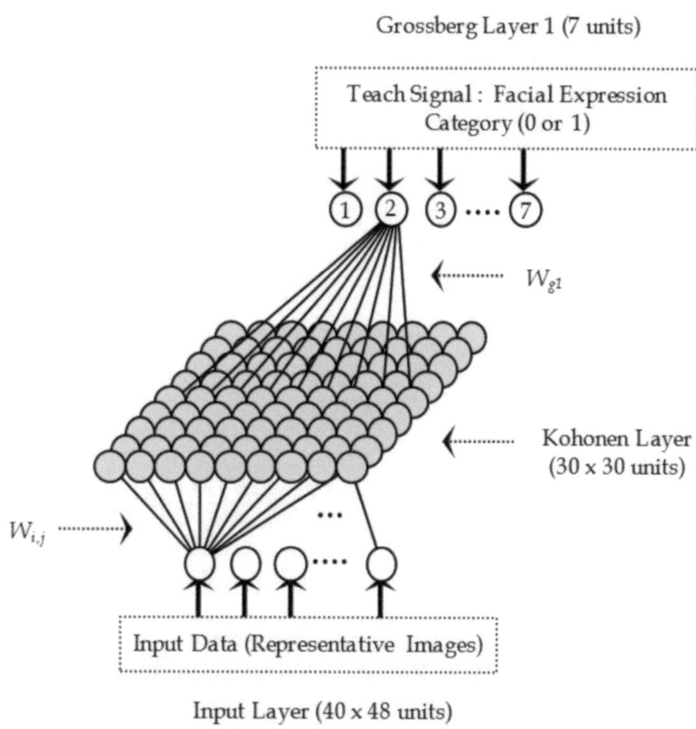

Figure 6. CPN architecture for generation of FEMap.

1. The CPN structure comprises an input layer of 40 × 48 units and a two- or three-dimensional Kohonen layer. In addition, Grossberg layer 1 of seven units was prepared; a teaching signal of six basic facial expressions and a neutral facial expression were input to it.

2. The representative images obtained in Section 4.1 were used as training data, and learning was carried out for each subject. As the teaching signal to Grossberg layer 1, 1 was

input to units that represent emotion categories of representative images; otherwise, 0 was input. The number of learning sessions was set to 20,000.

3. The weights (W_{g1}) of Grossberg layer 1 were compared for each unit of the Kohonen layer at the end of learning; the emotion category with the greatest value was used as the label of the unit. A category map generated by the processing described above was defined as a subject-specific FEMap.

4.3. Generation of emotion map

Although the facial expression patterns of an individual are unique, emotions expressed and recognized from facial expressions by humans are person-independent and universal. Therefore, it is necessary to match the grade of emotion based on a common index for each subject with the grade of change in facial expression patterns described in Section 4.2. The proposed method is based on the circumplex model proposed by Russell as a common index. Specifically, the coordinate values based on the circumplex model are input as teaching signals for the CPN, and the processing described in Section 4.2 is carried out simultaneously. Then, an EMap is generated for matching the grade of change in facial expression patterns with the grade of emotion. Figure 7 shows the procedure for generating the EMap, the details of which are provided below.

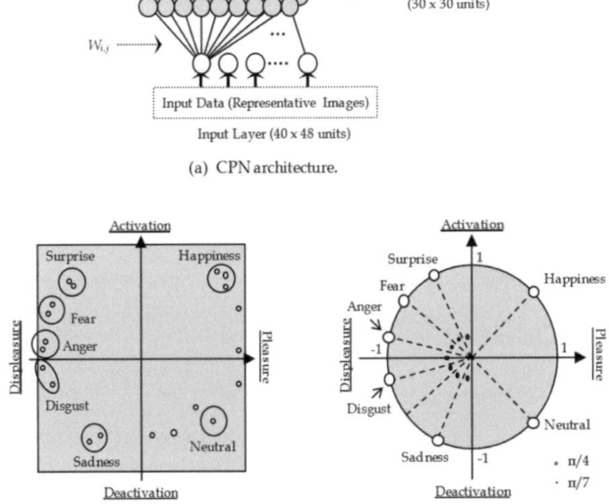

Figure 7. Procedure for generating EMap.

http://dx.doi.org/10.5772/51136

1. Grossberg layer 2 of one unit, which inputs the coordinate values of the circumplex model, was added to the CPN structure (Fig. 7(a)).

2. Each facial expression stimulus was arranged in a circle on a plane centered on "pleasantness" and "arousal" in the circumplex model (Fig. 7(b)). The proposed method expresses this circular space as the complex plane shown in Fig. 7(c), and complex numbers based on the figure were input to Grossberg layer 2 as teaching signals. For example, when the input training data represents the emotion category of happiness, the teaching signal for Grossberg layer 2 is $\cos(\pi/4) + i \sin(\pi/4)$.

3. This processing was repeated up to the maximum learning number.

4. Each unit of the Kohonen layer was plotted onto the complex plane at the end of learning, according to the values of the real and imaginary parts of the weight (W_{g2}) on Grossberg layer 2. Then, this complex plane was defined as a subject-specific EMap.

5. Evaluation experiment

5.1. Expression images

In general, open facial expression databases are used in conventional studies [14, 15]. These databases contain a few images per expression and subject. For this study, we obtained facial expression images of ourselves because the proposed method extracts subject-specific facial expression categories and representative images of each category from large quantities of data.

We discuss a neutral facial expression and six basic facial expressions, namely, anger, sadness, disgust, happiness, surprise, and fear. These expressions are deliberately manifested by a subject. The basic facial expressions were acquired as motion videos, including a process in which the neutral and basic facial expressions were manifested five times; each facial expression was manifested in turns. The motion videos were converted into static images (30 fps, 8-bit gray, 320 × 240 pixels). We processed a region containing facial components. Therefore, a face region image was extracted and normalized according to the following procedures.

1. A face was detected using Haar-like features [16]; a face region image normalized into a size of 80 × 96 pixels was extracted.

2. The image was processed using a median filter for noise removal. Then, smoothing processing was performed after dimension reduction of the image using coarse grain processing (40 × 48 pixels).

3. A pseudo-outline that is common to all the subjects was generated; the face region containing facial components was extracted.

4. 4. Histogram linear transformation was performed for brightness value correction.

Figure 8 shows an example of face region images after extraction and normalization. Table 1 lists the number of acquired frames and the number of frames extracted by the SOM as the training data for the CPN.

The data used in the study was acquired in accordance with ethical regulations regarding research on humans at Akita University, Japan.

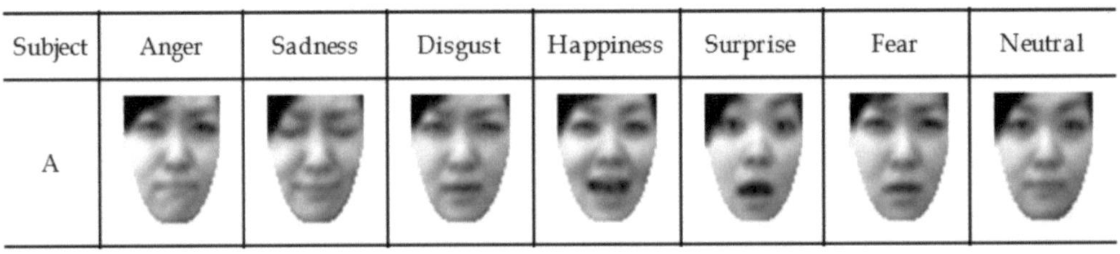

Figure 8. Examples of facial expression images.

Emotion Category	Anger	Sadness	Disgust	Happiness	Surprise	Fear	Neutral	Total
Acquired Frames	454	448	533	530	473	479	605	3,522
Training Data	30	30	40	40	20	30	340	530

Table 1. Number of acquired frames and training data.

5.2. Experiment details

This study examined the training data input method and the number of dimensions of the CPN mapping space. In particular, the following were examined.

i. Method 1: Learning was conducted using a CPN with a two-dimensional Kohonen layer of 30 × 30 units. Moreover, training data were randomly selected and input.

ii. Method 2: The Kohonen layer of the CPN was set to 30 × 30 units, as in Method 1. However, the training data for each emotion category were input by the same ratio.

http://dx.doi.org/10.5772/51136

iii. Method 3: Learning was conducted using a CPN with a three-dimensional Kohonen layer of 10 × 10 × 10 units. The training data input method is the same as that of Method 2.

6. Result and discussion

6.1. Discussion on training data input method

Tables 2 and 3 list the number of Kohonen layer units on the FEMap for Methods 1 and 2, respectively. Figure 9 and 10 shows the FEMaps and the EMaps generated using Methods 1 and 2.

Emotion Category	Anger	Sadness	Disgust	Happiness	Surprise	Fear	Neutral	Total
Number of Units	48	50	69	75	34	55	569	900
Ratio [%]	5.3	5.6	7.7	8.3	3.8	6.1	63.2	100.0

Table 2. Number of units on FEMap (Method 1).

Emotion Category	Anger	Sadness	Disgust	Happiness	Surprise	Fear	Neutral	Total
Number of Units	137	126	121	134	108	134	140	900
Ratio [%]	15.2	14.0	13.4	14.9	12.0	14.9	15.6	100.0

Table 3. Number of units on FEMap (Method 2).

Table 2 shows that the percentage of the neutral facial expression category is high. Moreover, although a mixed facial expression of a neutral expression and six basic expressions is generated, as shown in Fig. 10(a), a mixture of the six basic expressions is not generated. On the other hand, the number of units of each emotion category on the FEMap is roughly constant, as shown in Table 3, and many mixed facial expressions are generated between the expressions on the EMap, as shown in Fig. 10(b). These results suggest that the input ratio of the training data should be constant for every emotion category to effectively generate many mixed facial expressions.

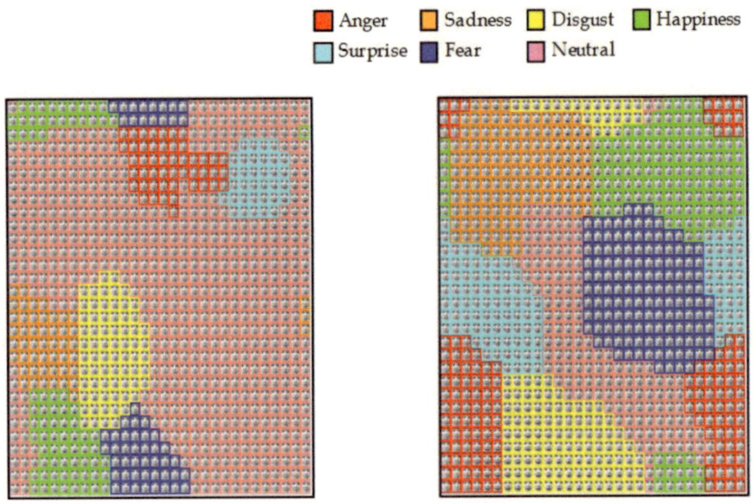

Figure 9. Generation results of FEMap using Methods 1 and 2.

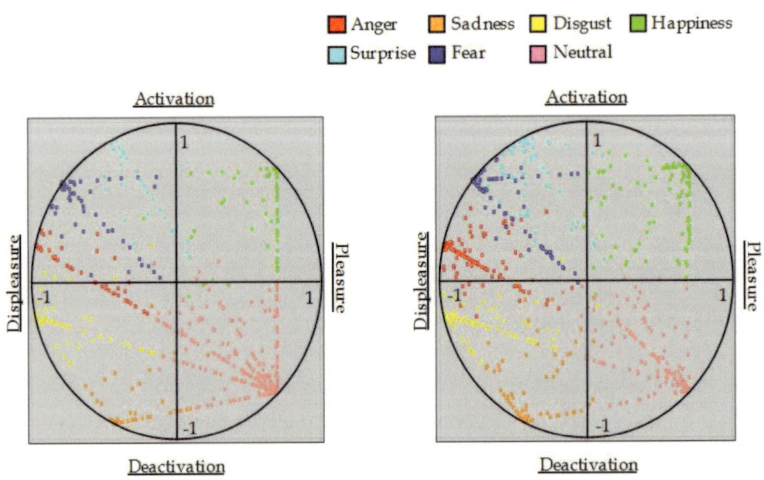

Figure 10. Generation results of EMap using Methods 1 and 2.

http://dx.doi.org/10.5772/51136

6.2. Discussion on number of dimensions of CPN mapping space

The EMap generated by Method 3 is shown in Fig. 11. Figure 12 shows the enlargement of the happiness region in the EMap generated by Methods 2 and 3.

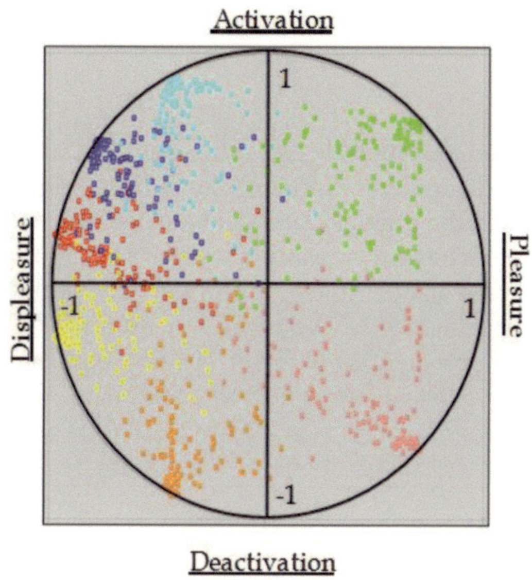

Figure 11. EMap generated by Method 3.

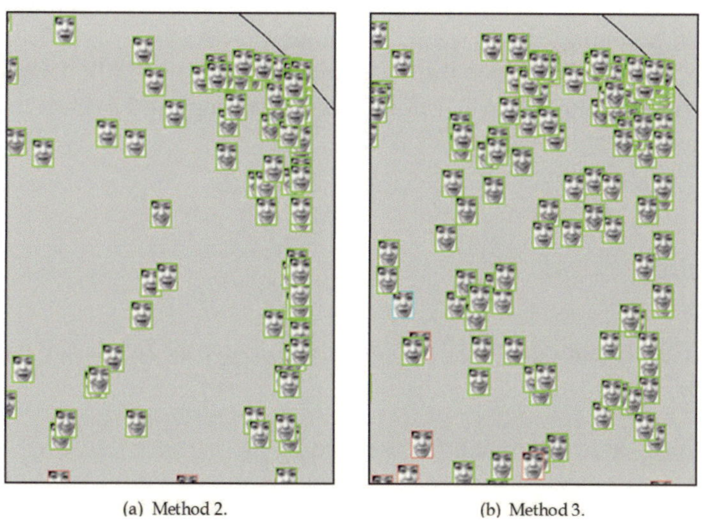

Figure 12. Enlargement of the happiness region in the Emap.

Although the number of Kohonen layer units in Methods 2 and 3 are almost equal (the former is 900 units and the latter is 1,000 units), the generation results of the EMaps differ significantly. In particular, many mixed facial expressions are radially generated from the coordinates of the teaching signal on the circumference, as shown in Fig. 11 and Fig. 12(b). The number of neighboring emotion categories on the FEMap increases as a result of an increase in the number of dimensions of the CPN mapping space.

7. Conclusion

In this chapter, we proposed a method for generating a feature space that expresses the correspondence between the changes in facial expression patterns and the degree of emotions. In addition, we investigated the training data input method and the number of dimensions of the CPN mapping space. The results clearly show that the input ratio of the training data should be constant for every emotion category and the number of dimensions of the CPN mapping space should be extended to effectively express a level of detailed emotion. We plan to experimentally evaluate emotion estimation using the generated feature spaces.

Acknowledgements

This work was supported by a Grant-in-Aid for Scientific Research on Innovative Areas "Face perception and recognition: Multidisciplinary approaching to understanding face processing mechanism (No.4002)" (23119717) from the Ministry of Education, Culture, Sports, Science and Technology, Japan.

This paper is based on "Generation of Emotional Feature Space for Facial Expression Recognition using Self-Mapping," by M. Ishii, T. Simodate, Y. Kageyama, T. Takahashi, and M. Nishida, which will be presented at the SICE Annual Conference 2012, an international conference on Instrumentation, Control, Information Technology and System Integration, to be held in Akita, Japan, from August 20-23, 2012.

Author details

Masaki Ishii[1*], Toshio Shimodate[2], Yoichi Kageyama[2], Tsuyoshi Takahashi[2] and Makoto Nishida[3]

*Address all correspondence to: ishii@akita-pu.ac.jp

1 Faculty of Systems Science and Technology, Akita Prefectural University, Japan
2 Graduate School of Engineering and Resource Science, Akita University, Japan
3 Akita University, Japan

References

[1] Pantic, M., & Rothkrantz, L. J. M. (2000). Automatic Analysis of Facial Expressions: The State of the Art. *IEEE Trans. Pattern Analysis and Machine Intelligence,* 22(12), 1424-1445.

[2] Tian, Y. L., Kanade, T., & Cohn, J. F. (2001). Recognizing Action Units for Facial Expression Analysis. *IEEE Trans. Pattern Analysis and Machine Intelligence,* 23(2), 97-116.

[3] Akamatsu, S. (2002). Recognition of Facial Expressions by Human and Computer [I]: Facial Expressions in Communications and Their Automatic Analysis by Computer. The Journal of the Institute of Electronics, Information, and Communication Engineers (in Japanese), 85(9), 680-685.

[4] Akamatsu, S. (2002). Recognition of Facial Expressions by Human and Computer [II]: The State of the Art in Facial Expression Analysis-1; Automatic Classification of Facial Expressions. The Journal of the Institute of Electronics, Information, and Communication Engineers (in Japanese), 85(10), 766-771.

[5] Akamatsu, S. (2002). Recognition of Facial Expressions by Human and Computer [III]: The State of the Art in Facial Expression Analysis-2; Recognition of Facial Actions. The Journal of the Institute of Electronics, Information, and Communication Engineers (in Japanese), 85(12), 936-941.

[6] Akamatsu, S. (2003). Recognition of Facial Expressions by Human and Computer [IV: Finish]: Toward Computer Recognition of Facial Expressions Consistent with the Perception by Human. The Journal of the Institute of Electronics, Information, and Communication Engineers (in Japanese), 86(1), 54-61.

[7] Fasel, B., & Luettin, J. (2003). Automatic Facial Expression Analysis: A Survey. *Pattern Recognition,* 36, 259-275.

[8] Russell, J. A., & Bullock, M. (1985). Multidimensional Scaling of Emotional Facial Expressions: Similarity from Preschoolers to Adults. *J. Personality and Social Psychology,* 48, 1290-1298.

[9] Yamada, H. (2000). Models of Perceptual Judgments of Emotion from Facial Expressions. Japanese Psychological Review in Japanese), 43(2), 245-255.

[10] Ishii, M., Sato, K., Madokoro, H., & Nishida, M. (2008). Generation of Emotional Feature Space based on Topological Characteristics of Facial Expression Images. Proc. IEEE Int. Conf. Automatic Face and Gesture Recognition All pages (CD-ROM), 6.

[11] Ishii, M., Sato, K., Madokoro, H., & Nishida, M. (2008). Extraction of Facial Expression Categories and Generation of Emotion Map Using Self-Mapping. IEICE Trans. Information and Systems (in Japanese), J91-D(11), 2659-2672.

[12] Kohonen, T. (1995). Self-Organizing Maps. *Springer Series in Information Sciences,* 10.1007/978-3-642-97610-0.

[13] Nielsen, R. H. (1987). Counter Propagation Networks. *Applied Optics*, 26(23), 4979-4984.

[14] Pantic, M., Valstar, M. F., Rademaker, R., & Maat, L. (2005). Webbased Database for Facial Expression Analysis. *Proc. IEEE Int. Conf. Multimedia and Expo*, 317-321.

[15] Gross, R. (2005). Face Databases, Handbook of Face Recognition. , S.Li and A.Jain, ed., Springer-Verlag

[16] Lienhart, R., & Maydt, J. (2002). An Extended Set of Haar-like Features for Rapid Object Detection. *Proc. IEEE Int. Conf. Image Processing*, 1, 900-903.

Chapter 8

A Self Organizing Map Based Motion Classifier with an Extension to Fall Detection Problem and Its Implementation on a Smartphone

Wattanapong Kurdthongmee

Additional information is available at the end of the chapter

http://dx.doi.org/10.5772/51002

1. Introduction

Automatic classification of human motions is very useful in many application areas. The characteristics of the motion types and patterns can be used as an indicator of one''s mobility level, latent chronic diseases and aging process [1]. The motion types can be employed to further make a decision if one is at risk; i.e. the motion type or the transition between the motion types may be risky and is likely to cause a fall. Alternatively, the motion types may be useful as an indication to request for a close observation/attention; i.e. a jogging is higher risk and requires a close attention than a normal walk especially for elderly people. The indication may be used to support the feature of a video surveillance system for monitoring elderly people. With respect to these examples of application areas in combination with the requirement to automate monitoring of elderly people as a result of "aging society", the demands for an automatic motion classification have been increased. To observe and make relation to motion types, either an acceleration sensor or video system has been widely accepted as useful.

In this chapter, we present the application of the self organizing map (SOM) to an automatic classification of basic, i.e. activities of daily live - ADL, human motions. To be specific, SOM is employed to solve the human motion classification problem. In our proposed approach, SOM is trained with motion parameters captured from a specific wearer and used to perform an adaptive motion types clustering and classification functions. This results in a codebook with different clusters of motion types whose parameters are similar. Instead of using a codebook alone, the algorithm is proposed in order to distinguish between different basic motion types whose motion parameters are similar and mapped to the same cluster as clearly reflected by the codecook. In addition, the frequency of occurrences from different motion types resulted from SOM classifications are used to make decision for the most probable motion type. By mean of SOM, it makes the resulting application adaptable to wearers of different ages and motion conditions. With the success of classification of different motion types, we propose extending the algorithm to perform fall detection. In this case, SOM is trained and labeled with a majority of data from fall curves. As the characteristics of the fall curves is almost similar to the motion types with rapid transition of acceleration, the motion type is employed to support the differentiation between fall and other rapid transition motion types. It can be summarized that the contributions of our research are twofolds. Firstly, the motion types classification algorithm employing SOM is proposed and validated for its correctness with respect to the continuous waveform of mixed motion types. Secondly, the motion types is successfully used to distinguish between fall and other motion types.

The rest of this chapter is organized as follows. Section 2 presents related work which is focused on the class of sensor attachment to body for motion classification and fall detection algorithms. The background of SOM, data capturing and SOM training and labeling stages are detailed in Section 3. The proposed algorithm for motion type classification and fall detection are then explained in Section 4. In Section 5, the validation results from the implementation of the proposed algorithms are given and discussed. In addition, the extensions of the algorithm to the fall detection problem is then given. Eventually, the implementation of the algorithm on the platform of choice for practical use is presented in Section 6. Finally, the chapter is concluded in Section 7..

2. Related Work

In this section, the survey of the previously proposed motion classification and fall detection algorithms are given. In general, the previously proposed motion classification algorithms can be classified into two categories: acceleration sensor based detection and video processing based detection. Motion classification using acceleration sensor has been widely studied and resulted in two difference classification schemes which are the threshold-based and statistical classification schemes [1]. Threshold-based motion classification takes advantage of known knowledge and information about the movements to be classified. It uses a hierarchical algorithm structure, a decision tree like, to discriminate between activity states. A set of empirically-derived thresholds for each classification subclass are required. A systematic approach for motion classification based on a hierarchical decision tree is presented by [2]. A generic classification framework presented in [3] consists of a hierarchical binary tree for classifying postural transitions, falling, walking, and other movements using signals from a wearable triaxial acceleration sensor. This modular framework also allows modifying individual classification algorithm for particular purposes.

Tilt sensing is a basic function provided by acceleration sensors which respond to gravity or constant acceleration. Therefore, human postures, such as upright and lying, can be distinguished according to the magnitude of acceleration signals along sensitive axes from only one acceleration sensor worn at the waist and torso [4, 6. However, the single-acceleration sensor approach has difficulty in distinguishing between standing and sitting as both are upright postures, although a simplified scheme with tilt threshold to distinguish standing and sitting has been proposed [4]. Standing and sitting postures can be distinguished by observing different orientations of body segments where multiple acceleration sensors are attached. For example, two acceleration sensors can be attached to the torso and thigh to distinguish standing and sitting postures from static activities [7, 8, 9]. Trunk tilt variation due to sit-stand postural transitions can be measured by integrating the signal from a gyroscope attached to the chest of the subject [5]. Sit-stand postural transitions can be identified according to the patterns of vertical acceleration from an acceleration sensor worn at the waist [6].

Acceleration signals can be used to determine walking in ambulatory movement. Walking can be identified by frequency-domain analysis [4, 10]. It is characterized by a variance of over 0.02 g in vertical acceleration and frequency peak within 1–3 Hz in the signal spectrum [10]. Discrete wavelet transform is used to distinguish walking on a level ground and walking on a stairway [11].

Motion classification using statistical schemes utilize a supervised machine learning procedure, which associates an observation (or features) of movement to possible movement states in terms of the probability of the observation. Those schemes include, for example, k-nearest neighbor (kNN) classification [8, 12], support vector machines (SVM) [13, 14], Naive Bayes classifier [15, 16], Gaussian mixture model (GMM) [17] and hidden Markov model (HMM) [18, 19]. Naive Bayes classifier determines activities according to the probabilities of the signal pattern of the activities. In GMM approach, the likelihood function is not a typical Gaussian distribution. The weights and parameters describing probability of activities are obtained by the expectation-maximization algorithm. Transitions between activities can be described as a Markov chain that represents the likelihood (probability) of transitions between possible activities (states). The HMM is applied to determine unknown states at any time according to observable activity features (extracted from accelerometry data) corresponding to the states. After the HMM is trained by example data, it can be used to determine possible activity state transitions.

From our point of view, there are several drawbacks of the previously proposed approaches. That is to say the differences in the collected data among different persons, or even within the same person but different time and sensor variable sampling rate, which are very common, are not taken into account. The previously proposed motion classifiers are almost all in the class of a pre-programmed system with the threshold for making decision from limited samples. This is in contrast to our proposed approach which relies on utilizing SOM to make it adaptable to a particular wearer. The movement nature of the wearer is taken into consideration and used for training and labeling and, in turn, used for fall detection and alert of the wearer. The details of our proposed algorithm are given in the next sections.

3. Background, Data Capturing and SOM Training and Labeling Stages

In this section, we briefly describe the background of SOM. The procedures for capturing data, the SOM training and labeling stages, and the proposed motion classification algorithm are then detailed.

3.1. A Brief Introduction to SOM

In general, SOM is one of the most prominent artificial neural network models adhering to the unsupervised learning paradigm [20]. It has been employed to solve problems in a wide variety of application domains. For the applications in engineering domain, it was elaborately surveyed and reported in [21]. Generally speaking, the SOM model consists of a number of neural processing elements (PEs) or "codebook". Each of the PE, i, which is called "codeword' is assigned an n-dimensional weight vector m_i where n is the dimension of an input data. During the training stage, the iteration t starts with the selection of one input data $p(t)$. $p(t)$ is presented to SOM and each codeword determines its activation by means of the distance between $p(t)$ and its own weight vector. The codeword with the lowest activation is referred to as the winner, m_c, or the best matching unit (BMU) at the learning iteration t, i.e.:

$$m_c(t) = min_i \quad p(t) - m_i(t) \quad . \tag{1}$$

The Euclidean distance (ED) is one of the most popular way to measure the distance between $p(t)$ and a codeword"s weight vector $m_i(t)$. It is defined by the following equation:

$$d(p(t), m_i(t)) = \sqrt{(p(t)_1 - m_i(t)_1)^2 + (p(t)_2 - m_i(t)_2)^2 + \ldots + (p(t)_n - m_i(t)_n)^2} \tag{2}$$

Finally, the weight vector of the winner codeword as well as the weight vectors of selected codewords in the vicinity of the winner are adapted. This adaptation is implemented as a gradual reduction of the component-wise difference between the input data and weight vector of the codeword, i.e.:

$$m_i(t+1) = m_i(t) + a(t) \quad h_{ci}(t) \quad [p(t) - m_i(t)]. \tag{3}$$

Geometrically speaking, the weight vector of codewords of the adapted units are moved a bit towards the input data. The amount of weight vector movement is guided by a learning rate, α , decreasing with time. The number of codewords that are affected by this adaptation is determined by a neighborhood function, h_{ci} which also decreases with time. This movement makes the distance between these codewords decrease and, thus, the weight vector of the codewords become more similar to the input data. The respective codeword is more likely to be a winner at future presentations of this input data. The consequence of adapting not only the winner alone but also a number of codewords in the neighborhood of the winner leads to a spatial clustering of similar input patterns in neighboring parts of the SOM.

Thus, similarities between input data that are presented in the n-dimensional input space are mirrored within the two-dimensional output space of SOM or SOM map. The training stage is terminated after the final SOM map is labelled with some known conditions.

The classification stage is very similar to the learning stage with some exceptions. That is to say there is no need to perform adaptation to the winner codeword and its neighbours of the SOM map with respect to the input data. Instead, the label of the winner codeword corresponding to the input data is returned and used for further interpretation; i.e. if the input data is mapped to the codeword with jogging motion type label.

3.2 The Motion Data Capturing and Preparation Procedures

Our proposed algorithm relies on using motion data which is captured from different basic daily activity types for training SOM. To efficiently and economically get such data, an application was developed to be executed on a smartphone instead of relying on an embedded data acquisition with a built-in acceleration sensor. A smartphone was targeted from the point of view that it provides all the necessary hardware to serve our purposes. A smartphone with an Android operating system was selected as it is an open platform device 22. The platform, in general, provides support for interfacing with a built-in triaxial acceleration sensor via Application Program Interfaces (APIs). With respect to the developed application, the following roles are performed during the data capturing stage:

- Capture motion data from a triaxial acceleration sensor in as fixed a sampling period manner as possible,
- Wirelessly transmit the captured motion data to the computer server via Bluetooth.

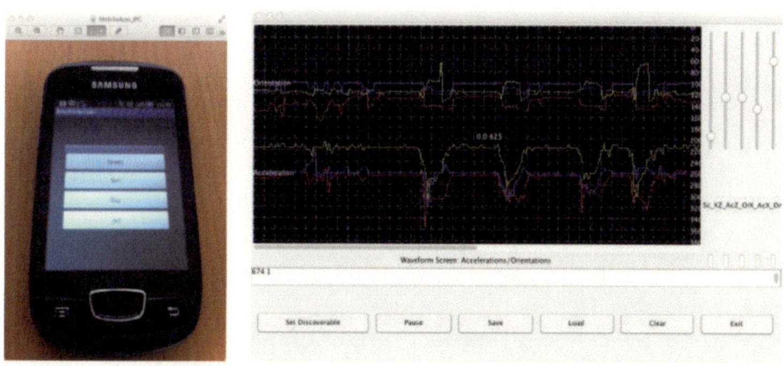

(a) (b)

Figure 1. (a) The main screen of the application running on the mobile phone and (b) the screen captured of a personal computer application.

The Mobile Sensor Actuator Link (MSAL) API was employed to implement the applications running both on a smartphone and a personal computer with the required functionalities. The API is an open source and freely available from Ericsson Laboratory 23. Figure 1 shows the main screen of the application running on the smartphone and the screen captured of a personal computer application. It is noted that the waveforms shown on the application screen in this case are three parameters along the x, y and z-axes from the acceleration sensors and the gyroscope. Only the parameters from the acceleration sensor are used in this experiment.

In the course of our experimentations, subjects were requested to perform the following motion types, which cover their basic daily activity types, while the smartphone with the installed application previously detailed was attached to their waist: {jogging (0), normal walk (1), walk upstairs and downstairs (1), stand-sit-stand (2), fall on the floor with support of bed (3), different types of fall on the arm chair (4), fast walk (5)}. The numbers in the parentheses represent the annotations of the motion types on the codebook resulted from the SOM labeling stage (to be described in Section 3.3. The first four and the last motion types were continuously captured for one minute and the fifth and sixth ones were requested to repeat 10 times each. The captured data for each motion type was saved by the server side application to a separate file. The captured motion data files for the first four and the last motion types required less preprocessing. This comes from the fact that these motion types could be performed almost continuously by subjects. As a result, the motion waveforms that represent these motion types have nearly continuous form. These data files were only required to convert from the raw data (separated a_x, a_y, and a_z) to be in the vector summed acceleration a form by applying Eq. 4. Doing this way created the data which are independent of the attachment orientation of the smartphone during data collection stage. Then, the time stamp t was attached to the vector summed acceleration data point by point in order to form the (a_i, t_i)-array. Figure 2 shows the motion waveforms in the vector summed acceleration form for 30 second periods of all captured motion types.

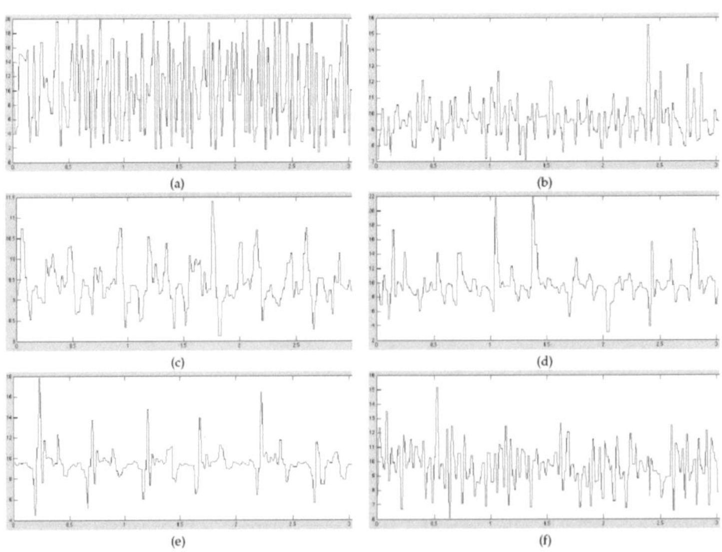

Figure 2. The motion waveforms in the vector summed acceleration form for 30 second periods of (a) jogging, (b) normal walk, (c) sit-stand-sit, (d) fall, (e) fall on the arm chair and (f) fast walk.

In contrast to the first group of captured data described earlier, the captured data files for the fifth and sixth motion types, which are the fall on the floor with support of bed and different types of fall on the arm chair, were required to preprocess. This was done in order to extract only motion waveforms, whose forms are (a_i, t_i), which were relevant to the falls.

$$a=\sqrt{a_x^2 + a_y^2 + a_z^2} \tag{4}$$

Followings are our findings from several experimentations during the training stage:

- the preprocessing stage for the motion types of "fall on the floor with support of bed" and "different types of fall on the arm chair" can be eliminated and replaced by using multiple set of training data from these two motion types.
- the combinations of following 5 motion parameters give rise to the highest degree of motion classification correctness: the origin of a segment (a_i), the endpoint of a segment (a_{i+1}), the endpoint of the adjacent segment (a_{i+2}), the slope of a segment, and the length of a segment. This can be represented by:

$$\left(a_i,\ a_{i+1},\ a_{i+2},\ \frac{(a_{i+1}-a_i)}{(t_{i+1}-t_i)},\ (a_{i+1}-a_i)\right) \tag{5}$$

All of the preprocessed data files were converted, from the vector summed acceleration and time stamp format, to be in the form defined by Eq. 5 on a segment by segment basis. At this point, the procedures taken to create the training data set ready for the training stage can be summarized as follows:

- Apply Eq. 4 to all elements of an array of raw acceleration data (a_x, a_y, a_z) in order to convert to an array of vector summed acceleration along with the time stamp format: (a_i, t_i). The process is applied to all arrays of raw acceleration data and gives rise to a set of T_m arrays where m is a motion type index.
- Create an array of $(S_j, S_{j+1}, S_{j+2}, O_j, m_j)$ by applying Eq. 5 to members at i, $i+1$, and $i+2$ of the T_m arrays. In addition, the motion type index, m, is added to all members of the T_m arrays.
- Merge all T_m arrays together by taking all data from the arrays whose motion types are jogging, normal walk, walk upstairs and downstairs, stand-sit-stand, and fast walk and using 3 repeats of fall on the floor with support of bed and different types of fall on the arm chair. All members of the merged arrays are then randomly rearranged. At this point, the training data with random mixture of motion data from all motion types, T, is obtained.

3.3. The SOM Training and Labeling Stages

In order to train and label SOM with the already prepared training data, the algorithms are implemented in the Matlab scripts. We keep the implementations to be as simple as possible as the algorithms will finally be exploited on the smartphone platform. Our training algorithm behaves by:

- single visiting to a member of the training data, T, of size k,
- using a simple learning function with linearly decayed learning rate. The learning rate is allowed to change 256 times with a linear decay rate of $\frac{1}{256}$. This is equivalent to changing the learning rate when $\frac{k}{256}$ members of training data is visited.
- using a simple neighborhood function of the form:

$$\beta(r, c) = a - \left(\sqrt{(r - r_{BMU})^2 + (c - c_{BMU})^2}\right)\frac{a}{2} \tag{6}$$

where $\beta(r, c)$ is the learning coefficient of the codeword at (r, c). α is the learning coefficient of the best matching unit (BMU) codeword whose index is at (r_{BMU}, c_{BMU}). Only the positive value of $\beta(r, c)$ is used to update the weight of the codeword.

For the labeling stage of the algorithm, the training data T is once again presented to the codebook resulted from the training stage. The BMU, whose index is at (r_{BMU}, c_{BMU}), is searched for a given input segment S_k which is a member of T. The matching frequency of the codeword at (r_{BMU}, c_{BMU}) is then incremented. Upon all S_k which is a member of T has been visited, the algorithm labels a codeword with the motion type whose frequency is the highest. It is noted that the matching frequency of a codeword is later used to make decision for the motion type of an unknown motion type segment. That is to say if an unknown motion type segment is found to match to the codeword at (r_m, c_m), its motion type is the motion type of the codeword at (r_m, c_m).

Figure 3 illustrates a codebook along with the projection maps on the training data planes for a configuration of 5×7 codewords. It can be clearly observed that the codewords are clustered very well. The separations between the clusters of slow transition motion types; normal walk (1), walk upstairs and downstairs (1), stand-sit-stand (2), and fast transition motion types; jogging (0), fall on the floor with support of bed (3), different types of fall on the arm chair (4), fast walk (5), are clearly noticeable. It, however, shows some imperfect clusters with mixed fast transition motion types; i.e. the cluster at the bottom left of the map which consists of these motion types: jogging (0), fall on the floor with support of bed (3), different types of fall on the arm chair (4) and fast walk (5). These can be interpreted that the fast transition motion types have some common motion parameters. This is confirmed by a section of comparative acceleration waveforms of the fast and slow transition motion types in Figure 4. At this point, it can be summarized that the codebook cannot be employed alone to the problem of motion classification. In the next section, we detail our proposed algorithm that makes use of the queried results from the SOM to improve the correctness of motion classification and to distinguish between each motion type in the fast transition group. The algorithm is also further designed to support detection of fall.

http://dx.doi.org/10.5772/51002

4. Our Proposed Algorithms

Our algorithm is proposed to compensate for the imperfect clustering of codebook mentioned earlier. It is illustrated in Algorithm 1. There are two inputs to the algorithm which are the codebook C and an unknown motion type segment S_t; i.e. the segment to be queried for its motion type with the form defined by Eq. 5. The codebook C is the one obtained from the training and labeling stages and assigned to the algorithm only once. It can, however, be changed to be specific to the motion conditions of users in practical usage. For a motion segment S_t, the algorithm finds the motion type, *segmentMotionType*, by querying the codebook. The set of query result is as follows: *{typeJogging, typeWalk, typeSitStandSit, typeFall, typeFallOnArmChair, typeFastWalk}*. Instead of using the query result right away which is very prone to error due to the imperfect clustering, the algorithm only registers the current segment motion type. This is performed by incrementing the counter at the corresponding index of the motion type in the *motionFrequency*-array. The algorithm keeps performing in this way for the new incoming segments without making decision for a period of *samplePeriod*. At the end of the Periodg, the motion type can be concluded that it is the one whose the occurrence frequency, or the value of the counter, within the *motionFrequency*-array is the highest. With respect to the algorithm, these processes are performed within the first if-condition. Upon finishing decision making of the motion type, the algorithm clears up the *motionFrequency*-array to ready it for the next period.

The algorithm described so far can be used to make decision between the motion types in the fast and slow transition groups. It, however, fails to distinguish between a jogging and a fall. The failure comes from the fact that these two motion types have fairly similar segment characteristics. These are confirmed by the codebooks (see Figure 3 in the region A, B and C) which show us that codewords of these two motion types seem to be close neighbors of each other. The algorithm is, therefore, incorporated with additional features to differentiate between these two motion types. Let's observe the second if-condition in Algorithm 1. First of all, the algorithm checks whether or not the segment under consideration is a falling edge whose slope is negative. If it is, the algorithm further uses the codebook query result, *segmentMotionType*, once again to check whether or not the segment is in the type of fall. Both testing results are used in combination with the current determination of the motion type result obtained from the first section of the algorithm. If the determination of the motion type result is of type jogging, it is likely that the segment under consideration is also of type jogging. Otherwise, the segment of type fall is detected alone and it is likely that a true fall is likely to occur under an additional condition that the endpoint of the segment, a_t, is less than a threshold.

In the next section, the experimental results after applying the proposed algorithm to the continuously captured motion data are presented.

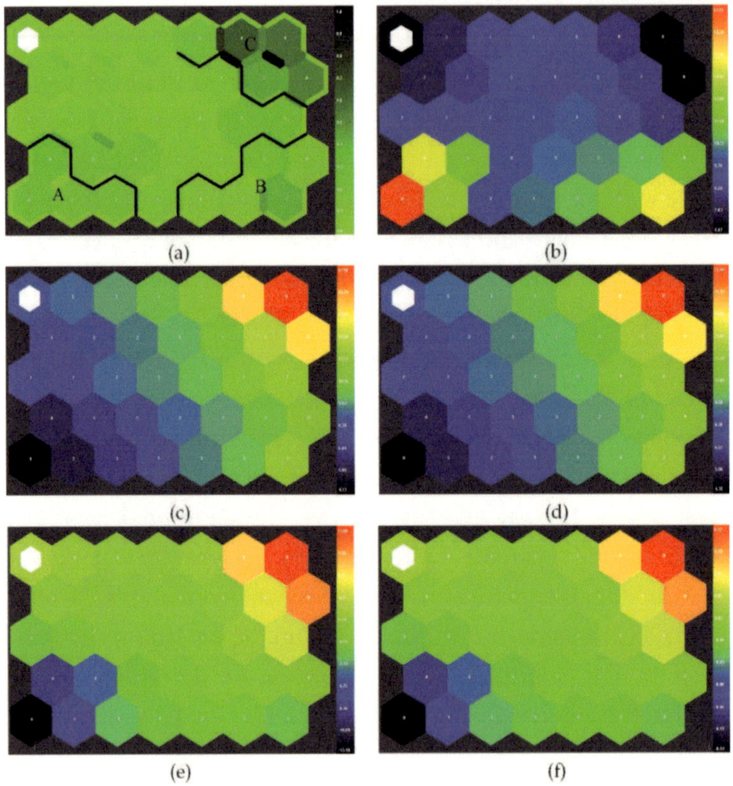

Figure 3. The codebook for a configuration of 5×7 codewords: (a) the original map, (b) - (f) the map projections on the origin of a segment (a_i), the endpoint of a segment (a_{i+1}), the endpoint of the adjacent segment (a_{i+2}), the slope of a segment, and the length of a segment, respectively. It is noted that the parameter value of a codeword is represented by a color whose value is shown on the right hand side bar.

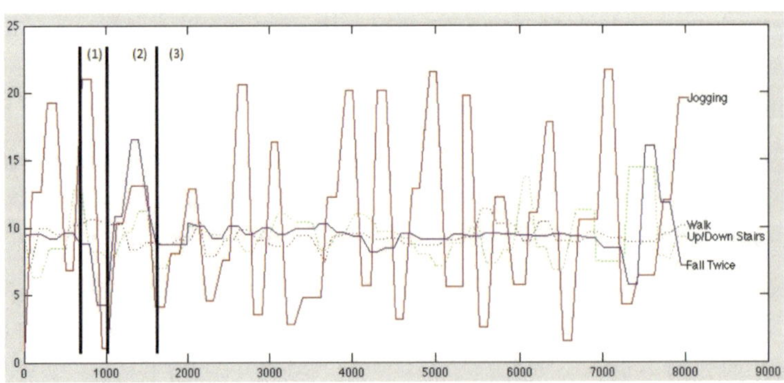

Figure 4. A section of comparative acceleration waveforms of the fast and slow transition motion types

5. Experimental Results and Discussions

During the course of our experimentations, the proposed algorithm was coded in Matlab script and verified its correctness with two sets of real and continuously captured motion data. The verification was performed on a personal computer. We avoided verifying the algorithm on a separate motion type waveform and reporting the false positive (FP) and fast negative (FN) results. It is true that this approach is commonly used in the previous publications. From our point of view, it makes more sense to perform verifications on the continuous motion data as it ensures that the proposed algorithm can be practically used. In addition, the weakness of almost all proposed algorithms in this application domain is that they do not point out clearly how to distinguish between fall and jogging or fast walk. They only focus on finding the representative, average and standard deviation, threshold slope of falls, from different people with different types of fall, in order to make a correct decision of fall. Our verification approach, however, has a weakness as it lacks a standard motion data to benchmark the proposed algorithm. This left us no choice apart from employing our captured motion data. Followings are the details of our motion data sets.

```
input : A codebook: C
input : a motion segment: S_t = {a_{t-1}, a_t, a_t, (a_t - a_{t-1})/(T_t - T_{t-1}), (a_t - a_{t-1})}
output: A classification result of 'Yes', if fall is detected.
/* Query SOM for the motion type of S_t segment. The query result is
   one of the following set: {typeJogging, typeWalk,
   typeSitStandSit, typeFall, typeFallOnArmChair, typeFastWalk}      */
segmentMotionType = SOMQuery(C, S_t);
motionFrequency(segmentMotionType) = motionFrequency(segmentMotionType) + 1;
/* Check if a period is longer than the duration to make decision of
   motion type.                                                      */
if stopWatch > samplePeriod then
    stopWatch = 0;
    /* Motion type is the highest frequency index in the
       motionFrequency-array.                                        */
    motionType = arg(max(motionFrequency));
    /* Reset motionFrequency                                         */
    motionFrequency(0..end) = 0;
end
/* Check if this is a falling edge segment.                          */
if a_t - a_{t-1} < 0 then
    if (segmentMotionType == typeFall) or (segmentMotionType == typeFastWalk) then
        /* Free-falling segment type is detected if the following case
           is true.                                                  */
        if motionType = typeJogging then
            if a_t < Threshold then
                return (Yes)
            else
                return (No)
            end
        else
            return (No)
        end
    end
end
```

Algorithm 1: A fall detection algorithm employing SOM and motion segments transition: Rising edge.

- Set 1: 78 seconds of normal walk, 41 seconds of fast walk, 37.5 seconds of jogging and 12 repeated falls with 10 seconds duration between a consecutive pair of falls.
- Set 2: Normal walk, fast walk, jogging, normal walk, fast walk, jogging, normal walk, fast walk, pause, fast walk, jogging and 10 repeated falls.

The experimental results with respect to these two sets of motion data are illustrated in Figure 5. In the figure, the green waveforms are the captured motion data in the vector summed acceleration form. The red waveforms are the motion types determined by the algorithm. The blue peaks are the positions of fall detected by the algorithm. The red waveforms and the blue peaks are automatically inserted by the algorithm during operation. The numbers labelled on the left bottom of the figures represent the motion type scale; i.e. the first motion type detected by the algorithm in Figure 5(a) is "1" which is a normal walk. It is noted that we avoid showing the motion type whose number is "0" (jogging) as it overlaps with the x-axis.

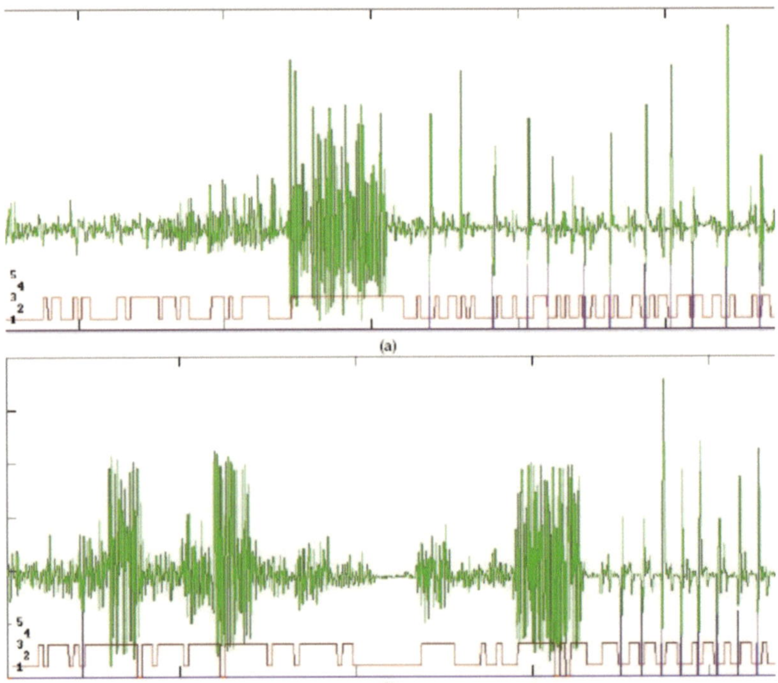

Figure 5. Experimental results after applying the algorithm to two different data: the green waveforms are the captured motion data, the red waveforms are the motion types and the blue peaks are the detected falls.

With respect to Figure 5, it can be seen that the algorithm, in conjunction with the configuration of codebook detailed in Section 3.3, is capable of detecting the changes in motion type. It is capable of detecting all fall curves in both motion data sets. It, however, cannot correctly handle the case of jogging. That is to say the algorithm reports the fast walk motion type instead of jogging. This is quite obvious in the middle of Figure 5(a) where the jogging motion type is captured. The interesting point of the detection results is found after magnifying the detected parts of fall curves as illustrated in Figure 6. Clearly, it can be seen that the algorithm is able to make decisions if falls occur almost one segment ahead of the first impact. This is equivalent to approximately 133 mS with respect to the data sampling period used during the data capturing stage. It is very useful from the point of view that there exists a system to get a pre-impact alert signal and handle in the way to prevent severe impact. This is an open question for our future research project.

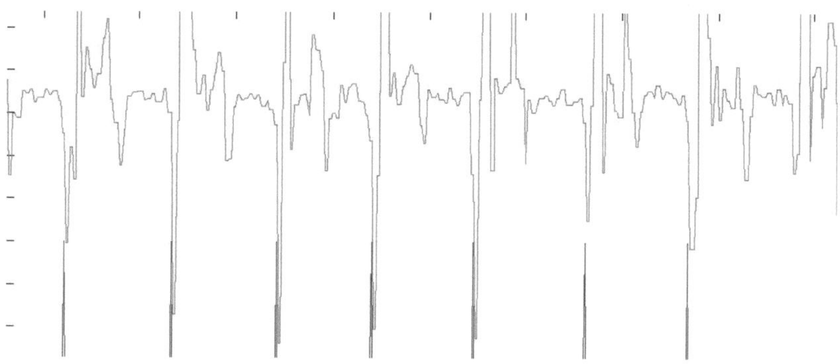

Figure 6. Magnifying the detected fall curves to show that the algorithm can make decision before the first impact.

After verifying the proposed algorithm with different configurations of SOM map, we found a configuration that gave rise to an acceptable correctness in term of motion classification result. This configuration has *8×8* codewords and the data preparation procedure differs from the previously described one in the way that it used only one, instead of three, data from the motion type of fall on the floor with support of bed. Figure 7 shows the classification results with respect to both motion data sets. The similarity between the verification results with respect to both data sets is that the algorithm can no longer detect fall. From Figure 7(a), the algorithm is capable of detection even a short period of normal walk with unusual waveforms which is the first peak of fast walk motion type. The fluctuations between normal and fast walks just a moment before jogging are also detected and correctly reported. In addition, the algorithm gives rise to a correct report during jogging motion type. The results in Figure 7(b) further confirms the correctness. The first two joggings are successfully detected. All motions ahead of the first jogging and in between the first and second and the second and the third joggings are correctly recognized and reported.

At this point, we are trying to give an answer to the question why two configurations of SOM map lead to different detection results. It can be said that the first configuration of training data is designed with the aim to make the abruptly changes of segment, fall segments - to be specific, detectable. In addition, the resulting SOM map must be capable of providing the current motion type to the algorithm. Because the motion type of either jogging or fast walk is used to reject the misjudgment of fall type. This is in contrast to the second configuration which is designed to distinguish among the continuous types of motion. In the first configuration, we provide the SOM with the majority of data from multiple sets of fall curves. This results in the SOM map whose majority of codewords are labelled with fall type. On the other hand, the second configuration, the data set from fall motion type is minority and makes the resulting map with only a small number of codewords whose label are of fall type. At the same time, it increases the number of codewords whose label with another motion type. When it comes to querying a segment, the possibility of matching a segment to the codeword with fall type is therefore low.

Another explanation is that when the data from the motion type of fall on the floor with support of bed is minority, it also reduces the number of fall curves within the data. This comes from the fact that the data from the motion type of fall on the floor does not consist of fall curves only. It also has some parts of standing, preceding all fall curves, and sit to stand transition. The sit to stand transition could have similar segments to walking. This results in lowering the number of codewords with fall type and increasing the chance of matching a queried segment to other motion type.

6. The Implementation for Practical Usability

With the positive verification results of the proposed algorithm detailed in the previous section, we then move ahead to implement the algorithm on the suitable platform. The aim of this implementation is to make it applicable in real life. We avoid employing a self-developed embedded system as a platform of choice. The reasons are that it is fairly difficult to design an embedded system with the least eye-catching, less power consumption, small size and high processing power. We have found that a smartphone platform which has been used during the data collection stage of our research is the most appropriate platform as detailed earlier. The algorithm is, therefore, integrated with some parts previously developed which are the acceleration sensor interfacing and background mode sensor sampling. In the prototype, the algorithm is partitioned into two parts: the background mode acceleration sensor query process and the main user interface application with features to support training and labeling stages and system setting. The background mode is programmed to execute with a fixed interval of 100 mS. In reality, this is only the best case sampling period as the operating system could be busy to service the process. However, it does not matter since the algorithm is designed to tolerate for this limitation. Once the acceleration parameters has already been sampled, the process dispatches the parameters to the main user interface application via an inter-process communication. This is done even the main user interface application is forced to operate in the background mode. It is ensured that either the fall detection or motion classification can be performed.

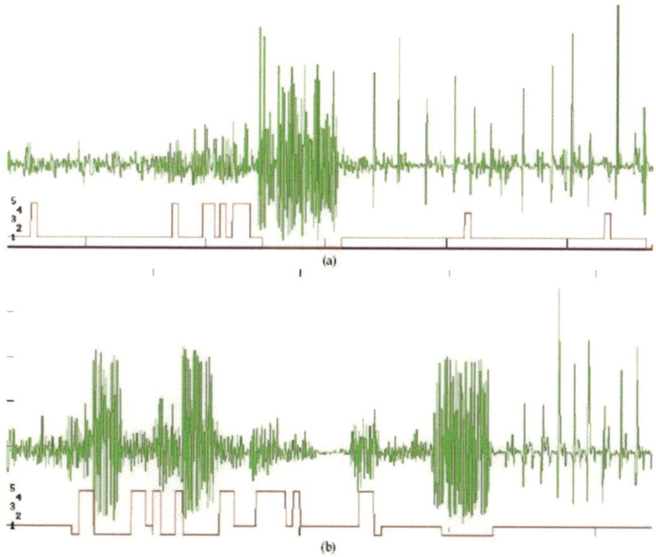

Figure 7. Experimental results after applying the algorithm to two different data: : the green waveforms are the captured motion data, the red waveforms are the motion types. In this case, the codebook is prepared to make the algorithm correctly classify motion types.

Figure 8 shows the screen captures of the main user interface application. In a normal operation mode, the screen of Figure 8(a) is displayed as a main user interface. The waveform shown on the screen is the real-time vector summed acceleration waveform. The button on the lower left is used to provide interaction with a user to change parameters setting (see 8(b)): a phone number to alert in case of fall and some parameters related to decision making of the algorithm. Figure 8(c) is an entry point to the training and labeling stages of the algorithm. It is activated as a result of pressing the "Train Mode"-button of the main user interface screen (Figure 8(a)).

In the training mode screen, the "Start Capturing"-button activates the application to enter data capturing for training and labeling stages. The application captures all motion types in order started from jogging and ended with fast walk with the capturing duration adjustable in the parameters setup screen. The application makes use of the internal data for all fall motion types without requiring a user to perform these risky motion types. When all motion types have already been captured, the application uses its own SOM implementation functions to perform training and labeling stages. The resulting codebook along with the labels can be visualized by use of a built-in feature of the application. Figure 8(d)-(f) shows the screen captures of the sample codebook. The codebook is displayed upon pressing a "Show Map"-button. It is noted that the codebook is useful as it provides a feedback to an operator in order to justify if the training and labeling stages result in a codebook with an acceptable quality. From our testing, we have found that the self training and labeling stages can be avoided and the default codebook can be used in most cases. The testing results for a bigger group of users is now under investigation.

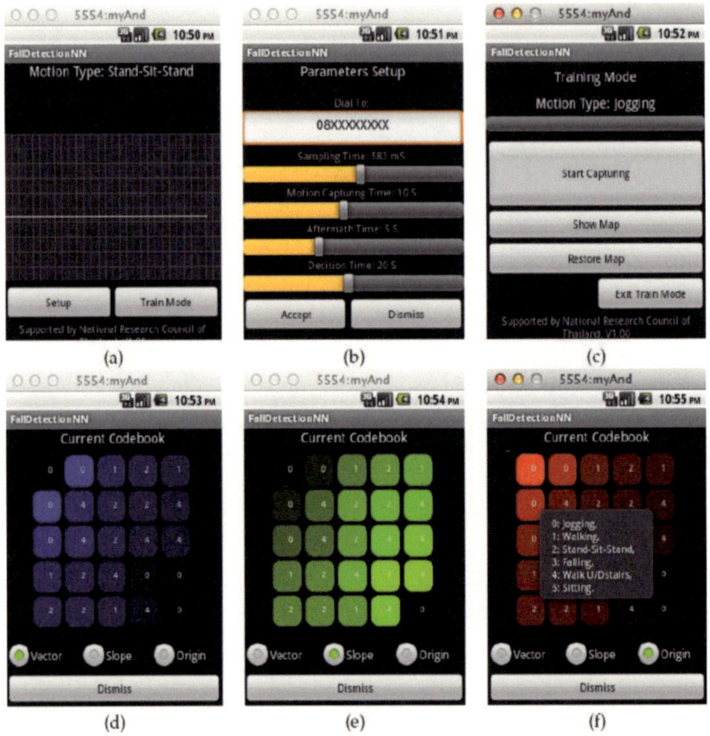

Figure 8. Screen captures of the main user interface application on an Android smartphone.

7. Conclusions

In this chapter, the novel motion classification algorithm in the class of body attachment sensor is proposed. A single triaxial acceleration sensor is employed by the algorithm with a capability to tolerate for a variable sampling rate. In contrast to previously proposed algorithms in the similar category which rely on using threshold techniques, our algorithm Employs the self organizing map neuron network to perform an adaptive motion types clustering and classification functions. The motion data from a wearer is used to train the SOM in order to cluster motion parameters in relation to motion type of the wearer. Later, the motion type is obtained by querying the trained SOM given a motion segment on a real-time basis. With the success of classification of different motion types, we propose extending the algorithm to perform fall detection. In this case, SOM is trained and labeled with a majority of data from fall curves. As the characteristics of the fall curves is almost similar to other motion types with rapid transition of acceleration, the motion type is employed to support the differentiation between fall and other rapid transition motion types. It can be summarized that the contributions of our research are twofolds. Firstly, the motion types classification algorithm employing SOM is proposed and validated for its correctness with respect to the continuous waveform of mixed motion types. Secondly, the motion types is successfully used to differentiate between fall and other motion types. The conducted experiments indicate that the algorithm gives rise to almost 100% of fall detection correctness with almost zero false for activities of daily living (ADLs). Above all, the algorithm can make decision if fall occurs one segment ahead of the first impact which is equivalent to approximately 133 mS. It is very useful from The point of view that there exists a system to get a pre-impact alert signal and handle immediately in the way to prevent severe impact. To make it applicable, the algorithm is successfully implemented on the smartphone platform based on an Android operating system.

Acknowledgements

This work was supported by National Research Council of Thailand under the project: Design and development of an elderly motion pattern classification and pre-fall alert system. The author would like to thank all anonymous reviewers for their comments in previous versions of this paper.

Author details

Wattanapong Kurdthongmee*

Address all correspondence to: kwattana@wu.ac.th

Walailak University, Thailand

References

[1] Yang, C. C., & Hsu, Y. L. (2010). A Review of Accelerometry-Based Wearable Motion Detectors for Physical Activity Monitoring. *Sensors*, 10(8), 7772-7788.

[2] Kiani, K., Snijders, C. J., & Gelsema, E. S. (1997). Computerized Analysis of Daily Life Motor Activity for Ambulatory Monitoring. *Technol. Health. Care 1997*, 5, 307-318.

[3] Mathie, M. J., Celler, B. G., Lovell, N. H., & Coster, A. C. F. (2004). Classification of Basic Daily Movements Using a Triaxial Accelerometer. *Med. Biol. Eng. Comput.*, 42, 679-687.

[4] Karantonis, D. M., Narayanan, M. R., Mathie, M., Lovell, N. H., & Celler, B. G. (2006). Implementation of a Real-Time Human Movement Classifier Using a Triaxial Accelerometer for Ambulatory Monitoring. *IEEE. Trans. Inf. Technol. Biomed.*, 10, 156-167.

[5] Najafi, B., Aminian,, K, Loew,, F, Blanc,, Y, & Robert, P. A. (2002). Measurement of Stand-Sit and Sit-Stand Transitions Using a Miniature Gyroscope and Its Application

in Fall Risk Evaluation in the Elderly. *IEEE Trans. on Biomedical Engineering*, 49(8), 843-851.

[6] Yang, C. C., & Hsu, Y., L. (2009). Development of a Wearable Motion Detector for Telemonitoring and Real-Time Identification of Physical Activity. *Telemed. J. E. Health*, 15, 62-72.

[7] Veltink, P. H., Bussmann, B. J., de Vries, W., Martens, W. L., & van Lummel, R. C. (1996). Detection of Static and Dynamic Activities Using Uniaxial Accelerometers. *IEEE. Trans. Rehabil. Eng.*, 4, 375-385.

[8] Foerster, F., Smeja, M., & Fahrenberg,, J. (1999). Detection of Posture and Motion by Accelerometry: A Validation Study in Ambulatory Monitoring. *Comput. Human. Behav.*, 15, 571-583.

[9] Lyons, G. M., Culhane K., M., Hilton, D., Grace, P. A., & Lyons,, D. (2005). A Description of an Accelerometer-Based Mobility Monitoring Technique. *Med. Eng. Phys.*, 27, 497-504.

[10] Ohtaki, Y., Susumago, M., Suzuki, A., Sagawa, K., Nagatomi, R., & Inooka,, H. (2005). Automatic Classification of Ambulatory Movements and Evaluation of Energy Consumptions Utilizing Accelerometers and a Barometer. *Microsyst. Technol.*, 11, 1034-1040.

[11] Sekine, M., Tamura, T., Togawa, T., & Fukui, Y. (2000). Classification of Waist-Acceleration Signals in a Continuous Walking Record. *Med. Eng. Phys.*, 22, 285-291.

[12] Bussmann, H. B., Reuvekamp, P. J., Veltink, P. H., Martens, W. L., & Stam, H. J. (1998). Validity and Reliability of Measurements Obtained with an "Activity Monitor" in People with and without a Transtibial Amputation. *Phys. Ther.*, 78, 989-998.

[13] Lau, H., Y., Tong, K. Y., & Zhu, H. (2009). Support Vector Machine for Classification of Walking Conditions of Persons after Stroke with Dropped Foot. *Hum. Mov. Sci.*, 28, 504-514.

[14] Zhang, T., Wang, J., Xu, L., & Liu, P. (2006). Fall Detection by Wearable Sensor and One-Class SVM Algorithm. *Intel. Comput. Signal Process. Pattern Recognit.*, 345, 858-863.

[15] Huynh, T., & Schiele, B. (2006). Towards Less Supervision in Activity Recognition from Wearable Sensors. *Proceedings of the 10th IEEE International Symposium on Wearable Computers, Montreux, Switzerland*, 11-14 October 2006, 3-10.

[16] Long, X., Yin, B., & Aarts, R. M. (2009). Single-Accelerometer-Based Daily Physical Activity Classification. *Proceedings of the 31st Annual International Conference of the IEEE EMBS, Minneapolis, MN, USA*, 2-6 September 2009, 6107-6110.

[17] Allen, F. R., Ambikairajah, E., Lovell, N. H., & Celler, B. G. (2006). Classification of a Known Sequence of Motions and Postures from Accelerometry Data Using Adapted Gaussian Mixture Models. *Physiol. Meas.*, 27, 935-951.

[18] Mannini, A., & Sabatini, A. M. (2010). Machine Learning Methods for Classifying Human Physical Activity from On-Body Accelerometers. *Sensors*, 10, 1154-1175.

[19] Pober, D. M., Staudenmayer, J., Raphael, C., & Freedson, P. S. (2006). Development of Novel Techniques to Classify Physical Activity Mode Using Accelerometers. *Med. Sci. Sports Exerc.*, 38, 1626-1634.

[20] Kohonen, T. (1990). The Self-Organizing Map. *Proc. of IEEE*, 78(9), 1990, 1464-1480.

[21] Kohonen,, T., Oja, E., Simula, O., Visa, A., & Kangas, J. (2002). Engineering applications of the self-organizing map. *Proc. of IEEE*, 84(10), 2002, 1358-1384.

[22] Android Developer. (2011). Android Developer Guide, Available from:, http://developer.android.com/index.html, 21-Dec-2011.

[23] Ericsson Labs. (2011). Mobile Sensor Actuator Link. https://labs.ericsson.com/developer-community/blog/mobile-sensor-actuator-link, 21-Dec-2011.

Chapter 9

Using Self-Organizing Maps to Visualize, Filter and Cluster Multidimensional Bio-Omics Data

Ji Zhang and Hai Fang

Additional information is available at the end of the chapter

http://dx.doi.org/10.5772/51702

1. Introduction

In the face of ever-growing of biological data at the genome scale (denoted as omics data) [1,2], investigators of virtually every aspect of biological research are shifting their attention to massive information extracted from omics data. The 'omics' refers to a complete set of biomolecules, such as DNAs, RNAs, proteins and other molecular entities. Omics data are produced by high-throughput technologies. At first, these technologies were known as cDNA microarray [3] and oligonucleotide chips [4]. Then, they were diversely evolved into ChIP-on-Chip [5] and ChIP-Sequencing [6,7], two-dimensional gel electrophoresis and mass spectrometry [8] and high-throughput two-hybrid screening [9]. Recently, they are highlighted by next-generation sequencing technologies such as DNA-seq [10] and RNA-seq [11]. Because of these technological advances, biological information can be quantified in parallel and on a genome scale, but at a much-reduced cost. Nearly, omics data cover every aspect of biological information and thus secure the studies being carried out from a genome-wise perspective. To name but a few examples, they can be used (i) to catalog the whole genome within a living organism (genomics), (ii) to monitor the gene expression at RNA level (transcriptomics) or at protein level (proteomics), (iii) to study the protein-protein interactions (interactomics) and transcription factor-DNA binding patterns (regularomics), and (iv) to characterize DNA or histone modifications exerting on the chromosomes (epigenomics). These multi-layer omics data not just constitute a global overview of molecular constituents, but also provide an opportunity for studying biological mechanisms. In contrast to conventional reductionism focusing on individual biomolecules, omics approaches allow the study of emergent behaviors of biological systems. This conceptual advance has led to the advent of systems biology [12], an interdisciplinary research field with the ultimate goal of *in silico* modeling of biological systems.

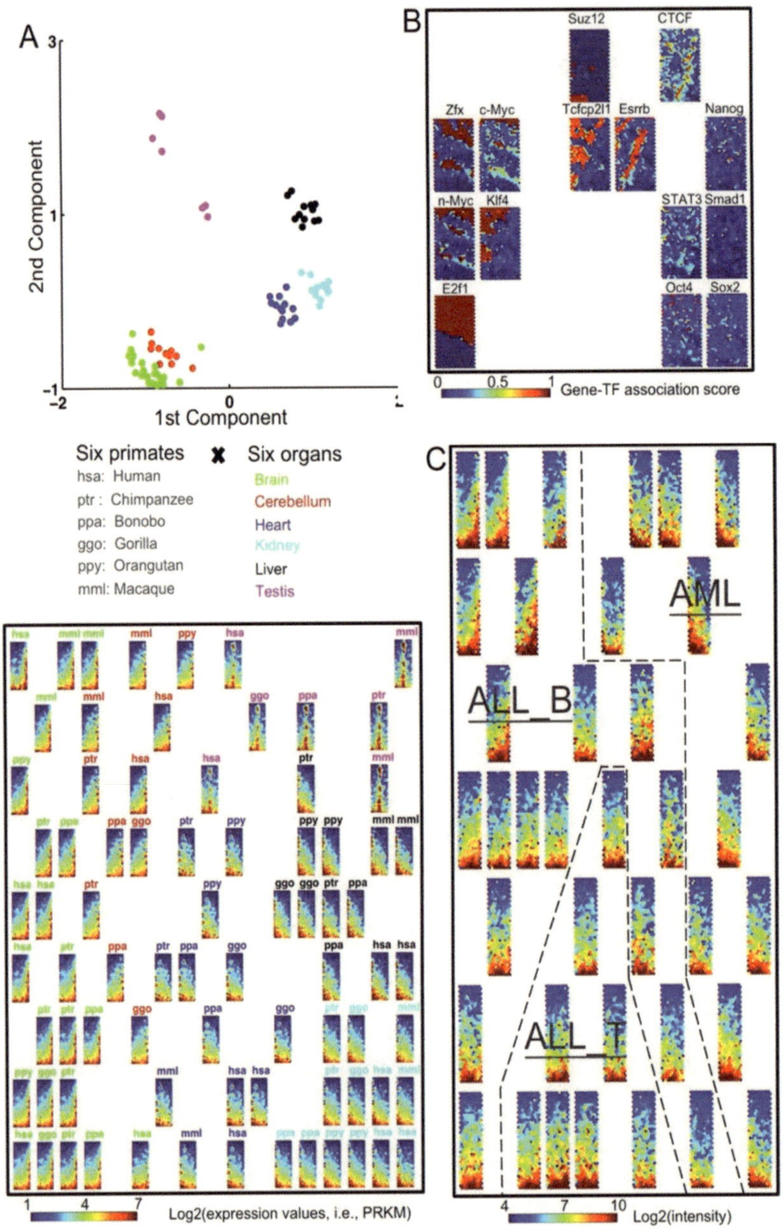

Figure 1. Reanalysis of three different sets of omics data by the reorganized CPPs. **(A)** Transcriptome evolution in mammalian organs. Sammon mapping onto the first two components is displayed in the top panel. Each dot corresponds to one of 36 samples, color-encoded based on their organ origins for the better visualization. The reorganized CPPs are shown in the bottom panel. Each component plane illustrates the sample-specific transcriptome map and is placed within a two-dimensional rectangular lattice (framed in black). Within each component plane, genes with the same or similar expression patterns are mapped to the same or nearby map nodes. When zooming out to look at between-planes/samples relationships, samples with the similar expression profiles are placed closer to each other. The title above each plane is texted in abbreviation and marked in color. The meanings of these abbreviations and colors are described in the middle panel. **(B)** Regularome of multiple transcription factors in embryonic stem cells. The reor-

ganized CPPs not only display regularome of each of 14 transcription factors, but also reveal their relationships by geometric closeness within the two-dimensional rectangular lattice. **(C)** Transcriptome profiling in cancer classification. The transcriptome similarities and distinctions among 38 leukemia samples are visualized by the reorganized CPPs. The dotted lines are used to intuitively indicate the boundary between the AML-ALL separation, and within the ALL, the boundary between its two subtypes (i.e., the ALL_B and ALL_T). Since each sample class occupies distinctive regions within the two-dimensional rectangular lattice, the sample labels are texted uniformly as indicated. AML: acute myeloid leukemia; ALL: acute lymphoblastic leukemia; ALL_B: B-cell ALL; ALL_T: T-cell ALL.

Today, all areas of biological science are confronted with ever-increasing amounts of omics data whereas interpretations of the data appear to lag far behind the rate of data accumulation [13]. It is largely due to a lack of understanding the complexity of the data, and is also partially explained by algorithms being applied inappropriately. For example, transcriptome data are tabulated as gene expression matrix, measuring expression levels of genes against experimental samples. Two factors limit the power of many conventional multivariate statistical methods. First, gene expression matrix contains data with low signal-to-noise ratio and missing values as well. Second, such matrix usually involves tens of thousands of genes but a much smaller number of samples, known as 'small sample sizes relative to huge gene volumes'. To overcome the limitations of conventional algorithms, bringing human intelligence into the data processing represents a crucial factor for the discovery of *bona fide* relationships between genes or samples, in which visual control is indispensible. Interestingly, early pioneered efforts on transcriptome data mining were primarily focused on data organization and visualization [14,15].

Visual inspection represents a crucial aspect in omics data mining, providing many potential benefits. However, such potential benefits are largely limited by using conventional algorithms such as hierarchical and K-mean clustering. Instead, we use the vector space model to conceptually express omics data. This model allows biological molecules (e.g., genes) to be automatically organized into data clouds in the virtual reality environment based on their numerical values across all samples tested. Take transcriptome data as an example, wherein each gene activity pattern (e.g., gene expression pattern) across N related samples could be referred to as a data point in an N-dimensional hyperspace. Tens of thousands of such data points would therefore form data clouds in the space. Accordingly, the methods used for the gene clustering or the projection/visualization of output results should respect the 'natural' structure of input expression matrix, that is, to preserve the shape and density (collectively called 'topological structure') of the data. Notably, the more similar activity the genes exhibit, the closer geometric space they occupy. Exploring geometric relationships in a topology-preserving manner provides a natural basis for discovering biologically meaningful knowledge. Such topological preservation is of particular significance at the exploratory phase of omics data mining since *a priori* knowledge of the data structure is usually unknown.

The self-organizing map (SOM), as a learning algorithm [16], appears to be suitable for topology-preserving analysis of multi-dimensional data. In an interactive manner, the SOM summarizes the input data by vector quantization (VQ) and simultaneously carries out topological preserving projection by vector projection (VP). More importantly, optimization of neighborhood kernels may control the extent to which the VP influences the VQ. For the sake of human-centric visualization, this algorithm usually produces a regular two-dimensional hexagonal grid of map nodes. Each map node is associated with a prototype vector in the high-dimensional space, collectively forming the codebook matrix. In terms of gene activity matrix (such as gene expression matrix) as input, the SOM produces a map, wherein (i) genes with the same or similar activity patterns (i.e., gene activity vectors) are mapped to the same or nearby map nodes, (ii) the density of genes mapped to this two-dimensional map follows the data density in the high-dimensional space. When all map nodes are color-encoded according to values in each component of prototype vectors, the resulting component map (or called 'component plane' due to a regular shape of the map [17]) can be used as a sample-specific presentation of gene activities. Based on this scheme, we have applied a method of component plane presentations (CPPs) to visualize microarray data analysis [18]. In essence, the CPPs take advantage of the visual benefits of the ordered SOM map to illustrate the codebook matrix in a sample-specific fashion.

In addition, we here aim to formally introduce a SOM-centric analytical pipeline, an extension to our previously proposed approaches [19], for in-depth mining of biological information. At the core is the plasticity of SOM neighborhood kernels in preserving local versus global topology of the input data to a varied degree. The remainder of this chapter is organized as follows. First, we will introduce the reorganized CPPs, originally called 'component plane reorganization' for correlation hunting [20], and illustrate the visual benefits in characterizing omics data of various types. Then, we will give a timeline review of the SOM in the context of its past applications in omics data. After that, we will focus on our proposed pipeline. Through a representative real-world case of transcriptome changes during early human organogenesis, we will provide a tutorial overview of how this pipeline can be used for the simultaneous visualizations of genes and samples, topology-preserving gene selection and clustering, and the temporal expression-active sub-network detection. Finally, we will conclude this chapter along with the future directions of the pipeline for the further developments.

2. The reorganized CPPs and the potential benefits for visualizing omics data of various types

As demonstrated in many applications [21-28], the CPPs enable straightforward and widespread use. They allow users to interpret omics data in a sample-specific fashion but without loss of information on tens of thousands of genes (still visible but being clustered and orderly organized). Very often users tend to mistake CPPs as microarray chips. It suggests the importance of sample-specific visualization of omics data from the biologists' point of view. Instead of the correction, we can further interpret the CPPs as a related set of microarray chips, in which probes (representing genes to be measured) are artificially reconfigured according to their patterns. Such metaphor might increase the circulation of the CPPs and thus the SOM within the omics community. Another way for increasing the circulation is to further improve the CPPs by adding new functionalities.

http://dx.doi.org/10.5772/51702

Since the SOM algorithm is robust to the missing data and rare outliers, the codebook matrix is not just an approximation to the input matrix, but can be more useful than previously thought. For instance, the codebook matrix can be further used to explore relationships between samples. It is an equivalent of reorganizing component planes by placing similar component planes closer to each other. Such reorganization can be realized by using a new SOM map (usually a rectangular lattice on a two-dimensional map) to train component plane vectors (i.e., column-wide vectors of output codebook matrix). To ensure the unique placement, each component plane mapped to this rectangular lattice can be determined in an order from the best matched to the next compromised one. Comparing to the ordinary ones, the CPPs being reorganized in such a way are rich in the information revealed; genes and samples can be simultaneously visualized in a single display. The organized CPPs are easier to interpret, especially when the number of samples (i.e., component planes) is relatively large and the relationships between samples are unclear. To give a sense of such visual benefits, we provide three examples involving omics data generated by different high-throughput technologies (Figure 1).

2.1. Transcriptome evolution in mammalian organs

Comparative study of different organs or of different species can be a useful approach for the insights into transcriptome features underlying phenotypic changes [29]. To demonstrate the power of our analysis tools in this regard, we first selected a recently published dataset comprising 13,277 one-to-one orthologous genes across six primates, each with six organs [30]. The data were generated by the RNA-seq technology, and expression levels were quantified by reads per kilobase of exon model per million mapped reads (RPKM). These reads were normalized across species/tissues on the basis of rank-conserved genes, followed by logarithm transformation. The higher the normalized and transformed RPKM indicates the higher expression levels. We projected samples onto two-dimensional space by Sammon mapping [31]. As showed in the top panel of Figure 1A, samples are grouped together according to the tissue origins except for the neural tissues (i.e. brain and cerebellum), which is slightly better than the originally published results using principle component analysis. When the reorganized CPPs were used instead, more informative relationships were revealed just by visual inspection (the bottom panel of Figure 1A). First, each component plane provides a sample-specific transcriptome map (rather than a dot). Second, samples are better separated even for the neural tissues. Last but not the least, there is much room left to label the samples; the species origins can be titled/colored above each plane. To conclude, the reorganized CPPs permit the direct comparisons of cross-species transcriptome evolution within the same tissue and cross-tissue trancriptome changes within the same species as well.

2.2. Regularome of multiple transcription factors in embryonic stem cells

Characterizing transcription factor (TF) binding sits from a genome-wise scale is the key to the understanding of pluripotency and reprogramming [32]. Also, such an approach has been widely used in various biological investigations. To further illustrate the visual benefits of using the SOM and the reorganized CPPs, we chose a second dataset generated by the ChIP-seq technology, which contained binding sites of 14 TFs at the promoter regions of 17,442 genes in mouse [33]. TF-gene association scores were calculated to estimate the strength of binding, with higher scores implying higher chance of a gene (in rows) being targeted by a TF (in columns). As shown in Figure 1B, the visual inspection of the reorganized CPPs suggests several features associated with this multiple TF regularome dataset: (i) binding profiles of five TFs (i.e., Nanog, Sox2, Oct4, Smad1 and STAT3) are similar both in the number and strength of target genes, being exclusively located into the bottom-right corner; (ii) another four TFs (i.e., n-Myc, c-Myc, Klf4 and Zfx) share much more common binding profiles than the rest, and are placed together; (iii) when examining regularome of two TFs (i.e., E2f1 and Suz12), their component planes are far apart, which is consistent with the observation that their binding profiles are mutually exclusive. Unlike the original publication, the reorganized CPPs spotlight these prominent features under a single informative display.

2.3. Transcriptome profiling in cancer classification

Cancer classification based on transcriptome profiling is one of the most popular applications [34]. For this regard, we chose a third dataset generated by oligonucleotide chip, consisting of 5,000 genes expressed at 38 leukemia samples [35]. These samples include 11 acute myeloid leukemia (AML) and 27 acute lymphoblastic leukemia (ALL) that can be further sub-typed into 19 B-cell ALL (ALL_B) and 8 T-cell ALL (ALL_T). This dataset is typically used as classification benchmark to evaluate the performance of the methods being tested. Here we used it for the reorganized CPPs to visualize three known classes and their boundaries. Figure 1C intuitively displays the AML-ALL distinction, each occupying its own landscape (AML on the right and ALL at the left). Within the ALL-occupied landscape, the partition between ALL-B and ALL-T can also be observed despite the fact that this benchmark dataset contains sample outliers (probably due to incorrect diagnosis of ALL samples). Since the cancer is a highly heterogeneous population with ambiguous boundary for the subpopulations/subtypes, the information provided by visualized data both in genes and samples is fairly important for the cancer classification and the identification of subtype-specific molecular signatures as well.

3. Timeline of the SOM-based applications in omics data mining

The SOM, originally proposed by Kohonen [36], is a special instance of artificial neural networks (ANNs) as an competitive learning algorithm inspired by the cortex of human brain.

Unlike other ANNs, a unique feature of SOM is that it can use neighborhood kernels to preserve and also control the topological structure of high-dimensional input data [16]. For this reason, the SOM has become a valuable tool and primary choice for visualizing and characterizing a relatively massive amount of data. Announced by Kohonen in the WSOM 2011 conference, there are already over 10,000 scientific papers published using SOM. The major contributions to this huge publication list come from its broad applications in engineering, economics and biomedicine [37,38].

Literature surveys of the bibliography suggest the existence of three periods, which can be used to summarize the past developments and applications of the SOM in multidimensional omics data. Namely, they are the opening, maturing, and turning periods along the timeline ahead. The opening period last from the year 1999 to 2001, in which the SOM was widely introduced into the field of genomics research. It attracted a great deal of interest by its superiority. Compared to other existing methods such as hierarchical clustering [14] at that time, it was scalable to large datasets, and was robust to noise and outliers. Also, two factors could explain the sudden popularity. At very end of the last century, there was a great need to develop effective tools for the extraction of the inherent biological information from explosive gene expression data. Another factor is that, although mathematically hard to understand, the computational implementation of the SOM algorithm was just available for the practical use, together with user-friendly documentations regarding data pre-processing, training and post-processing [17,39-41]. The following years (2002-2004) could be considered as the maturing period. During this period, biologists realized that it could be misleading without knowing the context of omics data. Accordingly, special attentions were given to visual potentials of the SOM when analyzing omics data. Also, numerous attempts were made to solve the problems associated with the algorithm itself, such as the requirements of pre-defined cluster numbers and the doubts on stability of clusters obtained. From the year 2005 on, the fewer advances have been achieved in gene expression data applications, although several combinations with other methods have also been reported. It can be explained by the shift from emphasis on the numeric gene expression data to the nonnumeric sequenced genomic data. This shift discourages the direct application of the SOM, and several variants of the SOM were instead tried. For these reasons, we call the third as the turning period. In the rest of this section, we will give a fair review of these three periods by focusing on successful applications and innovative improvements in the context of omics data mining.

3.1. Opening period by emerging gene expression data analysis

The SOM was first applied to interpret gene expression data of hematopoietic differentiation [15]. In the same year, several applications in other biological systems were also reported. These included the use of the SOM to analyze and visualize yeast gene expression data during diauxic shift [42], to process the developmental gene expression data during metamorphosis in Drosophila [43], and to discover and predict cancer classes based on gene expression data [35]. Thereafter, the exploratory nature of the SOM for the use was exploited in the context of gene expression data analysis [44,45]. In addition to expression data, the SOM was also proved as a powerful tool to characterize horizontally transferred genes by looking at the codon usage patterns of bacterial genomic data [46,47].

3.2. Maturing period for algorithm optimizations and improvements

Visual advantages of the SOM were systematically demonstrated in revealing relationships among genes of known functional classes [48], classifying tissues of different origins [49] and tumor origins [50], and both [51]. In particular, component plane-based visualizations were much appreciated [18,51-53]. As illustrated in the previous section, our experience of using reordered CPPs started with microarray data analysis. Such sample-specific presentations are intuitive to biologists, because it is straightforward to interpret biological significances of genes (being clustered) with respect to each sample [18]. Another major improvement during this period was the development of SOM variants, as highlighted by adaptive double SOM [54] and hierarchical dynamic SOM [55], to address the issue of how to identify unknown/consistent cluster number. The adaptive double SOM adapts its free parameters during the training process to find consistent cluster number, while hierarchical dynamic SOM uses growing SOM to hierarchically improve the clustering process. To account for the random initial conditions and to assess clustering stability, a generic strategy called resampling-based consensus clustering was also proposed to represent the consensus over multiple runs of the SOM algorithm with random restart [56]. Unfortunately, performance evaluations showed that consensus clustering for the SOM produced slightly worse results than that for the hierarchical clustering, and both were overtaken by another method based on nonnegative matrix factorization [57]. Using the SOM for the biological sequence analysis were also attempted, including the nonvectorial SOM algorithm for the clustering and visualization of a large protein sequences [58], the partitioning of similar protein sequences for the subsequent conserved local motif prediction [59], hidden genome signature visualization [60] and gene prediction [61].

3.3. Turning period with the emphasis on the nonnumeric data and the combination of the SOM with other methods

One of active attempts to analyze the DNA sequences was TF binding site identification [62] and sequence motif discovery [63], both using sequence motif representations as input vectors. Such DNA motif identifications were recently improved by using a heterogeneous node model [64]. Several variants of the SOM were reported to analyze microbial metagenomes for clustering and visualizing taxonomic groups. With the DNA oligonucleotide frequencies as input, emergent SOM was used for the increase in the projection resolution [65,66], growing SOM was used for speed improvements [67,68], and the main parameters of the SOM were studied for the accuracy [69]. Using other representations of genomic sequences was also reported in the hyperbolic SOM [70]. TaxSOM implementing the growing SOM and batch-learning SOM [71,72] was recently made available for the ease of use [73]. In terms of gene expression data, combinations with other methods were actively studied. The SOM was used as a data-filtering to improve classification performance of the support vector machine [74]. Multi-level SOM of SOM was proposed to determine the cluster number [75]. Minimum spanning tree and ensemble resampling were also employed to post-process the SOM for automatic clustering [76]. The combination of the SOM and the singular value decomposition (SVD) was suggested by us for topology-preserving gene selection [19].

4. A SOM-centric pipeline and its tutorial for the in-depth mining of transcriptome changes during early human organogenesis

The aforementioned three examples clearly show that the SOM with the reorganized CPPs enables straightforward and widespread use in a variety of omics data. From previous applications, a lesson can be learned that the popularity of the SOM during the opening period is not merely driven by the explosive gene expression data, but is also attributable to the availability of algorithm implementation and tutorial documentations. Accordingly, we attempt to develop a SOM-centric pipeline for maximizing its beneficial potentials in visualizing, selecting and clustering multidimensional omics data. Briefly, the implementation of pipeline starts with the preparation of data, in the form of gene activity matrix, to record biological activities of a large number of genes (rows) against related samples (columns). It is always advisable to pre-process raw data, such as normalization by rows and/or columns, and logarithmic transformation to approximate normal distribution. After that, it is highly recommended to simultaneously visualize genes and samples by the reorganized CPPs; these dual visualizations aim to effectively characterize data structure and to visually monitor data quality. Hybrid SOM-SVD is applied for topology-preserving gene selection, while the distance matrix-based clustering of the SOM (a special type of a SOM-based two-phase gene clustering) is used for topology-preserving gene clustering. The obtained genes clusters can facilitate many aspects of biological interpretations by applying enrichment analysis to examine whether clustered genes share functional, regulatory, or phenotypic characteristics. Also, the dominant patterns revealed by SOM-SVD can facilitate the graph mining tools for detecting temporal expression-active subnetworks. To demonstrate these multifaceted functionalities of this SOM-centric pipeline, we provide a tutorial overview of in-depth mining transcriptome changes during early human organogenesis, together with the necessary details of the underlying algorithms and the biological explanations.

Prior to the tutorial, it is necessary to clarify the technical issues with respect to the SOM used here. In terms of the SOM topology, the map size is heuristically determined based on the input training data, as suggested by the MATLAB SOM toolbox [77]. During the SOM training, the map is linearly initialized along two greatest eigenvectors of the input data. Then, map nodes compete to win the input data, followed by updating the winner node and its topological neighbors. This iterative training is implemented using the batch algorithm and contains two phases: rough phase and fine-tuning phase. To increase the reproducibility of the trained map, we purposely prolong the fine-turning phase until the successive fine-tunings reach a steady state; the quality of the SOM map (i.e., average quantization error and topographic error) does not change any more. Among various parameters associated with the SOM training, the neighborhood kernel is the most important one because it dictates the final topology of the trained map. In addition to the commonly used Gaussian function (see Equation 1), others, such as Epanechikov function (see Equation 2), Gut-gaussian function and Bubble function, can also be chosen depending on the tasks [77]. From the mathematical definitions as well as the practical comparisons using the same test of data, we have observed that Epanechikov neighborhood kernel puts more emphasis on local topological relationships than the other threes, suitable for the use in gene selection. On the other extreme, the Gaussian neighborhood kernel preserves global topology relationships to the most extent, and thus is ideal for the use in global gene clustering and visualization. As demonstrated below, the dual strengths of the SOM in preserving both local and global topological properties (via choosing different neighborhood kernels) can optimize the data processing from multi-aspects.

$$h_{ci}(t)=\max\left\{0,\ 1-\frac{\|\vec{r}_c-\vec{r}_i\|^2}{\sigma^2(t)}\right\} \tag{1}$$

$$h_{ci}(t)=\exp\left(-\frac{\|\vec{r}_c-\vec{r}_i\|^2}{2\sigma^2(t)}\right) \tag{2}$$

where the positive integer $\sigma(t)$ defines the width of the kernel at training time t, and $\vec{r}_c$ and $\vec{r}_i$ are respectively the location vectors of the winner node c and a node i on the two-dimensional SOM map grid.

4.1. Simultaneous visualizations of genes and samples

In our previous work [27], we have analyzed transcriptome data during early human organogenesis (hORG), which involves human embryos at six consecutive stages (Carnegie stages 9-14, S9-S14) with three replicates for each. Here, we use it for pipeline tutorials and for demonstrations on further improvements. After normalization and pre-filtering, the gene expression matrix contains expression values of 5,441 genes (in rows) × 18 samples (in columns; six developmental stages S9-S14 in triplicate R1-R3 for each) (available at the supplemental Table 1 in the original publication [27]). To account for variance stabilization and to focus on the relative expression across the samples, we further pre-process this matrix by base-2 logarithm transformation and the row-wise centering. From the hORG matrix, the gene expression vectors are input for the SOM training with the Epanechikov neighborhood kernel and the grid of 360 (30 × 12) hexagonal nodes. Each column of SOM codebook matrix corresponds to one component plane. The column-wise component plane vectors are then used to train a new SOM with the Gaussian neighborhood kernel (see [2]) and the grid of 40 (5 × 8) rectangular nodes. The placement of a component plane is determined in a sequential rank from the best-matching node (BMN) to the second BMN and so on (using Pearson correlation coefficients as the similarity metric). The above process repeats until all the component planes find the non-overlapping location in the rectangular lattice. As shown in Figure 2B, the reorganized CPPs enhance the visual convenience by placing component planes in a biologically meaningful manner. The relative geometric distance intuitively illustrates the correlations within the three replicates and across the six developmental stages. Remarkably, such simultaneous visualizations of genes and samples reveal developmental trajectory in the transcriptome landscape of early human organogenesis.

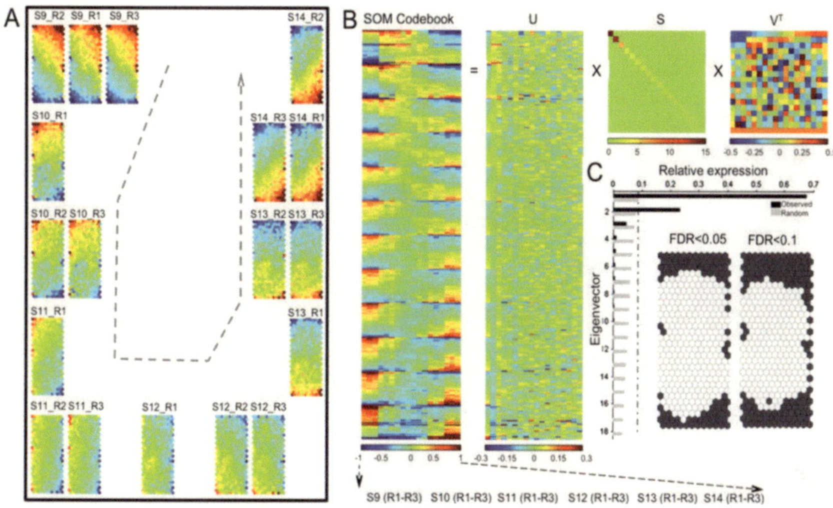

Figure 2. A tutorial on the simultaneous visualizations of genes and samples by the reorganized CPPs, and topology-preserving gene selection through the SOM-SVD. (A) The reorganized CPPs of transcriptome changes during early human organogenesis. Each component plane illustrates a sample-specific transcriptome map. Sample similarities and differences are also illustrated by the extent to which component planes are geometrically related to each other. Owing to simultaneous visualizations of genes and samples, the dotted line can be intuitively drawn to denote the developmental trajectory. (B) Decomposition of the SOM codebook matrix by SVD. This codebook matrix is linearly decomposed into three matrices of U, S and V^T. Values of eigensamples (columns of U), eigenexpressions (on-diagonal entries of S) and eigenvectors (rows of V^T) are color-encoded as indicated by bar underneath. (C) SOM node selection by false discovery rate (FDR) to account for multiple hypothesis tests. Bars on the left illustrate the relative contribution (in relative to the overall variation) of observed eigenvectors (filled in black) and randomized eigenvectors (filled in gray) from a randomization. The dominant eigenvectors are selected if their observed relative expression is larger than the maximum of random relative eigenexpression (as indicated by the vertical dotted line). On the right displays the SOM grid map with nodes being selected (in heavy gray) or not (in white) under the threshold of FDR as indicated.

4.2. Topology-preserving gene selection

In our recent work [19], we have developed hybrid SOM-SVD for topology-preserving selection of genes that show statistically significant changes in expression. Unlike conventional arbitrary or manual gene selection procedures, this approach permits the entire gene selection process to be realized automatically and on the basis of statistical inference. Through comparisons with other methods, this approach has demonstrated to be more effective in selecting cell cycle genes with a characteristic period. Also, the gene selection by hybrid SOM-SVD can facilitate the downstream clustering analysis, as direct application of the clustering method on unselected data may distort the topology of global clustering [19].

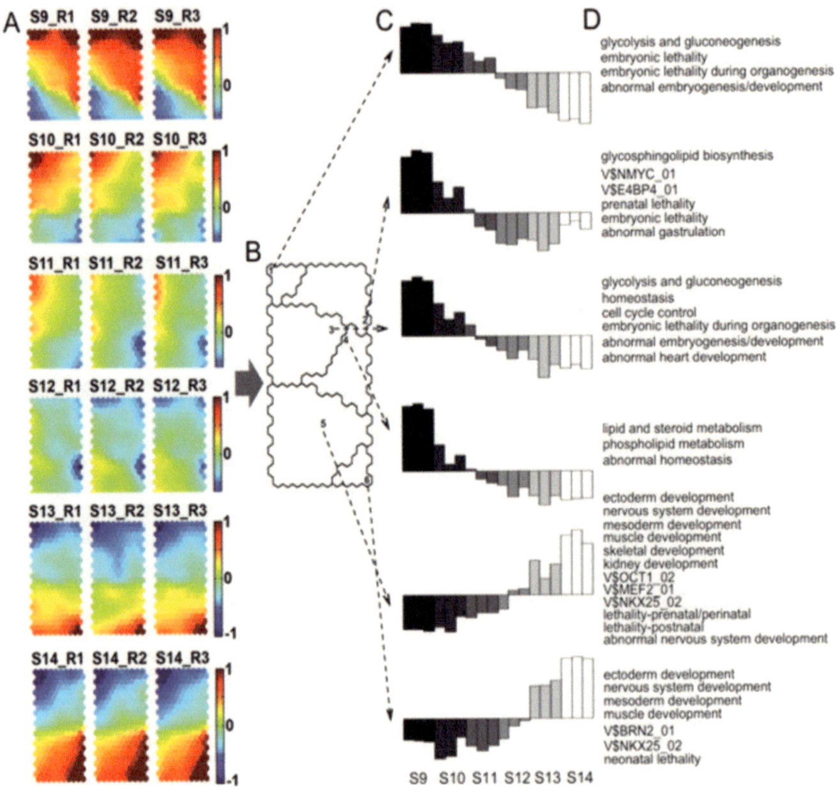

Figure 3. A tutorial on topology-preserving gene clustering by the distance matrix-based clustering of the SOM. (A) The CPPs of the SOM outputs using the input of the gene expression matrix selected by SOM-SVD. (B) Ideogram illustration of six gene clusters on a SOM grid map. The cluster index is marked in the seed node. From each seed node, the corresponding cluster is obtained through a region growing procedure. (C) Bar-graph display of SOM outputs in seed nodes. (D) Significant functional, regulatory and phenotypic features associated with gene clusters.

The hORG tabulated gene expression matrix (5,441 genes × 18 samples) is first subjected to non-linear transformation using the SOM algorithm with the Epanechikov neighbourhood kernel and the grid of 360 (30 × 12) hexagonal nodes. The resultant codebook matrix (i.e., 360 nodes in rows × 18 samples in columns) serves as an intermediate format for pattern recognition by SVD (Figure 2B). It is sequentially followed by two dominant eigenvector selection, SVD subspace projection and distance statistic construction, significant node assessment using the false discovery rate (FDR) procedure for multiple hypothesis tests, and finally the selection of significant nodes and their genes as defined by the BMN (Figure 2C).

A total of 2,148 genes are selected under an FDR cutoff of 0.1. The selected gene expression matrix (2,148 genes × 18 samples) forms the characteristic matrix, which can be used for further clustering analysis. Notably, the motivations behind the combination of the SOM with the SVD are: (i) the separation of features and artifacts by the SOM training with the Epanechikov neighbourhood kernel, (ii) the pattern recognition of features and artifacts by SVD decomposition, and (iii) the statistical selection of features by the FDR.

4.3. Topology-preserving gene clustering

Gene clustering in a topology-preserving manner is implemented using a SOM-based two-phase clustering algorithm that takes into account SOM neighborhoods. In the first phase, the gene expression vectors (preferably from gene expression matrix selected by SOM-SVD) are trained by SOM with the Gaussian neighbourhood kernel to better preserve the topology of the data. In the second phase, the resultant SOM map is divided into a set of clusters using a region growing procedure. By calculating the SOM distance matrix from U-matrix (i.e., distances between each map node and its neighbors) [78], this procedure starts with local minima of distance matrix as seeds, followed by the assignment of the remaining nodes to their corresponding clusters [79]. Like other hierarchical agglomerative or k-means partitive algorithms used at the second phase [40], this distance matrix-based algorithm can reduce the complexity of the clustering task from tens of thousands of genes to the hundreds of nodes in the SOM map. Unlike others, this distance matrix-based clustering of the SOM enables more reliable estimates of gene clusters in a topology-preserving manner. In our previous work [19], we have shown that, for the same data as input, using k-means clustering at the second phase could not result in topology-preserving gene clusters. Also, we have demonstrated the preferential use of the SOM-SVD gene selection ahead of the topology-preserving gene clustering. Otherwise, it would distort the topology of global clustering when directly applying on the unselected data.

Therefore, the gene expression matrix of 2,148 genes × 18 samples, as selected by the SOM-SVD, is used as input for the SOM-based two-phase gene clustering. Specifically, the input data is first trained using the SOM with 220 (22 × 10) nodes and Gaussian neighborhood kernel, and the SOM codebook matrix is displayed by CPPs in Figure 3A. The trained map is then divided using the region growing procedure. As showed in Figure 3B, the map nodes at the second phase of the gene clustering are continuously organized into six clusters according to neighborhood relationships and without any pre-knowledge of data structure. Since the seed nodes are identified as local minima (i.e., cluster centres), the pattern seen in a seed node can be viewed as the average expression pattern of genes mapped to that seed. More loosely, it can also be approximated as the overall pattern in the gene cluster obtained from the seed. As show in Figure 3C, seeds in clusters 1-4 display gradually decreasing expression patterns, while those for clusters 5-6 have gradual increasing pattern in expression. More importantly, gene clusters facilitate the downstream biological interpretations based on the paradigm of 'coexpression-cofunction-coregulation'. Such interpretations are coupled with external biological annotations such as Gene Ontology (GO) [80], conserved TF binding sites (in the form of positional weighted matrix) from the UCSC Genome Browser database [81] and mammalian phenotype ontology [82]. Using these diverse annotations, enrichment analysis is conducted to identify functional, regulatory and phenotypic features that are shared by genes being clustered together. Figure 4D lists shared features associated with each gene cluster. Genes in clusters 1-3 are functionally related to cellular metabolism and homeostasis, are possibly regulated by survival-related transcription factors, and are largely linked to embryonic lethality and abnormal embryogenesis. By contrast, genes in cluster 5-6 are functionally involved in the establishment of organ morphogenesis, are regulated by organogenesis-specific TFs, and are primarily linked to postnatal lethality and diverse organ/system defects.

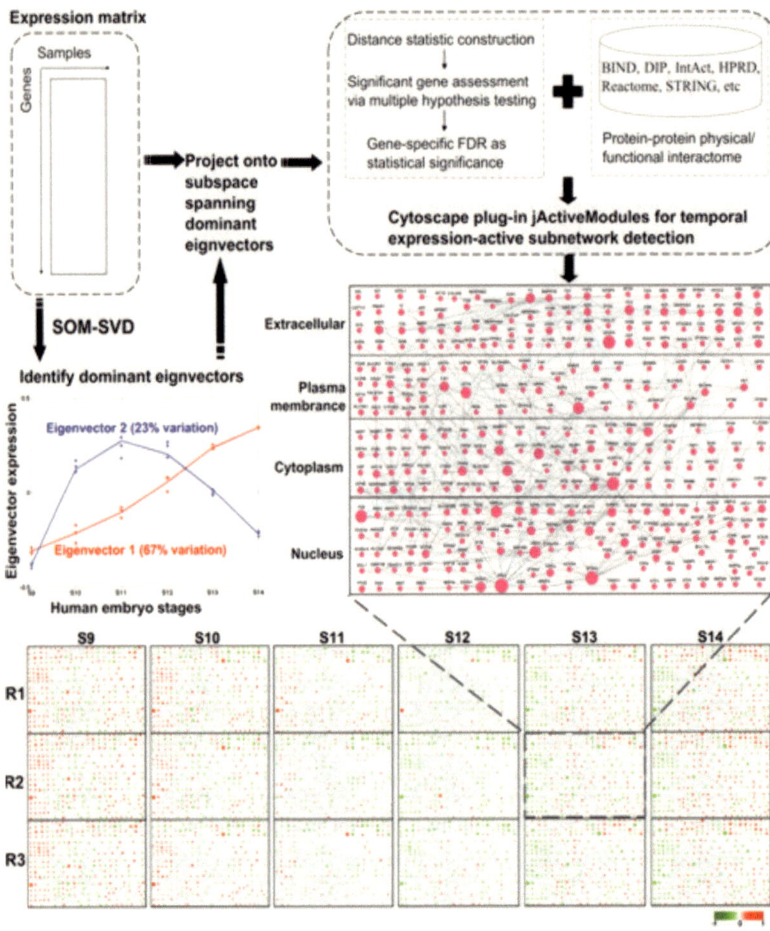

Figure 4. A tutorial on temporal expression-active subnetwork detection by jActiveModules. The Cytoscape plug-in jActiveModules, as a subgraph-searching tool, requires the input of both a user-predefined network being searched against and a gene-specific metric to measure the significance of expression change (top-right corner). For the network to be input, the existing protein physical interaction databases such as BIND, DIP, IntAct, HPRD, Reactome can be compiled together, which can be further complemented by the functional interactions from the database like STRING to improve the network coverage. For the temporal change measure, the dominant eigenvectors identified by SOM-

SVD analysis can be used (top-left corner). As suggested here, it consists of three steps, including gene projection onto the subspace spanning dominant eigenvectors, distance statistic construction, significant gene assessment through multiple hypothesis tests for FDR calculation. The gene-specific FDR is then used as the significance of expression change. With both data as input, jActiveModules uses the simulated annealing to detect expression-active subnetworks containing genes with expression patterns highly similar to dominant eigenvectors as identified by SOM-SVD analysis. The middle-right panel displays the detected temporal expression-active subnetwork, the layout of which is reconfigured according to subcellular localization. By overlaying gene expression data from each of 18 samples (i.e., three replicates R1-R3 in rows × six stages S9-S14 in columns) onto the subnetwork, each plane (such as S13_R2 as highlighted in dot lines) illustrates sample-specific subnetwork with genes/nodes color-encoded based on their expression values as indicated underneath (bottom panel). Similar to the CPPs, such plane visualization permits the monitoring of the subnetwork expression changes, indicative of this subnetwork activity being dynamically changed during early human organogenesis.

4.4. Temporal expression-active subnetwork detection

A temporal expression-active subnetwork is the connected region of an interactome/ network, constrained by that this subnetwork should contain genes that show significant changes in expression over a biological process. Such active subnetworks can bring the value of omics data into the higher level. Biologically, genes do not act alone but are interconnected into cohesive networks. Methodologically, the integration of two or more sources of omics data can increase the chance of identifying biologically meaningful knowledge than either data source. Temporal expression-active subnetworks can be viewed as the integration of the context-independent interactome (static, unionizing all possible interactions) and the context-specific transcriptome (dynamic, involving only genes being expressed under the conditions). The Cytoscape plug-in jActiveModules [83] is one of algorithms that have been successfully used for identifying expression-active subnetworks. In addition to a user-predefined network, it also requires the input of a gene-specific metric to measure the significance of expression change. This method is effective for the transcriptome data obtained from the 'case-control' experimental design because the significance of expression change can be evaluated by testing the differences. In a time-series setting, however, this method can be problematic. Although any two-successive expression change can result in the corresponding expression-active subnetworks, these subnetworks may not overlap at all and ignore the temporal dependency. It is appealing to identify subnetworks that are cohesively active across the whole time series. For the use of jActiveModules in this purpose, we propose to calculate a gene-specific FDR as a measure of significance in temporal expression. The basic idea is to weigh genes according to their similarity with dominant eigenvectors (as identified by SOM-SVD). Similar to the calibration strategy, genes with expression pattern similar to the dominant eigenvector expression are up-weighed; otherwise down-weighed.

Schematic flowchart in Figure 4 illustrates a temporal expression-active subnetwork during early human organogenesis. Brief explanations can be found in the legend. Here, we only detail the steps of how to calculate the gene-specific FDR from gene expression matrix (denoted as M with G genes × N samples) and the L dominant eigenvectors (e.g., the first 2 dominant eigenvectors identified by SOM-SVD analysis in Figure 2). Let $\vec{x}$ be gene expression vector, and $\Re^L$ be SVD subspace spanning by the L dominant eigenvectors. We project $\vec{x}$ onto $\Re^L$, obtaining projection vector $\vec{q} \in \Re^L$. In $\Re^L$, we compute the Euclidian distance (distance statistic, DS) of projection vector $\vec{q}$ away from the coordinate-wise zero point. The

DS measures similarity between gene expression and the dominant eigenvector expression, with the larger value indicating the higher similarity. When comparing multiple hypothesis tests simultaneously, we assess statistical significance of gene-specific *DS* by a method of FDR, described as follows. For the matrix *M*, we first use the above procedure to obtain a list of *DS*, being ranked as$DS_{r1} \leq DS_{r2} \leq \cdots \leq DS_{rG}$. Then, obtain $b = 1, \ldots, B$ randomized matrix M^b, which is generated by randomly permuting matrix *M* in both row and column directions. Analogously, compute projection values of randomized gene expression vector $\vec{x}^b$ on the chosen *L* dominant eigenvectors to obtain projection vector and calculate the distance statistic DS^b, and rank the distances:$DS_{r1}^b \leq DS_{r2}^b \leq \cdots \leq DS_{rG}^b$. Finally, assess statistical significance in terms of FDR for each gene. For the ri^{th} gene as ordered, compute the number of genes called significant ($rG - ri + 1$), and the median number of genes falsely called significant by calculating the median number of genes among each of the *B* sets of reference data, whose DS_{rj}^bsatisfy:$DS_{rj}^b \geq DS_{ri}$, $j = 1, \ldots, G$. Thus, FDR for the ri^{th} ordered gene is quantized as the median number of falsely called genes divided by the number of genes called significant.

5. Conclusion

A great number of advances in the SOM have been made during the past decades. The applications in the omics data mining are largely driven by the persuasive gene expression data, as well as by the availability of the user-friendly tools. The ongoing applications are to analyze the nonnumeric genomic sequenced data, probably combined with other existing methods. In principle, the same SOM procedures could also be applied to the nonnumeric sequenced data, if these sequenced data could be numerically transformed in an appropriate way (such as regularome data illustrated in Figure 1B). We envisage that these massive omics data, whether be quantified numerically or not, offer an unprecedented opportunity for the next-wave applications of the SOM. It requires the better appreciation of its dual strengths in preserving both local and global topological properties through adjusting neighborhood functions. To guide towards this direction, we have extended our previous approach into a SOM-centric pipeline, and through a real-world transcriptome data, have demonstrated its practical usefulness in achieving multifaceted functionalities. Below, we discuss future directions for further improvements.

Owing to the advantage in simultaneously displaying genes and samples, the reorganized CPPs have been demonstrated powerful for use in a variety of omics data (Figure 1). As an improvement to the ordinary CPPs, geometric location within a rectangular lattice has been utilized to reveal natural relationships between samples. At the current state, the ambiguous boundary is identified by visual inspection (Figure 1C). In the future, an automatic procedure is needed to avoid any subjective intervention from human. Another issue regarding the reorganized CPPs is limited space left for displaying component planes, especially when hundreds of samples are involved. One of the possible solutions is to use the tree-like structure [84]. The tree-structured is a natural way to link together component planes that have been clustered into different groups. Each node of the tree is a set of component planes visualized by the reorganized CPPs. Further efforts in this direction can increase the value of the reorganized CPPs in transcriptome profiling-based cancer classifications.

Another promising direction is to improve the stability of the gene clusters obtained by SOM-based two-phase clustering algorithm. The obtained clusters not only depend on random variations in the data, which has been reduced through the SOM-SVD gene selection (Figure 2), but also the stochastic nature of the SOM algorithm. As a result, distance matrix from U-matrix would differ from multiple runs, which will affect the determination of the seed nodes (i.e., local minima of distance matrix; Figure 3). The strategies like consensus clustering [56] could be used for the improvements.

The use of the SOM in network-level interpretations of omics data is poorly attempted in the literature. We have showed such possibility of aiding in temporal expression-active subnetwork detections (Figure 4). However, the SOM here only plays an indirect role. It has been reported to be used in the social network mining [85]. Much more work remains to be done so that the SOM could be directly applied to the intereactome data. Since the networked data are primarily represented as an adjacent matrix, the SOM of the matrix data (rather than the vectors) seems to be possible too [86].

Author details

Ji Zhang[1,2*] and Hai Fang[1,2]

*Address all correspondence to: jizhang@sibs.ac.cn

1 State Key Laboratory of Medical Genomics, Shanghai Institute of Hematology and Sino-French Center for Life Science and Genomics, Rui-Jin Hospital affiliated to Shanghai Jiao Tong University School of Medicine, China

2 Institute of Health Sciences, Shanghai Institutes for Biological Sciences, Chinese Academy of Sciences, China

References

[1] Ledford, H. (2010). Big science: The cancer genome challenge. *Nature*, 464(7291), 972-974.

[2] Toft, C., & Andersson, S. G. (2010). Evolutionary microbial genomics: insights into bacterial host adaptation. *Nat Rev Genet*.

[3] Schena, M., Shalon, D., Davis, R. W., & Brown, P. O. (1995). Quantitative monitoring of gene expression patterns with a complementary DNA microarray. *Science*, 270(5235), 467-470.

[4] Lockhart, D. J., Dong, H., Byrne, M. C., Follettie, M. T., Gallo, M. V., Chee, M. S., Mittmann, M., Wang, C., Kobayashi, M., Horton, H., & Brown, E. L. (1996). Expression monitoring by hybridization to high-density oligonucleotide arrays. *Nat Biotechnol*, 14(13), 1675-1680.

[5] Ren, B., Robert, F., Wyrick, J. J., Aparicio, O., Jennings, E. G., Simon, I., Zeitlinger, J., Schreiber, J., Hannett, N., Kanin, E., Volkert, T. L., Wilson, C. J., Bell, S. P., & Young, R. A. (2000). Genome-wide location and function of DNA binding proteins. *Science*, 290(5500), 2306-2309.

[6] Carroll, J. S., Meyer, C. A., Song, J., Li, W., Geistlinger, T. R., Eeckhoute, J., Brodsky, A. S., Keeton, E. K., Fertuck, K. C., Hall, G. F., Wang, Q., Bekiranov, S., Sementchenko, V., Fox, E. A., Silver, P. A., Gingeras, T. R., Liu, X. S., & Brown, M. (2006). Genome-wide analysis of estrogen receptor binding sites. *Nat Genet*, 38(11), 1289-1297.

[7] Johnson, D. S., Mortazavi, A., Myers, R. M., & Wold, B. (2007). Genome-wide mapping of in vivo protein-DNA interactions. Science;, 316(5830), 1497-1502.

[8] Domon, B., & Aebersold, R. (2006). Mass spectrometry and protein analysis. *Science*, 312(5771), 212-217.

[9] Walhout, A. J., & Vidal, M. (2001). High-throughput yeast two-hybrid assays for large-scale protein interaction mapping. *Methods*, 24(3), 297-306.

[10] Shendure, J., & Ji, H. (2008). Next-generation DNA sequencing. *Nat Biotechnol*, 26(10), 1135-1145.

[11] Wang, Z., Gerstein, M., & Snyder-Seq, M. (2009). RNA-Seq: a revolutionary tool for transcriptomics. *Nat Rev Genet*, 10(1), 57-63.

[12] Hood, L., Heath, J. R., Phelps, M. E., & Lin, B. (2004). Systems biology and new technologies enable predictive and preventative medicine. *Science*, 306(5696), 640-643.

[13] Treangen, T. J., & Salzberg, S. L. (2012). Repetitive DNA and next-generation sequencing: computational challenges and solutions. *Nat Rev Genet*, 13(1), 36-46.

[14] Eisen, M. B., Spellman, P. T., Brown, P. O., & Botstein, D. (1998). Cluster analysis and display of genome-wide expression patterns. *Proc Natl Acad Sci U S A*, 95(25), 14863-14868.

[15] Tamayo, P., Slonim, D., Mesirov, J., Zhu, Q., Kitareewan, S., Dmitrovsky, E., Lander, E. S., & Golub, T. R. (1999). Interpreting patterns of gene expression with self-organizing maps: methods and application to hematopoietic differentiation. *Proc Natl Acad Sci U S A*, 96(6), 2907-2912.

[16] Kohonen, T. (2001). Organizing Maps. Third, extended edition Springer

[17] Vesanto, J. (1999). SOM-based data visualization methods. *Intelligent Data Analysis*, 3(2), 111-126.

[18] Xiao, L., Wang, K., Teng, Y., & Zhang, J. (2003). Component plane presentation integrated self-organizing map for microarray data analysis. *FEBS Lett.*

[19] Fang, H., Du, Y., Xia, L., Li, J., Zhang, J., & Wang, K. A. (2011). A topology-preserving selection and clustering approach to multidimensional biological data. *OMICS.*

[20] Vesanto, J., & Ahola, J. Hunting for Correlations in Data Using the Self-Organizing Map. In Proc. of International ICSC Congress on Computational Intelligence Methods and Applications (CIMA'99), Rochester, New York, USA, June 22-25

[21] Xu, K., Guidez, F., Glasow, A., Chung, D., Petrie, K., Stegmaier, K., Wang, K. K., Zhang, J., Jing, Y., Zelent, A., & Waxman, S. (2005). Benzodithiophenes potentiate differentiation of acute promyelocytic leukemia cells by lowering the threshold for ligand-mediated corepressor/coactivator exchange with retinoic acid receptor alpha and enhancing changes in all-trans-retinoic acid-regulated gene expression. *Cancer Res*, 65(17), 7856-7865.

[22] Zheng, P. Z., Wang, K. K., Zhang, Q. Y., Huang, Q. H., Du, Y. Z., Zhang, Q. H., Xiao, D. K., Shen, S. H., Imbeaud, S., Eveno, E., Zhao, C. J., Chen, Y. L., Fan, H. Y., Waxman, S., Auffray, C., Jin, G., Chen, S. J., Chen, Z., & Zhang, J. (2005). Systems analysis of transcriptome and proteome in retinoic acid/arsenic trioxide-induced cell differentiation/apoptosis of promyelocytic leukemia. *Proc Natl Acad Sci U S A*, 102(21), 7653-7658.

[23] Du, Y., Wang, K., Fang, H., Li, J., Xiao, D., Zheng, P., Chen, Y., Fan, H., Pan, X., Zhao, C., Zhang, Q., Imbeaud, S., Graudens, E., Eveno, E., Auffray, C., Chen, S., Chen, Z., & Zhang, J. (2006). Coordination of intrinsic, extrinsic, and endoplasmic reticulum-mediated apoptosis by imatinib mesylate combined with arsenic trioxide in chronic myeloid leukemia. *Blood*, 107(4), 1582-1590.

[24] Fang, H., Wang, K., & Zhang, J. (2008). Transcriptome and proteome analyses of drug interactions with natural products. *Curr Drug Metab*, 9(10), 1038-1048.

[25] Wang, K., Fang, H., Xiao, D., Zhu, X., He, M., Pan, X., Shi, J., Zhang, H., Jia, X., Du, Y., & Zhang, J. (2009). Converting redox signaling to apoptotic activities by stress-responsive regulators HSF1 and NRF2 in fenretinide treated cancer cells. *PloS one*, .

[26] Bi, Y. F., Liu, R. X., Ye, L., Fang, H., Li, X. Y., Wang, W. Q., Zhang, J., Wang, K. K., Jiang, L., Su, T. W., Chen, Z. Y., & Ning, G. (2009). Gene expression profiles of thymic neuroendocrine tumors (carcinoids) with ectopic ACTH syndrome reveal novel molecular mechanism. *Endocr Relat Cancer*, 16(4), 1273-1282.

[27] Fang, H., Yang, Y., Li, C., Fu, S., Yang, Z., Jin, G., Wang, K., Zhang, J., & Jin, Y. (2010). Transcriptome analysis of early organogenesis in human embryos. *Dev Cell*, 19(1), 174-184.

[28] Wu, K., Dong, D., Fang, H., Levillain, F., Jin, W., Mei, J., Gicquel, B., Du, Y., Wang, K., Gao, Q., Neyrolles, O., & Zhang, J. (2012). An Interferon-Related Signature in the

Transcriptional Core Response of Human Macrophages to Mycobacterium tuberculosis Infection. *PloS one*, e38367.

[29] Khaitovich, P., Enard, W., Lachmann, M., & Paabo, S. (2006). Evolution of primate gene expression. *Nat Rev Genet*, 7(9), 693-702.

[30] Brawand, D., Soumillon, M., Necsulea, A., Julien, P., Csardi, G., Harrigan, P., Weier, M., Liechti, A., Aximu-Petri, A., Kircher, M., Albert, F. W., Zeller, U., Khaitovich, P., Grutzner, F., Bergmann, S., Nielsen, R., Paabo, S., & Kaessmann, H. (2011). The evolution of gene expression levels in mammalian organs. *Nature*, 478(7369), 343-348.

[31] Sammon, J. W. (1969). A Nonlinear Mapping for Data Structure Analysis. *IEEE Trans. Comput.*, 18(5), 401-409.

[32] Plath, K., & Lowry, W. E. (2011). Progress in understanding reprogramming to the induced pluripotent state. *Nat Rev Genet*, 12(4), 253-265.

[33] Chen, X., Xu, H., Yuan, P., Fang, F., Huss, M., Vega, V. B., Wong, E., Orlov, Y. L., Zhang, W., Jiang, J., Loh, Y. H., Yeo, H. C., Yeo, Z. X., Narang, V., Govindarajan, K. R., Leong, B., Shahab, A., Ruan, Y., Bourque, G., Sung, W. K., Clarke, N. D., Wei, C. L., & Ng, H. H. (2008). Integration of external signaling pathways with the core transcriptional network in embryonic stem cells. *Cell*, 133(6), 1106-1117.

[34] Alizadeh, A. A., Eisen, M. B., Davis, R. E., Ma, C., Lossos, I. S., Rosenwald, A., Boldrick, J. C., Sabet, H., Tran, T., Yu, X., Powell, J. I., Yang, L., Marti, G. E., Moore, T., Hudson, J,., Jr, Lu, L., Lewis, D. B., Tibshirani, R., Sherlock, G., Chan, W. C., Greiner, T. C., Weisenburger, D. D., Armitage, J. O., Warnke, R., Levy, R., Wilson, W., Grever, M. R., Byrd, J. C., Botstein, D., Brown, P. O., & Staudt, L. M. (2000). Distinct types of diffuse large B-cell lymphoma identified by gene expression profiling. Nature; , 403(6769), 503-511.

[35] Golub, T. R., Slonim, D. K., Tamayo, P., Huard, C., Gaasenbeek, M., Mesirov, J. P., Coller, H., Loh, M. L., Downing, J. R., Caligiuri, M. A., Bloomfield, C. D., & Lander, E. S. (1999). Molecular classification of cancer: class discovery and class prediction by gene expression monitoring. *Science*, 286(5439), 531-537.

[36] Kohonen, T. (1982). Self-organized formation of topologically correct feature maps. *Biological Cybernetics*, 43(1), 59-69.

[37] Oja, M., Kaski, S., & Kohonen, T. (2002). Bibliography of Self-Organizing Map (SOM) Papers : 1998-2001 Addendum. *Neural Networks*, 3(1), 1-156.

[38] Po, M., Honkela, T., & Kohonen, T. (2009). Bibliography of self-organizing map (som) papers: 2002-2005 addendum. *TKK Reports in Information and Computer Science, Helsinki University of Technology, Report TKK-ICS-R23*.

[39] Juha, V., Johan, H., Esa, A., & Juha, P. (1999). Self-Organizing Map in Matlab: the SOM Toolbox.

[40] Vesanto, J., & Alhoniemi, E. (2000). Clustering of the self-organizing map. *IEEE Trans Neural Netw*, 11(3), 586-600.

[41] Siponen, M., Vesanto, J., Simula, O., & Vasara, P. An approach to automated interpretation of SOM. In Advances in Self-Organizing Maps: Springer: (2001). , 2001, 89-94.

[42] Toronen, P., Kolehmainen, M., Wong, G., & Castren, E. (1999). Analysis of gene expression data using self-organizing maps. *FEBS Lett*, 451(2), 142-146.

[43] White, K. P., Rifkin, S. A., Hurban, P., & Hogness, D. S. (1999). Microarray analysis of Drosophila development during metamorphosis. *Science*, 286(5447), 2179-2184.

[44] Kaski, S. (2001). SOM-Based Exploratory Analysis of Gene Expression Data. N, Yin H, Allinson L, and Slack J. London: Springer , 2001124-131.

[45] Torkkola, K., Gardner, R. M., Kaysser-Kranich, T., & Ma, C. (2001). Self-organizing maps in mining gene expression data. *Inf. Sci.*

[46] Kanaya, S., Kinouchi, M., Abe, T., Kudo, Y., Yamada, Y., Nishi, T., Mori, H., & Ikemura, T. (2001). Analysis of codon usage diversity of bacterial genes with a self-organizing map (SOM): characterization of horizontally transferred genes with emphasis on the E. coli O157 genome. *Gene*.

[47] Wang, H. C., Badger, J., Kearney, P., & Li, M. (2001). Analysis of codon usage patterns of bacterial genomes using the self-organizing map. *Mol Biol Evol*, 18(5), 792-800.

[48] Nikkila, J., Törönen, P., Kaski, S., Venna, J., Castrén, E., & Wong, G. (2002). Analysis and visualization of gene expression data using self-organizing maps. *Neural Netw.*

[49] Covell, D. G., Wallqvist, A., Rabow, A. A., & Thanki, N. (2003). Molecular classification of cancer: unsupervised self-organizing map analysis of gene expression microarray data. *Mol Cancer Ther*, 2(3), 317-332.

[50] Buckhaults, P., Zhang, Z., Chen, Y. C., Wang, T. L., St, Croix. B., Saha, S., Bardelli, A., Morin, P. J., Polyak, K., Hruban, R. H., Velculescu, V. E., & Shih, Ie. M. (2003). Identifying tumor origin using a gene expression-based classification map. *Cancer Res*, 63(14), 4144-4149.

[51] Wang, J., Delabie, J., Aasheim, H., Smeland, E., & Myklebost, O. (2002). Clustering of the SOM easily reveals distinct gene expression patterns: results of a reanalysis of lymphoma study. *BMC Bioinformatics*.

[52] Sultan, M., Wigle, D. A., Cumbaa, C. A., Maziarz, M., Glasgow, J., Tsao, M. S., & Jurisica, I. (2002). Binary tree-structured vector quantization approach to clustering and visualizing microarray data. Bioinformatics (Oxford, England) Suppl 1S , 111-119.

[53] Hautaniemi, S., Yli-Harja, O., Astola, J., Kauraniemi, Pi., Kallioniemi, A., Wolf, M., Ruiz, J., Mousses, S., & Kallioniemi-P, O. (2003). Analysis and Visualization of Gene

Expression Microarray Data in Human Cancer Using Self-Organizing Maps. Mach. Learn.

[54] Ressom, H., Wang, D., & Natarajan, P. (2003). Clustering gene expression data using adaptive double self-organizing map. *Physiol Genomics*, 14(1), 35-46.

[55] Hsu, A. L., Tang, S. L., & Halgamuge, S. K. (2003). An unsupervised hierarchical dynamic self-organizing approach to cancer class discovery and marker gene identification in microarray data. *Bioinformatics (Oxford, England)*, 19(16), 2131-2140.

[56] Monti, S., Tamayo, P., Mesirov, J., & Golub, T. (2003). Consensus Clustering: A Resampling-Based Method for Class Discovery and Visualization of Gene Expression Microarray Data. *Machine Learning*, 52(1), 91-118.

[57] Brunet, J. P., Tamayo, P., Golub, T. R., & Mesirov, J. P. (2004). Metagenes and molecular pattern discovery using matrix factorization. *Proc Natl Acad Sci U S A*, 101(12), 4164-4169.

[58] Kohonen, T., & Somervuo, P. (2002). How to make large self-organizing maps for nonvectorial data. *Neural Netw*.

[59] Yang, Z. R., & Chou, K. C. (2003). Mining biological data using self-organizing map. *J Chem Inf Comput Sci*, 43(6), 1748-1753.

[60] Abe, T., Kanaya, S., Kinouchi, M., Ichiba, Y., Kozuki, T., & Ikemura, T. (2003). Informatics for unveiling hidden genome signatures. *Genome Res*, 13(4), 693-702.

[61] Mahony, S., Mclnerney, J. O., Smith, T. J., & Golden, A. (2004). Gene prediction using the Self-Organizing Map: automatic generation of multiple gene models. *BMC Bioinformatics*.

[62] Mahony, S., Hendrix, D., Golden, A., Smith, T. J., & Rokhsar, D. S. (2005). Transcription factor binding site identification using the self-organizing map. *Bioinformatics (Oxford, England)*, 21(9), 1807-1814.

[63] Liu, D., Xiong, X., Das, Gupta. B., & Zhang, H. (2006). Motif discoveries in unaligned molecular sequences using self-organizing neural networks. *IEEE Trans Neural Netw*, 17(4), 919-928.

[64] Lee, N. K., & Wang, D. (2011). SOMEA: self-organizing map based extraction algorithm for DNA motif identification with heterogeneous model. BMC Bioinformatics Suppl 1S16.

[65] Ultsch, A, & Orchen, F. (2005). ESOM-Maps: tools for clustering, visualization,and classification with Emergent SOM.

[66] Dick, G. J., Andersson, A. F., Baker, B. J., Simmons, S. L., Thomas, B. C., Yelton, A. P., & Banfield, J. F. (2009). Community-wide analysis of microbial genome sequence signatures. *Genome biology R85*.

[67] Chan, C. K., Hsu, A. L., Halgamuge, S. K., & Tang, S. L. (2008). Binning sequences using very sparse labels within a metagenome. *BMC Bioinformatics*.

[68] Chan, C. K., Hsu, A. L., & Tang, S. L. (2008). Halgamuge SK.Using growing self-organising maps to improve the binning process in environmental whole-genome shotgun sequencing. *J Biomed Biotechnol*.

[69] Gatherer, D. (2007). Genome signatures, self-organizing maps and higher order phylogenies: a parametric analysis. *Evol Bioinform Online*, 3211-236.

[70] Martin, C., Diaz, N. N., Ontrup, J., & Nattkemper, T. W. (2008). Hyperbolic SOM-based clustering of DNA fragment features for taxonomic visualization and classification. *Bioinformatics (Oxford, England)*, 24(14), 1568-1574.

[71] Abe, T., Sugawara, H., Kanaya, S., Kinouchi, M., & Ikemura, T. (2006). Self-Organizing Map (SOM) unveils and visualizes hidden sequence characteristics of a wide range of eukaryote genomes. *Gene*, 36527-34.

[72] Abe, T., Hamano, Y., Kanaya, S., Wada, K., & Ikemura, T. (2009). A Large-Scale Genomics Studies Conducted with Batch-Learning SOM Utilizing High-Performance Supercomputers.

[73] Bio-Inspired Systems: Computational and Ambient Intelligence. (2009). 5517829-836.

[74] Weber, M., Teeling, H., Huang, S., Waldmann, J., Kassabgy, M., Fuchs, B. M., Klindworth, A., Klockow, C., Wichels, A., Gerdts, G., Amann, R., & Glockner, F. O. (2011). Practical application of self-organizing maps to interrelate biodiversity and functional data in NGS-based metagenomics. *ISME J*, 5(5), 918-928.

[75] Wu, W., Liu, X., Xu, M., Peng, J. R., & Setiono, R. A. (2005). A hybrid SOM-SVM approach for the zebrafish gene expression analysis. *Genomics Proteomics Bioinformatics*, 3(2), 84-93.

[76] Ghouila, A., Yahia, S. B., Malouche, D., Jmel, H., Laouini, D., Guerfali, F. Z., & Abdelhak, S. (2009). Application of Multi-SOM clustering approach to macrophage gene expression analysis. *Infect Genet Evol*, 9(3), 328-336.

[77] Newman, A. M., & Cooper, J. B. (2010). AutoSOME: a clustering method for identifying gene expression modules without prior knowledge of cluster number. *BMC Bioinformatics*.

[78] Vesanto, J. (2000). SOM Toolbox for Matlab 5: Helsinki University of Technology. ;.

[79] Vellido, A., Lisboa, P. J. G., & Meehan, K. (1999). Segmentation of the on-line shopping market using neural networks. *Expert Systems with Applications*, 17(4), 303-314.

[80] Vesanto, J., & Sulkava, M. (2002). Distance matrix based clustering of the Self-Organizing Map. *Artificial Neural Networks- Icann*, 2415951-956.

[81] Ashburner, M., Ball, C. A., Blake, J. A., Botstein, D., Butler, H., Cherry, J. M., Davis, A. P., Dolinski, K., Dwight, S. S., Eppig, J. T., Harris, M. A., Hill, D. P., Issel-Tarver,

L., Kasarskis, A., Lewis, S., Matese, J. C., Richardson, J. E., Ringwald, M., Rubin, G. M., & Sherlock, G. (2000). Gene ontology: tool for the unification of biology. The Gene Ontology Consortium. Nat Genet; , 25(1), 25-29.

[82] Dreszer, T. R., Karolchik, D., Zweig, A. S., Hinrichs, A. S., Raney, B. J., Kuhn, R. M., Meyer, L. R., Wong, M., Sloan, C. A., Rosenbloom, K. R., Roe, G., Rhead, B., Pohl, A., Malladi, V. S., Li, C. H., Learned, K., Kirkup, V., Hsu, F., Harte, R. A., Guruvadoo, L., Goldman, M., Giardine, B. M., Fujita, P. A., Diekhans, M., Cline, M. S., Clawson, H., Barber, G. P., Haussler, D., & James, Kent. W. (2012). The UCSC Genome Browser database: extensions and updates 2011. Nucleic Acids Res (Database , 40(D918-923), 918-923.

[83] Smith, C.L., & Eppig, J.T. (2009). The mammalian phenotype ontology: enabling robust annotation and comparative analysis. *Wiley Interdiscip Rev Syst Biol Med,* 1(3), 390-399.

[84] Ideker, T., Ozier, O., Schwikowski, B., & Siegel, A. F. (2002). Discovering regulatory and signalling circuits in molecular interaction networks. Bioinformatics (Oxford, England) Suppl 1S , 233-240.

[85] Barreto, S. M. A., & Pérez-Uribe, A. (2007). Improving the correlation hunting in a large quantity of SOM component planes: classification of agro-ecological variables related with productivity in the sugar cane culture. In Proceedings of the 17th international conference on Artificial neural networks.

[86] Boulet, R., Jouve, B., Rossi, F., & Villa, N. (2008). Batch kernel SOM and related Laplacian methods for social network analysis. *Neurocomput.*

[87] Seo, S., & Obermayer, K. (2004). Self-organizing maps and clustering methods for matrix data. *Neural Netw.*

Chapter 10

Application of Self-Organizing Maps in Text Clustering: A Review

Yuan-Chao Liu, Ming Liu and Xiao-Long Wang

Additional information is available at the end of the chapter

http://dx.doi.org/10.5772/50618

1. Introduction

Text clustering is one of the most important text mining research directions. Despite the loss of some details, clustering technology simplifies the structure of data set, so that people can observe the data from a macro point of view.

After clustering process, the text data set can be divided into some different clusters, making the distance between the individuals in the same cluster as small as possible, while the distance between the different categories as far away from each other as possible.

Similar as text classification, text clustering is also the technology of processing a large number of texts and gives their partition.What is different is that text clustering analysis of the text collection gives an optimal division of the category without the need for labeling the category of some documents by hand in advance, so it is an unsupervised machine learning method. By comparison, text clustering technology has strong flexibility and automatic processing capabilities, and has become an important means of effective organization and navigation of text information. Jardine and van Rijsbergen made the famous clustering hypothesis: closely associated documents belong to same category and the same request [1]. Text clustering can also act as the basic research for many other applications. It is a preprocessing step for some natural language processing applications, e.g., automatic summarization, user preference mining, or be used to improve text classification results. YC Fang, S. Parthasarathy, [2] and Charu [3] use clustering techniques to cluster users' frequent query and then the results to update the FAQ of search engine sites.

Although both text clustering and text classification are based on the idea of class, there are still some apparent differences: the classification is based on the taxonomy, the category distribution has been known beforehand. While the purpose of text clustering is to find the topic structure of documents [4] [5] [6] [7] [8] [9] [10]. Yasemin Kural [11] made a lot of experiments and compared the clustering mode and linear array mode for search engine, the results show that the former can indeed increase information access efficiency greatly.

Although there are many clustering methods, SOM has attracted many researchers in recent years. In this chapter, we reviewed the application of Self-Organizing Maps in Text Clustering. Our recent works on SOM based text clustering are also introduced briefly. The remaining of this chapter is organized as follows. Section 2 gives a review about the advances in text clustering and SOM; section 3 presents our recent work on application of self-organizing maps in text clustering. Then in section 4 some conclusions and discussions are given.

2. The Advances In Text Clustering And SOM

2.1. Text Clustering And Its Recent Research And Development

Text clustering is an unsupervised process that is not dependent on the prior knowledge of data collection, and based solely on the similarity relationship between documents in the collection to separate the document collection into some clusters. The general mathematical description of text clustering can be depicted as follows:

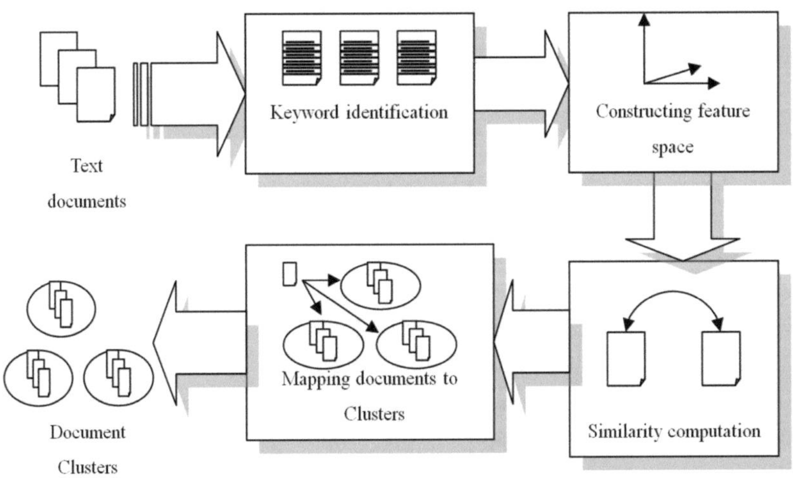

Figure 1. The main framework for text clustering system.

Suppose $C=\{d_1, d_2, \ldots, d_n\}$ is a collection of documents to be clustered, each document d_i can be represented as high-dimensional space vector$d_i=\{w_1, w_2, \ldots, w_i\}$ by the famous vector space model (VSM), where w_i means the weight of d_i on feature j. The purpose of text clustering is to divide C into $C_1, C_2, \ldots, C_x$, $C_1 \cup C_2 \cup \ldots \cup C_x = C$, here $1 \le i \ne j \le k$. For hard clustering, each document can belong to only one class, i.e. $C_i \cap C_j = \Phi$. Whereas for soft clustering, one document may belong to multiple clusters. Membership degree μ_{ij} can be used to denote how much d_i belongs to cluster C_j.

Compared with other data types, text data is semi-structured. This makes man database-based algorithms does not apply to text clustering.

One important preprocessing step for text clustering is to consider how the text content can be represented in the form of mathematical expression for further analysis and processing. The Common method is Salton's vector space model [12] (Vector Space Model, VSM). The basic idea is: one feature space are constructed firstly, each dimension means one term, which comes from the key words of each document. Then each document is represented as one vector in this feature space. The document vector is usually a sparse vector as the dimension is very huge.

Dimensionality reduction is an essential step in text clustering. There are several techniques to reduce the dimension of the high-dimensional feature vector. PCA (Principal Component Analysis) method is one of the widely used dimension reduction techniques. Given an n × m-order document-term matrix, the k eigenvectors of the PCA with an m × m-order covariance matrix is used to reduce the dimension of the word space, and ultimately resulted in a k-term space dimension, which is much smaller than m.

LSI (Latent Semantic the Indexing) method is also widely used in the field of information retrieval, dimensionality reduction. It is in essence similar with the PCA. LSI make singular value decomposition not on covariance matrix, but on the initial n × m-order document–term matrix, and then selecting these singular eigenvectors as representative, thereby reduces the dimension.

Another problem is how to extract important features from documents. Mark P. Sinka and David W. Corne [13] argue that stop word removal will improve the text clustering effect. They also pointed out that after obtaining all unique words in the collection, you can only keep some high-frequency words to construct the space. Anton V. Leouski and W. Bruce Crof demonstrated that for each document, it is necessary to select only some important words to represent the document, and can basically meet the needs of the cluster without impacting clustering results. Literature [14] proposed a method to extract the key words in the document as features Literature [15] use latent semantic indexing (LSI) method to compress the dimension of the clustering feature space. Besides, ZhengYu Niu [16] and STANISŁAW OSIŃSKI [17], etc also performed research on feature selection.

Assume there are five documents doc1 doc2, doc3, doc4, and doc5. For each document, the first steps are segmenting, stop word removal, and word frequency counting. In order to improve the clustering efficiency, only the words which frequency is above a certain threshold value are used to construct the feature space. Studies have shown that such a treatment will not have an adverse impact on the clustering quality. Then the feature space can be constructed by using the term set which comes from all these terms. Each document is represented as a vector in the feature space. Fig.2. depicts the preprocessing steps for text clustering.

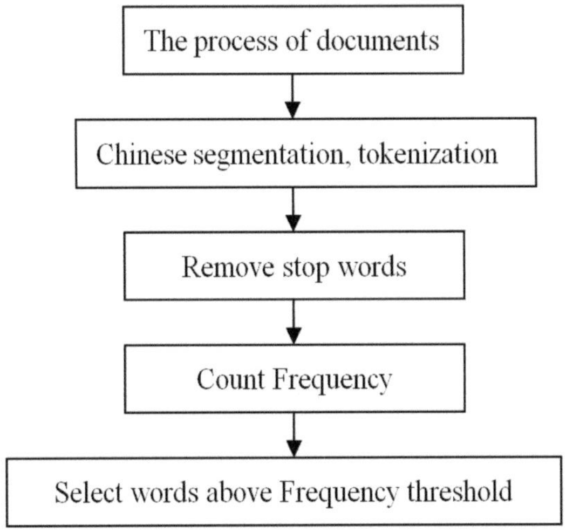

Figure 2. the preprocessing steps of text document for text clustering.

Suppose the feature space is (apple, banana in the cat, window), and feature words frequency threshold is 2, then the following example document-term matrix can be formed:

	(Apple,	banana,	cat,	window)
doc1 = (	5,	3,	0,	4)
doc2 = (	4,	6,	0,	3)
doc3 = (	0,	3,	7,	5)
doc4 = (	8,	0,	9,	0)
doc5 = (	5,	0,	0,	3)

As all documents are represented as the vector in the same feature space, thus it is more convenient for computing the document similarity. In fact, the similarity calculation is very frequent for most clustering algorithms. In addition, as there are usually many common words in different documents, the actual dimension of the feature space is less than the sum of the number of words selected from each document.

The evaluation of word importance. Take a science paper as an example, it is shown that about 65% to 90% author-marked keywords can be found in the main content in the original paper[18]. This means that by importance evaluation, the key words can be extracted from documents to represent the main content. Basically, keyword extraction can be seen as a supervised machine learning problems; this idea is first proposed by Turney [19]. Turney also make a comparative study based on genetic algorithms and decision tree-based keywords extraction algorithm. Factors which can denote the word importance includes word frequency, word location (title, caption and etc.). Many researches showed that high-frequency words are the more important words. Some typical keyword extraction system has been listed in table 1.

name	websites
NRC's Extractor	http://ai.iit.nrc.ca/II_public/extractor/
Verity's Search 97	http://www.verity.com/
KEA	http://www.nzdl.org/Kea/
GenEX	http://extractor.iit.nrc.ca/
Microsoft office 2003	http://www.microsoft.com/
Eric Brill's Tagger	ftp://ftp.cs.jhu.edu/pub/brill/Programs/

Table 1. Some Classical Keyword Extraction Systems.

2.2. Two Clustering strategies in Text Clustering: whole clustering and incremental clustering

There are two common Clustering strategies, and both need to measure the similarity of the document.

The first strategy is the "complete" strategy, or called "static" strategy. During the clustering process, the documents collection did not change neither adding documents, nor removing documents. At the beginning of clustering, the documents in the collection are fixed. In the clustering Method based on this policy, an N*N similarity matrix can be generated from the beginning and there are $N(N-1)/2$ similarity values in the matrix. As it will compare the similarity among any documents, the computation is very costly.

The second strategy is the strategy of "incremental"[20]. In many occasions, the document collection can be increased at any time in the clustering process. When adding a document, it will be merged into the existing cluster, or you can separate it as a new category. While increasing documents, it may be necessary to perform re-clustering.

There are some methods to calculate the similarity or distances between different clusters: 1) the shortest distance method (single link method). If G_p, G_q are two different clusters, $D_s(p, q)=\min\{d_{ij} \mid i\in G_p,\ j\in G_q\}$; 2) the longest distance method. If G_p, G_q are two different clusters, $D_s(p, q)=\max\{d_{ij} \mid i\in G_p,\ j\in G_q\}$;3) Group average method. $D_s^2(p, q)=\frac{1}{n_p n_q}\sum_{\substack{i\in G_p \\ j\in G_q}} d_{ij}^2$;4)

The centric method. $\overline{x_G}=\frac{1}{L}\sum_{i=l}^{L} x_i$ Mean Quantization Error (abbreviated as MQE) is adopted as convergence condition as performed by Ref. [10-12]. Since MQE can measure the average agglomeration degree of clustering results, when its value is less than a threshold such as 0.01 (which is adopted by Kohonen in Ref. [21]), this dynamic algorithm stops.

$$MQE=\frac{\sum_{j=1}^{C}\sum_{Di\in Cj}\frac{|Di-Nj|^2}{|Cj|}}{C} \quad (1)$$

Where, C represents the quantity of clusters. Nj represents one neuron. Cj represents the cluster, which includes the data that are more similar to Nj than to other neurons. |Cj| represents the quantity of the data included by Cj. Di represents one datum among Cj.

2.3. SOM And Its Application For Text Clustering

Self-organizing map network (SOM, for abbreviation) is first proposed by T.Kohonen Professor in University of Helsinki in Finland, also known as the Kohonen network [22]. Kohonen believes that a neural network will be divided into different corresponding regions while receiving outside input mode, and different regions have different response characteristics for corresponding input mode, and this process can be done automatically. SOM network has the following main properties: 1) The cluster center is the mathematical expectation of all the documents in this cluster; 2) "cluster" of input data, and maintaining the topological order. Fully trained SOM network can be viewed as a pattern classifier. By inputting a document, the neurons representing the pattern class-specific in the output layer will have the greatest response.

The self-organizing map is proposed based on this idea, which is similar to the self-organization clustering process in human brain[23] [24]. SOM clustering method has been successfully used in the field of digital libraries, text clustering and many other applications [25] [26] [27] [28].

The running process of the SOM network can be divided into two stages: training and mapping. In the training phase, the samples were input randomly. For a particular input pattern, there will be a winning node in the output layer, which produces the greatest response. At the beginning of the training phase, which node in the output layer will generate the maximum response is uncertain. When the category of the input pattern is changed, the winning node of the two-dimensional plane will also change. Due to the lateral mutual excitatory effects, Nodes around the winning node have a greater response, so all the nodes of the winning node and its neighborhood will both perform different levels of adjustment.

SOM adjust the weights of the output layer nodes with a large number of training samples, and finally each node in the output layer is sensitive to a specific pattern class. When the class characteristics of the two clusters are close, the nodes on behalf of these two clusters are also close in position.

After the training of the SOM network, the relation between output layer nodes and each input pattern can be determined, then all the input patterns can be mapped onto the nodes in the output layers, which is called mapping steps.

SOM method usually requires pre-defining the size and structure of the network. There are some methods which can achieve this purpose [29][30][31]. The basic idea is to allow more rows or columns to be dynamically added to the network, make the network more suitable for the simulation of the real input space.

SOM method requires the definition of neighborhood function and learning rate function beforehand. There is no fixed pattern in Kohonen model on the choice of neighborhood function and learning rate function, they are generally selected based on the heuristic information [32][33]. H.Yin proposed BSOM, which is SOM method based on Bayesian [34]. The basic idea is to minimize the KL distance of the data density and neural models. KL distance can measure the distance or deviation between the environment probability density and real probability density, its value is generally a positive number. Learning process can be done within a fixed range of the winner neuron. The BSOM therefore gives a new perspective on the role of the conventional SOM neighborhood function. In addition, Filip, Mulier and Vladimir Cherkassky studied the learning rate function strategy in SOM [35]. The experimental results show that the location of the neurons may be over affected by the last input data. Filip, Mulier, Vladimir Cherkassky has improved the learning rate function and neighborhood function, to make impact of the input training data on the neuron location more uniform.

2.4. The Comparison Of SOM With Other Text Clustering Methods

Besides from SOM, There are also two widely used text clustering methods: AHC clustering method and K-means clustering method. The basic steps of AHC for text clustering method are as follows:

1. Calculate the document similarity matrix;
2. Each document is seen as a cluster firstly;
3. Merge the nearest two clusters into one;
4. Update the similarity matrix, i.e, re-calculating of the similarity of the new cluster with the current cluster; if there are only one cluster, then go to step 5), otherwise go to step 3);
5. End.

Researchers often use two different methods to cut the hierarchical relationships. One is to use the number of clusters as segmentation standard; another method is using the similarity as the segmentation standard, that is, when the similarity between two clusters is lower than a given threshold, the clustering algorithm will stop. Besides, it has been shown that the clustering entropy [36] can be used as the termination conditions of the hierarchical clustering method:

$$En = \left(\sum_{j-l}^{k}\sum_{i-l}^{n} e(p_i^{(j)}, p_0^{(j)})\right) + \sum_{j-l}^{k} e(p_0^{(j)}, c_0) \tag{2}$$

The first expression in the right side of the formula is the intra-cluster entropy; the second means the inter-cluster entropy. When En is smallest, the clustering result achieves optimum value. c_0 is the center of all the samples. $p_i^{(j)}$ is the i documents for cluster j. $p_0^{(j)}$ is the center of the jth clusters. K is the number of clusters, n_j is the number of documents in cluster j.

K-means clustering algorithm is the typical dynamic partition method [37] [38] [39] [40]. The basic steps [41] are as follows:

1. Randomly select K documents, which represent initial cluster centroids.
2. Assign each document to the cluster that has the closest centroid.
3. When all documents have been assigned, recalculate the K centroids.
4. Repeat Steps 2 and 3 until the centroids no longer change.
5. Output the separation of these documents, i.e. different clusters.

For K-means, if the k value selected is inappropriate or the choice of initial accumulation point is uneven, the clustering process will be delayed and the clustering results are also adversely affected. Traditionally, there are mainly two methods to select the initial cluster center: 1) randomly select k points; 2) use empirical method to select the initial cluster centers. In addition, the researchers also made some of the more complex but very effective method: 1) the gravity center method. The basic idea is: first calculate the gravity center of all the samples as the first point; then select a positive number as the minimum critical distance. Input all the samples in turn, if the input sample has distance greater than d, it will be deemed as a new clustering point; 2) the density method. Two positive numbers d1 and d2 ($d1d2$) are first set, form the ultra-dimensional ball using d1 as the radius, which density is calculated as the number of samples in that ball. Select the sample with the maximum density as the first center; select the sample with the second maximum density.

Generally, SOM has proven to be the most suitable document clustering method. It can map documents onto two-dimensional diagram to show the relationship between the different documents. SOM can depict text in more figurative and better visual way. High-dimensional space can be transformed into two-dimensional space, and the similarity between the input data in the multi-dimension space is well maintained in the two-dimensional discrete space, the degree of similarity between the high dimensional spatial data can also be transformed into the location proximity of representation space, which can maintain the topological order. SOM also has the following advantages: 1) noise immunity; 2) visualization; 3) parallel processing.

Text Clustering is a high-dimensional application and closely related to the semantic features. The above characteristics of SOM make it very suitable for text clustering.

2.5. Dynamic clustering of SOM

Self-Organizing-Mapping (abbreviated as SOM) is one of the most extensively applied clustering algorithm for data analysis, because of its characteristic that its neuron topology is identical with the distribution of input data. However, the inconvenience, that it needs to predefine two parameters of cluster quantity and neuron topology, prevents it from prevailing in online situation.

As indicated by Ref. [42][43][44], many methods have been proposed to cluster dynamic data. For example, Dhillon et al. [45] proposed a dynamic clustering algorithm to help analyze the transfer of information. Unfortunately, this algorithm is time-consuming and impractical, since it needs to run several times. Ghaseminezhad and Karami [46] improve this algorithm by employing SOM structure, which forms an initial neuron topology at first and then dynamically tunes its topology once input data are updated. However, its neuron topology is fixed in advance and too rigid to be altered.

In order to enable neuron topology easily to be altered, some self-adaptive algorithms have been proposed. The prominent merit of them is that they don't need to set any assumption about neuron topology in advance. For example, Melody in Ref. [47] initializes a neuron topology of small scale at first and then gradually expands it following the update of input data. Tseng et al in Ref. [48] improve this algorithm by tuning neuron topology in virtue of dynamically creating and deleting the arcs between different neurons.

Unfortunately, aforementioned self-adaptive algorithms have two defects. One is that, when neuron topology isn't suitable for current input data, they will insert or split neurons, whereas, these newly created neurons may locate out of the area where input data distribute. The other is that, they fail to preserve topology order. Therefore, they can't perform competitive learning as transitional SOM based algorithms, which will generate some dead neurons and they will never be tuned. The detailed discussions are indicated in Ref. [49][50].

For avoiding predefining cluster quantity, some scalable SOM based clustering algorithms are proposed, such as GSOM in Ref. [51] and GHSOM in Ref. [52]. Nevertheless, neuron topologies of them are fixed as liner, cycle, square or rectangle in advance. These kinds of topologies are too rigid, and hardly to be altered.

In order to solve this problem, some topology adaptive algorithms have been proposed, such as GNG in Ref. [53], PSOM in Ref. [54], and DASH in Ref. [55]. These algorithms free of predefining neuron topology and can automatically construct it to let it conform to the distribution of input data.

3. Our Recent Work On Application Of Self-Organizing Maps In Text Clustering

3.1. The Conceptual SOM Model For Text Clustering

Most of the existing text clustering methods simply use word frequency vector to represent the document, with little regard to the language's own characteristics and ontological knowledge. When documents are clustered using conventional "SOM plus VSM" way, it is hard to grasp the underlying semantic knowledge and consequently the clustering quality may be adversely affected. However, we notice that the documents in same cluster are very relevant to each other even though there are few common words shared by these documents, so the relevance calculation among documents can be simplified by the relevance calculation of words in documents.

Y.C. Liu et al. have proposed a conceptional self-organizing map model (ConSOM) [56]for text clustering, in which neurons and documents are represented by the vector in extended concept space and that in traditional feature space. It has been shown that by importing concept relevance knowledge, SOM can achieve better performance than traditional mode due to its semantic sensitivity. Figure 3 give the basic principle for ConSOM. After both extended concept space and traditional feature space are constructed, all documents and neurons are represented by two vectors: traditional vector VF purely formed by word frequency and extended concept vector VC, as shown in Fig. 3. Table 2.presents Concept Representation of Word in HowNet.

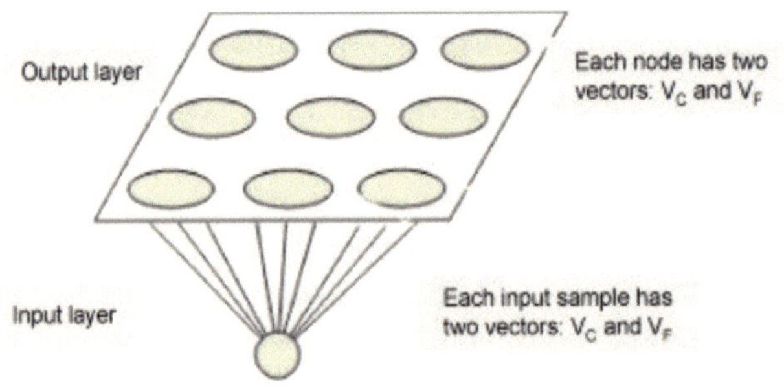

Figure 3. The basic principle of ConSOM.

<table>
<tr><td>NO.=124922
W_C=医生：G_C=N：E_C=NULL：W_E=Dr.：G_E=N：E_E=NULL：DEF={human|人:HostOf={Occupation|职位},domain={medical|医},{doctor|医治:agent={~}}}</td></tr>
<tr><td>NO.=048622
W_C=患者：G_C=N：E_C=NULL：W_E=patient：G_E=N：E_E=NULL：
DEF={human|人:domain={medical|医},{SufferFrom|罹患:experiencer={~}},{doctor|医治:patient={~}}}</td></tr>
<tr><td>NO.=124949
W_C=医院：G_C=N：E_C=NULL：W_E=hospital：G_E=N：E_E=NULL：
DEF={InstitutePlace|场所:domain={medical|医},{doctor|医治:content={disease|疾病},location={~}}}</td></tr>
</table>

Table 2. Concept Representation of Word in HowNet.

3.2. Fast SOM Clustering Method For Large-Scale Text Clustering

Conventional data clustering methods frequently perform unsatisfactorily for large text collections due to 3 factors:1) there are usually large number of documents to be processed; 2) the dimension is very huge for text clustering; 2) the computation complexity is very high. So it is very necessary to improve the computation speed.

As similarity computation is very crucial for text clustering, and has much impact on clustering efficiency, Y. liu and etc[57]. propose one novel feature representation and similarity computation method to make SOM text clustering much faster. Each document is coded as the collection of some keywords extracted from the original document, and will directly be input to SOM, whereas each output layer node of SOM are coded as numerical vector as that of most Kohonen Networks.

In order to directly separate documents into different groups, ring topology is adopted as our SOM structure, thus the number of groups can be any integral values. Like Kohonen Networks, it consists of two layers, input layer and output layer; each node in output layer corresponds to one cluster. Only neurons need to be represented as high-dimension vector, whereas the document will be coded as indexes of keywords.

3.3. The Variant Of SOM Model For Dynamic Text Clustering

Figure 5 shows the ring output layer topology of V-SOM [58]. The advantage of this topology is that sector number (node number) can be any integers, and it will be possible to reflect topic distribution of the input documents more finely and make full use of neurons. Besides, the number of neighboring neurons for each neuron is same, thus it can help avoid edge effect which usually happens by using rectangular or hexagonal topology. Neurons can be inserted gradually to avoid lack-of-use phenomenon of neurons. R^2 cluster criterion is used to find suitable network size which can reflect topic distribution of input documents.

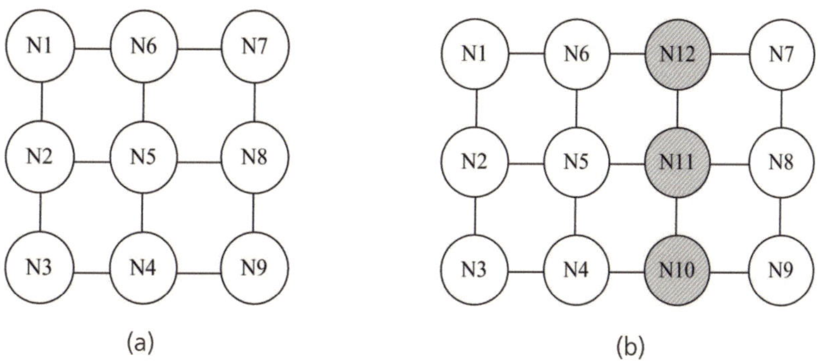

Figure 4. The rectangular topology of GHSOM (N10, N11, N12 in Figure1. (b) are the newly inserted neurons).

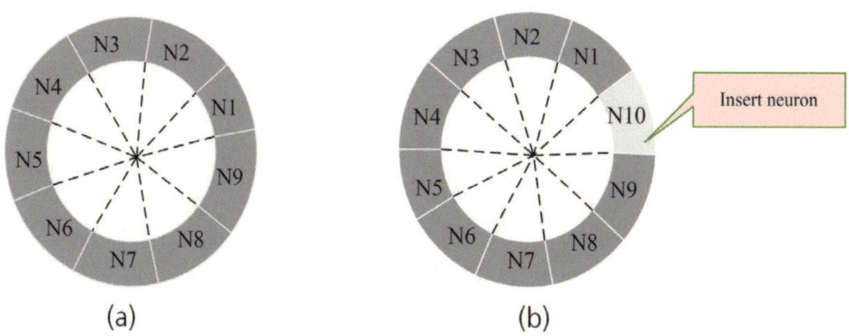

Figure 5. The Ring Topology of V-SOM. N10 Is The Inserted Node In Figure (b).

4. Conclusions and discission

In conclusion, SOM has obvious advantage in terms of topology preserving order, anti-noise ability. By using self-organizing map network as the main framework of the text clustering, semantic knowledge can also be easily incorporated so as to enhance the clustering effect.

First, SOM can better handle the dynamic clustering problem through various kinds of dynamic vari-structure model. E.g. V-SOM model, which combine the decomposition strategy and neuronal dynamic expansion, under the guidance of clustering criterion function, dynamically and adaptively adjust the network structure, thus the clustering results can better reflect the topic distribution of input documents.

Second, semantic knowledge can be easily integrated into the SOM. Due to the diversity and complexity of language, same concept may also have different forms of expression. The traditional "VSM+SOM" mode rely solely on the frequency of feature words, and cannot grasp and embody semantic information. We use HowNet as a source of conceptual knowledge and perform effective integration with statistical information in order to enhance the sensitive ability of the clustering. if there are clusters with hidden common concept, they will be merged into one cluster, even if they are less common words shared by these documents.

Finally, the SOM's unique training structure provides convenience for the realization of parallel clustering and incremental clustering, thus contributing to improve the efficiency of clustering. Incremental clustering also makes it more suitable for dynamic clustering of web documents.

Author details

Yuan-Chao Liu , Ming Liu and Xiao-Long Wang

Address all correspondence to: lyc@insun.hit.edu.cn

School of Computer Science and Technology, Harbin Institute of Technology, China

References

[1] Jardine, N., & van Rijsbergen, C. J. (1971). The use of hierarchic clustering in information retrieval. *Information Storage and Retrieval*, 7(1), 217-240.

[2] Fang, Y. C., Parthasarathy, S., & Schwartz, F. (2002). Using Clustering to Boost Text Classification. *In Proceedings of the IEEE ICDM Workshop on Text Mining*, 101-112.

[3] Charu. (2004). On using Partial Supervision for Text Categorization. *IEEE Transactions On Knowledge And Data Engineering*, 16(2), 245-258.

[4] Croft, W. B. (1978). Organizing and searching large files of documents. *Ph.D. Thesis*, University of Cambridge.

[5] Hearst, M. A., & Pedersen, J. O. (1996). Reexamining the cluster hypothesis: Scatter/ Gather on retrieval results. *Proceedings of the 19th International ACM SIGIR Conference on Research and Development in InformationRetrieval (SIGIR'96)*, 76-84.

[6] Leouski, A. V., & Croft, W. B. (1996). An evaluation of techniques for clustering search results. *Technical Report IR-76*, Department of Computer Science, University of Massachusetts, Amherst.

[7] Allen, R. B., Obry, P., & Littman, M. (1993). An interface for navigating clustered document sets returned by queries. *Proceedings of the ACM Conference on Organizational Computing Systems*, 166-171.

[8] Cutting, Douglass R., Karger, David R., & etc. Scatter/Gather. (1992). A Cluster-based Approach to Browsing Large Document Collections. *SIGIR'92*, 318-329.

[9] Voorhees, E. M. (1986). The efficiency of Inverted Index and Cluster Searches. *In: Proceedings of the ACM Conference on R&D in IR. Pisa*, 1986, 164-174.

[10] El -Hamdouchi, A., & Willett, P. (1989). Comparison of Hierarchic Agglomerative Clustering Methods for Document Retrieval. *The Computer Journal*, 32(3), 220-227.

[11] Kural, Yasemin, Robertson, Steve, & Jones, Susan. (2001). Clustering Information Retrieval Search Outputs. *Information Processing & Management*, 1630-1700.

[12] Salton, G., Wong, A., & Yang, C. (1975). A vector space model for automatic indexing. Communications of the ACM ., 18(11), 613-620.

[13] Seung-Shik, Kang. (2003). Keyword-based Document Clustering. *The 6th International Workshop on Information Retrieval with Asian Languages*, 132-137.

[14] Lerman, K. (2004). Document Clustering in Reduced Dimension Vector Space. *Proceedings of CSAW'04*.

[15] Niu, Z. Y., Ji, D. H., & Tan, C. L. (2004). Document clustering based on cluster validation. *13th Conference on Information and Knowledge Management. CIKM 2004*, Washington DC, USA, 501-506.

[16] Osiński, S. (2004). Dimensionality Reduction Techniques for Search Results Clustering. *MSc. thesis*, University of Sheffield, UK.

[17] Wang, B. B., Mc Kay, R. I., Hussein, A., Abbass, , et al. (2003). A comparative study for domain ontology guided feature extraction1. Darlinghurst, Australia. *In Proc of 26th Australian Computer Science Conference (ACSC2003)*, Australian Computer Society Inc., 69-78.

[18] Witten, I. H., Paynter, G. W., Frank, E., Gutwin, C., & Nevill-Manning, C. G. (1999). KEA: Practical automatic keyphrase extraction. *Proceedings of DigitalLibraries 99 (DL'99)*, ACM Press, 254-256.

[19] Turney, P. (2002, July). Mining the Web for Lexical Knowledge to Improve Keyphase Extraction: Learning from Labeled and Unlabeled Data. *P. Source: NRC/ERB-1096,* NRC Publication Number: NRC 44947.2002.

[20] Zamir, O., & Etzioni, O. (1999). Grouper: A dynamic clustering interface to web search results. *Computer networks,* 31, 1361-1374.

[21] Herbert, J. P., & Yao, J. T. (2009). A Granular Computing Framework for Self-Organizing Maps. *Neurocomputing,* 72, 2865-2872.

[22] Niklasson, L., Bodén, M., & Ziemke, . (1998). Self-organization of very large document collections: State of the art. *Proceedings of ICANN98, the 8th International Conference on Artificial Neural Networks,* 65-74.

[23] Lin, X., Soergel, D., & Marchionini, G. (1991). A self-organizing semantic map for information retrieval. *Proceedings of the annual international ACM SIGIR conference on research and development in information retrieval,* 262-269.

[24] Su, K. Lamu-Chun, Chang, Hsiao-te, & Chou, Chien-hsing. (1996). Approach to interactive exploration. *In proc int'l conf knowledge discovery and data mining(KDD'96),* 238-243.

[25] Miikkulainen, R. (1990). Script recognition with hierarchical feature maps. *Connection science,* 2, 83-101.

[26] Merkl, D. (1993). Structuring software for reuse: the case of self-organizing maps. Piscataway, NJ, IEEE Service Center. *Int. Joint Conf. on Neural Networks,* III, 1993, 2468-2471.

[27] Roussinov, D., & Ramsey, M. (1998). Information forage through adaptive visualization. *The Third ACM Conference on Digital Libraries,* 303-304.

[28] Rauber. (1999). LabelSOM: On the labeling of self-ofganizing maps. *In proc int'l joint conf neural networks(IJCNN'99).*

[29] Martinetz, T. M., & Schulten, K. J. (1991). A "neural-gas" network learns topologies' in Kohonen. *Artificial neural networks,* 397-402.

[30] Fritzke, B. (1995). Growing grid-a self-organising network with constant neighbourhood range and adaptation strength. *Neural Process. Letters,* 2, 9-13.

[31] Bauer, Ha., & Villmann, T. (1997). Growing a hypercubical output space in a self-organising feature map. *IEEE Transactions on Neural Networks,* NN-8(2), 218-226.

[32] Ritter, H., Martinetz, T., & Schulten, K. (1992). *Heurd Computation and Self-Organizinp Maps: Introduction,* Addison-Wesley.

[33] Kohonen, T. (1990). The self-organizing map. *Proc. of the IEEE,* 9, 1464-1479.

[34] Yin, H., & Allinson, N. M. (1990). Bayesian self-organising map for gaussian mixtures. *IEEE Proceedings: Vision, Image and Signal Processing,* 148(4), 234-240.

[35] Mulier, F., & Cherkassky, V. (1994). *Learning rate schedules for self-organizing maps, In Proceedings of 12th International Conference on Pattern Recognition*, 2, 224-228.

[36] Jung , Yunjae. (2001). Design and Evaluation of Clustering Criterion for Optimal Hierarchical Agglomerative Clustering. *Phd. thesis,* University of Minnesota.

[37] Steinbach, M., Karypis, G., & Kumar, V. (2000). A comparison of document clustering techniques. *In KDD Workshop on Text Mining.*

[38] Larsen, Bjornar, & Chinatsu, Aone. (1999). Fast and effective text mining using linear-time document clustering. *In Proc. of the Fifth ACM SIGKDD Int'l Conference on Knowledge Discovery and Data Mining,* 16-22.

[39] Aggarwal, Charu C., Gates, Stephen C., & Yu, Philip S. (1999). On the merits of building categorization systems by supervised clustering. *In Proc.of the Fifth ACM SIGKDD Int'l Conference on Knowledge Discovery and Data Mining,* 352-356.

[40] Cutting, D. R., Pedersen, J. O., Karger, D. R., & Tukey, J. W. (1992). Scatter/gather: A cluster-based approach to browsing large document collections. Copenhagen. *In Proceedings of the ACM SIGIR,* 318-329.

[41] Luke, Brian T. (1999). *K-Means Clustering,* http://fconyx.ncifcrf.gov/~lukeb/kmeans.html.

[42] Martin, S., & Detlef, N. (2006). Towards the Automation of Intelligent Data Analysis. *Applied Soft Computing,* 6, 348-356.

[43] Zhou, X. Y., Sun, Z. H., Zhang, B. L., & Yang, Y. D. (2006). Research on Clustering and Evolution Analysis of High Dimensional Data Stream. *Journal of Computer Research and Development,* 43, 2005-2011.

[44] Huang, S., Chen, Z., Yu, Y., & Ma , W. Y. (2006). Multitype Features Coselection for Web Document Clustering. *IEEE Transactions on Knowledge and Data Engineering,* 18, 448-459.

[45] Dhillon, I. S., Guan, Y. Q., & Kogan, J. (2002). Iterative Clustering of High Dimensional Text Data Augmented by Local Search. *In: Proceedings of the Second IEEE International Conference on Data Mining,* 131-138, IEEE Press, Japan.

[46] Ghaseminezhad, M. H., & Karami, A. (2011). A Novel Self-Organizing Map (SOM) Neural Network for Discrete Groups of Data Clustering. *Applied Soft Computing,* 11, 3771-3778.

[47] Melody , Y. K. (2001). Extending the Kohonen Self-Organizing Map Networks for Clustering Analysis. *Computational Statistics & Data Analysis,* 38, 161-180.

[48] Tseng, C. L., Chen, Y. H., Xu, Y. Y., Pao, H. T., & Fu, H. C. (2004). A Self-Growing Probabilistic Decision-Based Neural Network with Automatic Data Clustering. *Neurocomputing,* 61, 21-38.

[49] Tsai, C. F., Tsai, C. W., Wu, H. C., & Yang, T. (2004). ACODF: A Novel Data Clustering Approach for Data Mining in Large Databases. *Journal of Systems and Software*, 73, 133-145.

[50] Lee, S., Kim, G., & Kim, S. (2011). Self-Adaptive and Dynamic Clustering for Online Anomaly Detection. *Expert Systems with Applications*, 38, 14891-14898.

[51] Alahakoon, D., , S., Halganmuge, K., & Srinivasan, B. (2000). Dynamic self-organizing maps with controlled growth for knowledge discovery. *IEEE Transactions on Neural Networks*, 11(3), 601-614.

[52] Merkl, Rauber D., & Dittenbach, M. (2002). The growing hierarchical self-organizing map: exploratory analysis of high-dimensional data. *IEEE Transactions on Neural Networks*, 13(6), 1331-1341.

[53] Qin, A.-K., & Suganthan, P.-N. (2004). Robust growing neural gas algorithm with application in cluster analysis. *Neural Networks*, 17(8-9), 1135-1148.

[54] , L., Robert, K., & Warwick, K. (2002). The plastic self organising map. Hawaii. *Proceedings of the 2002 International Joint Conference on Neural Networks, IEEE*, 727-732.

[55] Hung, C., & Wermter, S. (2003). A dynamic adaptive self-organising hybrid model for text clustering. Melbourne. *Proceedings of the Third IEEE International Conference on Data Mining, IEEE*, Florida, USA, 75-82.

[56] Liu, Yuanchao, Wang, Xiaolong, & Wu, Chong. (2008, January). ConSOM: A conceptional self-organizing map model for text clustering. *Neurocomputing*, 71(4-6), 857-862.

[57] Liu, Yuan-chao, Wu, Chong, & Liu, Ming. (2011, August). Research of fast SOM clustering for text information. *Expert Systems with Applications*, 38(8), 9325-9333.

[58] Liu, Yuanchao, Wang, Xiaolong, & Liu, Ming. (2009). V-SOM: A Text Clustering Method based on Dynamic SOM Model. *Journal of Computational Information Systems*, 5(1), 141-145.

Chapter 11

Non-Linear Spatial Patterning in Cultural Site Formation Processes - The Evidence from Micro-Artefacts in Cores from a Neolithic Tell Site in Greece

Dimitris Kontogiorgos

Additional information is available at the end of the chapter

http://dx.doi.org/10.5772/51193

1. Introduction

Micro-artefacts (i.e., cultural particles smaller than 2mm in diameter), due to their abundance and incorporation into the sedimentary matrix of an archaeological deposit, constitute a significant part of the cultural particles present [21]. Micro-artefact analysis is extensively complex due to the different micro-artefact categories that may appear in an archaeological context and also because of the numerous cultural (and non-cultural/natural) formation processes that may have been involved in the creation of characteristics specific to an archaeological context.

Recently, the use of a non-linear method (i.e., spherical-SOFM) on micro-artefact data has shown that the method is able to recognize and to provide a visual representation of micro-artefact patterns prior to performing any statistical analysis on the data, providing a quick view into possible relationships or differences that may occur between temporally, spatially, and culturally different archaeological contexts (i.e., pits and ditches from the Neolithic Tell site at Paliambela (Pieria region-Northern Greece) which unusually comprises an extended settlement component [8].

It was shown that the spherical-SOFM non-linear method revealed patterns among the data that linear methods were unable to classify. Furthermore, the method attempted to overcome the difficulties posed by the friable nature of different micro-artefact classes (for example, unburnt clay, burnt clay, bone, shell, or charcoal). Material characteristics and the process of micro-artefact generation, including the effects of post-depositional processes, were considered as important factors in the search for strong pattern recognition [9]. The analysis has shown that similar classes of micro-artefacts in three analyzed data sets were characterized by different non-linear associations, further suggesting that these were possibly formed through different cultural formation processes [8].

Figure 1. Map of Greece, showing the location of Paliambela (Source:'Paliambela excavation' archive).

The use of the spherical-SOFM non-linear method was also able to recognize and to provide a visual representation of micro-artefact patterns in archaeological contexts (i.e., a colluvial deposit from a Hellenistic Theatre in NW Greece) affected *only* by natural formation processes [10, 11].

The implication of the applied non-linear method (i.e., spherical-SOFM) is that it has the 'ability' to demonstrate the dynamics of cultural or natural formation processes in leaving non-linear 'signals' in archaeological contexts being in a *'non equilibrium'* state until the time of recovery. Therefore, the rationality for developing such recognitions in archaeological contexts is to release the dynamics of formation processes since archaeological patterning is arguably (at least for the most part) the result of the interplay between many complex processes, both cultural and non-cultural (natural) [2, 28, 1, 16]. Therefore, this type of recognition is of critical importance also in core-data, since this type of data provide broader spatial information and are more sensitive in both cultural and natural formation processes.

Section 2 briefly describes how the spherical self-organizing map creates a 3D visual or graphical representation of the data. Section 3 presents a summary of previous geoarchaeological work on core-data from the Neolithic Tell site at Paliambela (Pieria region-Northern

http://dx.doi.org/10.5772/51193

Greece) while section 4 and section 5 offer the results of this study and some concluding remarks, respectively.

2. Spherical self-organizing feature map

The Spherical Self-Organizing Feature Map (S-SOFM), introduced by Kohonen [7], maps n-dimensional data into a low-dimensional space. The spherical SOFM [17] the low-dimensional space is a tessellated sphere that is formed by subdividing an icosahedron. Every vertex on this sphere is a strategic location of an n-dimensional vector that represents an ensemble of similar data vectors which are assigned to the vector during the mapping operation. It is therefore necessary to visually enhance variations in the data using the physical attributes of the mapping lattice. The benefit of a spherical lattice in the implementation of the S-SOFM is that the enclosed space can be used to generate a 3D visual representation of some physical aspect of the n-dimensional data.

Conventional implementation of the S-SOFM method have used a 2D lattice as the low-dimensional space, and associations in the data are visualized by means of a terrain map, wherein elevation represents some aspect of the vector(s) at that location [27, 24]. Relative similarity between data vectors mapped into the sphere can be visualized by introducing distortions in the sphere accompanied by changes in the colour. Informative characteristics of the data are reflected as distortions and colour gradations on the surface of the sphere. The formulation of these measures is a non-trivial task and often application dependent. The measures reflect desired data correlations (either linear or non-linear) and must be defined by the researcher who is familiar with the underlying data set. It is this aspect of the S-SOFM that differs from existing literature about the self-organizing feature map. The S-SOFM utilizes the spherical lattice of the S-SOFM space to generate a visual form of the clustered data that is more intuitive and easy to perceive. A visual form of the data is created by scaling the radial distance of the vertices on the sphere in proportion to a measure characterizing some physical aspect of the data. Examples illustrating the various implementations of the spherical SOFM on different data and the use of possible measures to create spherical SOFM graphical representations are discussed in Sangole [17] and Sangole and Knopf [18].

3. Summary of previous work on core-data from the Neolithic Tell site at Paliambela (Pieria region-Northern Greece-Fig.1)

Coring, as a minimally destructive technique, facilitates the definition of subsurface units, provides a clear view of the buried surfaces on which occupations took place [23]. The macroscopic examination of all twelve cores drawn from the subsurface investigation conducted on the tell, revealed three basic stratigraphic units: bedrock, occupation deposits and a topsoil layer. Given, therefore, their relative macrostratigraphic similarity and the rather broad stratigraphic resolution/delineation required from the cores at Paliambela, three cores (out of 12) were selected for analysis (i.e., nos 1083-84-85, Fig.2). These were judged to provide good site coverage from east to west, and thus offer information regarding the depth and thickness of the cultural deposits on the tell, on a coarse temporal and spatial scale.

The analysis of three cores (out of twelve) defined the stratigraphy of the site on a coarse temporal and spatial scale. The culturally sterile bedrock was identified at ca 2m depth and the initial human occupation probably started on top of the bedrock, because remnants of any overlying palaeosol have not been recognised, suggesting that this might have been stripped or reworked by subsequent human activity.

The analysis of the occupation deposits revealed significant variation, both temporal and spatial, in micro-artefacts (burnt clay, unburnt clay, shell, bone and charcoal) and so, presumably, in human activity on the site. This indicates that the surviving occupation deposits built up sufficiently rapidly and bury and preserve variable concentrations of micro-artefacts. In short, the analysis of the cores revealed that the tell component of the site might have been the product of long term anthropogenic accretion of sediment and artefactual material that created a low mound, with 0.5-2m of *surviving* occupation debris. [8].

4. Non-linear micro-artefact patterning as a general indicator of differences in cultural site formation processes

4.1. Laboratory procedures

The laboratory procedure followed in micro-artefact analysis used two divisions of the phi (ϕ) scale, that is -2.00ϕ and 0ϕ. Contents of the bulk samples were passed through a stack of 4mm (-2.00ϕ) and 1mm (0ϕ) sieves. The material retained in the 1mm sieve created the sub-sample that was processed for micro-artefacts and an optical microscope was used for identifications. Five micro-artefact categories were identified in the deposits from the cores: unburnt clay (e.g., from mudbricks, wattle and daub constructions), burnt clay (i.e., burnt specimens of the previous category), shell (marine shells), bone (animal bone), and charcoal (charred organic particles).

Shell, bone and charcoal were easily distinguished, but the more problematic distinction between unburnt clay and burnt clay was based on the following observations: unburnt clay grains were often very fragile even in this small fraction and were, in most cases, subdiscoidal, ranging in colour from light grey to dark grey; burnt clay fragments were, in most cases, spherical particles of brownish colour, and relatively more solid than the unburnt clay ones.

In the core samples (total number: 120 sediment samples, ca. 1000kg each), the total sub-sample was sorted for micro-artefacts and the total mass for each material class was weighed on an electronic precision balance. Physically sorting the total sub-sample for micro-artefacts, followed by weighing of each category, provides a representative picture of the micro-artefacts present in a sample and is feasible when small sample sizes are involved in analysis, as in the case of the cores.

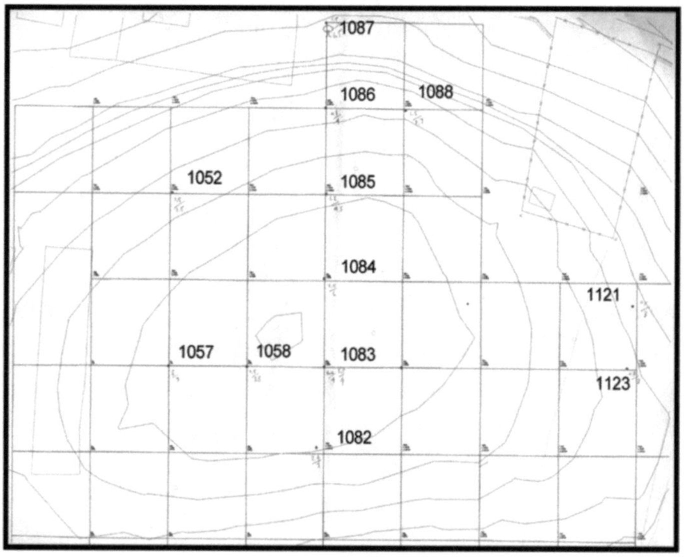

Figure 2. Contour map of the Neolithic tell showing the location of the Cores. Contours at 10m (Source: 'Paliambela excavation' archive).

Micro-artefact density (*D*) was obtained by using the following equation: $D = m/v$, where *m* is the weight of each material class, and *v* is the volume of each sample. This method is rather simple but needs the total sub-sample to be sorted for micro-artefacts and the various material types to be weighed in a high precision electronic balance.

The construction of the S-SOFM graphical representation was based on a database of 120 five-dimensional records, each dimension representing a micro-artefact category. Every row represented the point-counting results. Figure 3 shows the formation of three distinct white regions that correspond to the micro-artefact core-data from the site. A non-linear structure lies within this statistical space which can be distinguished into three separate sub-structures. The spherical-SOFM pattern recognition procedure provides a comprehensive preliminary visual representation of inherent non-linear characteristics in data, serving as the initial step in the analysis of the multidimensional micro-artefact data. In this study three meaningful components were revealed – which appeared to be the determinants for the constitution of the analysed data set. This further suggests that the three groups of contexts (i.e., micro-artefacts from the three cores) from the site were possibly formed through different formation processes.

It is important to mention that the five classes of micro-artefacts set for analysis -i.e., micro-shell, micro-bone, microfragments of charcoal, microfragments of burnt clay, and microfragments of unburnt clay- generate from an interpretatively complicated set of larger artefacts, those made of friable materials -the so called 'size unstable' [22].

The preservation of such materials in an archaeological context indeed, is closely connected not only with the length of deposition but also with the rate and type of weathering [22].

Moreover, micro-artefacts provide different information than do larger artefacts and definitely should not be used simply to reflect 'noise' in larger artefacts [6].

Therefore, the researcher cannot assume that, for example, chronologically distant archaeological contexts will provide similar or different micro-artefact patterning due to the many factors that may account for the observed pattern. The implication is that it enhances attempts for developing interpretations on micro-artefact patterning by providing strong pattern recognition.

The observation of this pattern in cultural indicators such as micro-artefacts should be related at least in part (and arguably for the most part) with differences in the spatial organization of activities carried out in the site and ending up in the deposits. In other words, it should be related with spatial differences in cultural formation processes. That these differences in cultural processes had become so embedded in the sedimentary traces of the deposits arguably reflects *long-term continuity* of distinct patterns of spatial organisation of behaviour.

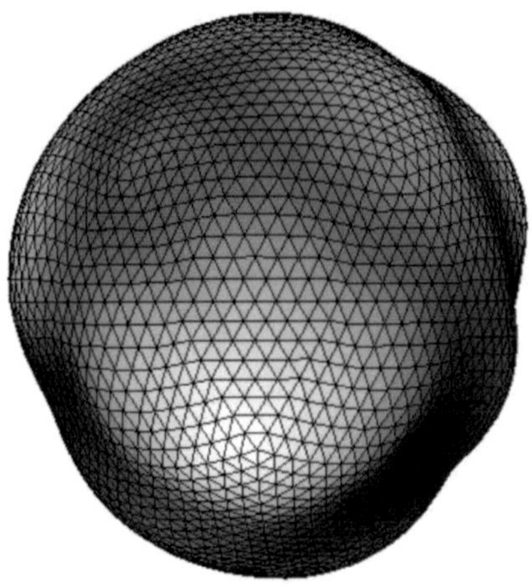

Figure 3. View of the S-SOFM graphical representation showing the formation of three distinct white regions – corresponding to micro-artefact core-data (each for a core).

In this study, the critical prerequisite was rather the depiction of the existence of differences in formation processes (and arguably of cultural formation processes) and of spatial content between different contexts (i.e., cores) from the site, on a broad spatial and temporal scale, than a detailed presentation of the spatial and temporal use of space on the tell settlement or of differences in formation processes between different activity areas across the site.

Despite the natural and cultural agents/processes that have disorganized the site's behavioural contexts, the archaeological sediments from Paliambela still preserve significant nonlinear behavioural information. The spatial differences in cultural formation processes arguably reflect long-term continuity of distinct patterns of spatial organisation of behaviour. The term 'continuity' is conceptualized here as the cultural product of different social systems (Neolithic or later) that inhabited Paliambela. Their cultural outcomes, embedded in and decoded from the archaeological sediments, contributed significantly to the site's formation, transforming it into a cultural product. Therefore, the archaeological sediments of Paliambela, enclose significant cultural information, and this study has demonstrated the potential of the non-linear method to help identify this information.

5. Conclusions: The importance of understanding formation processes in a non-linear world

Since Schiffer's [19] original recognition of the importance of studying and understanding the formation processes of the archaeological record, many authors have pointed out their critical importance [5, 12, 13, 25]. Moreover, it is now widely accepted that variability is introduced into the archaeological record through cultural and non-cultural formation processes which distort systemic patterns as well as creating their own patterns [20].

The unit of analysis appropriate for identifying formation processes is, according to Schiffer [20] the deposit, but "viewing the deposit as a single discrete depositional event or process has its problems, as a single depositional process can give rise to materials in different deposits, and conversely, a single deposit can contain the products of many different depositional processes" [20].

However, despite the recognised importance of cultural and natural processes in the formation of the archaeological record, studies addressing the interpretative potential of micro-artefacts remain relatively limited, although micro-artefacts, due to their abundance and incorporation in an archaeological deposit constitute a significant part of the cultural particles present and may provide information on the cultural and natural formation processes occurring in a deposit [4, 3, 26, 6, 21].

Dunnel and Stein [6] outline some of the important characteristics of micro-artefacts that compel their consideration as archaeological data of the first order. They note, that information content may be different for micro-artefacts than for larger artefacts and they may be most informative about different things (e.g., particle transport and site formation processes). Equally important, processes that generate microscopic artefacts vary depending on material and context [6]. These last two issues, differing information content and differing formation processes within the micro-scale are important reasons for undertaking micro-artefact analysis [6].

Then again, attempting to define cultural and natural formation processes in a site focusing, for example, either in their variability or in the proportional correlation among micro-artefact classes may be misleading because their archaeological significance rests upon understanding the interaction among, the almost, numerous variables within a sequence which would determine their transport potential.

The example offered in this study indicates that similar types of micro-artefacts within different archaeological contexts across the site exhibit significant non-linear information plausibly as a result of different types of formation processes that were assumed to imply, for the most part, differences in cultural formation processes. In any case, stronger interpretation can only be achieved by strong micro-artefact pattern recognition [9, 10] especially in cases of archaeological deposits sensitive to cultural formation processes.

Without underestimating the effects of natural processes or rather 'naively' expecting cultural factors to account for all the extant variability in an archaeological site, it seems that drawing logical connections between geoarchaeological data and past human activities upgrades and enhances cultural interference upon natural factors in a site's formation. The study of micro-artefacts, those cultural particles included into archaeological sediments, although by no means conclusive, can be utilised to identify forms of behaviour enacted within a site, when strong pattern recognition has been achieved [8].

New ways of describing differences in archaeological assemblages could only be effective if we could connect them with past human behaviour in a non static physical environment. The identification of cultural formation processes, spatially and temporally, on the micro-level in a complex site, as Paliambela, indicates that such discrimination is possible through the application of a certain methodology. More importantly, it calls for awareness of the multiplicity of scales at which these cultural processes can be traced. Although not exhaustive, the non linear spherical self organizing feature map method has provided a higher resolution with which to view the archaeological information encoded within archaeological sediments.

Author details

Dimitris Kontogiorgos

Wiener Laboratory, American School of Classical Studies at Athens, Athens, Greece

References

[1] Ball, P. (2004). Critical mass: How one thing leads to another. Portsmouth, NH: Heinemann.

[2] Bentley, R. A., & Maschner, H. D. G. (2003). Complex systems and archaeology. *Salt Lake City: University of Utah Press.*

[3] Fladmark, K. R. (1982). Microdebitage analysis: initial considerations. *Journal of Archaeological Science*, 9, 205-220.

[4] Hassan, F.A. (1978). Sediments in archaeology: Methods and implications for palaeoenvironmental and cultural analysis. *Journal of Field Archaeology*, 197-213.

[5] Goldberg, P., Nash, D. T., & Petraglia, M. D. (1993). Press Formation Processes. *Archaeological Context Madison, Wisconsin: Prehistory.*

[6] Dunnell, R. C., & Stein, J. K. (1989). Theoretical issues in the interpretation of microartifacts. *Geoarchaeology*, 31-42.

[7] Kohonen, T. Self-organized formation of topologically correct feature maps. *Biological Cybernetics*, 198(43), 59-69.

[8] Kontogiorgos, D. (2008). Geoarchaeological and microartifacts analysis of archaeological sediments. *A case study from a Neolithic Tell site in Greece. Nova Science Publishers Inc., New York.*

[9] Kontogiorgos, D., Leontitsis, A., & Sangole, A. (2007). Telling a non linear story: The investigation of microartefacts non linear structure. *Journal of Archaeological Science*, 1532-1536.

[10] Kontogiorgos, D., & Preka, K. (2009). From Neolithic to Hellenistic. A Geoarchaeological Approach to the Burial of the a Hellenistic Theatre: The Evidence from Particle Size Analysis and Microartifacts. *On Site Geoarchaeology on a Neolithic Tell Site in Greece: Archaeological Sediments,Microartifacts and Softwear Development, Kontogiorgos, D. Ed., Nova Science Publishers, Inc., New York*, 71-80.

[11] Kontogiorgos, D., & Leontitsis, A. (2011). Is it Visible? *Micro-artefacts Non-Linear Stucture and Natural Formation Processes In: Self-Organizing Maps and Novel Algorithm Design. Intech open access Publishers. Vienna, Austria.*, 643-648.

[12] Mc Guire, R. H. (1995). Behavioural Archaeology: Reflections of a Prodigal Son. *J. M. Skibo, W. H.Walker and A. E. Nielsen (eds.) Expanding Archaeology*, 162-177, Salt Lake City, University of Utah Press.

[13] Reid, J. J. (1995). Four Strategies after Twenty Years: A Return to Basics. *J. M. Skibo, W. H. Walker and A. E. Nielsen (eds.) Expanding Archaeology*, 15-21, Salt Lake City, University of Utah Press.

[14] Rosen, A.M. (1986). *Cities of Clay: The Geoarchaeology of Tells.University of Chicago Press, Chicago.*

[15] Rosen, A. M. (1989). Ancient Town and City Sites: A View from the Microscope. *American Antiquity*, 564-578.

[16] Ormerod, P. (2005). *Why most things fail: Evolution, extinction, and economics*, London, Faber & Faber.

[17] Sangole, A. (2003). Data-driven modeling using spherical self-organizing feature maps. *PhD thesis, University of Western Ontario*, Canada, Universal Publishers, 1-58112-319-1.

[18] Sangole, A., & Knopf, G. K. (2003). Visualization of random ordered numeric data sets using self-organized feature maps. *Computers and Graphics*, 963-976.

[19] Schiffer, M. B. (1972). Archaeological Context and Systemic Context. *American Antiquity*, 156-165.

[20] Schiffer, M. B. (1987). *Formation Processes of the Archaeological Record*, University of New Mexico Press, Albuquerque.

[21] Sherwood, S. C. (2001). Microartifacts. *Goldberg, P., Holliday, V.T., and Ferring, R., Eds., Earth Sciences and Archaeology*, Kluwer Academic/ Plenum Publishers, New York, 327-351.

[22] Sherwood, S. C., Simek, J. F., & Polhemus, R. R. (1995). Artifact size and spatial process: macro- and microartifacts in a Mississipian House. *Geoarchaeology*, 429-455.

[23] Stein, J.K. (1986). Coring archaeological sites. *American Antiquity*, 505-527.

[24] Ultsch, A., & Siemon, H. P. (1990). Kohonen's self-organizing feature maps for exploratory data analysis. *Proceedings of the International Neural Network Conference. Dordrecht, The Netherlands*, 305-308.

[25] Tani, M. (1995). Beyond the Identification of Formation Processes: Behavioural Inference Based on Traces Left by Cultural Formation Processes. *Journal of Archaeological Method and Theory*, 231-252.

[26] Vance, E. D. (1987). Microdebitage and archaeological activity analysis. *Archaeology*, 58-59.

[27] Vesanto, J. S. O. (1999). SOM-based data visualization methods. *Journal of Intelligent Data Analysis*, 111-126.

[28] Watts, D.J. (2003). *Six degrees: The science of a connected age.London: Random House.*

Chapter 12

Spatial Clustering Using Hierarchical SOM

Roberto Henriques, Victor Lobo and
Fernando Bação

Additional information is available at the end of the chapter

http://dx.doi.org/10.5772/51159

1. Introduction

The amount of available geospatial data increases every day, placing additional pressure on existing analysis tools. Most of these tools were developed for a data poor environment and thus rarely address concerns of efficiency, high-dimensionality and automatic exploration [1]. Recent technological innovations have dramatically increased the availability of data on location and spatial characterization, fostering the proliferation of huge geospatial databases. To make the most of this wealth of data we need powerful knowledge discovery tools, but we also need to consider the particular nature of geospatial data. This context has raised new research challenges and difficulties on the analysis of multidimensional geo-referenced data. The availability of methods able to perform "intelligent" data reduction on vast amounts of high dimensional data is a central issue in Geographic Information Science (GISc) current research agenda.

The field of knowledge discovery constitutes one of the most relevant stakes in GISc research to develop tools able to deal with "intelligent" data reduction [2, 3] and tame complexity. More than prediction tools, we need to develop exploratory tools which enable an improved understanding of the available data [4].

The term cluster analysis encompasses a wide group of algorithms (for a comprehensive review see [5]). The main goal of such algorithms is to organize data into meaningful structures. This is achieved through the arrangement of data observations into groups based on similarity. These methods have been extensively applied in different research areas including data mining [6, 7], pattern recognition [8, 9], and statistical data analysis [10]. GISc has also relied heavily on clustering algorithms [11, 12]. Research on geodemographics [13-16], identification of deprived areas [17], and social services provision [18] are examples of the relevance that clustering algorithms have within today's GISc research.

One of the most challenging aspects of clustering is the high dimensionality of most problems. While in general describing phenomena requires the use of many variables, the increase in dimensionality will have a significant impact on the performance of clustering algorithms and the quality of the results. First, it will increase the search space affecting the clustering algorithm's efficiency, due to the effect usually known as the "curse of dimensionality" [19]. Second, it will yield a more complex analysis of the output, as the clusters are more difficult to characterize due to the contribution of multiple variables to the final structure. Thus, in a typical clustering problem, the user is asked to select a low number of variables that optimize the phenomena's description.

However, to produce an accurate representation of the phenomenon, it is sometimes necessary to measure it from several perspectives. A typical example is the use of census variables to study the socio-economic environment in an urban context. Usually, the census covers a wide range of themes describing the characteristics of the population such as the demography, households, families, housing, economic status, among others[20]. In these cases, some variables are strongly correlated, independently of the subject they are covering. In fact, with the increase in dimensionality, there is a higher probability of correlation between variables. In addition, due to the spatial context of census data, variables have strong spatial autocorrelation [21]. Spatial autocorrelation measures the degree of dependency among observations in a geographic space. This spatial autocorrelation corroborates Tobler's [22] first law (TFL) which expresses the tendency of nearby objects to be similar.

To GIScientists, clusters are usually more representative and easier to understand if they present spatial contiguity. However, several reasons can cause the clusters to present spatial discontinuity. Among these, the scale or zoning scheme of the geographical units, known as the modifiable areal unit problem (MAUP) [23] can affect the expected spatial patterns. In addition, the combination of different variables, that presents distinct levels of spatial autocorrelation, affects the clusters' spatial patterns.

Traditional clustering methods, in which self-organizing maps [24] are included, are very sensitive to divergent variables. Divergent variables are those that present significant differences to the general tendency. These variables have a great impact in the clustering process and are crucial in the final partition. For instance, when clustering using a set of variables where all, except one, present spatial autocorrelation, the divergent variable will have a higher impact than the others. In most cases, the clusters created will not follow the spatial arrangement suggested by the majority of the variables, but will get distorted by the variables presenting odd spatial distributions.

To avoid this problem a hierarchical structure may be used to explore and cluster geospatial data. Variables are grouped in themes, and each theme will be independently clustered. These partial clusters are then used to create a global partition.

One well-known clustering method is the Self-Organizing Map (SOM) proposed by Kohonen [24]. One of the interesting properties of SOM is the capability of detecting small differences between objects. SOM have proved to be a useful and efficient tool in finding

http://dx.doi.org/10.5772/51159

multivariate data outliers [25-27]. SOM has also been widely used in the GIScience field in the exploration and clustering of geospatial data [28-33, 34, 35].

In this chapter, we propose the use of Hierarchical SOMs to perform geospatial clustering. Several characteristics of geospatial data make it a good candidate to benefit from the HSOM specific features. The classic layer organization used in GIScience fits perfectly the layered structure of HSOM. HSOM provides an appropriate framework to perform the clustering task based on individual themes, which can then be compared with the clusters created from the combination of several themes. HSOM is less sensitive to divergent variables because these will only have a direct impact on their theme.

There are many types of hierarchical SOM, so we propose a taxonomy to classify existing methods according to their objectives and structure.

2. Background

2.1. Self-Organizing Maps

Teuvo Kohonen proposed the Self-organizing maps (SOM) in the beginning of the 1980s [36]. The SOM is usually used for mapping high-dimensional data into one, two, or three-dimensional feature maps. The basic idea of an SOM is to map the data patterns onto an n-dimensional grid of units or neurons. That grid forms what is known as the output space, as opposed to the input space that is the original space of the data patterns. This mapping tries to preserve topological relations, *i.e.* patterns that are close in the input space will be mapped to units that are close in the output space, and *vice-versa*. The output space is usually two-dimensional, and most of the implementations of SOM use a rectangular grid of units. To provide even distances between the units in the output space, hexagonal grids are sometimes used [24]. Each unit, being an input layer unit, has as many weights as the input patterns, and can thus be regarded as a vector in the same space of the patterns.

When training an SOM with a given input pattern, the distance between that pattern and every unit in the network is calculated. Then the algorithm selects the unit that is closest as the winning unit (also known as best matching unit- BMU), and that pattern is mapped on to that unit. If the SOM has been trained successfully, then patterns that are close in the input space will be mapped to units that are close (or the same) in the output space. Thus, SOM is 'topology preserving' in the sense that (as far as possible) neighbourhoods are preserved through the mapping process.

The basic SOM learning algorithm may be described as follows:

Let

$\boldsymbol{X}$ be the set of n training patterns $\boldsymbol{x}_1, \boldsymbol{x}_2, \ldots \boldsymbol{x}_n$

$\boldsymbol{W}$ be a $p \times q$ grid of units $\boldsymbol{w}_{ij}$ where i and j are their coordinates on that grid

α be the learning rate, assuming values in $]0,1[$, initialised to a given initial learning rate

r be the radius of the neighbourhood function $h(\boldsymbol{w}_{ij}, \boldsymbol{w}_{mn}, r)$, initialised to a given initial radius

Repeat

    For $m = 1$ to n

        For all $\boldsymbol{w}_{ij} \in \boldsymbol{W}$,

            Calculate $d_{ij} = \|\boldsymbol{x}_m - \boldsymbol{x}_{ij}\|$

        Select the unit that minimizes d_{ij} as the winner $\boldsymbol{w}_{winner}$

        Update each unit $\boldsymbol{w}_{ij} \in \boldsymbol{W}: \boldsymbol{w}_{ij} = \boldsymbol{w}_{ij} + \alpha h(\boldsymbol{w}_{winner}, \boldsymbol{w}_{ij}, r)\|\boldsymbol{x}_m - \boldsymbol{w}_{ij}\|$

        Decrease the value of α and r

Until α reaches 0

The learning rate α, sometimes referred to as η, varies in [0, 1] and must converge to 0 to guarantee convergence and stability in the training process. The decrease of this parameter to 0 is usually done linearly, but any other function may be used. The radius, usually denoted by r, indicates the size of the neighbourhood around the winner unit in which units will be updated. This parameter is relevant in defining the topology of the SOM, deeply affecting the output space unfolding.

The neighbourhood function h, sometimes referred to as or N_c, assumes values in [0, 1], and is a function of the position of two units (a winner unit, and another unit), and radius, r. It is large for units that are close in the output space, and small (or 0) for faraway units.

2.2. Hierarchical SOM

Hierarchical SOMs [37-41] share many characteristics with other methods such as the multi-layer SOMs [42, 43], multi-resolution SOMs [44], multi-stage SOMs [45, 46], fusion SOMs [47] or Tree-SOMs [48].

All these methods share the idea of constructing a system using SOMs as building blocks. They vary in the way these SOMs interact with each other, and with the original data. We consider as Hierarchical SOMs, those where, at some stage, one of the SOMs receives as inputs the outputs of another SOM, as will be described later. This type of structure resembles a multi-layer perceptron (MLP) neural network in the sense that multiple layers exist connected in a feed-forward way. However, Hierarchical SOMs have completely different training algorithms and types of interaction between layers.

General multilayer SOMs may have many completely different interactions between layers. As an example, a data pattern may be mapped onto a given SOM, and then all data patterns mapped to that unit may be visualized on a second SOM. Another common type of architecture presents several SOMs in linked windows [49], providing an environment where a data pattern is visualised simultaneously in several SOMs. We do not consider these as Hierarchical SOMs because the outputs of one SOM are not used to actively train another SOM, nor does the second SOM, in any way, use information from the first map to map the original data patterns.

We consider that, to be recognized as a Hierarchical SOM, the interaction between different SOMs must be of the train/map type. This type of interaction is one where the outputs of one SOM are used to train the other SOM, and this second one maps (represents) the original data patterns using the outputs of the first one. If these two characteristics are not present, we consider we do not have a true Hierarchical SOM, because it is the train/map relationship that establishes a strict subordination between SOMs that in turn is necessary for a hierarchy to exist.

The train/map type of interaction encompasses different specific ways of passing information from one SOM to another. As an examples, when a data pattern is presented to the first level SOM, it may pass the information onto the second level by passing the index of the best matching unit (BMU), the quantization error, the coordinates of the BMU, all activation values for all units of the first level, or any other type of data. The important issue is that whatever data is passed on, it is used to train the second level SOM. A particular case of output of one SOM layer may be the original data pattern itself, or an empty data pattern. This is the case of a first level gating SOM that filters which data patterns are sent to each upper level SOM: it may or may not pass the pattern, depending on some characteristic.

Still, many different configurations are possible for Hierarchical SOMs. They may vary in the number of layers used, in the different ways connections are made and even in the information sent through each connection.

2.3. Why use Hierarchical SOMs (HSOM)?

There are mainly two reasons for using a Hierarchical SOM (HSOM) instead of a standard SOM:

- A HSOM can require less computational effort than a standard SOM to achieve certain goals;
- A HSOM can be better suited to model a problem that has, by its own nature, some sort of hierarchical structure.

The reduction of computational effort can be achieved in two ways: by reducing the dimensionality of the inputs to each SOM, and by reducing the number of units in each SOM. Instead of having a SOM that uses all components of the input patterns, we may have several SOMs, each using a subset of those components, and in this way we minimize the effect of the "curse of dimensionality" [19]. The distance functions used for training the different SOMs will be simpler, and thus faster to compute. This simplicity will more than compensate for the increase in the number of different functions that have to be computed. Speed gains can also be achieved by using fewer units in each SOM. The finer distinction between different clusters (units) can be achieved in upper level SOMs that will only have to deal with some of the input patterns. This "divide and conquer" strategy will avoid computing distances and neighbourhoods to units that are very different from the input patterns being processed in each instant.

The second reason for using HSOMs is that, in general, they are better suited to deal with problems that present a hierarchical/thematic structure. In these cases, HSOM can map the natural structure of the problem, by using a different SOM for each hierarchical level or thematic plane. This separation of the global clustering or classification problem into different levels may not only represent the true nature of the phenomena, but it may also provide an easier interpretation of the results, by allowing the user to see what clustering was performed at each level. GIS science applications, as already discussed, have a strong thematic structure that can be expressed with a different SOM for each theme, and an upper level (hierarchically superior) SOM, that fuses the information to produce globally distinct clusters.

HSOMs are often used in application fields where a structured decomposition into smaller and layered problems is convenient. Some examples include: remote sensing classification [45], image compression [28], ontology [43, 50], speech recognition [51] pattern classification and extraction using health data [52-54], species data [55], financial data [56], climate data [57],,music data [58, 59] and electric power data [60].

3. Taxonomy for Hierarchical SOMs

Based on the survey of the work made on the field, we propose the following taxonomy to classify the HSOM methods (Fig.1).

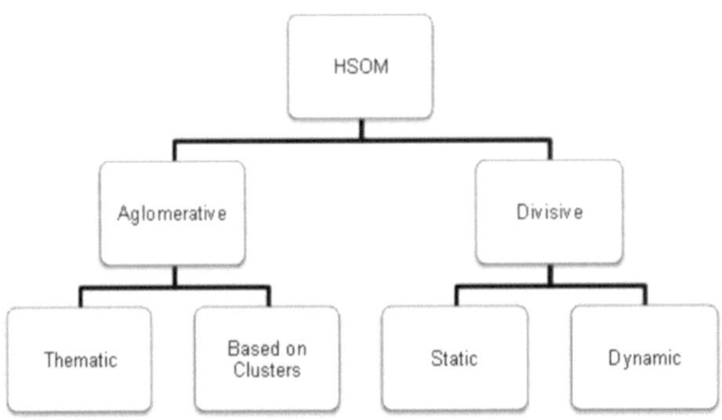

Figure 1. HSOM taxonomy.

This is a possible taxonomy for the HSOM based on their objective and on the type of structure used. Therefore, the first partition groups HSOM methods in two main types: the agglomerative and divisive HSOMs (Fig.2). This partition results from the type of approach adopted in each HSOM method. In an agglomerative HSOM, we usually have several SOMs in the first layer (i.e., the layer directly connected to the original data patterns), and then fuse the outputs in a higher level SOM, while in the divisive HSOM, we will usually have a single SOM in the first layer, and then have several SOMs in the second layer.

In the agglomerative HSOM (Fig.2a), the level of data abstraction increases as we progress up the hierarchy. Thus, usually the first level on the HSOM is the more detailed representation (or a representation of a particular aspect of the data) and, as we ascend in the structure, the main objective is to create clusters that will be more general and provide a simpler, and arguably easier, way of seeing the data.

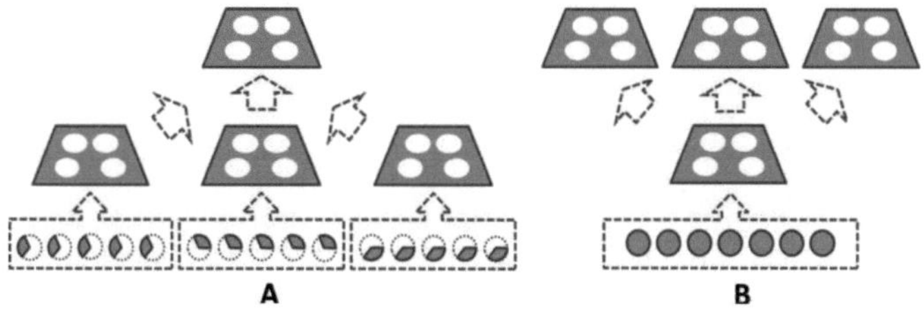

Figure 2. Types of hierarchical SOMs: a) agglomerative and; b) divisive.

In the divisive HSOM (Fig.2b), the first level is usually less accurate and uses small networks. The main objective of this level is to create rough partitions, which will be more detailed and accurate as we ascend in the levels of HSOM.

In the second taxonomic level, agglomerative HSOMs can be divided into thematic and based on clusters while divisive HSOMs can be divided into static or dynamic. In the following, we will present a description on each category.

3.1. Thematic agglomerative HSOM

The first class of agglomerative HSOMs is named Thematic. The name results from the fact that the input space is regarded as a collection of subspaces, each one forming a theme. Fig.3 presents a diagram exemplifying how HSOM methods are generally structured in this category.

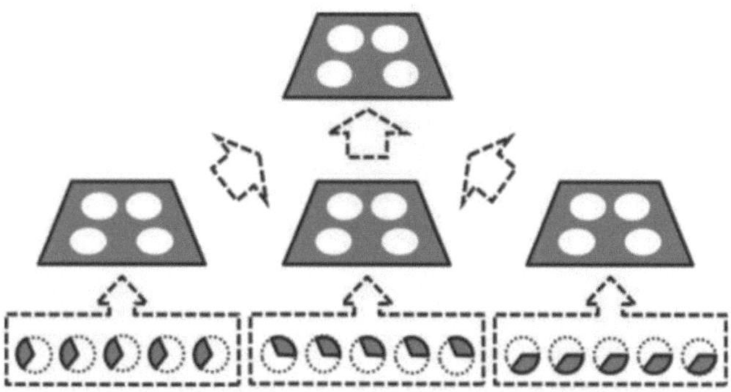

Figure 3. Thematic HSOMs

In a thematic HSOM, the variables of the input patterns are grouped according to some criteria, forming several themes. For instance, in the case of census data, variables can be grouped into different themes such as economic, social, demographic or other. Each of these themes forms a subspace that is then presented to an SOM, and its output will be used to train a final merging SOM. As already stated, the type of output sent from the lower level SOM to the upper level can vary in different applications.

In Fig.3, each theme is represented by a subset of the original variables. Assuming that each original data pattern (with all its variables) would get represented by a grey circle, a portion of that circle is used to represent the subset of each data pattern used in each theme.

This structure presents several advantages when performing multidimensional clustering. The first advantage is the reduction of computation caused by the partition of the input space into several themes. This partition also allows the creation of thematic clusters that, per se, may be interesting to the analyst. Thus, since different clustering perspectives are presented in the lower level, these can be compared to the global clustering solution allowing the user to better understand and explore the emerging patterns.

3.2. Agglomerative HSOM based on clusters

This category is composed by two levels, each using a standard SOM (Fig.4). The first level SOM learns from the original input data, while its output is used in the second level SOM. The second level SOM is usually smaller, allowing a coarser, but probably easier to use, definition of the clusters. In this architecture, if only the coordinates of the bottom level SOM are passed as inputs to the top level, each unit of the top level SOM is BMU for several units from the first level. In this case, the top level is simply clustering together units of the bottom level, and the final result is similar to using a small standard SOM. However, this method has the advantage of presenting two SOMs mapping the same data with different levels of detail, without having to train the top level directly with the original patterns. Fig.4 presents the diagram of this category of HSOM.

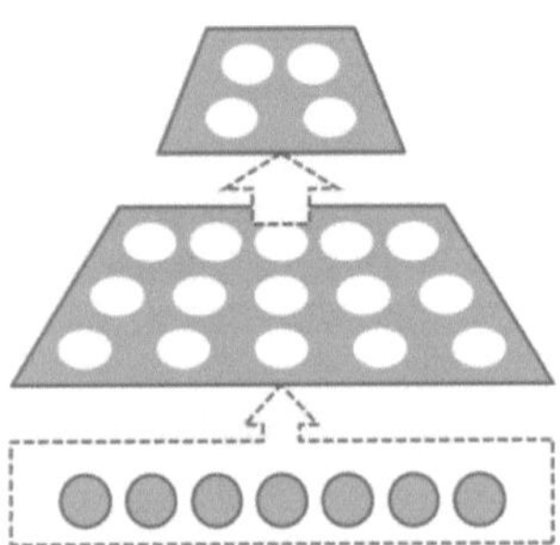

Figure 4. HSOMs based on clusters

A HSOM based on clusters will be significantly different from a standard SOM if, instead of using only the coordinates of the BMU, more information is passed as input to the top level. As an example, one might use both the coordinates and the quantization error of the input patterns as inputs to the top level. In this case, the top level SOM will probably cluster together patterns that have high quantization error (i.e. patterns that are badly represented) in the first level. Thus the top level SOM could be used to detect input patterns that, by being misrepresented in the first level, require further attention.

The name proposed for this class (HSOM based on clusters) stems from the fact that the bottom level SOM uses the full patterns to obtain clusters, and the information about those clusters is the input to the top level SOM. Depending on what cluster information is passed on, the HSOM based on clusters may be similar or very different from the standard SOM.

3.3. Static divisive HSOM

In this category, the HSOM has a static structure, defined by the user. The number of levels and the connections between SOMs are predefined according to the objective. Fig.5 presents two examples of HSOM structures possible in this category.

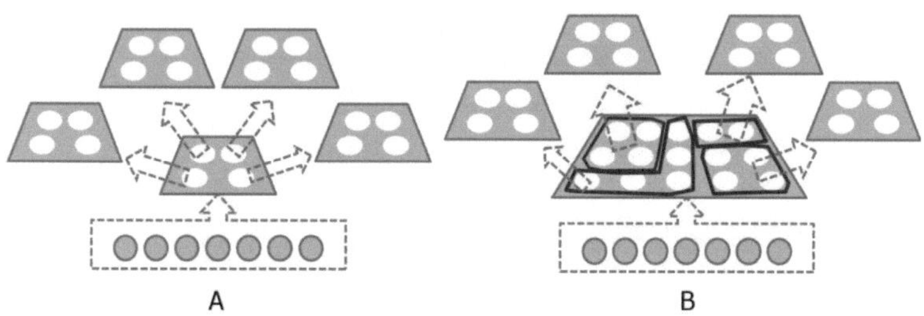

Figure 5. Static HSOMs: a) structure in which each unit will originate a new SOM and; b) structure in which a group of units will originate a new SOM.

In the first case (Fig.5a) the bottom level SOM creates a rough partition of the dataset and, in a second level, an SOM is created for each unit of the first level SOM. Each of these second level SOMs receive as input only the data patterns represented by its origin unit in the bottom level that acts as a gating device.

In the second case (Fig.5b), each top level SOM receives data from several bottom level units. This allows different levels of detail for different areas of the first level SOM.

The main advantages of Static divisive SOMs over large standard SOMs are the reduction of computational effort due to the small number of first level units (and only some of the top level units will be used in each case), and the possibility of having different detail levels for different areas of the SOM. If, for example, we want to train a 100x100 unit SOM, we may use a bottom level SOM with 10x10 units, and a series of 10x10 unit SOMs to form a mosaic in the second level. While each training pattern will require the computation of 10.000 distances in the first case, it will require only 100+100=200 distances in the second.

3.4. Dynamic divisive HSOM

Finally, the category of dynamic divisive HSOMs is characterized by the structure's self-adaptation to data. These methods, also known as Growing HSOM [61], allow the growth of the structure during the learning phase. Two types of growth are allowed: horizontal and vertical growth. The first concerns the increase in the number of units of each SOM, while the second concerns the increase of the number of layers in the HSOM (Fig.6).

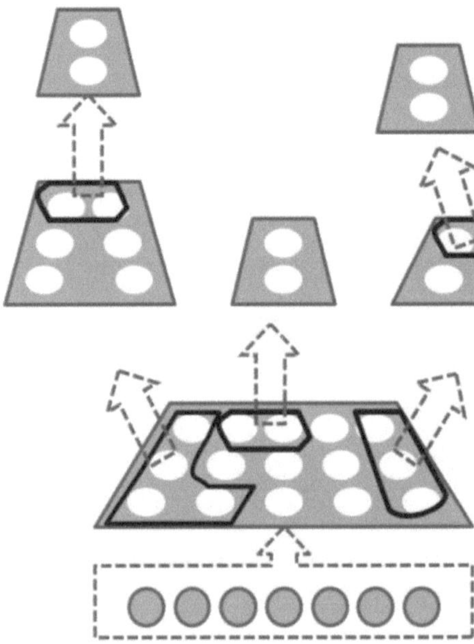

Figure 6. Dynamic HSOMs

A diagram of this type of HSOM is shown in Fig.6. The size of each level SOM and the number of levels is defined during the learning phase and relies on some criteria such as the quantization error.

4. Some HSOM implementations proposed in the literature

One of the first works related to HSOM was proposed by Luttrell in [40]. In his work, hierarchical vector quantization is proposed as a specific case of multistage vector quantization. This work stresses the difference in the input dimensionality between standard and hierarchical vector quantization and proves that distortion in a multistage encoder is minimised by using SOM.

[38] analyses the HSOM as a clustering tool. The structure proposed is based on choosing, for each input vector, the index of the best-matching unit from the first level to train the second level map. The first level produces many small mini-clusters, while the second produces a smaller number of broader and more understandable clusters.

HSOM has proved to be quite valuable for processing temporal data, often using different time scales at different hierarchical levels. An example is the work of [58, 60], where the authors use HSOM to perform sequence classification and discrimination in musical and electric power load data. Another example is [62] where HSOM is used to process sleep apnea data.

Another class of HSOM is proposed in [61]with the Growing Hierarchical Self-Organizing Map (GHSOM). This neural network model is composed of several SOMs, each of which is allowed to grow vertically and horizontally. During the training process, until a given criterion is met, each SOM is allowed to grow in size (horizontal growth) and the number of layers is allowed to grow (vertical growth) to form a layered architecture such that relations between input data patterns are further detailed at higher levels of the structure. One of the problems of GHSOM is the definition of the two thresholds used to control the two types of growth. Several authors proposed some variants to this method to better define these criteria. One example is the Enrich-GHSOM [50]. Its main difference is the possibility to force the growth of the hierarchy along some predefined paths. This model classifies data into a predefined taxonomic structure. Another example of a GHSOM variant is the RoFlex-HSOM extension [57]. This method is suited to non-stationary time-dependent environments by incorporating robustness and flexibility in the incremental learning algorithm. RoFlex-HSOM exhibits plasticity when finding the structure of the data, and gradually forgets (but not catastrophically) previous learned patterns. Also,[63] proposed a Tension and Mapping Ratio extension (TMR) to the GHSOM. Two new indexes are introduced, the mapping ratio (MR) and the tension (T) that will control the growth of the GHSOM. MR measures the ratio of input patterns that get better represented by a virtual unit, placed between two existent units. T measures how similar are the distances between all the units.

Another example of HSOM is proposed in [64] with the Hierarchical Overlapped SOM (HOSOM). The process starts by using just one SOM. After completing the unsupervised learning, each unit is labelled. Then, a supervised learning method is used (LVQ2) and units are merged or removed, based on the number of mapped patterns. After this, a new LVQ2 is applied and, based on the classification quality, additional layers can be created. The process is then repeated for each of these layers.

A similar structure is presented in [65], which proposes a cooperative learning algorithm for the hierarchical SOM. In the first layer, some BMUs are selected, and for each of these BMUs a SOM in the second layer is created. Input patterns used in this second level SOM are derived from the original BMU.

Ichiki *et al.*[43] propose a hierarchical SOM do deal with semantic maps. In this proposal, each input pattern is composed by two parts: the attribute and the symbol,$X_i=[X_{ai} X_{si}]$.The attribute part$X_{ai}$is composed by the variables describing the input pattern, while the symbol partX_{si} is a binary vector. The first level SOM is trained using both parts of the patterns, while the second level SOM only uses the symbol set and information from the first level.

HSOM has also been used for phoneme recognition [51]. The authors use sound signal attributes in a first level SOM to classify the phonemes into pause, vocalised phoneme, non-vocalised phoneme, and fricative segment. After phonemes are classified, a feature frequency-scale vector is used to train the corresponding second level SOM.

A different approach called tree structured topological feature map (TSTFM) is presented in [37]. This approach uses a hierarchical structure to search for the BMU, thus reducing computation times. While the purpose of this approach is strictly to reduce computation times, its tree searching strategy is in effect a series of static divisive HSOMs.

Miikkulainen [41] proposes a hierarchical feature map to recognize an input story (text) as an instance of a particular script by classifying it in three levels: scripts, tracks and role bindings. At the lowest level, a standard SOM is used for a gross classification of the scripts. The second level SOMs receives only the input patterns relative to its scripts, and different tracks are classified at this level. Finally, in the third level a role classification is made.

Table 1 provides a classification using the proposed taxonomy for the HSOM discussed above.

Method	Classification in proposed taxonomy		Main objective
	1st level	2nd level	
[40]	Agglomerative	thematic	Vector quantization
[38]	Agglomerative	cluster based	Clustering
[58][60]	Agglomerative	cluster based	Sequential data classification and discrimination
[61]	Divisive	dynamic	Exploratory data mining
[50]	Divisive	static	Exploratory data mining
[57]	Divisive	dynamic	Exploratory data mining
[63]	Divisive	dynamic	Exploratory data mining
[64]	Divisive	static	Exploratory data mining
[65]	Divisive	static	Clustering
[43]	Agglomerative	cluster based	Create Semantic maps
[51]	Agglomerative	thematic	Phoneme recognition
[37]	Divisive	static	Clustering
[59]	Agglomerative	thematic	Capture the various levels of information in a musical piece
[41]	Divisive	static	Story recognition

Table 1. Comparison table of HSOM methods

4.1. GeoSOM Suite's HSOM implementation

The GeoSOM Suite is a public domain software package for working with SOMs that is particularly oriented towards geo-referenced datasets. It is implemented in Matlab® and uses the public domain SOM toolbox [66]. A standalone graphical user interface (GUI) was built, allowing non-programming users to evaluate the SOM and GeoSOM algorithms. GeoSOM, proposed in [67], is an extension of SOM, specially oriented towards spatial data mining. The GeoSOM Suite is freely available at [68]. The purpose of GeoSOM Suite is to: 1) present spatial data; 2) train maps with the SOM and GeoSOM algorithms; 3) produce several repre-

http://dx.doi.org/10.5772/51159

sentations (views) of the data and; 4) establish dynamic links between views, allowing an interactive exploration of the data.

The GeoSOM Suite implementation of HSOM uses a thematic agglomerative hierarchical SOM (see taxonomy in Fig.1). Fig.7 presents a scheme of the HSOM where several thematic SOMs are created, according to the themes used.

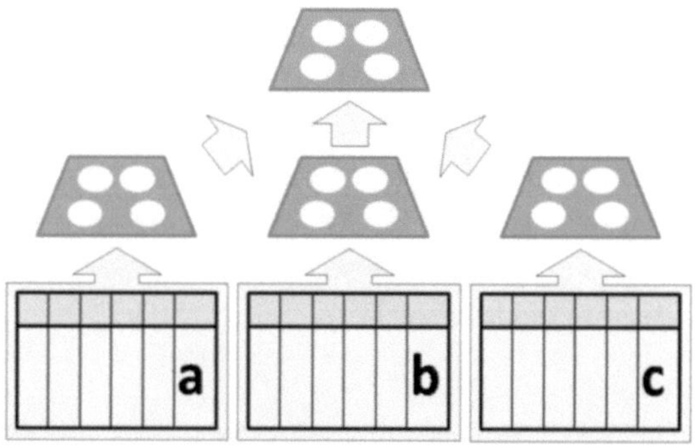

Figure 7. Hierarchical SOM (HSOM) used in this paper. Labels a, b and c refer to different themes.

This HSOM divides the input data space into several subspaces according to different themes. Fig.7 shows an example of HSOM using three themes: a, b and c. Each of these themes can be viewed as a subspace created by a subset of variables from the dataset. For instance, if theme a is demography, some of the possible variables to use in it are the age structure, the number of inhabitants, the number of births, etc.

Each of these data subspaces is used to train a SOM, and its output will be used to train a final merging SOM. When compared to the standard SOM, this approach has the advantage of setting an equal weight for each theme.

Generally, HSOM implemented can be described as follows:

Let

$\boldsymbol{X}$ be the set of n training patterns $\mathbf{X}_1, \mathbf{X}_2, \ldots \mathbf{X}_n$.

$\boldsymbol{X}_i$ be a vector with $\boldsymbol{m}$ components $\mathbf{d}_1, \ldots \mathbf{d}_m$

$\mathbf{t}$ be a theme composed by k_t components of $\mathbf{X}_i$ from $\mathbf{d}_1, \ldots \mathbf{d}_{kt}$

$\mathbf{s}_t$ be a thematic SOM map relative to the theme t, i.e. a SOM trained with the components of $\boldsymbol{X}_i$ belonging to theme $\mathbf{t}$.

$\mathbf{o}_i$ be the image of $\boldsymbol{X}_i$ in the maps S_t, i.e. the concatenation of the outputs of all the maps S_t when pattern$\boldsymbol{x}_i$ is presented.

$\boldsymbol{O}$ be the set of all.

$\mathbf{o}_i$

This set constitutes the modified training set for the top level SOM.

Do

1 For each theme t

2 Train each thematic SOM map s_t in a standard way using as input the relevant

components of ***X***

3 Create the set of modified training patterns ***O*** as a concatenation of the possible outputs of maps S_t, using for each input pattern:

a. The coordinates of its BMU.

b. Its quantization error.

c. Its distance to each unit(i.e., all quantization errors).

4 Train the top level SOM using as input the set of modified training patterns ***O***.

GeoSOM Suite's implementation of HSOM is shown in Fig.8. GeoSOM suite presents an interface where the user can choose the HSOM inputs, based on the SOMs created before, and/or the original variables. Thus, to create a structure like the one presented in Fig.7, the user must create three first level SOMs. Each of these SOMs will use the variables relative to one theme. Then the user can create the HSOM by choosing as input data the outputs obtained from the three SOMs. Fig.8 presents a screen-shot of GeoSOM Suite in which this selection and the HSOM parameterization is shown.

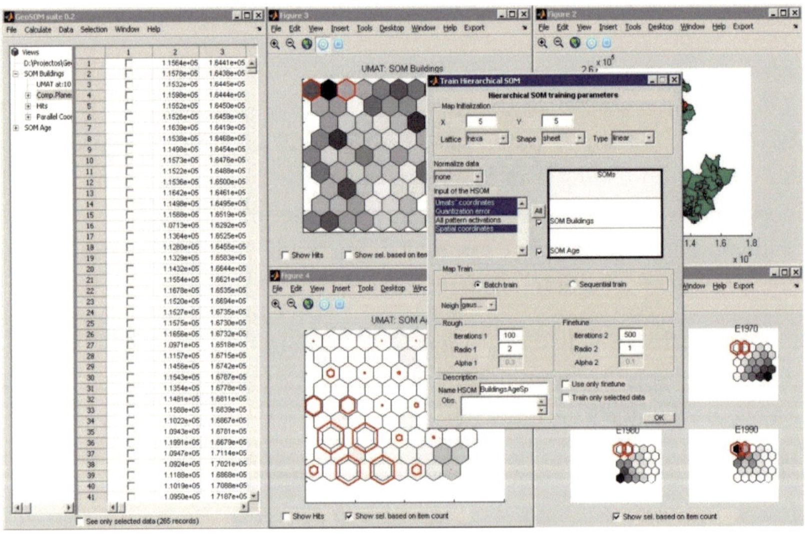

Figure 8. HSOM implementation in GeoSOM suite. In this example, two SOMs are trained using buildings and population age data. An HSOM is parameterized using these two SOM's outputs (BMU coordinates and quantization error) and the geographical coordinates of each ED.

5. Conclusions

In this chapter we presented a case for using Hierarchical Self-Organizing Maps (HSOM) when analysing high dimensional spatial data. We showed that several different approaches can be used to construct HSOM, and presented a taxonomy for them. We pointed out strengths and shortcomings of the different variants, and reviewed several previous proposals of HSOM in the light of the proposed taxonomy. Finally, we presented an implementation of a HSOM that is particularly well suited for spatial analysis. This implementation is publically available for general use at [68].

Author details

Roberto Henriques[1*], Victor Lobo[1,2] and Fernando Bação[1]

*Address all correspondence to: roberto@isegi.unl.pt

1 ISEGI, Universidade Nova de Lisboa Campolide, Portugal

2 CINAV, PO Navy Research Center, Alfeite, Portugal

References

[1] Openshaw, S., & Openshaw, C. (1997). *Artificial Intelligence in Geography*, John Wiley & Sons, Inc., 329.

[2] Gahegan, M. (2003). Is inductive machine learning just another wild goose (or might it lay the golden egg)? *International Journal of Geographical Information Science*, 17(1), 69-92.

[3] Miller, H., & Han, J. (2001). Geographic Data Mining and Knowledge Discovery. London, UK, Taylor and Francis., 372.

[4] Openshaw, S. (1994). What is GISable spatial analysis? in New Tools for Spatial Analysis Eurostat Luxembourg , 36-44.

[5] Jain, A. K., Murty, M. N., & Flynn, P. J. (1999). *Data clustering: a review., ACM Comput. Surv*, 31(3), 264-323.

[6] Fayyad, U. M., Piatetsky-Shapiro, G., & Smyth, P. (1996). From Data Mining to Knowledge Discovery: An Overview. , in Advances in Knowledge Discovery and Data Mining, U.M. Fayyad, et al., Editors., AAAI Press/ The MIT Press. , 1-43.

[7] Miller, H., & Han, J. (2001). Geographic data mining and knowledge discovery an overview. , in Geographic Data Mining and Knowledge Discovery, H. Miller and J. Han, Editors., Taylor and Francis London, UK , 3-32.

[8] Fukunaga, K. (1990). Introduction to statistical pattern recognition. nd ed: Academic Press Inc.

[9] Duda, R. O., Hart, P. E., & Stork, D. G. (2001). *Pattern Classification*, Wiley-Interscience.

[10] Kaufman, L., & Rousseeuw, P. J. (1990). Finding groups in data : an introduction to cluster analysis. Wiley series in probability and mathematical statistics. Applied probability and statistics , New York John Wiley & Sons ., 342.

[11] Han, J., Kamber, M., & Tung, A. K. H. (2001). Spatial clustering methods in data mining: A survey, in Geographic Data Mining and Knowledge Discovery. H.J. Miller and J. Han, Editors., Taylor and Francis London. , 188-217.

[12] Plane, D. A., & Rogerson, P. A. (1994). The Geographical Analysis of Population: With Applications to Planning and Business,. New York, John Wiley & Sons.

[13] Feng, Z., & Flowerdew, R. (1998). Fuzzy geodemographics: a contribution from fuzzy clustering methods,. in Innovations in GIS 5, S. Carver, Editor, Taylor & Francis London , 119-127.

[14] Birkin, M., & Clarke, G. (1998). GIS, geodemographics and spatial modeling in the UK financial service industry. *Journal of Housing Research*, 9, 87-111.

[15] Openshaw, S., Blake, M., & Wymer, C. (1995). Using Neurocomputing Methods to Classify Britain's Residential Areas Available from: http://www.geog.leeds.ac.uk/papers/95-1/.

[16] Openshaw, S., & Wymer, C. (1995). . Classifying and regionalizing census data, in Census users handbook,. S. Openshaw, Editor, GeoInformation International Cambrige, UK , 239-268.

[17] Fahmy, E., Gordon, D., & Cemlyn, S. (2002). Poverty and Neighbourhood Renewal in West Cornwall. in Social Policy Association Annual Conference Nottingham, UK.

[18] Birkin, M., Clarke, G., & Clarke, M. (1999). GIS for Business and Service Planning, in Geographical Information Systems. , M. Goodchild, et al., Editors.,Geoinformation Cambridge

[19] Bellman, R. (1961). Adaptive Control Processes: A Guided Tour,. Princeton, New Jersey, Princeton University Press.

[20] Rees, P., Martin, D., & Williamson, P. (2002). Census data resources in the United Kingdom, in. The Census Data System, P. Rees, D. Martin, and P. Williamson, Editors., Wiley Chichester , 1-24.

[21] Goodchild, M. (1986). Spatial Autocorrelation. *CATMOG*, 47, Norwich, Geo Books.

[22] Tobler, W. (1973). A continuous transformation useful for districting. *Annals, New York Academy of Sciences*, 219, 215-220.

[23] Openshaw, S. (1984). The modifiable areal unit problem. Norwich, England, Geo-Books- CATMOG 38.

[24] Kohonen, T. (2001). Self-Organizing Maps. rd edition ed, Berlin Springer

[25] Muñoz, A., & Muruzábal, J. (1998). Self-organizing maps for outlier detection. *Neurocomputing*, 18(1-3), 33-60.

[26] Hadzic, F., Dillon, T. S., & Tan, H. (2007). Outlier detection strategy using the self-organizing map. in Knowledge Discovery and Data Mining: Challenges and Realities, X.Z.I. Davidson, Editor, Information Science Reference Hershey, PA, USA , 224-243.

[27] Nag, A., Mitra, A., & Mitra, S. (2005). Multiple outlier detection in multivariate data using self-organizing maps title. *Computational Statistics*, 245-264.

[28] Barbalho, J. M., et al. (2001). Hierarchical SOM applied to image compression. in International Joint Conference on Neural Networks,. IJCNN'01. 2001. Washington, DC

[29] Céréghino, R., et al. (2005). Using self-organizing maps to investigate spatial patterns of non-native species. *Biological Conservation*, 459-465.

[30] Green, C., et al. (2003). Geographic analysis of diabetes prevalence in an urban area. *Social Science & Medicine*, 57(3), 551-560.

[31] Guo, D., Peuquet, D. J., & Gahegan, M. (2003). ICEAGE: Interactive Clustering and Exploration of Large and High-Dimensional Geodata. *GeoInformatica*, 229-253.

[32] Koua, E., & Kraak, M. J. (2004). Geovisualization to support the exploration of large health and demographic survey data. *International Journal of Health Geographics*, 3(1), 12.

[33] Oyana, T. J., et al. (2005). Exploration of geographic information systems (GIS)-based medical databases with self-organizing maps (SOM): A case study of adult asthma. in Proceedings of the 8th International Conference on GeoComputation Ann Arbor University of Michigan

[34] Skupin, A. (2003). A novel map projection using an artificial neural network. in Proceedings of 21st International Cartographic Conference Durban, South Africa: ICC.

[35] Bação, F., Lobo, V., & Painho, M. (2008). Applications of Different Self-Organizing Map Variants to Geographical Information Science Problems. in Self-Organising Maps: Applications in Geographic Information Science P. Agarwal and A. Skupin, Editors. , 21-44.

[36] Kohonen, T. (1982). Self-organized formation of topologically correct feature maps. *Biological Cybernetics*, 59-69.

[37] Koikkalainen, P., & Oja, E. (1990). Self-organizing hierarchical feature maps. in International Joint Conference on Neural Networks, IJCNN Washington, DC, USA

[38] Lampinen, J., & Oja, E. (1992). Clustering properties of hierarchical self-organizing maps. *Journal of Mathematical Imaging and Vision*, 261-272.

[39] Kemke, C., & Wichert, A. (1993). Hierarchical Self-Organizing Feature Maps for Speech Recognition. in Proc. WCNN'93, World Congress on Neural Networks Lawrence Erlbaum.

[40] Luttrell, S. P. (1989). Hierarchical vector quantisation. *Communications, Speech and Vision, IEE Proceedings I*, 136(6), 405-413.

[41] Miikkulainen, R. (1990). Script Recognition with Hierarchical Feature Maps. *Connection Science*, 2(1), 83-101.

[42] Luttrell, S. P. (1988). Self-organising multilayer topographic mappings. in IEEE International Conference on Neural Networks San Diego, California

[43] Ichiki, H., Hagiwara, M., & Nakagawa, M. (1991). Self-organizing multilayer semantic maps. in International Joint Conference on Neural Networks, IJCNN-91. Seattle.

[44] Graham, D. P. W., & D'Eleuterio, G. M. T. (1991). A hierarchy of self-organized multiresolution artificial neural networks for robotic control. in International Joint Conference on Neural Networks, IJCNN-91. Seattle.

[45] Lee, J., & Ersoy, O. K. (2005). Classification of remote sensing data by multistage self-organizing maps with rejection schemes. in Proceedings of 2nd International Conference on Recent Advances in Space Technologies, RAST 2005.Istanbul, Turkey

[46] Li, J. M., & Constantine, N. (1989). Multistage vector quantization based on the self-organization feature maps. in Visual Communications and Image Processing IV..SPIE

[47] Saavedra, C., et al. (2007). Fusion of Self Organizing Maps. in Computational and Ambient Intelligence , 227-234.

[48] Sauvage, V. (1997). The T-SOM (Tree-SOM). in Advanced Topics in Artificial Intelligence , 389-397.

[49] Bação, F., Lobo, V., & Painho, M. (2005). Geo-SOM and its integration with geographic information systems. , in WSOM 05, 5th Workshop On Self-Organizing Maps: University Paris 1 Panthéon-Sorbonne , 5-8.

[50] Chifu, E. S., & Letia, I. A. (2008). Text-Based Ontology Enrichment Using Hierarchical Self-organizing Maps. in Nature inspired Reasoning for the Semantic Web (NatuReS 2008) Karlsruhe, Germany.

[51] Kasabov, N., & Peev, E. (1994). Phoneme Recognition with Hierarchical Self Organised Neural Networks and Fuzzy Systems- A Case Study. in Proc. ICANN'94, Int. Conf. on Artificial Neural Networks Springer

[52] Douzono, H., et al. (2002). A design method of DNA chips using hierarchical self-organizing maps. in Proceedings of the 9th International Conference on Neural Information Processing. ICONIP'02. Orchid Country Club, Singapore

[53] Hanke, J., et al. (1996). Self-organizing hierarchic networks for pattern recognition in protein sequence. *Protein Science*, 5(1), 72-82.

[54] Zheng, C., et al. (2007). Hierarchical SOMs: Segmentation of Cell-Migration Images. in Advances in Neural Networks- ISNN 2007 , 938-946.

[55] Vallejo, E., Cody, M., & Taylor, C. (2007). Unsupervised Acoustic Classification of Bird Species Using Hierarchical Self-organizing Maps. in Progress in Artificial Life , 212-221.

[56] Tsao, C. Y., & Chou, C. H. (2008). Discovering Intraday Price Patterns by Using Hierarchical Self-Organizing Maps. in JCIS-2008 Proceedings, Advances in Intelligent Systems Research.. Shenzhen, China Atlantis Press

[57] Salas, R., et al. (2007). A robust and flexible model of hierarchical self-organizing maps for non-stationary environments. *Neurocomput*, 70(16-18), 2744-2757.

[58] Carpinteiro, O. A. S. (1999). A Hierarchical Self-Organizing Map Model for Sequence Recognition. *Neural Processing Letters*, 9(3), 209-220.

[59] Law, E., & Phon-Amnuaisuk, S. (2008). Towards Music Fitness Evaluation with the Hierarchical SOM. in Applications of Evolutionary Computing , 443-452.

[60] Carpinteiro, O.A.S., & Alves da Silva, A.P. (2001). A Hierarchical Self-Organizing Map Model in Short-Term Load Forecasting. *Journal of Intelligent and Robotic Systems*, 105-113.

[61] Dittenbach, M., Merkl, D., & Rauber, A. (2002). Organizing And Exploring High-Dimensional Data With The Growing Hierarchical Self-Organizing Map. in Proceedings of the 1st International Conference on Fuzzy Systems and Knowledge Discovery (FSKD 2002) Orchid Country Club, Singapore.

[62] Guimarães, G., & Urfer, W. (2000). Self-Organizing Maps and its Applications in Sleep Apnea Research and Molecular Genetics,. , University of Dortmund- Statistics Department

[63] Pampalk, E., Widmer, G., & Chan, A. (2004). A new approach to hierarchical clustering and structuring of data with Self-Organizing Maps. *Intell. Data Anal*, 8(2), 131-149.

[64] Suganthan, P. N. (1999). Hierarchical overlapped SOM's for pattern classification. *Neural Networks, IEEE Transactions on*, 10(1), 193-196.

[65] Endo, M., Ueno, M., & Tanabe, T. (2002). A Clustering Method Using Hierarchical Self-Organizing Maps. *The Journal of VLSI Signal Processing*, 32(1), 105-118.

[66] Vesanto, J., et al. (1999). Self-organizing map in Matlab: the SOM Toolbox. in Proceedings of the Matlab DSP Conference Espoo, Finland: Comsol Oy

[67] Bação, F., Lobo, V., & Painho, M. (2004). Geo-self-organizing map (Geo-SOM) for building and exploring homogeneous regions. *Geographic Information Science, Proceedings*, 3234, 22-37.

[68] Lobo, V., Bação, F., & Henriques, R. (2009). GeoSOM suite. 15-11-2009]; Available from: www.isegi.unl.pt/labnt/geosom

Chapter 13

Self-Organizing Maps: A Powerful Tool for the Atmospheric Sciences

Natasa Skific and Jennifer Francis

Additional information is available at the end of the chapter

http://dx.doi.org/10.5772/54299

1. Introduction

Self-organizing maps (SOMs) are a powerful tool used to extract obscure diagnostic information from large datasets. In the context of issues related to threats from greenhouse-gas-induced global climate change, SOMs have recently found their way into atmospheric sciences, as well. In meteorology SOMs provide a means to visualize the complex distribution of synoptic weather patterns over a region of interest (Hewitson and Crane 2002), explore extreme weather and rainfall events (Hong et al. 2005, Zhang et al. 2006, Uotila et al. 2007), classify cloud patterns (Tian et al. 1999, Ambroise et al. 2000) and reveal causes and effects of climate changes projected using global climate models (Lynch et al. 2006; Cassano et al. 2007, Skific et al. 2009a, 2009b).

The SOMs' unsupervised learning algorithm reduces the dimension of large data sets by grouping similar multi-dimensional fields together and organizing them into a two-dimensional array (Kohonen 2001). To a trained operational meteorologist the interpretation of SOMs is intuitive, as they are reminiscent of synoptic charts arranged adjacent to one another according to their similarity (much like tracking a weather system in time, as is done in synoptic meteorology, Hewitson and Crane 2002). Although still largely underutilized, SOMs are gradually becoming more widely used for applications in atmospheric science. Unlike most traditional clustering algorithms, SOMs attempt to conserve space continuum, utilizing the information from the provided data. The resulting clusters will therefore have some resemblance because the process of SOM creation assumes that a single sample of data will contribute to the creation of more than one cluster, as the whole neighborhood around the best matching cluster is also updated in each step of training. It will also result in a more detailed presentation of particular features appearing on neighboring clusters, if the information from the original data enables it to do so. On the other hand, as the SOMs attempts to span a continuous data space, some of the resulting clusters may have only a few members ascribed to them, in the attempt to overlap the data gap or the region where data information exists but is very sparse.

This chapter provides a brief summary of several experiments using SOMs to explore how Arctic climate will change by the end of the 21st century. It demonstrates how the SOM technique can be adapted to quantify a change in a meteorological variable of interest and possibly reveal the underlying mechanism driving that change.

2. Data preparation

In this application, the high-dimensional data subjected to SOM analysis are daily fields of sea-level pressure (SLP) anomalies simulated by the Community Climate System Model, version 3 (CCSM3), for time periods from 1960 to1999, 2010 to 2030, and 2070 to 2089. The latter two periods are extracted from a simulation for the "worst-case scenario: of greenhouse gas emissions for the 21st century as specified by the Special Report on Emission Scenarios, SRES A2 (Nakicemovic and Swart 2000). These scenarios are based upon assumptions for future greenhouse gas pollution, land use, global economic development, etc. The SLP fields are then interpolated from the original 1.4º x 1.4º grid to a 200 km x 200 km Equal Area-Scalable Earth (EASE) grid (Armstrong et al. 1997), covering the area north of 60ºN and consisting of 51 x 51 grid points. Interpolation to an equal area grid avoids errors that might occur owing to equal weighting in the SOM algorithm of the original latitude-longitude grid boxes, which decrease in size toward the pole.

Daily SLP anomalies are then derived by subtracting the gridpoint SLP from the domain-averaged SLP for each daily field (Cassano et al. 2007). The spatial distribution of the daily SLP anomalies represent the SLP gradient, which drives the strength and direction of the circulation, without being influenced by fluctuations in the area-mean absolute SLP values. Areas with elevation higher than 500 m are removed from the fields because pressure reduction to sea level can lead to unrealistic singularities emerging in the SOM training, which then obscure the realistic patterns.

3. SOM methodology

The SOM consists of a two-dimensional grid of clusters or nodes, which in this case is a grid of SLP anomaly maps. Each node i corresponds to an n-dimensional weight or reference vector, m_i, where n is the dimension of the input data, treated as a vector created from the gridpoints in each sample.

The initial step of this routine is the creation of a first-guess array, which consists of an arbitrary number of nodes and corresponding reference vectors. In this study we use a grid of 35 nodes, creating a 7x5 array. Slightly smaller and larger SOM matrices were tested to deter-

http://dx.doi.org/10.5772/54299

mine a suitable number of nodes for this analysis. If the matrix is too small, some characteristic atmospheric patterns may not be represented; if it is too big, adjacent patterns will be too similar and visualization is unwieldy. The 7x5 matrix appears to capture and separate the important differences in pressure patterns. Moreover, the results are not affected by small differences in the matrix size (see Skific et al. 2009a).

The reference vectors are created at the beginning using linear initialization, which consists of first determining the two eigenvectors with the largest eigenvalues, then letting these eigenvectors span the two-dimensional linear subspace (Kohonen 2001). We use the covariance matrix of the input SLP dataset to determine the two eigenvectors. In this case the centroid of a rectangular array of initial reference vectors identified with array points corresponds to the mean of the sea level pressure values, and the vectors identified with the corners of the array correspond to the largest eigenvalues. By initiating a SOM in this way, the procedure starts with an already ordered set of weights, then training begins with the convergence phase. Linear initialization helps achieve faster convergence, which is an advantage of this procedure over other methods (i.e., random initialization), but the SOM results are not sensitive to the selected initialization method. In the process of training, each data sample (i.e., one daily map of SLP) is presented to the SOM in the order it occurs in the original data set.

The similarity between the data sample and each of the reference vectors is then calculated, usually as a measure of Euclidean distance in space. In this process, the "best match" node is identified as that with the smallest Euclidean distance between its reference vector and the data sample. Only the vectors for the best-matching node and those that are topologically close to it in the two-dimensional array are updated. The updating scheme is shown below

$$m_i(t+1)=m_i(t)+h_{ci}(t)\cdot[x(t)-m_i(t)],$$

where t is a discrete-time coordinate, m_i is a reference vector, x is a data sample, and h_{ci} is a neighborhood function (Kohonen 2001), usually in the form of the Gaussian function,

$$h_{ci}=a(t)\cdot\exp(-\frac{\| r_c-r_i\|^2}{2\sigma^2(t)}.$$

α is the training rate function (usually an inverse function of time), r is the location vector in the matrix, $||r_c-r_i||$ corresponds to the distance between the best-matching node (location r_c) and each of the other nodes (location r_i) in the two-dimensional matrix, and σ defines the width of the kernel, or a relative distance between nodes, often referred to as the radius of training. The training procedure is controlled by the training rate α, the training radius r, and the duration of training, which is fixed at 20 times the number of data samples. This choice is based on the "rule of a thumb" for optimal training length, which should be longer than 500 times the vector size (see Kohonen 2001). The initial value of r is 4, and decreases linearly in time. The training scheme is repeated several times, with the training rate reduced by an order of a magnitude each time. At the end of each trial the mean quantization error is calculated, defined as

$$mqe=\frac{\sqrt{\sum_{i=1}^{M}(x_i-m_c)^2}}{M},$$

where x_i is a data sample, M is the number of samples, and m_c is its best matching unit out of 35 reference vectors. A smaller mean quantization error indicates a closer resemblance between m_c and the daily SLP anomaly fields. Once the smallest mean quantization error is found, we then fine-tune the training by varying the training rate slightly around that value and calculating the error for each trial. The training is complete once the smallest mean quantization error is identified, as the reference vectors from that training best approximate the data space of interest. The final reference vectors are then mapped onto a 2D grid, with their locations in the matrix corresponding to their matching nodes. The maps in the resulting matrix represent the predominant patterns in which the atmosphere tends to reside, or alternatively the centroid of the particular data cluster.

Although the measure of similarity between the data and the reference vector is linear, it is this iterative training procedure that allows the SOM to account for the non-linear data distributions (Hewitson and Crane 2002). The non-linear approximation of the data space is therefore a great advantage of the method compared to some other approaches, such as empirical orthogonal functions (EOFs) (Reusch et al. 2005).

4. SOMs application in practical meteorology

4.1. Detection of regional climate change

Once the SOM has been trained and the final set of reference vectors has been identified, daily fields of SLP anomalies can be mapped to the best-matching pattern to form clusters of daily maps that are most similar to each pattern. This is achieved by finding the pattern in the SOM that minimizes the Euclidean distance between itself and the daily field. Once all the SLP anomaly fields have been assigned to a node, the frequencies of occurrence (FO) can be determined, i.e., the fraction of daily fields that reside in each cluster. Ascribing a particular daily SLP sample to a specific circulation pattern in the SOM also enables an analysis of associated variables (such as temperature, precipitation, cloud amount, etc.) for the same days as those in each cluster. By mapping the new variable onto a particular SLP-derived cluster, the matrix of maps for any other variable can be used to describe the conditions associated with a specific circulation regime. The following examples elaborate this procedure in more detail.

Figure 1a shows dominant circulation regimes in which Arctic atmosphere resides, according to the CCSM3 model output described above. These clusters or neuronal weights form a discrete approximation of the data distribution, which in the process of SOM creation, become organized on a 2D grid. Clusters near each other on the grid are more similar than clusters farther away. Most distinct patterns are situated in the corners of the map, while the cluster positions on the master SOM and their mutual distances approximate the probability density function of a given dataset. This technique results in an overlap among neighboring clusters because the process of training a single data sample will contribute to defining the neighboring clusters as well, not only to the most similar one.

http://dx.doi.org/10.5772/54299

In this example, the clusters in the lower right side of the master SOM are characterized by a pronounced low pressure center in the North Atlantic and Pacific region, and high pressure over the Eurasian continent. These features bare close resemblance to the North Atlantic Oscillation (NAO), the most dominant SLP mode of variability in the high-latitude winter atmosphere. The upper right side of the master SOM has cluster groups characterized by a pronounced low pressure in the North Atlantic that extends farther northward and eastward, towards the Norwegian and Barents Seas. A strong high-pressure ridge generally resides over the western Arctic in these clusters. The lower left corner of the map contains clusters with low pressure over the Arctic, while in the clusters of the upper left corner low (high) pressure is generally present in the western (eastern) Arctic. The clusters in the middle of the map show a weak or moderate ridge over the central Arctic region.

Further insight about the relationships between adjacent nodes is provided by the so-called Sammon map (Figure 1b). This distortion surface is a projection of Euclidean distance between neighboring nodes of the SOM matrix (Figure 1a) to a set of 2D vectors, following a Sammon mapping algorithm (Sammon 1969). Numbers 1 to 35 on the distortion surface correspond to the nodes on the SOM matrix, from the upper left to the bottom right corner of the map. Generally, the closer two nodes are together on the Sammon map, the more similar they are to each other. Although the distortion surface generally conforms to the expected rectangular shape of the SOM matrix (Figure 1a), some more detailed relationships between the nodes are revealed. One can see that nodes on the left of the SOM are closer in Euclidean space than those on the right. This shows that node distribution approximates the multi-dimensional distribution function, as the nodes are more closely spaced in regions where data density is higher, i.e., where nodes have more members in their group. The Sammon map is also useful for visualizing the process of creating the SOM. If one were to draw a Sammon projection at each step of SOM training, each iteration would look like a wrinkled tablecloth that is gradually becoming less wrinkled, until at the end of the training, it resembles its familiar rectangular shape (Figure 1c).

To better understand the origin and characteristics of circulation patterns in the master SOM, we create monthly histograms of CCSM3 mean SLP for each node in the SOM. Figure 2 shows a matrix of histograms corresponding to the master SOM (Figure 1). The x-axis of each histogram is a month, while the y-axis is the number of times that this particular cluster was a best match for an individual daily SLP map during that month. The histograms illustrate the frequency with which a particular regime occurs during each month. As mentioned earlier, the clusters on the right side are recognized as the NAO pattern, which is most common in winter. The histograms for these clusters confirm that the non-summer days are most likely to have these patterns. A single cluster in the upper left corner of the master SOM also describes non-summer circulation patterns. These cold-season histograms show that the clusters with pronounced low pressure in the North Atlantic along with a ridge over the Eurasian continent or over the western Arctic occur most frequently in the winter months. Come spring, although still present, these patterns become less frequent through summer, then increase again in fall. These patterns thus depict the annual cycle of development and intensification of the Icelandic low, influenced by strong temperature gradients along the sea ice margins (Serreze 1995; Serreze et al. 1997a), "splitting" of lows moving in from the south and southwest by the high orographic barrier of Greenland (Serreze and Barry 2005), and lee-side vorticity production off the southeast coast of Greenland (Petersen et al. 2003). The vigorous synoptic activity in the Atlantic is also related to the large moist static energy transport into the Arctic through this sector (Overland et al. 1996). Features towards the middle left side of the master SOM are primarily summer patterns, with increased FOC as the warmest season approaches. They are characterized by either weak low pressure, most commonly in the western Arctic, or a weak atmospheric ridge over the central Arctic.

(a)

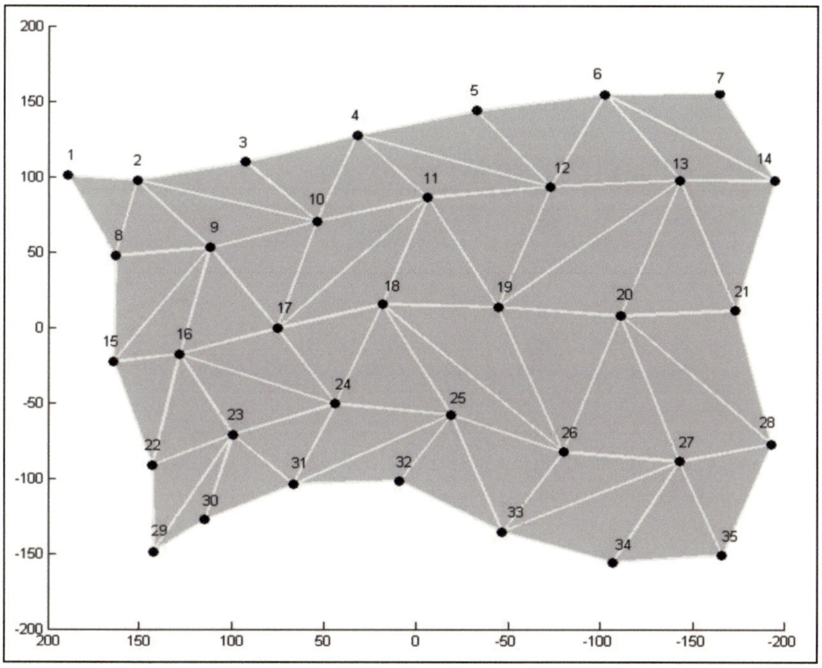

(b)

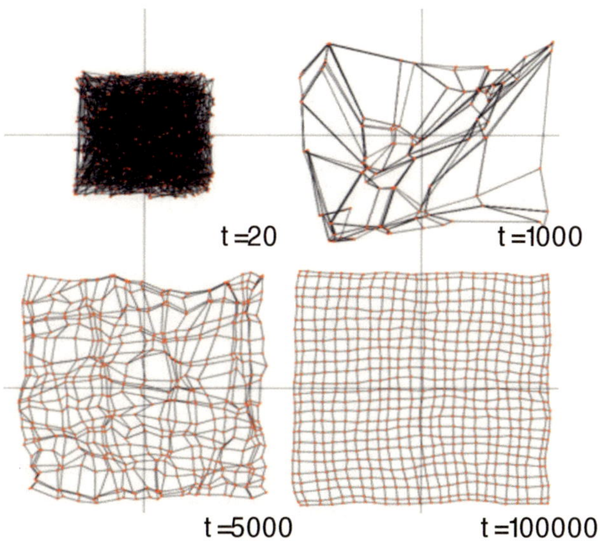

(c)

Figure 1. a: Master SOM of sea level pressure anomaly patterns (hPa) derived from daily SLP anomaly fields CCSM3 (1960-1999, 2010-2030, and 2070-2089), and from the ECMWF Reanalysis (ERA-40) from 1958 to 2001. b: Sammon map of the SOM matrix shown in Figure1 a.c: Projections of reference vectors in 2-dimensional space for various stages of map training (from Kohonen, 1990).

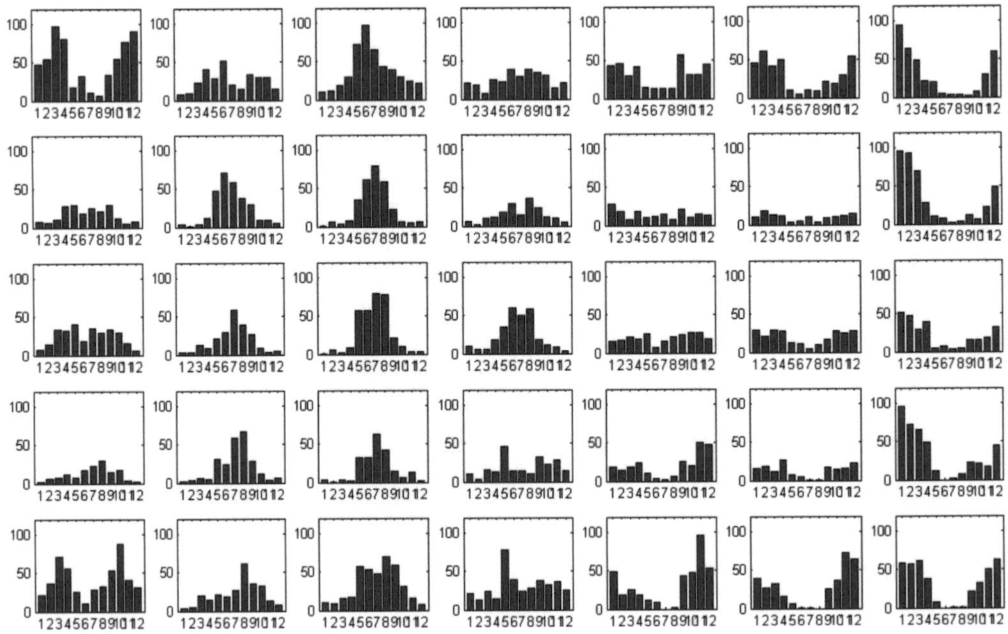

Figure 2. Frequency of occurrence displayed as monthly histograms for each node in the master SOM. The x–axis is month, y-axis is the number of times that node was the best matching unit during that month.

The SOM algorithm keeps track of which days in the data record fall into which of the clusters, thus one can analyze other variables corresponding to the same days that exhibit that circulation regime. This is a highly valuable tool for attributing causes for variations in particular variables. We illustrate this tool by investigating fields of cloud fraction.

Figure 3 shows cluster-averaged cloud fraction for the CCSM3 1971-1999 period. The fact that the minimum values are near 50% indicates that the Arctic is a very cloudy place. Low stratus clouds account for over 80% of the total cloud cover in this region. Clusters on the right side of the map correspond to the cold-season regimes, and as expected, these are characterized by lower values of cloud fraction, typically around 50% for the central Arctic region. Summer patterns, located in the middle left of the SOM, show the most extensive cloud cover for the central Arctic, ranging around 75%. The projection of cloud features on a geographic map assist in understanding the reasons for observed cloud patterns. Variability over the central Arctic, for example, is primarily driven by the seasonality in the low-level stratus, which is related to the availability of moisture. In summer when the surface is melting, evaporation increases and clouds are more abundant than in the much colder winter months when evaporation is small (Beesley and Moritz 1999). The Atlantic sector, in contrast, is frequently overcast, reflecting abundant moisture and intense cyclonic activity, particularly during the winter season. Large cloud fractions over the Scandinavian Peninsula in winter patterns (right side of the map) are due to orographic uplift at the continental boundary. Heavy overcast is also seen along the land-ocean boundary in the summer patterns (in the middle left of the SOM). These areas of increased cloudiness likely reflect summer cyclonic activity in connection with the development of the summer Arctic frontal zone. This discontinuity is sustained by differential heating between the Arctic Ocean (at temperatures kept at the melting point) and snow-free land, as well as sharpening of the baroclinicity by coastal orography (high topography can "trap" the cold ocean air). Increased summer cloud fraction over Eurasia and northwestern Canada likely also reflects increased cyclogenesis over land areas and more abundant convective clouds, in contrast to the winter months that are dominated by low stratus.

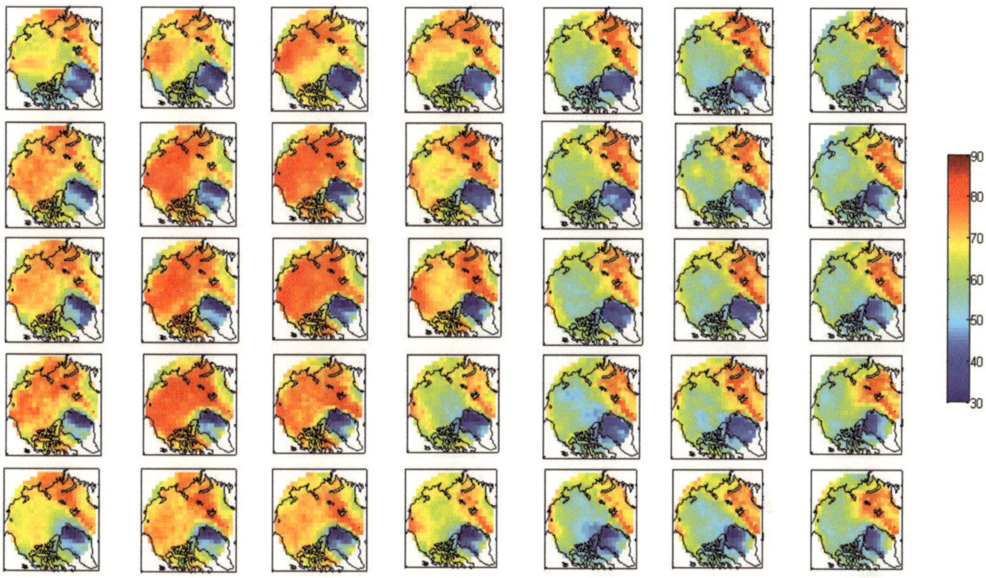

Figure 3. Node- averaged cloud fraction (in %) ascribed to a corresponding SLP pattern of the master SOM.

Another related variable that is highly dependent on cloud characteristics is the downward longwave (infrared) radiation flux (DLF). This is an important quantity for studies of the Arctic energy balance, as no energy is received from the sun during the 6-month polar night. Figure 4 shows cluster-averaged downward longwave flux (DLF), corresponding to each circulation pattern on the master SOM (Fig 1). The spatial pattern of the mean DLF is similar to the distribution of total cloud fraction (Fig 3), underscoring the close relationship between DLF and cloud properties. During the cold season (patterns on the right of the matrix) the highest values of DLF occur in the Atlantic sector, where cloud cover is extensive both horizontally and vertically, water vapor is abundant, and temperatures are relatively warm. The surface elevation of central Greenland is above much of the cloud cover, which along with low temperatures and humidity values, results in low DLF values in all clusters and seasons. Higher values of DLF for the clusters on the left side of the map, corresponding to the summer patterns, are related to seasonal increase of surface temperature and atmospheric water vapor.

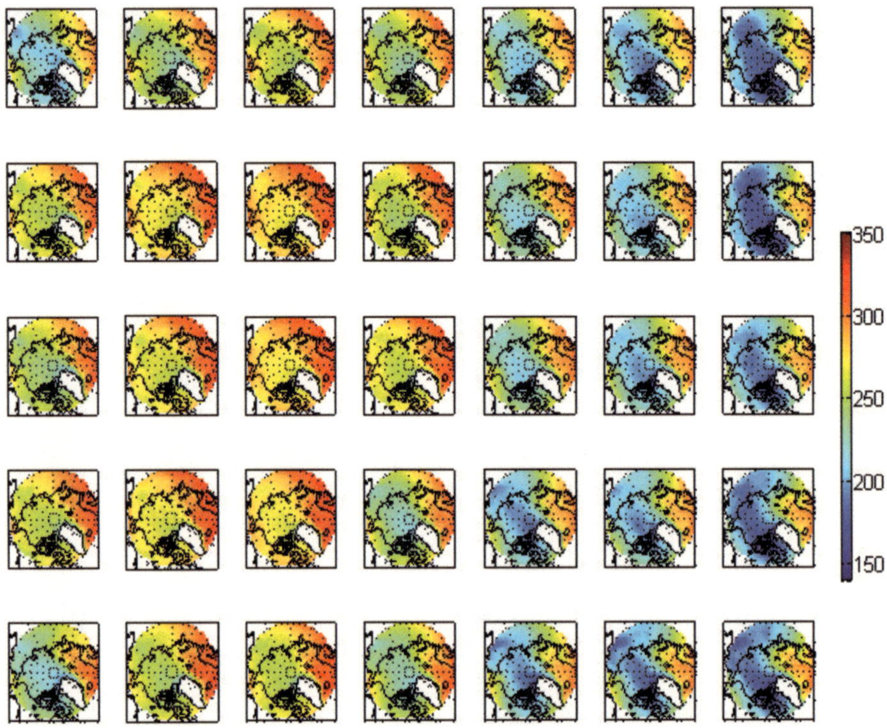

Figure 4. Node-averaged downward longwave flux (W m^{-2}) ascribed to each individual SLP pattern on the master SOM.

In addition to investigations of relationships between circulation patterns and corresponding atmospheric variables, the SOM analysis also allows an assessment of changing tendencies for the atmosphere to reside in particular circulation patterns. These kinds of questions are relevant to climate-change studies (for example, whether summer-like patterns are becoming more frequent as the climate warms, or whether the relative locations of high and low pressure centers are shifting.

The top two panels of Figure 5 display the percentage of winter and summer days that fall into each node during the late 20th century. Corresponding to the histograms shown in Figure 2, it is clear winter days tend to exhibit the circulation patterns along the right side of the master SOM, while summer patterns occur in nodes in the center left. By calculating frequencies of occurrence (FO) in two time periods, one can determine whether the atmospheric circulation patterns are shifting. We present an example in the lower panel of Figure 5 that assesses changes in the FOs of each cluster on the master SOM from the late 20th century (1971-1999) to the late 20st century (2070-2089). Black solid (dashed) contours show areas of significantly (> 95% confidence) higher (lower) difference in frequency of occurrence. The range in a 95% confidence interval,

$$\pm 1.96\sqrt{\frac{p_1(1-p_2)}{n_2}+\frac{p_2(1-p_2)}{n_2}},$$

where $p_1(1\text{-}p_1)/n_1$ and $p_2(1\text{-}p_2)/n_2$ are variances of two independent, random, binomial processes, p_1 and p_2 are the expected frequencies of occurrence for the two time periods (p=1/35), n_1 is the number of samples in the first data set, and n_2 is the number of samples in the second data set (for more details see Cassano et al., 2007). Because this statistical test does not account for the effects of serial correlation in the daily SLP fields, and thus likely overestimates the degrees of freedom, we determine an approximation for the effective degrees of freedom by dividing the number of samples of the two data sets by 7. This value is determined from the serial correlation of the SLP time series, which indicates that the atmosphere tends to reside in a circulation regime for about one week. This procedure decreases the degrees of freedom, thus establishing a higher threshold for determination of a significance level.

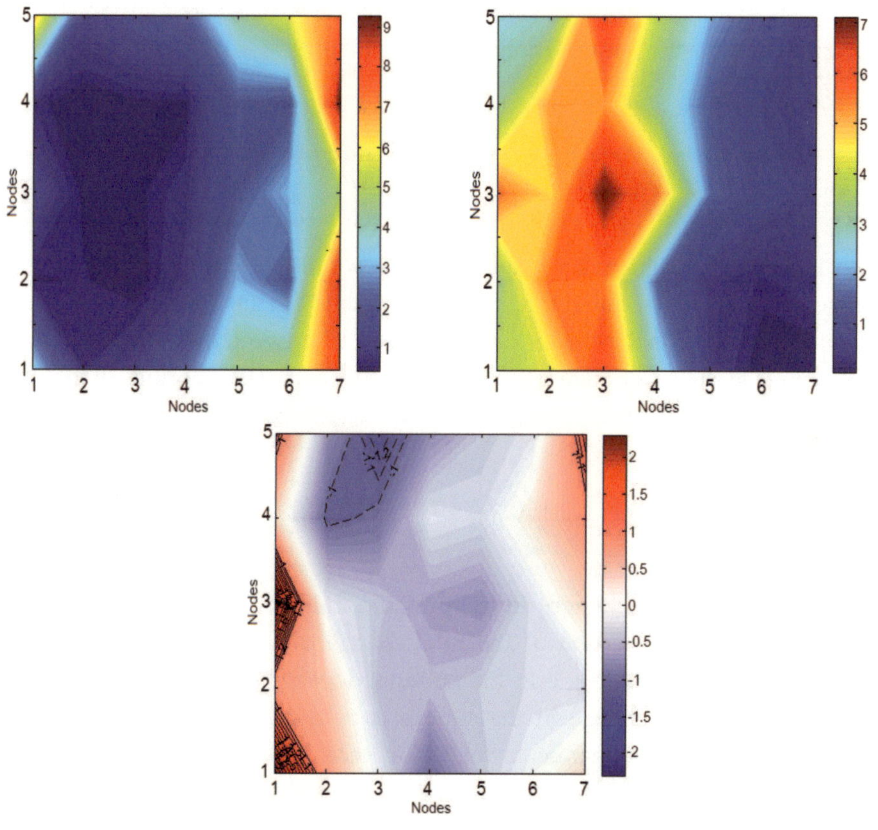

Figure 5. Frequency of occurrence (FO) of winter (DJF) days (upper left) and summer (JJA) days (upper right) in CCSM3. Frequencies are presented as percent of total days of the 1971-1999 period that map into each node of the master SOM. Change in FO from the late 20th century to the late 21st century is shown in bottom panel. Significantly larger (smaller) differences are indicated with solid (dashed) lines, with a level of confidence above 95%.

A pronounced, statistically significant increase is apparent in patterns with low pressure over the central Arctic (left of the master SOM, Figure 1), as well as those with strong high pressure across the western Arctic region and strong low pressure in the Atlantic sector and eastern Arctic (upper right SOM). The clusters in the middle, mostly dominated by a weak or a moderate high pressure over the central Arctic, decrease significantly. Taken together these changes represent a decrease in pressure over the central Arctic in this greenhouse-gas-forced model projection, but SOMs and their corresponding FOs allow for a more detailed, quantified look at regional variability in pressure change.

4.2. Attribution of regional climate change

This section demonstrates how the SOM technique can be adapted to better understand what processes are driving the change in a variable of interest. Cassano et al. (2007) formulated a method that separates the factors contributing to a temporal change in a variable of interest into the portion caused by a change in the FO of daily maps in a cluster, the portion due to a change in the cluster-mean value of the physical variable, and a third due to a combination of the two effects. The equation is given as follows:

$$\Delta x = \sum_{i=1}^{N} (x_i + \Delta x_i)(f_i + \Delta f_i) - x_i f_i \tag{1}$$

where Δx is the total change in a variable between two different time periods, x_i is the cluster-averaged variable in the initial time period, f_i is the FO of the daily maps in cluster i during the initial period, Δf_i is the change in FO for cluster i between the two periods of interest, Δx_i is the change in the cluster-averaged variable between the two periods of interest, and N is the total number of clusters ($N = 35$ in this study). Expanding (1):

$$\Delta x = \sum_{t}^{N} = 1(x_i \Delta f_i + f_i \Delta x_i + \Delta x_i \Delta f_i). \tag{2}$$

The first term, $x_i \Delta f_i$ relates changes in the pressure field to changes in the FO of circulation patterns. It shows a portion of the total change owing to shifts in the frequencies with which daily SLP fields reside in the patterns depicted in the SOM. A change in this distribution represents a change in the surface circulation, and thus we loosely refer to this contribution as the "dynamic factor." The second term, $f_i \Delta x_i$, relates to temporal changes in the variable of interest averaged over all days that belong to a cluster. In the case of cloud fraction, changes of this type are likely caused mainly by thermodynamic effects – such as changes in the horizontal and vertical distribution of water vapor, varying moisture and temperature gradients, or changes in evaporation—thus we refer to this contribution as the "thermodynamic factor" (Cassano et al. 2007; Skific et al. 2009a; 2009b). The third term in Eq. 2 represents the contribution from the interaction of both changing pattern frequency and the cluster-averaged variable. This term tends to be small compared to the other two.

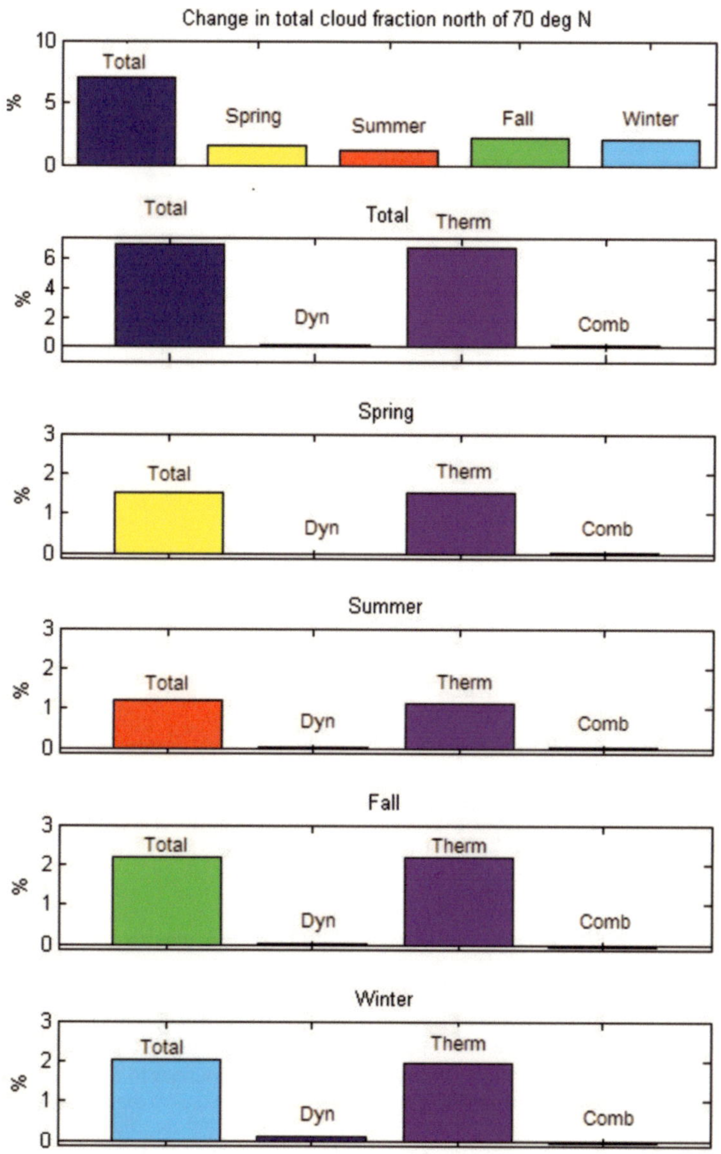
Change in total cloud fraction north of 70 deg N
Total
Spring
Summer
Fall
Winter
%
Total
Total
Dyn
Therm
Comb
Spring
Summer
Fall
Winter

(a)

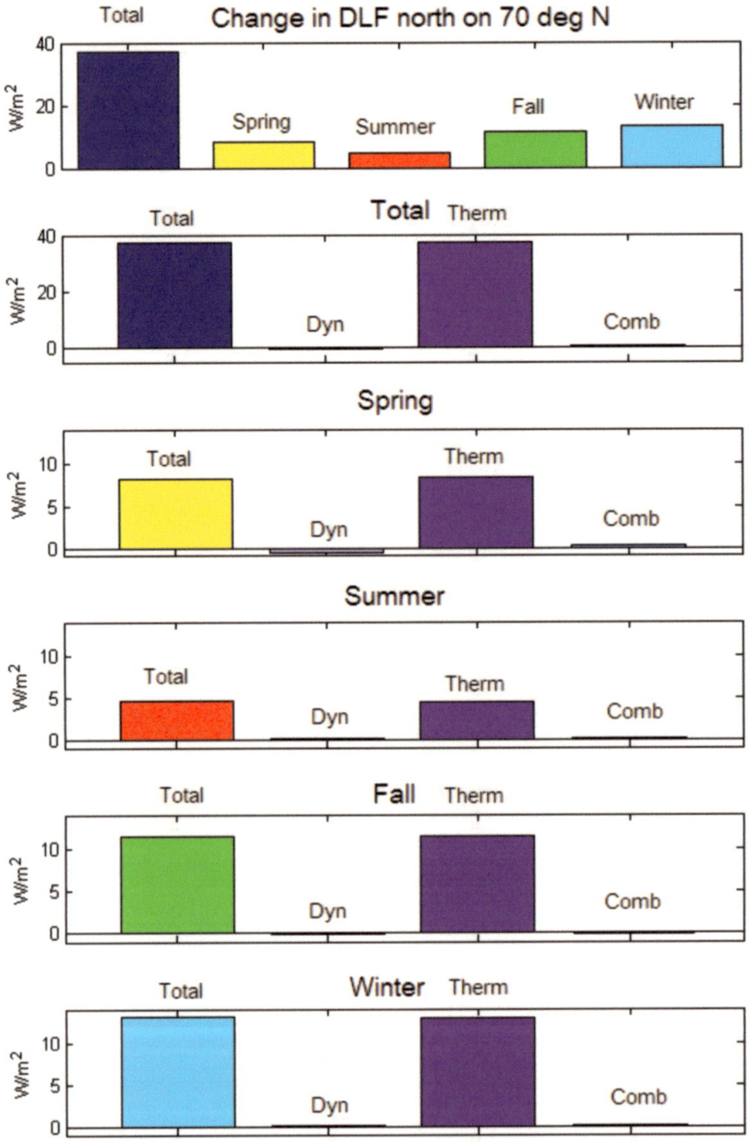

(b)

Figure 6. a: Annual and seasonal changes in total cloud fraction (%) in the region north of 70°N in the CCSM3 from the late 20thcentury (1971-1999) to the late 21st century (2070-2089). Contributions to the total change from the dynamic, thermodynamic, and combined terms are also shown b: Annual and seasonal changes in downward longwave flux (DLF, in W m^{-2}) over the region north of 70°N in the CCSM3 from the 20th century (1971-1999) to the late 21st century (2070-2089). Contributions to the total change from the dynamic, thermodynamic, and combined terms are also shown.

We therefore utilize the derived master SOM and the aforementioned procedure to determine a portion of a total change in cloud fraction (Figure 6a) and DLF (Figure 6b) from the late 20th century to the late 21st century due to dynamics, thermodynamics, and their combination. The experiment focuses on both the annual and seasonal changes. Total cloud fraction north of 70ºN is projected to increase by 6.5% by the end of the 21st century, with largest changes expected to occur in the fall and winter (increase in cloud fraction of about 2%). The figures show that for both variables, the increase is caused mainly by the thermodynamics factor, while the contribution to cloud and DLF changes from shifting FO of particular pressure patterns is relatively small. Thermodynamic processes driving the cloud changes are likely related to local temperature changes and their effects on cloud formation, such as changes in precipitable water that would lead to changes in cloud amount even under the same dynamics, changes in the temperature and humidity profiles, and changes in relative humidity owing to changes in evaporation. The largest increase in cloud fraction in this model run occurs in the fall season and smallest in the summer (Figure 6a). These changes are driven by the projected increases in surface temperature, which are strongest in fall and winter. It also suggests that the seasonality in cloud cover over the Arctic is primarily driven by low-level stratus (Serezze and Barry 2005), as they constitute about 80% of the total cloud cover over the central Arctic Ocean. They are greatly affected by the changes in surface temperature through its affect on the stratification of the atmospheric boundary layer. Fall and winter seasons have experienced the largest changes in surface temperature in connection with the loss of sea ice and resulting increased absorption of solar energy into the Arctic Ocean.

DLF increases most in the winter (by 12.6 W m^{-2}, Figure 6b), which points to the sensitivity of DLF to surface temperature, water vapor, and cloud cover. Small summer increases in both cloud amount and DLF because surface temperature is fixed at the melting point while sea ice melts, and a heavy overcast of low clouds persists through the melt season. These relatively constant conditions dictate small changes in DLF. Because the model projects only a small increase in summer surface temperature by the end of the 21st century, it is expected that cloud fraction and DLF will not increase substantially either.

Changes in both cloud fraction and DLF are driven mainly by processes that occur for a fixed circulation regime, which implies that the same synoptic pattern with similar pressure gradients will generate more clouds and thus a larger DLF occur by the end of the 21st century. Because clouds are an important element of Arctic energy budget, these changes will feed back on surface temperatures, leading to even higher surface temperatures.

5. Conclusion

Here we present examples of our application of SOMs to understanding changes in the Arctic climate system as greenhouse gas concentrations continue to increase. The purpose of this exercise is to illustrate the power and adaptability of the SOM technique for a variety of scientific applications. Understanding and possibly predicting potential drivers of the Arctic climate change has great implications for society as a whole, such as sea-level rise, mid-latitude weather patterns, marine and terrestrial productivity, to name only a few. Linkages between the dramatic changes within the Arctic and the global system remain poorly understood in present conditions, thus the uncertainty regarding future changes will remain an important focus for global-change research.

Changes in Arctic cloud fraction and downward longwave flux, and mechanisms responsible for those changes, are presented through the rather simple and conceptually appealing neural network technique of SOMs, introduced in Cassano et al. (2007), and further elaborated in Skific et al. (2009a, 2009b). Given the recent and rapid changes of the Arctic climate system and uncertainties associated with many climate feedbacks over this region, this technique offers a valuable contribution toward attributing these changes to either shifts in the dominant atmospheric circulation patterns or to thermodynamically driven changes in the set of variables associated with them.

Author details

Natasa Skific and Jennifer Francis*

*Address all correspondence to: francis@imcs.rutgers.edu

Institute of Marine and Coastal Sciences, Rutgers University, New Brunswick, NJ, USA

References

[1] Ambroise, C.; Seze, G. Badran F, and S. Thiria, 2000: Hierarchical clustering of self-organizing maps for cloud classification, *Neurocomputing*, 30, 47–52, ISSN 0925-2312

[2] Armstrong, R, M. J. Brodzik, and A. Varani, 1997: The NSIDC EASE-Grid: Addressing the need for a common, flexible, mapping and gridding scheme. *Earth System Monitor*, 7(3), 3 pp.

[3] Beesley, J.A., and R.E. Moritz, 1999: Toward an explanation of the annual cycle of cloudiness over the Arctic Ocean. *J. Climate*, 12, 395-415.

[4] Cassano, J.J, P. Uotilla, A.H. Lynch, E.N. Cassano, 2007: Predicted changes in Synoptic Forcing of Net Precipitation in Large Arctic River basins During the 21st century, *J. Geoph. Res- Biogeosciences*, 112, G04S49, doi:10.1029/2006JG000332.

[5] Hewitson, B.C., and R.G. Crane, 2002: Self-organizing maps: applications to synoptic climatology. *Clim. Res.*, 22, 13-26.

[6] Hong, Y.; Hsu, K., Sorooshian, S. and X. Gao, 2005: Self-organizing nonlinear output (SONO): A neural network suitable for cloud patch-based rainfall estimation at small scales, *Water Resources Research*, 41, No. W03008,

[7] Kohonen, T., 2001:*Self-organizing maps*. 3d ed. Springer-Verlag, 501 pp.

[8] Lynch, A.H., P. Uotila, J.J. Cassano, 2006: Changes in synoptic weather patterns in the polar regions in the 20th and 21st centuries, Part 2: Antarctic. International Journal of Climatology, 26(9), 1181-1199.

[9] Nakicemovic, N. and R. Swart, 2000: Intergovernmental Panel on Climate Change Special Report on Emission Scenarios. Cambridge University Press, 570 pp.

[10] Overland, J.E., P. Turet, and A.H. Oort, 1996: Regional variations of moist static energy flux in the Arctic. *J. Climate*, 9(1), 54-65.

[11] Petersen, G.N., Olafsson, H., and J.E. Krisjansson, 2003: Flow in the lee of idealized mountains and Greenland. *J. Atmos. Sci*, 60, 2183-2195.

[12] Reusch, D.B., R. Alley and B.C. Hewitson, 2005: Relative performance of self-organizing maps and principal component analysis in pattern. Extraction from synthetic climatologic. *Polar Geography*, 29, 188-212.

[13] Sammon, J.W., 1969: A nonlinear mapping for data structure analysis. *IEEE Transactions on Computers*, 18, 401–409.

[14] Serreze, M.C., and R.G. Barry, 2005: *The Arctic Climate System*. Cambridge University Press, 146 pp.

[15] Carse, F., Barry, R.G., and J.C. Rogers, 1997a: Icelandic Low cyclone activity: climatological features, linkages with the NAO, and relationships with recent changes in the Northern Hemisphere circulation. *J. Climate*, 10, 453-464. 1995: Climatological aspects of cyclone development and decay in the Arctic. *Atmosphere-Ocean*, 33, 1-23.

[16] Skific, Natasa, Jennifer A. Francis, John J. Cassano, 2009a: Attribution of Projected Changes in Atmospheric Moisture Transport in the Arctic: A Self-Organizing Map Perspective. *J. Climate*, 22, 4135–4153.

[17] Skific, Natasa, Jennifer A. Francis, and John J. Cassano 2009b: Attribution of Seasonal and Regional Changes in Arctic Moisture Convergence, *J Clim*, *22*(19), 5115.

[18] Tian, Bin, M.A. Shaikh, M.R. Azimi-Sadjadi,T.H.V. Haar, and D.L. Reinke, 1999: A study of cloud classification with neural networks using spectral and textural features, *IEEE Transactions on Computers*, 10(1),138-151.

[19] Uotila, P.; Lynch, A. H., Cassano J. J. and R.I. Cullather, 2007: Changes in Antarctic net precipitation in the 21st century based on Intergovernmental Panel on Climate Change (IPCC) model scenarios, *Journal of Geophysical Research*, 112, D10107.

[20] Uppala, S.M., P.W. Kallberg, A. J. Simmons, U. Andrae, V.D. Bechtold, M, Fiorino, J.K. Gibson, J. Haseler, A. Hernandez, G. A. Kelly, X. Li, K. Onogi,S. Saarinen, N. Sokka, R. P. Allan, E. Andersson, K. Arpe, M. A. Balmaseda, A. C. M. Beljaars, L. Van De Berg, J. Bidlot, N. Bormann, S. Caires, F. Chevallier, A. Dethof, M. Dragosavac, M. Fisher, M. Fuentes, S. Hagermann, E. Holm, B.J. Hoskins, L. Isaksen, P.A.E.M. Janssen, A.P. McNally, J.F. Mahfouf, J.J. Morcreete, N.A. Rayner, R.W. Saunders, P. Si-

mon, A. Sterl, K. E. Trenberth, A. Untch, D. Vasiljevic, P. Viterbo, and J.Wollen, 2005: The ERA-40 reanalysis. *Quart. J. Royal. Met. Soc.*, 131, 2961-3012.

[21] Zhang, R.; Wang, Y., Liu, W., Zhu, W, and J. Wang, 2006: Cloud classification based on self-organizing feature map and probabilistic neural network, *Proceedings of the 6th World Congress on Intelligent Control and Automation*, June 21 - 23, 2006, Dalian, China, 41-45, ISSN 0272-1708

Chapter 14

Image Simplification Using Kohonen Maps: Application to Satellite Data for Cloud Detection and Land Cover Mapping

Suzanne Angeli, Arnaud Quesney and
Lydwine Gross

Additional information is available at the end of the chapter

http://dx.doi.org/10.5772/51352

1. Introduction

In this study, we present classification results obtained by applying Kohonen maps to Earth observation data. Earth observation refers to the use of sensors onboard artificial satellites dedicated to the monitoring of the Earth surface-atmosphere system geophysical properties. These sensors may perform passive or active remote sensing.

In the domain of Earth Observation, the information delivered by optical telescopes is most of the time multi-spectral, meaning that several light wavelengths are measured from near ultraviolet to thermal infrared, depending on the mission [1, 2, 3]. In Synthetic Aperture Radar (SAR) imagery, if most of the time only one information is available (the unpolarised backscatter cross-section in the SAR emitted wavelength), recent satellite missions [4, 5, 6] deliver polarised response, leading to two to four variables. In both cases (optical and SAR), Earth Observation interpretation is thus a multivariate problem.

Physical theory used to interpret passive observations is called radiative transfer, while electromagnetism is used to interpret active sensor measurements. In both cases, the interpretation of satellite images corresponds to the inversion of the physical theory that explains observation as a function of geophysical parameters describing surface properties and atmosphere. Because satellite imagery is geo-referenced, this retrieval leads to cartographic maps of Earth-atmosphere geophysical variables (atmosphere gas contents, aerosols and clouds optical thickness, vegetation chlorophyll content, surface soil moisture, sea surface salinity etc.).

But physically interpreting satellite imagery requires a classification step prior to the retrieval of geophysical parameters. Indeed, for the same bio-geophysical variable, the physical inversion scheme may be different depending on the processed pixel location on Earth. As an example, the chlorophyll concentration in $mg.m^{-3}$ is not estimated by the same algorithm if the observed pixel is located on a continental land surface or on liquid water surface. Moreover, because physical inversion is often an ill-posed problem, an identification step is required to simplify this problem by a priori knowledge introduction (variables initialisation or default values). Indeed, land cover maps are often used as auxiliary inputs of physical inversion. A good example is the land SMOS (Soil Moisture and Ocean Salinity) processing chain [7] which requires soil properties and land cover classifications. These data give useful information over the observed surfaces and allow their modelling trough a reduced number of free parameters which remain to retrieve (soil moisture, optical thickness of the vegetation cover).

Physicists generally use very simple methods to classify the pixels according to their geophysical content: they apply thresholds or threshold cascades, equivalent to decision trees based on linear tests, on spectral information or spectral information linear compositions. The choice of the tested variables at each node of the decision tree is based on physical knowledge, the thresholds values are found empirically by an operator on a few observation cases. Typical examples are the MODIS (Moderate Resolution Imaging Spectroradiometer) level 2 cloud mask [8] and the Météo-France ECOCLIMAP classification of land cover at 1 km of resolution [9].

But these kinds of algorithms are very costly in time to develop, and are often imperfect because remote sensing problems cannot be stacked into linear subspaces. Indeed, for most applications, classification problems on SAR and optics imageries are non linear and continuous, and should be addressed by Bayesian theory. Moreover, because thresholds are very sensitive, each time a new sensor is launched, physicists have to redefine the decision trees or the thresholds values. We thus decided to attempt more automatic and more mathematically adapted solution to the problem of satellite observation geophysical identification.

In order to underline the achieved progress when using Kohonen maps instead of linear decision trees, we applied the Mixed Topological Map algorithm (MTM) [10] to two well-known classification problems in satellite imagery: cloud detection on low resolution (LR) optics imagery and land cover mapping on high resolution (HR) optics imagery. In the first use-case, we compared the results obtained by the MTM on MODIS data algorithm with the Level 2 MODIS cloud mask [8]. We showed that cloud detection is largely improved over bright surfaces like snow and deserts using the MTM algorithm. In the second use-case, because no real-time labelled land cover is available at high resolution spatial scale, we validated our results by projecting HRG sensor images (Haute Résolution Géométrique [11]) classified by the MTM algorithm on Google Earth cartographic background, showing that temporally stable structures (down-town areas, rivers and forests) are correctly detected.

We propose to organise this chapter into four paragraphs. The first paragraph describes our methodology. The second one details the application of the MTM algorithm to MODIS data for cloud detection and includes a cloud detection state of the art. The third paragraph describes the application of the MTM algorithm to HRG data for land cover mapping. Finally, a general conclusion detailing satellite imagery classification improvements using Kohonen map is proposed, and an overview of possible continuations of the methodology is presented.

2. Methodology

The amount of satellite data available is very large (more than several tenth of millions of pixels are available each day with low resolution sensors), and thus, statistical methods are well adapted to develop automatic classification of remote sensing observations. On the other hand, the amount of in situ data (ground truth) which could be used as target data for a supervised learning is very small, meaning not representative, compared to the amount of available input data (remote sensing pixels). Therefore, applicable statistical tools are unsupervised, and in-situ data are to be used as test (or validation) data.

Because Kohonen maps are unsupervised algorithms, and moreover because they preserve the genuine space topology (close neurons on a Kohonen map represent close data according to the dissimilarity that is used during the learning phase), they are good candidates to address remote sensing data classification. Indeed, topology conservation is essential to facilitate the a posteriori physical interpretation of the results, like neurons identification. As an example, it allows propagating labels to neighbourhood on the Kohonen map (automatically or not [12]). Another advantage of Kohonen maps is that they are adapted to multivariate non Gaussian distributions (like we have in remote sensing data ensembles), and they allow the simultaneous process of quantitative and qualitative variables [10].

Our methodology can be described by three steps: the first step is the data ensembles preparation for learning, labelling and testing a Kohonen map, the second step is a Kohonen map learning and labelling phase, and the third step is the application of a calibrated Kohonen map to satellite images.

Indeed, the first step corresponds to posing the problem, i.e. encoding the variables to improve the performance of the targeted classification. This encoding may thus be different from a problem to another.

The second step realisation (the learning phase) also may differ from a problem to another because some choices have to be done concerning learning algorithm and parameters (as an example do we proceed the calibration of the map with or without a priori label, do we choose a probabilistic map or not, which dissimilarity shall we use etc.), concerning Kohonen map architecture (typically the size of the map), and last concerning the method to label the map, depending on the quantity and the nature of the available a priori knowledge.

The third step of the method (the application of a calibrated Kohonen map to classify pixels), may be completed by an image processing algorithm to arrange the results if they are too noisy, which may be the case for high and very high resolution optical images or SAR imagery. In this case, the radiometric value of a pixel is replaced by the value of its corresponding neuron weights prior to the image processing application, in order to simplify the problem.

In paragraphs 3 and 4, these three steps are detailed in the case of our two use-cases: cloud detection and land cover mapping using optical imagery.

2.1. Data preparation

In the case of optical imagery, if exception is made of future European Spatial Agency (ESA) Sentinels missions, the lower spatial resolution, the less available spectral bands, for evident reasons of data volumetry management. Typically, HR sensors are radiometers equipped with wide band-pass filters from the green (G) to the near infrared (NIR) and are referred to as broadband radiometers (BBR), while LR sensors are radiometers equipped with about ten narrow band-pass filters (sometime more) from the blue (B) to the short-wave infrared (SWIR), and are referred to as multispectral imagers (MSI). Moreover, a very few MSI like PARASOL [13] and MISR [14] are multidirectional and polarised, leading to several tenth of variables by pixel.

As our methodology is general and applicable to both BBR and MSI, we decided the following: each pixel will be represented by all its available spectral information, but avoiding the bands that are sensitive to gas absorption, which are too sensitive to atmosphere content. A data is thus an optical pixel defined by several spectral bands, in our case irregularly distributed from the blue to the SWIR. No geometrical information (solar and viewing angles, solar and satellite azimuth angles) is taken into account in the definition of a data vector, but irradiances (e.g. in $W. m^{-2}. sr^{-1}. nm^{-1}$) are transformed into reflectances (dimensionless) prior to further computations. Moreover, in order to improve classification quality, we completed the available spectral information with new variables, created from reflectance data with various kinds of transformations.

Red (R), green (G) and blue (B) bands were converted into other colour spaces:

1. The CMYK (Cyan, Magenta, Yellow and Key (black)) space is the colour model used in colour printing. The black component is used to increase the black density which can be obtained by addition of magenta, cyan and yellow.

2. The HSV colour model can be seen as a cylinder space of three components: Hue gives the colour in degree, Saturation corresponds to the colour intensity in percent and Value is the colour brightness in percent.

3. The CIE L*a*b* (more often called Lab) space have been created by the CIE (Commission Internationale de l'Eclairage) so that distances between colours are closer to colour differences for human eyes. The L* variable indicates the lightness in percent. The colour is explained by two axes: between green (negative) and red (positive) in the component a* and between blue (negative) and yellow (positive) in the component b*.

Moreover, we applied a gamma correction on RGB bands to increase their contrasts [15]. This transformation consists in taking the puissance of the corresponding channel. We used as exponentiation the value 0.45, generally used for sRGB space. This kind of correction is currently used to adjust screen or camera.

Some physical indexes were created from spectral bands, like normalized difference indices. They are commonly used by scientists to detect different kind of earth surfaces and their temporal variations:

- The Normalized Difference Vegetation Index (NDVI) is the most common vegetation index used. It is created from near-infrared (NIR) and red (R) bands and used by physicists in order to control the vegetation variation :

$$NDVI = \frac{NIR - R}{NIR + R} \tag{1}$$

- The Normalized Difference Snow Index (NDSI) [16] is made from green (G) and mid-infrared (MIR) bands. The difference between visible and thermal bands allows us discriminating snow and cloud :

$$NDSI = \frac{G - MIR}{G + MIR} \tag{2}$$

- The Normalized Difference Built-up Index (NDBI) [17] is created from mid-infrared (MIR) and near-infrared (NIR) bands. This index enables distinguishing urban areas :

$$NDBI = \frac{MIR - NIR}{MIR + NIR} \tag{3}$$

The shape of the spectrum produced for each pixel by spectral bands reflectances is a very useful indication. Each type of earth surface has its own shape. In order to add this information in the database, we fitted the spectrum of each pixel by a polynomial approximation using wavelengths values. Depending on the number of spectral bands of the studied sensor, we used a three or four degree for the polynomial. The calculation of the spectrum derivative by a simple polynomial derivative is also possible but, in our case, adding these variables does not allow to improve the classification. Polynomial coefficients are additional information and they are added in the database.

Some qualitative variables may also be added to the variables vector, like information about the observed background or the weather, if they are available. They are used in order to interpret our classification results by comparison to these existing qualitative image masks. If a mask concerning the targeted classification is available (which is the case for MODIS, because a cloud mask is distributed as a Level 2 product), this mask is taken as a priori label, and it is added to the data vector by the way of integer variables.

All variables were independently normalized between 0 and 1 in order to ensure that they have the same weight during the Kohonen learning phase, except of the integer variables (e.g. a priori labels).

We then posed the problem by taking the imagery pixels as independent data, which, on a local spatial scale is false, but by sub-sampling images on the full Earth become true. Pixels for which one variable is missing are not put in the databases.

For the learning database constitution, that must be representative of the problem, we decided to equally represent the different observable land covers, in order to avoid under representation of certain geophysical cases. Indeed, choosing a natural sampling of Earth would lead to a massive representation of water pixels in the data distribution. Moreover, each type of forest, crop, field, desert, and city are equally important from a physical point of view. In the case of cloud detection, we did the same according to the weather, by collecting the same pixel number for each kind of clouds on each earth surface type.

We also constituted a labelling database, smaller than the learning database, in which a priori knowledge is equally represented considering the targeted classes. This database will be used to control or to create the neurons labels, depending on which Kohonen map algorithm will be used during the learning phase. It is constituted by pixels taken from as many identified areas as desired classes, as examples: urban area, forest area, crop area etc.

Finally, the testing database is constituted by all the data that has not been used for the learning database or the labelling database constitution.

2.2. Calibration and labelling of a Kohonen map

First step of our methodology is the Kohonen map calibration using the learning database. As already stated, we chose to use the MTM algorithm [10]. This algorithm is a classical topological map algorithm in which the use of binary variables is allowed. This is done by declaring which variables from the input vector are continuous and which ones are binary, and then applying the Euclidian distance to the continuous variables and the Hamming distance to the binary variables. The cost function is thus constituted by the sum of two parts: one is the classical cost function used by the Kohonen Batch algorithm [18] and is based on the continuous variables (this cost function is denoted E_{som} in the following); the other part is the cost function used in the denoted BinBatch algorithm [19] and is based on the binary variables (denoted E_{bin}).

For the learning phase, the classical Kohonen iterative scheme is applied, following two steps: the assignment step and the optimisation step. The assignment step consists in associating, for each iteration, each data of the learning database to its closer neuron considering a current neighbourhood function (which size decreases at each iteration), using a ponderated sum of the Euclidian distance and the Hamming distance. The optimisation step consists in calculating the new value of the weights of each neuron using the input vectors assigned to it. The neurons weights are defined as the concatenation of the mean of the inputs continuous part, and the median of the inputs qualitative part. Iteratively performing the assignment and the optimisation steps leads to the minimisation of E_{som} and E_{bin}.

In the case of cloud detection, because a priori labels were available, the MTM algorithm was used to calibrate a Kohonen map, using binary masks completing the radiometric information, and giving an equivalent ponderation to the radiometric information and the binary masks. But in the case of the land cover mapping, no a priori knowledge was available, thus the MTM code was applied without binary part in the input vector, which means that we used a classical Kohonen algorithm only. For both cases, we use a exponential neighbourhood function.

Second step of our methodology is the Kohonen map neurons labelling, according to the targeted classes of each problem. If a priori labels are present in the learning database, the MTM algorithm automatically labels each neuron by majority vote. If no a priori labels are present in the learning database, we project the labelling database on the Kohonen map and label the neurons by majority vote.

To finalise the resulting classification, we have to control the learned label and regroup them in order to match the desired classes. A control is performed on images which have not been used for the labelling (testing data set). Controls of the labels are applied on images and with respect to the topology of the Kohonen map. One label must correspond to neighbour labelled neurons on this map. If neurons are unidentified, they may be corrected manually or automatically (as example by hierarchical clustering [12]).

2.3. Operation of a Kohonen map

Once calibrated and labelled on a representative learning data set, the Kohonen map may be used in an operational mode, i.e. using only the assignment algorithm in order to associate a winning neuron, and thus a winning label, to each new pixel presented to the map.

This process is sufficient in the case of LR imagery in order to obtain smooth and easy to interpret classified image masks, superimposable on the processed satellite product. But it may be insufficient in the case of LR imagery, because in this case images have much more high frequencies in their radiometric values, and thus the result of the Kohonen map labelling may seem noisy to a human eye.

In the case of LR imagery only, we thus decided to apply image processing to achieve the process of pixel classification. It is also needed because of the radiometric high frequencies values, but it is also justified because of the local spatial pixel correlation that may be very high in LR imagery (and is much smaller in HR imagery). A lot of algorithms may be used to complete or correct the first classification result given by a Kohonen map: from simple local filters computed on a local window like mean or median filters, to more sophisticated image processing solutions like growing region algorithms [20].

In this study, to achieve the classification, we simply chose to perform a majority vote between labels on a local window, because we wanted to avoid costly algorithms in calculus time. We thus do not use any radiometric information to perform this post-processing. But if we had chosen some real image processing algorithm, we would have replaced each pixel radiometric value by its winning neuron weights value before perform the image processing scheme. By this way, we would have simplified the problem (by removing radiometric highest frequencies) and gain calculus and scientific performance on the resulting classification. In other study cases, we perform this simplification prior to change detection.

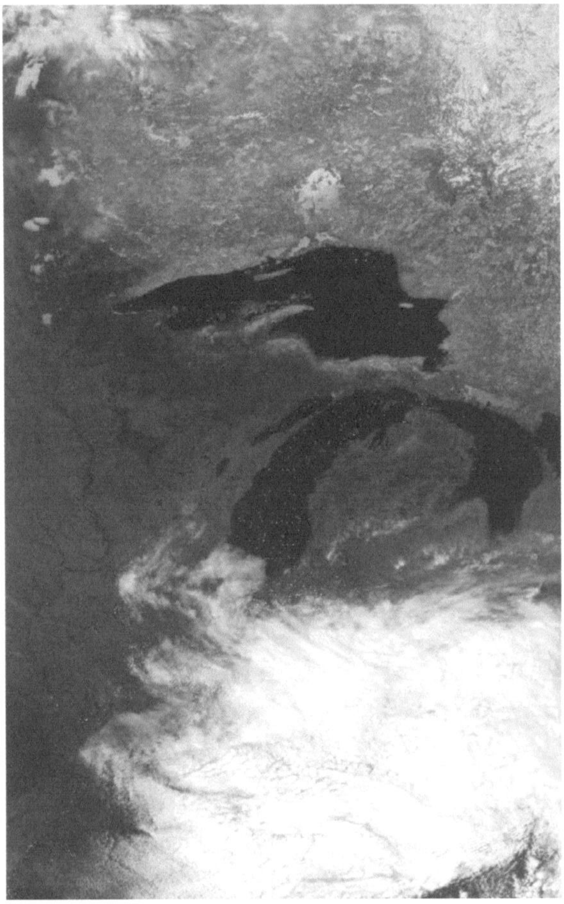

Figure 1. RGB composite image from MODIS data, North of Great Lakes, Canada.

3. First use-case: Cloud detection

The determination of the presence of global cloudiness is essential because clouds play a critical role in the radiative balance of the Earth and must be accurately described to assess climate and potential climate change. Moreover, the presence of cloudiness must be accurately determined to retrieve properly many atmospheric and surface parameters. For many of these retrieval algorithms even thin cirrus represents contamination.

Visible and infrared window threshold approaches are largely used in the cloud detection because they allow separating easily bright, dense, and cold surfaces. However, some surface conditions such as snow covers, ice cover, bright desert surfaces, or even salty areas could be detected as clouds by these classical tests. Moreover, some cloud types such as thin cirrus, low stratus at night, and small cumulus are difficult to detect because of insufficient contrast with the surface radiance.

In brief, cloud detection is a difficult and recurrent problem when using a sensor which does not provide information in the thermal infra-red. Classical threshold methods on reflectance data are insufficient, even though a lot of attempts have been made to create decision trees depending on latitude, seasons and observed surfaces [21], because the detection problem is continuous and non linear if all kind of Earth surfaces and all types of cloud optical thicknesses are taken into account.

We thus decided to challenge one of these classical algorithms by a Kohonen map used for classification. MODIS sensor has been chosen because of its important number of spectral bands (eight for land observation from visible to mid infrared) and because of the availability of validated, but not perfect, cloud detection masks deduced from a decision tree [8]. In order to calibrate the MTM algorithm on the entire Earth, fourteen sites were chosen everywhere on the planet. For each site, five satellite images (MODIS Calibrated Radiances Level 1B products, MYD021KM collection 5.1) were selected at different seasons for their balanced cloud proportion (you can see an example on Figure 1).

3.1. Data preparation for cloud detection on MODIS data

Multiple Level 2 cloud masks (MYD35_L2 collection 5) were combined to have five "weather" labels (clear sky, thin clouds, thick clouds, shadows and indeterminate pixels) and six background labels (water, coastal, glitter, snow/ice, land and desert) (Figure 2). These labels allowed the random selection of the same amount of pixels by background type and weather type (about 100 000 per combination), avoiding indefinite weather pixels, leading to a learning database containing a total number of two millions pixels.

The learning and testing databases were built using the eight spectral bands, with a gamma correction for RGB bands. Moreover, we decided to add new colour spaces: Lab, CMYK and HSV. As H component of HSV is a circular angle between 0° and 360°, it had been separated into two variables corresponding to its sine and cosine. A polynomial regression of degree four was applied for each pixel of the database and we added their polynomial coefficients. We also computed the NDVI index in order to improve the discrimination efficiency between cloud and snow or ice.

First, we performed a Linear Discriminant Analysis using the four weather labels to control the linearity of the problem. It clearly appeared that linear models cannot discriminate thin clouds from thick clouds. During this descriptive analysis of the database, we also studied the correlation matrix of variables. It seemed that some components of new colour space are correlated, such as K component of CMYK and L component of Lab. Then, we computed another Linear Discriminant Analysis deleting correlated variables and using only two classes: clear weather (regrouping clear sky and shadows) and cloudy weather (regrouping thin and thick clouds). Results were better than the first one but not enough discriminant. It was then justified to attempt the use of MTM algorithm in order to distinguish several cloud optical depths.

As a result of this prior study, we decided to put the cloud probability result obtained by the second Linear Discriminant Analysis in the input vector constituting learning and testing databases of the Kohonen map, as a new pre-processing variable. We also added two qualitative variables to the input vector: weather labels and background labels, in order to take advantage of the MTM algorithm binary variable processing.

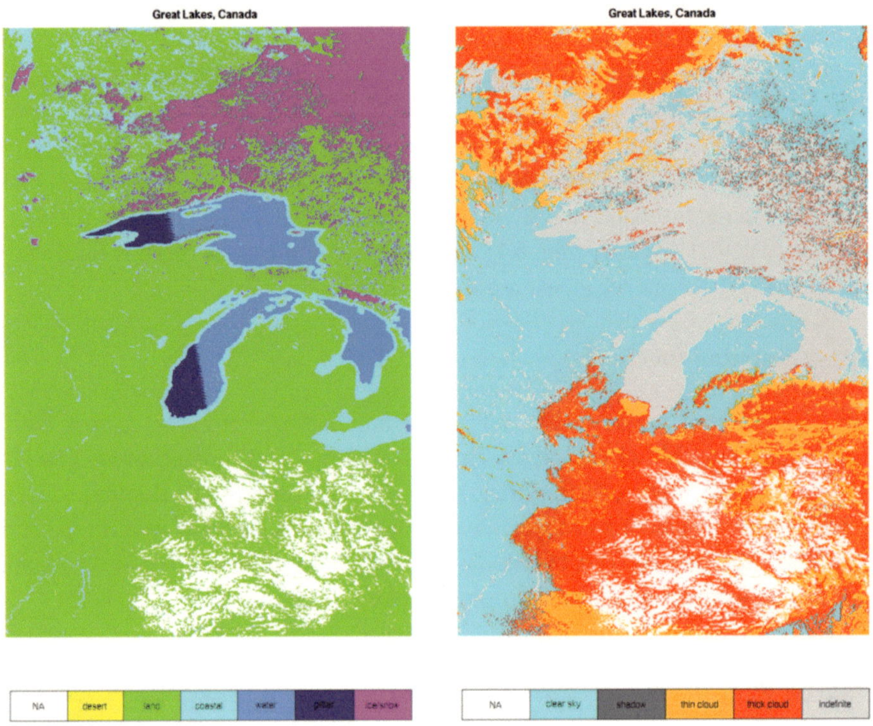

Figure 2. Example of background labels (on the left) and weather labels (on the right) created from MODIS masks. White pixels correspond to non available data. North of Great Lakes, Canada.

3.2. Calibration and labelling of a Kohonen map for cloud detection on MODIS data

The MTM algorithm was then applied to the learning database, in order to calibrate a 20 by 20 neurons map. After a short study of the first results, it was decided to make the following changes:

- coastal pixels were removed from the database, because they were radiometrically unstable,
- glitter pixels were changed to water pixels, because they correspond to a particular case of water observation,
- shadows were declared as clear sky, because they correspond to a particular case of clear sky observation,

• For thick clouds, there was no distinction between backgrounds, that's why we created a new background for them (equivalent to undetermined background).

Figure 3. Example of cloud detection made by the MTM algorithm, two optical depths thresholds: "thick" in red, "thin" in yellow, (black pixels correspond to non available data). North of Great Lakes, Canada.

After these modifications, a new 20 by 20 neurons map was produced with pre-classified neurons by the MTM algorithm. In order to correct the map (and at the same time the MODIS mask), three test images were chosen with different backgrounds and under different latitudes: an image of Great Lakes in Canada, to see the difference between snow/ice and cloud (top of Figure 3), another image on Sahara to discriminate cloud with sand, and the last image on Mediterranean Sea with glitter. For each neuron, we studied corresponding pixels on the three images, and corrected its label when necessary, respecting the Kohonen map topology (see paragraph 2.2).

3.3. Operation of a Kohonen map for cloud detection on MODIS data

Using confusion matrices between MODIS Level 2 cloud mask and the MTM results computed on the test database (in operation mode only), we showed that we entirely retrieved MODIS level 2 mask results in confident cases and improved it on indefinite cases. As it can be seen on Great Lakes image, undefined pixels on water appear as clear sky and our cloud detection classification makes less error on snow and ice. More precisely, if we compare Figure 2 –right and Figure 3, to Figure 1, we can see that fewer pixels are undefined in the case of presence of snow, and that fewer pixels are over-detected as clouds. This is confirmed when computing confusion matrices on this image (Tables 1 and 2), where we can see that 11.7% of the pixels are declared as thick or thin clouds by the MODIS mask but declared as clear sky by the MTM algorithm, and 28.5% of the pixels are declared as undefined by the MODIS mask although declared as clear sky by the MTM algorithm (Table 1).

		Results of the MTM algorithm		
		Clear sky	**Thin cloud**	**Thick cloud**
MODIS	Clear sky	33,104	0,022	0,000
cloud	Thin cloud	6,277	1,364	5,484
mask	Thick cloud	5,397	3,241	16,315
	Undefined	28,486	0,153	0,157

Table 1. Confusion matrix (distribution of pixels in %) comparing results of the MTM algorithm after correction and MODIS cloud mask on the image of North of Great Lakes, Canada.

Table 2 shows the confusion matrix computed between the two algorithms on pixels declared as snow by the MODIS background mask. We can see that all snow pixels are declared as clear sky by the MTM algorithm, while 45.5% of them were declared undefined by the MODIS cloud mask.

We can note by the examination of these matrices that we do not have the same definition of thin cloud between MODIS and MTM classification, because we did not chose the same corresponding cloud optical thickness. On the Great Lakes image, 5.5% of the pixels declared as thin cloud by MODIS are declared as thick cloud by the MTM algorithm.

3.4. Generalisation to other sensors

Some other sensors have their own cloud masks too, that could be used to perform the same kind of study, but they are made by threshold values using generally fewer spectral bands than MODIS, leading to lesser quality reference cloud mask. In order to create cloud detection masks for other sensors, we thus decided to create pseudo-sensors (Landsat [2], Pleiades [3], Sentinel 2 [22], etc.) using the learning and testing MODIS databases, keeping only MODIS closest spectral bands to the targeted sensors. As an example, learning and testing databases containing the bands 1, 2, 3 and 4 of a pseudo HRG sensor were constituted using the MODIS bands 4, 1, 2 and 6, respectively.

		Results of the MTM algorithm		
		Clear sky	**Thin cloud**	**Thick cloud**
MODIS	Clear sky	54,459	0,009	0,000
cloud	Thin cloud	0,005	0,000	0,000
mask	Thick cloud	0,002	0,000	0,000
	Undefined	45,506	0,190	0,000

Table 2. Confusion matrix (distribution of pixels in %) for pixels labelled as snow or ice by MODIS mask, comparing results of the MTM algorithm after correction and MODIS cloud mask on the image of North of Great Lakes, Canada.

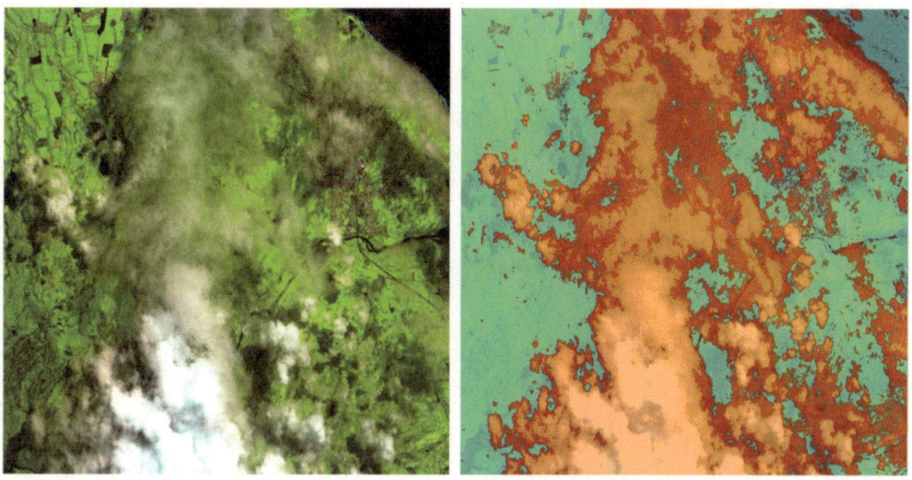

Figure 4. On the left: RGB composite image of SPOT 5 HRG Level 1B data, On the right: results of the MTM algorithm calibrated using pseudo HRG data and applied to SPOT 5 HRG real data (in orange: thick clouds, in red: thin clouds and in blue: clear sky), Reunion Island, France.

We logically showed that the lesser the bands, the more difficult to discriminate clouds from bright targets. But the performance is decreasing more rapidly when using classical linear algorithms; we thus still encourage the use of Kohonen maps, even when less multi-spectral information is available (Figure 4).

4. Second use case: Land cover mapping

Human actions have a negative impact on biodiversity. Construction of roads and urban expansion fragment living environment of wildlife. Some species need a minimum area to live and the reduction of their habitats can lead to their extinctions. In order to decrease these effects, some infrastructures help wildlife to overpass or underpass roads such as amphibians' tunnels and animals' bridges. Satellite data can help governments to detect urban and natural surfaces from the sky and see if natural areas are sufficiency vast and connected. Moreover, land cover mapping has a lot of applications in the sector of urbanism; we thus decided to test the MTM algorithm [10] on this problem in order to verify its applicability to HR data processing.

4.1. Data preparation for land cover mapping on HRG data

We chose to use SPOT 5 (Satellite Pour l'Observation de la Terre) HRG Level 1B images at 20 metres of spatial resolution [11]. Only four spectral bands (at 545 nm, 645 nm, 885 nm and 1.665 nm) are available. The HRG spectral information is thus very different from the MODIS one. Moreover, unlike the MODIS use-case, we did not have any qualitative information to help us to label the data. The database was generated from zooms on seven cities in France and their surrounding landscape (three cities around Bordeaux, three cities on Reunion Island and three zooms on different sector in Toulouse) at different seasons and latitudes. These zooms were made in order to have as many urban pixels as natural pixels on each of them.

Because there are only four spectral bands, adding new variables like physical indexes is very important (please refer to the Methodology chapter). For this specific problem, we choose to add to the database the NDVI, the NDBI, the NDSI, polynomials coefficients computed on a three degree polynomial, and a gamma correction was applied on green and red bands (see paragraph 2.1). As no blue band is available on HRG sensor, we could not create new colour spaces. Thus, the database was made of eleven variables when we had only four reflectances in entry.

In order to constitute the learning database, about four millions pixels were randomly chosen and controlled in order to have the same amount of pixels in each town and each type of vegetation from the nine chosen images.

In this study, no labels are available for HRG pixels, we thus created the labelling database from available images: four labelled sub-databases, corresponding to the four backgrounds expected to be distinguished (water, city, crop and forest), were created by several little zooms on images. However, this labelled database was not entirely consistent; as an example, some gardens and trees could be found on little zooms made on city, despite all of our attention.

4.2. Calibration and labelling of a Kohonen map for land cover mapping on HRG data

The MTM algorithm was applied on the database on a 20 by 20 neurons square map, with 100 learning iterations. Because no validated a priori knowledge was available concerning the targeted classes, no qualitative variables were used during the learning phase. The labelling database was used to label the Kohonen map by majority vote after the learning phase (please refer to the Methodology paragraph), but because this database was not completely consistent, we kept in mind that it only gave us a first idea of the Kohonen map labelling.

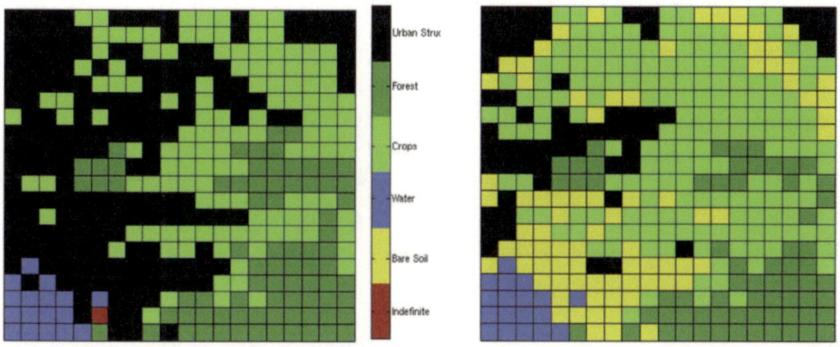

Figure 5. Kohonen activation map obtained by majority vote (on the left) and the same activation map after correction on the image of Toulouse (on the right).

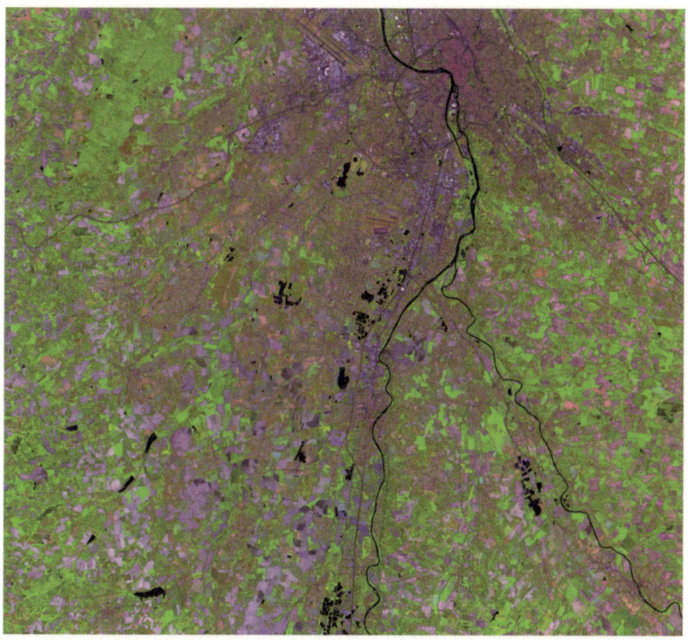

Figure 6. RGB composite image (B4, B3, B2, respectively) of SPOT 5 HRG data, May 21st 2011, Toulouse, France.

After the projection of the labelling database on the map, only one neuron could not be clearly attributed to a class and had been flagged as "indefinite" (Figure 5 - left). In order to correct the Kohonen map, a visual rectification was made with the help of three representations of Toulouse: the RGB image computed with the original HRG data (RGB composite image from bands B4 B3 B2, of May 21st 2011, Figure 6), Google Maps website and the French website Géoportail created by IGN (Institut Géographique National) and BRGM (Bureau de Recherches Géologiques et Minières). It appeared that a new class, distinguishing bare soil, had to be taken into account. This new class was added to the corrected Kohonen map (Figure 5 - right). Results of Kohonen classification before and after the map correction are shown on Figure 7 (on the Toulouse image).

4.3. Operation of a Kohonen map for land cover mapping on HRG data

During the Kohonen map correction, we decided to favour crop, water and forest from city pixels and then to add a new step, consisting in a sliding window filter, favouring city pixels (please refer to the paragraph 2.3). After a sensitivity study of the window length and of classes' priority, two window filters were applied:

- A first 7 by 7 window filter had been used on classes image of Toulouse with the following algorithm: if one pixel of the window is of class town: pixel is town, else if one pixel of the window is of class water: pixel is water, else a majority vote on the window was made between forest, crop and bare soil.
- Then, a second 7 by 7 window filter had been applied with a majority vote without class priority.

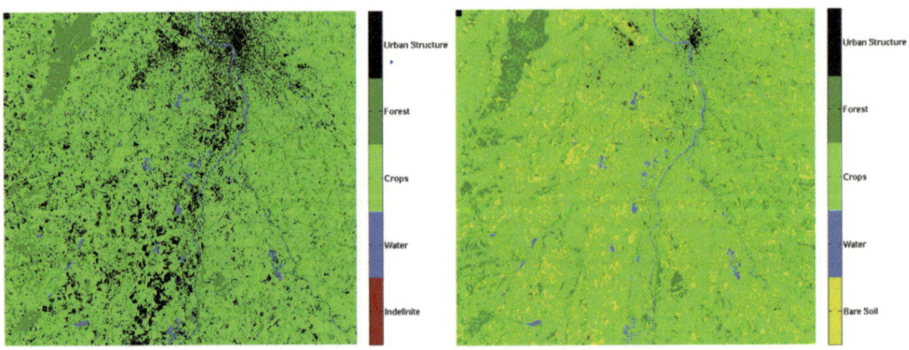

Figure 7. Visualisation of the activation map obtained by majority vote, before (left) and after correction (right) of the neurons labelling. May 21st 2011, Toulouse, France.

These filters allowed us to correct Kohonen maps classification taking into account spatial information (see Figure 8). In order to finalize this product for scientists and governmental administrations, we will have to add real geolocated information to this image, such as roads and already done infrastructures. Indeed, on this interpreted SPOT 5 HRG image of Toulouse, we can distinguish highways, but they do not appear continuous. Other roads are not visible because of the resolution of the sensor. We will have to reconstruct them with the help of a geolocated map of roads, and using different information depending on the targeted product.

As an example, if we target environment control, we will have to include animal bridges which can appear as discontinuities in the road and have to be kept as animal movement possibilities. Moreover, we need to have information about existing wildlife crossing which are not visible by satellite such as amphibians' underpass tunnels. On the other hand, bridges detected over rivers are real road detections. This also means that post-processing will not be the same depending on map application. For example, road bridges are not useful for fishes study.

Results were visually validated on Google Earth cartographic background, showing a slight over-detection of urban structures (Figure 9). But the method seems to be adapted to perform automatic land cover mapping, which is generally done manually in operational structures today. Indeed, relatively timely stable structures were well retrieved, as rivers, forests and urban down-town buildings.

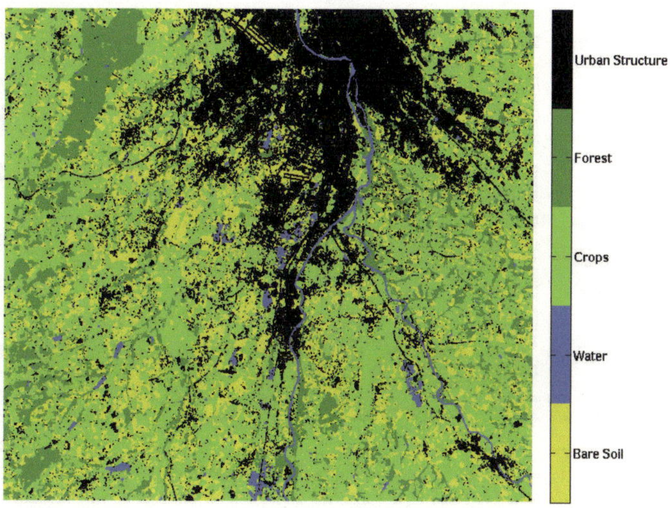

Figure 8. Results of the classification after the image processing step, May 21st 2011, Toulouse, France.

In order to finalize this study, the next step will be the geolocation of roads and other infrastructures made for animals. Once this information will be added in the database, the study of the living environment of each type of animals can be done. Indeed, we also have an algorithm able to reproduce animals' moves from a starting pixel, which can be used in order to visualize their displacements for a chosen kind of land cover. Moreover, this methodology needs to be validated on another city.

5. Conclusion

Application of Kohonen map to satellite cloud detection and land cover mapping problems has been presented, as an alternative to classical decision trees algorithms based on linear tests (e.g. thresholds applied to radiometric information). General methodology using the MTM algorithm [10] is explained (paragraph 2) and then detailed for the two use cases, which correspond to low resolution (LR) imagery and high resolution (HR) imagery, respectively (paragraphs 3 and 4).

Results show that in the case of cloud detection, the use of the MTM algorithm improves significantly the detection results over bright targets as snow, ice, and deserts, reducing false detections and indetermination, when comparing the MTM results to the operational MODIS Level 2 cloud mask. These results are very important for scientists, as cloud and snow/ice masks are used as one of the necessary inputs for computing the radiative budget of the planet.

Figure 9. Automatic land cover detection by Kohonen map (city in black, bare soil in yellow, crop in light green, forests in dark green, water in blue): validation by projection on Google Earth. Toulouse, France.

In the case of land cover mapping, results show that a fully automatic algorithm may be used to rapidly interpret HR imagery, producing instantaneous cartographic maps for a wide range of applications, from environment survey to urbanism. The classification results, interpreted as number of pixels of each targeted class in the image, may also be used to index the images in voluminous satellite databases, improving the extraction of useful information from them. Moreover, because Kohonen map neurons correspond to radiometric information, they may also be used to radiometrically simplify voluminous HR images prior to further image processing, like change detection as we propose in paragraph 2.3, or even prior to save them in satellite databases for volumetry economy purpose. This would be done by saving only the image of the winning neurons of each pixel (which would be one integer image and not about a tenth of radiometric bands), associated to the table of corresponding radiometric vectors.

Finally, because Kohonen maps are simple solution for multivariate classification, we think it will allow the fusion of optic and SAR imagery, in the case of well geographically co-registered missions.

Acknowledgements

The MODIS L1B data were obtained through the online Data Pool at the NASA Land Processes Distributed Active Archive Center (LP DAAC), USGS/Earth Resources Observation and Science (EROS) Center, Sioux Falls, South Dakota (http://lpdaac.usgs.gov/get_data).

We thank the French spatial agency (Centre National des Etudes Spatiales, CNES) Kalideos project (http://kalideos.cnes.fr) for SPOT 5 HRG imagery courtesy. The cloud detection study was funded by the CNES Recherche and Technology program, Observation de la Terre axis n°4 (Méthodes pour l'Extraction d'Informations des Images).

Author details

Suzanne Angeli, Arnaud Quesney and Lydwine Gross*

*Address all correspondence to: lydwine.grosscolzy@capgemini.com

Capgemini Technology Services, Scientific Office, 15 avenue du Docteur Grynfogel, BP 53655, 31036 Toulouse Cedex 1, France

References

[1] European Space Agency. (2011). *Medium Resolution Imaging Spectrometer (MERIS) Product Handbook* [3], http://envisat.esa.int/handbooks/meris/.

[2] NASA's Earth Observing System. (2012). *Landsat 7.*, http://eospso.gsfc.nasa.gov/eos_homepage/mission_profiles/docs/Landsat7.pdf.

[3] Centre National d'Etudes Spatiales. (2006). *Main characteristics of the Pleiades mission*, http://smsc.cnes.fr/PLEIADES/GP_mission.htm.

[4] Deutsche Forschungsanstalt für Luft- und Raumfahrt. (2007). *TerraSAR-X Ground Segment, Level 1b Product Format Specification* [1.3 (TX-GS-DD-3307)], 257, http://sss.terrasar-x.dlr.de/.

[5] Earth Observation Research Center, Japan Aerospace eXploration Agency. (1997). *ALOS user Handbook (NDX-070015),* http://www.eorc.jaxa.jp/ALOS/en/doc/alos_userhb_en.pdf.

[6] Agenzia Spaziale Italiana. (2007). *COSMO-SkyMed System Description & User Guide, Rev. A (ASI-CSM-ENG-RS-093-A),* 49, http://www.cosmo-skymed.it/docs/ASI-CSM-ENG-RS-093-A-CSKSysDescriptionAndUserGuide.pdf.

[7] Kerr, Y., Waldteufel, P., Wigneron, J. P., & Font, Berger. (2003). *The Soil Moisture and Ocean Salinity Mission IGAARS 2003, Toulouse.*

[8] Ackerman, S., Strabala, K., Menzel, P., Frey, R., Moeller, C., Gumley, L., Baum, B., Wetzel, Seemann. S., & Zhong, H. (2006). *Discriminating clear sky from cloud with MODIS. Algorithm theoretical basis document MOD35,* 129.

[9] PELCOM project. (2000). Development of a consistent methodology to derive land cover information on a European scale from remote sensing for environmental modelling. *PELCOM FINAL REPORT- DGXII. Editor C.A. Mücher,* 299.

[10] Lebbah, M., Chazottes, A., Thiria, S., & Badran, F. (2005). *Mixed Topological Map, ESANN 2005 proceedings-European Symposium on Artificial Neural Networks. Bruges, April,* 26-29, 357-362.

[11] © ASTRIUM-© Cnes 2004-2010. (2012). 2011, *SPOT: accuracy and coverage combined,* http://www.astriumgeo.com/files/pmedia/public/r233_9_geo_0013_spot_en_2012_03.pdf.

[12] Niang, A., Gross, L., Thiria, S., & Badran, S. (2003). *Automatic neural classification of ocean colour reflectance spectra at the top of the atmosphere with introduction of expert knowledge. RSE,* 86, 257-271.

[13] Breon, F. M., Buriez, J. C., Couvert, P., Deschamps, P. Y., Deuze, J. L., Herman, M., Goloub, P., Leroy, M., Lifermann, A., Moulin, C., Parol, F., Seze, G., Tanre, D., Vanbauce, C., & Vesperini, M. (2002). *Scientific results from the POLarization and Directionality of the Earth's Reflectances (POLDER). Adv. Space Res.,* 30(11), 2383-2386.

[14] Jovanovic, V., Miller, K., Rheingans, B., & Moroney, C. (2012). *Multi-angle Imaging SpectroRadiometer (MISR) Science Data Product Guide (JPL D-73355),* http://eosweb.larc.nasa.gov/PRODOCS/misr/DPS/MISR_Science_Data_Product_Guide.pdf.

[15] Pascale, D. (2003). *A Review of RGB color spaces...from xyY to R'G'B',* http://www.babelcolor.com/download/A%20review%20of%20RGB%20color%20spaces.pdf,, 17-19.

[16] Salomonson, V. V., & Appel, I. (2006). Development of the Aqua MODIS NDSI Fractional Snow Cover Algorithm and Validation Results. *IEEE TRANSACTIONS ON GEOSCIENCE AND REMOTE SENSING,* 44(7).

[17] Xu, H. (2007). *Extraction of Urban Built-up Land Features from Landsat Imagery Using a Thematic oriented Index Combination Technique, Photogrammetric Engineering & Remote Sensing,* 73(12), 1381-1391.

[18] Kohonen, T. (1994). *Self-Organizing Map*, Springer, Berlin.

[19] Lebbah, M., Thiria, S., & Badran, F. (2000). *Topological Map for Binary Data, Proceedings of ESANN 2000, Bruges*, 26, 27-28.

[20] Baatz, M., & Schäpe, A. (2000). Multiresolution Segmentation: an optimization approach for high quality multi-scale image segmentation. *Journal of Photogrammetry and Remote Sensing*, 58(3-4).

[21] Heidinger, A. K., Anne, V. R., & Dean, C. (2002). Using MODIS to estimate cloud contamination of the AVHRR data-record. *Journal of Atmospheric and Oceanic Technology*, 19, 586-601.

[22] European Space Agency. (2010). *Sentinel 2 payload data ground segment, product definition document (GMES-GSEG-EOPG-TN-09-0029).*, http://emits.esa.int/emits-doc/ESRIN/Sentinel-2/ProductsDefinitionDocument(PDD).pdf.